**Study Guide**

# West Federal Taxation
# Taxation of Business Entities

**2004 Edition**

**James E. Smith, Ph.D., CPA**
College of William and Mary

**William A. Raabe, Ph.D., CPA**
Ohio State University

**David M. Maloney, Ph.D., CPA**
University of Virginia

**Eugene Willis, Ph.D., CPA**
University of Illinois at Urbana

Prepared by

**Debra L. Sanders**
Washington State University

THOMSON
SOUTH-WESTERN

Australia · Canada · Mexico · Singapore · Spain · United Kingdom · United States

THOMSON

SOUTH-WESTERN

**Study Guide**

**Taxation of Business Entities 2004 Edition**

James E. Smith, William A. Raabe, David M. Maloney, Eugene Willis
prepared by Debra L. Sanders

**VP/Editorial Director:**
Jack W. Calhoun

**VP/Editor-in-Chief:**
George Werthman

**Acquisitions Editor:**
Jennifer L. Codner

**Developmental Editor:**
Craig Avery

**Marketing Manager:**
Heather MacMaster

**Production Editor:**
Lora Arduser

**Manufacturing Coordinator:**
Doug Wilke

**Senior Design Project Manager:**
Michelle Kunkler

**Cover Designer:**
Ann Small/a small design studio

**Cover Images:**
© William J. Hebert/Getty Images, Inc.

**Printer:**
Globus Printing
Minster, OH



Printed in the United States of America
1 2 3 4 5 06 05 04 03

ISBN: 0-324-19071-9



For more information
contact South-Western,
5191 Natorp Boulevard,
Mason, Ohio, 45040.
Or you can visit our Internet site at:
http://www.swlearning.com

# CONTENTS

# PREFACE

**This *Study Guide* accompanies the 2004 edition of *West's An Introduction to Business Entities.* The textbook is designed for a one semester undergraduate or graduate course in Federal taxation. Thus, because the scope of the text is quite broad, you will be required to digest a large amount of fairly complex information in a short period of time.**

**In recognition of the difficulty of such a task, this *Study* Guide was created. It offers you an additional review of the content of the text chapters in outline form, to allow a rapid perusal. Moreover, additional problems and exercises are contained in the *Study Guide* for review. These exercises are presented in a self-evaluation format, with the suggested solutions directly following the exercises, so that you can receive immediate feedback as to the accuracy of your answers. These problems take a number of different formats, including true and false, fill-in-the-blank, multiple choice, and short answers. I believe that this arrangement will maximize your understanding of the text material in a reasonable period of time.**

**It is important that you use this *Study Guide* as an *aid* to mastering the material in the textbook, and *not* as a replacement for it. I suggest that you incorporate the *Study Guide* into your regular study routine, perhaps by reviewing the Chapter Highlights after reading the text, and then working the *Study Guide* problems before attempting those assigned in the text.**

**Any questions you may have about the *Study Guide*, error and omissions, or any suggestions you have to improve this manual may be sent to me at my e-mail address: *dsanders@wsu.edu***

Debra L. Sanders, Professor
Washington State University
May 2003

# Chapter 1
# Introduction to Taxation

## CHAPTER HIGHLIGHTS

A proper analysis of the United States tax system begins with an examination of the tax structure and types of taxes employed in the US. Knowledge of historical principles that guided the development of the system, and investigating the various motivations that underlie existing provisions of the tax law will help in understanding the US tax system. This chapter also introduces the various taxable and nontaxable business entities and provides an overview of tax planning.

I. The Structure of Taxes (Tax Terminology)
   A. Taxes have two components: tax rate and tax base.
   B. Tax Rates – Rates can be structured to yield:
      1. Proportional tax: The rate of tax remains constant over the tax base (sales tax);
      2. Progressive tax: Tax rates increase as the tax base grows larger (Federal income, gift & estate tax); or,
      3. Regressive tax: Tax rates decrease as the tax base grows larger (Federal employment taxes such as FUTA and FICA).
   C. Tax Base – Most taxes are levied on one of the following tax bases:
      1. Transactions (including sales and estate & gift taxes);
      2. Property or wealth (including real estate taxes and ownership of property);
      3. Privileges and rights (including ability to use the corporate form or to be in certain profession, excise taxes, and custom duties); or
      4. Income (can be on gross or net income).

II. Types of Taxes
   A. After income taxes, transaction taxes usually affect more US taxpayers than other taxes. In many countries transaction taxes are even more important than income taxes.
   B. Taxes on the Production and Sale of Goods: Levied on the sale, consumption, or production of commodities or services. Examples of transaction taxes include:
      1. Excise Taxes
         a. Levied by Federal and state governments on exchanges of specified commodities (oil, alcohol, phone service, and tobacco) or services. Excise taxes may be levied on producers, resellers or consumers.
         b. May have significant impact on specific industries.

c. Although excise tax rate is generally proportional, rates may vary greatly from state to state.

2. Sales and Use Taxes

a. Major sources of income for most state and local governments and covers a broad base of transactions.

b. Items subject to tax vary by state and rates may vary by locality.

c. The rate is proportional and collected by retailers.

d. For various reasons, states may suspend the general sales tax either permanently on some items or have a tax holiday for short intervals.

e. Use tax imposed on items bought in a lower sales tax locality and transported for use in another locality. The rate is usually the same as the sales tax rate. Difficult to enforce on many purchases.

3. Value Added Tax (VAT)

a. In many countries around the world, the VAT has gained acceptance as a major source of revenue.

b. It is a sales tax levied on the value added at each stage of production.

C. <u>Employment Taxes</u>: As imposed by Federal and state governments, these taxes include

1. FICA taxes (Federal Insurance Retirement Act)

a. Tax imposed on the self-employed, employees, and their employers. Accounts for about 1/3 of the Federal revenues; only income taxes provides more Federal revenue.

b. Proceeds finance retirement (Social Security) and medical costs (Medicare)

(1) Employee rate is 6.2% for Social Security (SS) up to $87,000 for 2003 ($84,900 for 2002) and 1.45% for Medicare (no ceiling). Total of 7.65% if income is $87,000 or less. Employer matches the contributions.

(2) Self-employed pay the employee and employer portions. This is 12.4% (2 X 6.2%) for SS and 2.9% (2 X 1.45%) for Medicare. Income limits are the same as for employees. So total of 15.3% if income is $87,000 or less.

2. FUTA (Federal Unemployment Tax Act)

a. Generally has a state counterpart. Amounts finance state unemployment compensation benefits. As with FICA, this is a regressive tax.

b. The rate is generally 6.2% of first $7,000 of wages and paid only by the employer. States may impose special tax on employees to provide disability benefits and/or supplemental unemployment benefits.

c. Federal credit of up to 5.4% for unemployment taxes paid to the state.

D. <u>Death Taxes</u>: Levied by Federal and state governments on the right to transfer property at death. Intended to prevent large concentrations of wealth.

1. Estate Taxes are imposed on the decedent and inheritance taxes are imposed on the recipient. Federal imposes estate taxes and states may levy either or both types.

2. The tax base is the fair market value (FMV) of the property owned by the decedent at death less allowable deductions (funeral costs, administration

expenses, certain taxes, liabilities of decedent, charitable contributions, and martial deduction) plus prior taxable gifts.

3. Federal Estate Taxes uses a progressive rate scheme. Rates range from 18% to 49% in 2003. However, transfers may avoid some or all taxation through the application of the unified transfer tax credit. For 2003 this credit eliminates tax $1 million of taxable estate. The amount of the credit is $345,800.
4. State inheritance taxes are based on the heirs relationship to the decedent.

E. Gift Taxes: Also imposed on the right to transfer property but these transfers are during the owner's lifetime. A few states impose gift taxes.

1. Base for the tax is the FMV at the date of the gift of the property transferred.
2. Uses same tax rates as estate taxes; that is, the estate and gift taxes are *unified.* Unified Transfer Tax Credit for gifts is frozen at $345,800 ($1million of gifts).
3. Gifts of $11,000 or less per donee per donor per year are not taxable due to the *annual exclusion* available. Married couples may elect *gift splitting* which increases the exclusion to $22,000.

F. Property Taxes: Usually based on ownership or levied on wealth or capital. Those based on value are known as *ad valorem taxes* (at value taxes). These taxes are generally imposed by state and local governments.

1. Real Property Taxes are important sources of revenue to localities. The taxes are generally not imposed on Federal and State government property or property owned by charities. Other exemptions or special rates may exist for certain types of property and certain groups of individuals.
2. Personal Property Taxes may be imposed on property not classified as reality. Taxes on property devoted to personal use has inconsistent taxpayer compliance. Personalty used in business, however, has better compliance. Automobile property tax base may be weight rather than value.

G. Taxes on Privileges and Rights: Usually are excise taxes. Examples of these taxes are:

1. Custom Duties are taxes on the right to move goods across national boarders. Tend to be the instrumentality for applying the protectionist policy of the US.
2. Franchise and Occupational Taxes are taxes on the privilege of doing business or practicing a profession in a state or local jurisdiction.
3. Severance Taxes are imposed by some states on the extraction of natural resources. They are an important source of income in some states.

H. Income Taxes

1. Levied by the Federal, most states, and some local governments.
2. Generally income taxes imposed on corporations, estates, trusts, and individuals. Most taxing jurisdictions use a pay-as-you-go system for collecting taxes.
3. History of US Taxation
   a. First income tax in Massachusetts Bay Colony in 1634.
   b. An income tax on individuals was used to provide financing for the Civil War. When the war ended, the tax was repealed.

c. After an economic depression in 1893, a new individual income tax was enacted, but the Supreme Court in *Pollock v Farmer's Loan and Trust Co.* held the tax to be unconstitutional because it was a direct tax.

d. A corporate income tax was adopted in 1909 and in *Flint v Stone Tracy Co.* the Supreme Court found the tax constitutional because it was an indirect tax on the right to do business as a corporation.

e. The Sixteenth Amendment, which sanctioned both the Federal individual and corporate income taxes, was ratified in 1913. The present income tax on individuals was enacted in October 1913.

f. The maximum tax rates changed over time from 6% in 1913 to 77% in 1918 during World War I. In 1925 the maximum rate was reduced back to 25%. By World War II (1945) 74% of Americans paid income taxes. In 1943 the pay-as-you-go system was enacted.

4. Tax Structure – The basic tax formula for all taxable entities is fairly similar.

a. Income is broadly included in the tax base whereas deductions must be specifically provided for in the law.

b. Tax rates are progressive; from 10% to 35% (after the Tax Act of 2003) for individuals and from 15% to 35% for corporations.

c. The taxation of individuals employs an intermediate sum called adjusted gross income (AGI) to distinguish between the two types of individual deductions: *for* AGI, and *from* AGI.

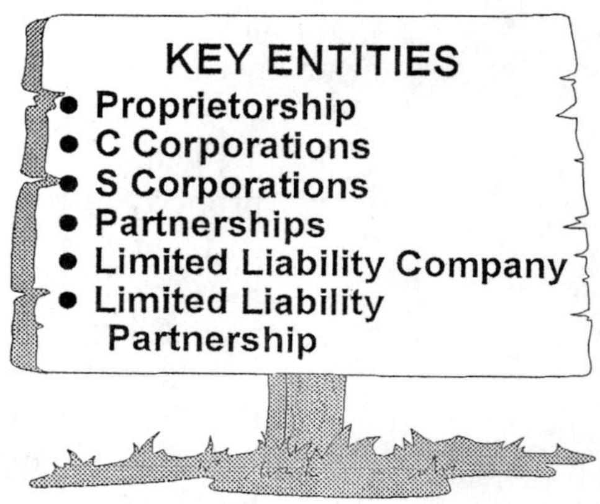


5. State and Local income Taxes –
Most states and a few cities impose income taxes. The calculation of taxes usually relies to some degree on Federal income tax law and computations.

III. Income Taxation of Business Entities

A. <u>Proprietorships</u> –

1. This simple form of business is not a separate entity from the individual owner.
2. Its profits are reported on the taxpayer's personal return.

B. <u>Corporations</u> –

1. Separate corporate taxable entities are called C corporations or regular corporations. Those corporate entities not generally subject to taxation are called Sub S corporations or S corporations.
2. Both of these types of corporations, however, must file tax returns.

C. <u>Partnerships</u> –

1. While required to file a return, a partnership is not a separate taxable entity and is not subject to taxation.
2. The financial results of the partnership *flow-through* to the partners and appear on their tax returns.

D. <u>S Corporations</u> –

1 These entities have the legal characteristics of C corporations but are flow-through entities like partnerships. Financial results of S corporations appear on the shareholders' tax returns.

2. Thus, they avoid the double taxation problems of C corporations.

E. Limited Liability Companies & Partnerships –

1. These entities follow the same tax rules as partnerships
2. They have the added benefit of limited liability for their owners.

F. Dealings Between Individuals and Entities –

1. There are important tax consequences for transactions involving the owners and their business entities.
2. There are numerous tax law provisions governing these transactions.

IV. Tax Planning Fundamentals

A. Overview of Tax Planning

1. A distinction exists between legal tax planning – *tax avoidance*, and illegal tax planning or evading taxes – *tax evasion*.
2. Clients expect practitioners to advise as to how to structure transaction in order to minimize their taxes. This is called *tax planning*.

B. General Framework for Income Tax Planning

1. A primary purpose of tax planning is to minimize a taxpayer's total tax liability.
2. The key to good tax planning is assessing the nontax as well as the tax considerations of any business decisions.

C. Tax Minimization Strategies Related to Income

1. Avoid income recognition – Use tax exclusions. Numerous available to individuals but not many are provided for corporations.
2. Postponement recognition of income to achieve tax deferral – Although there are tax provisions to keep taxpayers from shifting income and expenses across periods, some opportunities still exist.

D. Tax Minimization Strategies Related to Deductions

1. Maximize deductible amounts – Corporations should maximize the dividends received deduction.
2. Accelerate recognition of deductions to achieve tax deferral – Accrual basis corporations can deduct charitable contributions in the year preceding the payment if certain requirements are met.

E. Tax Minimization Strategies Related to Tax Rates

1. Shift net income from high-bracket years to low-bracket years – This strategy will reduce the total amount of taxes paid by the entity.
2. Shift net income from high-bracket taxpayers to low-bracket taxpayers – Although there are several tax rules to keep taxpayers from shifting income from high-bracket taxpayers to low-bracket taxpayers, some opportunities still exist.
3. Shift net income from high-taxing jurisdictions to low-taxing jurisdictions – The country, state or county income is earned in can make a difference in the amount of taxes that are paid.
4. Control the character of the income and deductions – Changing an item's character from tax-disfavored to tax-favored income (ordinary to capital gain) or deduction (nondeductible to deductible) is beneficial to the taxpayer.
5. Avoid double taxation – Choose entity forms that reduce or eliminate the possibility of the same income be tax twice; once at the entity level and another at the owner level.

F. Tax Minimization Strategies Related to Credits
   1. Maximize tax credits – Credits reduce the tax liability dollar for dollar and are not affected by the taxpayer's tax rate.
   2. A deduction, on the other hand, reduces income dollar for dollar. Its tax benefit is dependent on the tax bracket of the taxpayer.

G. Thinking Outside the Framework
   1. The general framework for income tax planning is presented in Figure 1-3 in the text.
   2. Determining the Tax Burden
      a. Of the three kinds of tax rates, *marginal, average,* and *effective,* the marginal rate is the most useful for tax planning purposes. It is the tax rate on the next dollar of income.
      b. The current taxes as well as the present value of future taxes should be considered.
      c. In determining the tax amount of taxes paid both *explicit* taxes (directly paid) and *implicit* (paid indirectly through higher prices, etc) should be considered.

V. Understanding the Federal Tax Law

A. Although the major objective of the Federal tax law is to raise revenue, economic, social, equity, and political considerations also play a significant role in the design of specific tax provisions.

B. Revenue Needs
   1. The foundation of the income tax system is to raise revenues to cover the cost of government operations.
   2. However, the revenues from taxes may not equal the expenditures by the US Congress and resulting in deficit spending.
   3. Congress uses several approaches to reduce deficit spending such as limiting the number of years a tax benefit is available or using phase-ins or phase-outs.

C. Economic Considerations
   1. The tax law is increasingly being used to accomplish economic goal of the government.
   2. Attempts at stimulation or temperance of the national economy, and encouragement or discouragement of specific activities or industries, have led to a large number of recent amendments to the Code.

D. Social Considerations
   1. The tax system is also used for social considerations, particularly with regard to individual taxation.
   2. Tax-favored treatment concerning certain employer provided benefits, child care costs, charitable contributions, and education costs are responses to various social goals.
   3. On the other hand, expenditures that are contrary to public policy are discouraged by tax laws.

E. Equity Considerations
   1. Attempts are made to maintain a sensitivity in the law regarding taxpayers in various circumstances. Of course, definitions of equity often produce heated debate among interested parties.
   2. Nevertheless, the tax law offers:

        a. Relief from multiple taxation,
        b. Deferral of tax liability until the taxpayer has the *wherewithal to pay* (funds available with which to pay a tax),
        c. Mitigation of hardships caused by the annual accounting period concept,
        d. Relief from the eroding results of inflation.

F. Political considerations
    1. As might be expected, political considerations are evident in the tax law.
    2. The effect of these considerations largely results in special interest legislation, political expediency situations, and state and local government influences.

G. The Internal Revenue Service
    1. The IRS has contributed to the tax system by encouraging amendments in specific provisions in the tax law.
    2. In its capacity as the protector of the national revenue, the IRS has been instrumental in securing legislation designed to curtail flagrant tax avoidance practices and to ease administration of the tax laws.

H. Federal Courts
    1. In addition to interpreting the tax law, the Federal courts have influenced tax law by formulating certain judicial concepts that provide guidance in the application of various tax provisions.
    2. Also, key court decisions have been instrumental in Congressional changes to the Internal Revenue Code.

## TEST FOR SELF-EVALUATION - CHAPTER 1

**True or False**

Indicate which of the following statements are true or false by circling the correct answer.

T F 1. The Federal government raises a large portion of its revenue through property taxes on real estate.

T F 2. A value added tax resembles a national sales tax.

T F 3. The corporate income tax came into existence in 1913 with the passage of the 16th amendment.

T F 4. Property taxes are a form of *ad valorem* taxes.

T F 5. The estate tax is a regressive tax whereas the gift tax is a proportional tax.

T F 6. If tax rates increase as the tax base grows larger, the tax is regressive.

T F 7. An excise tax is a tax on the use, consumption, or storage of property.

T F 8. The primary purpose of some tax laws is to simplify for the IRS the collection of tax revenues and the administration of the tax law.

T F 9. State governments use the sales tax as one of their primary sources of tax revenues.

T F 10. The effective tax rate is the relevant rate to apply in tax planning decisions.

T F 11. Tax evasion and tax avoidance essentially have the same meaning.

T F 12. While many states impose estate and/or inheritance taxes, only a few states impose gift taxes.

T F 13 Some provisions of the Federal tax law, particularly those dealing with taxation of corporations, can be explained as trying to encourage certain social results.

T F 14 A corporation maximizing its dividend received deduction is an example of deduction tax planning strategy.

T F 15. A $1,000 deduction and a $1,000 credit will be of equal value to a corporation.

T F 16. While most states levy an excise tax on gasoline, liquor, and tobacco, the rates among states can vary dramatically.

T F 17. Deferring tax liabilities until the taxpayer has the funds available with which to pay is called the wherewithal to pay concept.

**Fill-in-the-Blanks**

Complete the following statements with the appropriate word(s) or amount(s).

1. The ________ Amendment, ratified in ________, authorized the Federal income tax on individuals.
2. ________ taxes are on assets owned by the taxpayer and usually based at fair market value.
3. Taxes on income may be imposed at the ________, ________, and ________ levels of government.
4. Relief from multiple taxation is an example of the effect of ________ considerations in the development of the tax law.
5. An accrual corporation receiving a current deduction for charitable contributions paid in the firs 2 ½ months of the following year is an example of ________ tax planning strategy.
6. Prepaid subscriptions and dues not being taxable until earned but prepaid rents being taxable when received is an example of ________ considerations in the tax law.
7. The tax business entities available for an enterprise are ________, ________, ________, ________, and ________.
8. With respect to employment taxes, the ________ tax is paid equally by the employer and employee, while ________ taxes are paid by only the employer.
9. The _____-_____-_____-_____ feature of the income tax system compels employers to withhold a specific portion of an employee's wages for taxes.
10. A severance tax is an example of a(n) ________ tax because it is levied on the activity of extracting natural resources.
11. Changing the character of income and expenses from tax-disfavored to tax-favored categories is a tax minimization strategy related to ________.
12. A(n) ________ tax is a tax on the right to receive property from a decedent.
13. The purpose of the ________ system is to provide funds that states can use to provide unemployment benefits.
14. In ________ court case, the Supreme Court found that the income tax of 1983 was unconstitutional because it was a direct tax.
15. A(n) ________ tax is paid directly to a government whereas a(n) ________ tax is paid through higher prices or lower returns on tax-favored investments.
16. The first tax in America was introduced in the ________ Colony in ________.

## Multiple Choice

Choose the best answer for each of the following questions.

____ 1. When the tax base is $10,000, the tax liability is $3,000. When the tax base is $100,000, the tax liability is $40,000. This tax has a rate structure that is:

a. Regressive.
b. Progressive.
c. Proportional.
d. *Ad Valorem*.

____ 2. When the tax base is $10,000, the tax liability is $765. When the tax base is $50,000, the tax liability is $3,825. This tax is an example of:

a. Federal income tax.
b. FUTA tax.
c. FICA tax.
d. Gift tax.

____ 3. Which of the following statements is *false*.

a. Bracket creep is when the tax brackets adjust each year for inflation.
b. Installment sale treatment demonstrates the wherewithal to pay concept.
c. The allowance of a deduction for state and city income taxes is to help alleviate the effect of multiple taxation.
d. The United States believes what is good for small business is good for the economy as a whole.

____ 4. The Federal gift and estate taxes are:

a. Progressive Taxes.
b. Transaction Taxes.
c. Unified Taxes.
d. All of the above.

____ 5. Which of the following is a tax minimization strategy.

a. Shift deductions from high-bracket tax years to low-bracket tax years.
b. Accelerate recognition of income to achieve tax deferrals.
c. Maximize deductions over credits.
d. Convert the character of income from ordinary to capital gains..

____ 6. Shifting income from parents in the highest tax bracket to a child in the lowest tax bracket is an example of which tax minimizing strategy.

a. Shifting from high-bracket taxpayers to low-bracket taxpayers.
b. Avoiding double taxation.
c. Shifting from high-bracket tax years to low-bracket tax years.
d. Avoiding income recognition through exclusions.

____ 7. Which of the following is an example of social considerations affecting the tax law.

a. The alternative minimum tax.
b. Deductions for contributions to retirement plans.
c. The accelerated depreciation system.
d. The installment sales method.

____ 8. The concept of equity appears in tax provisions to provide all of the following except:

a. Alleviate the effect of multiple taxation.
b. Cope with inflation.
c. Mitigate the effect of the application of the annual accounting period concept.
d. Encourage certain business activities.

____ 9. Which of the following statement is *false*.

a. The basic Federal income tax formula is similar for all taxable entities.
b. Taxpayers can make gifts of $11,000 or less without paying a transfer tax if because of the unified credit.
c. States generally rely on the Federal income tax laws for their income taxation.
d. City income taxes usually apply to income earned in the city regardless of whether the taxpayers live in the city or not.

____ 10. The Federal courts have influenced tax law by all of the following except:

a. Formulating certain judicial concepts that serve as guidance in the application of various tax provisions.
b. Interpreting statutory provisions and administrative pronouncements.
c. Making key decisions that have led to changes in the Internal Revenue Code.
d. Changing Congressional intent as to the application of Federal tax law.

____ 11. Which of the following statements is *true* regarding taxes on the sale of goods.

a. Excise taxes are currently a major source of revenue for the United States.
b. Excise taxes are levied only at the Federal level.
c. Sales taxes are levied by many states and localities but not at the Federal level.
d. States that do not have a sales tax usually have a use tax.

____ 12. Which of the following is not a tax on privileges and rights:

a. Use taxes.
b. Customs duties.
c. Franchise taxes.
d. Occupational taxes.

____ 13. The VAT is:

a. A type of income tax popular in Europe and Canada.
b. Levied at each stage of production on the value added by the producer.
c. The Federal sales tax collected in the United States.
d. A minor revenue generator for most of the countries employing it.

____ 14. Over time, the Internal Revenue Service has worked to

a. Secure passage of legislation designed to curtail tax loopholes.
b. Make administration of the tax law easier.
c. Make adjustments based on substance, rather than the form of a transaction.
d. All of the above.

____ 15. Which of the following statements is true regarding Federal income taxes.

a. The first income tax passed in 1916 was at a rate of 1 percent.
b. Income tax rates have ever been higher than 75%.
c. The Federal tax law is based on the idea that all income from whatever source derived is subject to Federal income tax.
d. All expenses unless specifically denied are allowed as deductions for Federal income taxes.

____ 16. Most taxes are levied on one of the tax bases listed below except:

a. Appreciation in value.
b. Property or wealth.
c. Income.
d. Transactions.

____ 17. Zolla earned $100,000 as an executive in 2003. How much FICA did Zolla pay (rounded to the nearest dollar)?

a. $6,200.
b. $6,655.
c. $6,844.
d. $7,650.
e. None of the above.

____ 18. Assume the same facts question # 17. How much FUTA did Zolla pay in 2003 (rounded to the nearest dollar)?

a. $56.
b. $378.
c. $434.
d. $696.
e. None of the above.

____ 19. What would Zolla's FICA tax be if the $100,000 was self-employment income (rounded to the nearest dollar)?

a. $7,650.
b. $12,400.
c. $13,688.
d. $15,300.
e. None of the above.

____ 20. Which of the following entities are separate taxable entities.

a. Proprietorships.
b. Corporations.
c. Partnerships.
d. S Corporations.
e. Limited Liability Companies.
f. b., d., and e. are taxable.

# SOLUTIONS TO CHAPTER 1 QUESTIONS

## True or False

1. F Property taxes are imposed by and important to state and local governments.
2. T
3. F Corporate income tax came into existence in 1909.
4. T
5. F The estate and gift taxes are unified into one taxing system which is progressive.
6. F The tax is progressive.
7. F The tax described is the use tax.
8. T
9. T
10. F The marginal is the most appropriate rate to use in tax planning.
11. F Tax evasion is illegal whereas tax avoidance is legal.
12. T
13. F Tax provisions dealing with taxation of individuals encourage social results. Tax provisions dealing with taxation of corporations encourage economic results.
14. T
15. F A $1,000 deduction is less valuable than a $1,000 credit for any taxpayer.
16. T
17. T

## Fill-in-the-Blanks

1. 16th, 1913
2. Property or Ad valorem
3. Federal, state, local
4. equity
5. Accelerating recognition of deductions to achieve tax deferrals
6. political
7. proprietorship, corporations, partnerships, S corporations, and limited liability companies or limited liability partnerships
8. FICA (social security and Medicare), FUTA (unemployment)
9. pay-as-you-go
10. excise
11. tax rates
12. Inheritance
13. FUTA
14. *Pollock v. Farmers Loan and Trust Co.*
15. explicit, implicit
16. Massachusetts Bay, 1634

## Multiple Choice

| | | |
|---|---|---|
| 1. | b | On a tax base of $10,000 the effective tax rate was 30% and, as the tax base increased to $100,000, the effective tax rate increased to 40%. |
| 2. | c | FICA is made up of two components: social security at a rate of 6.2% and Medicare health insurance with a rate of 1.45% for a combined rate of 7.65%. However, the Social Security base has a ceiling of $87,000 for 2003. |
| 3. | a | Bracket creep occurs when taxpayers are pushed into higher tax brackets because of increases in their wages to compensate for inflation. Indexing the tax brackets adjusts for bracket creep. |
| 4. | d | |
| 5. | d | |
| 6. | a | |
| 7. | b | Retirement plan deductions are for social considerations. The AMT is to insure that all taxpayers with substantial economic income pay a minimum amount of taxes, accelerated depreciation is to stimulate the economy, and installment sales treatment is based on the wherewithal to pay, an equity concept. |
| 8. | d | Encouraging certain business activities is an economic consideration. |
| 9. | b | Individuals may make gifts of $11,000 per person per year without using any of their unified credit. |
| 10. | d | The courts cannot change Congressional intent. |
| 11. | c | The importance of excise taxes has steadily declined, states do impose excise taxes, only states with sales taxes impose use taxes. |
| 12. | a | Use tax is a tax on the sale of goods. |
| 13. | b | VAT a *sales tax* that is major source of revenue for those countries which use it. The United State does not currently have a VAT tax. |
| 14. | d | |
| 15. | c | All income is subject to Federal taxation. The first tax act was in 1913 not 1916, tax rates have been higher than 77% and *no* deductions are allowed unless specifically provided for in the law. |
| 16. | a | Taxes are not generally solely on appreciation. Privileges and rights is the fourth base omitted from the list. |
| 17. | c | $6,844. (87,000 X 6.2%) + (100,000 X 1.45%). |
| 18. | e | Only the employer pays FUTA so Zolla paid zero FUTA. |
| 19. | c | $13,688. ($87,000 X 12.4%) + ($100,000 X 2.9%). |
| 20. | b | Only corporations are separate taxable entities. |

Chapter 2
Working with the Tax Law

## CHAPTER HIGHLIGHTS

There are three primary sources of Federal tax law: statutory, administrative, and judicial. Each of these sources contributes significantly to the development and evolution of tax law. Therefore, each of these influences must be considered and understood when working with the tax law. Numerous resources are available to assist individuals in their study of the tax law or when investigating a tax problem. If thorough research is to be performed, it is important that the researcher consider all aspects of the law's development and status, from its origin up to the very day that the research is being conducted.

I. Tax Sources -- The sources of Federal tax law are *statutory*, *administrative* and *judicial*.
   A. Statutory Sources of the Tax Law
      1. Until the Internal Revenue Code of 1939, statutory tax provisions were found in the individual acts of Congress. The codification in 1939 arranged all the Federal tax provisions into a logical and separate sequence of Federal statutes.
      2. The code was renamed in 1954 after an extensive rearrangement of the sections and continued until it was renamed again in 1986. Tax acts now amend or add new sections to the Internal Revenue Code of 1986.
      3. The Legislative Process – Generally originates in the *House Ways and Means Committee*. After passage by the House, the bills are sent to the *Senate Finance Committee* and then passed by the Senate. The Senators can amend the bill on the senate floor. It is unlikely that the bills passed by the House and the Senate will be identical. Therefore, the differences between the House and Senate versions are resolved by the *Joint Conference Committee*. The final version is approved by both houses of Congress, and finally, signed by the President.
      4. The Code – Arranged by subtitles, chapters, subchapters, parts, sections, subsections, paragraphs and subparagraphs.
         a. References to the Code usually begins with the Section number followed by the lower division indicators.
         b. Specific areas of the Code are commonly referred to by the Subsection designation. For example, Corporate tax rules are in Subsection C.
      5. Effect of Treaties -- Tax treaties with foreign countries have been established with the intent of assisting tax enforcement and mitigating double taxation. Neither a tax law nor a tax treaty automatically takes precedence. When there is a conflict, the most recent takes prevails as authority.

B. Administrative Sources of the Tax Law

1. Administrative pronouncements are either issued by the IRS or the US Treasury Department.
2. Regulations
   a. Regulations are issued by the Treasury and are general interpretations of the Code. They are arranged in the same sequence as the Code but a number is added in the front followed by a period.
   b. New Regulations and changes in existing Regulations are first issued in a proposed form to permit taxpayers to comment on them. This notice-and-comment is distinctive feature of Regulations. These Proposed Regulations carry little weight in the Tax Court.
   c. Temporary Regulations are issued when immediate guidance on a new tax law is important. They are issued without the notice-and-comment period and expire within 3 years.
   d. Final Regulations are published in the *Federal Register* and may be classified as *interpretive, legislative, or procedural.*
      (1) Interpretive Regulations rephrase and elaborate what is stated in the Committee Reports issued when the section was enacted. They are rarely overturned.
      (2) Legislative Regulations occur when Congress effectively delegates its legislative powers to the Treasury Department. They have the same force as law.
      (3) Procedural Regulations are *housekeeping* type instructions that neither establish or explain tax laws.
3. Revenue Rulings, Revenue Procedures, and Letter Rulings
   a. These pronouncements are issued by the National Office of the IRS and are specific interpretations of the tax law.
   b. They carry less weight than Regulations.
   c. Revenue Rulings and Revenue Procedures provide guidance to IRS personnel and taxpayers in handling routine tax matters. They are published weekly in the *Internal Revenue Bulletin* and semiannually the bulletins are published in a bound volume called the *Cumulative Bulletin.*

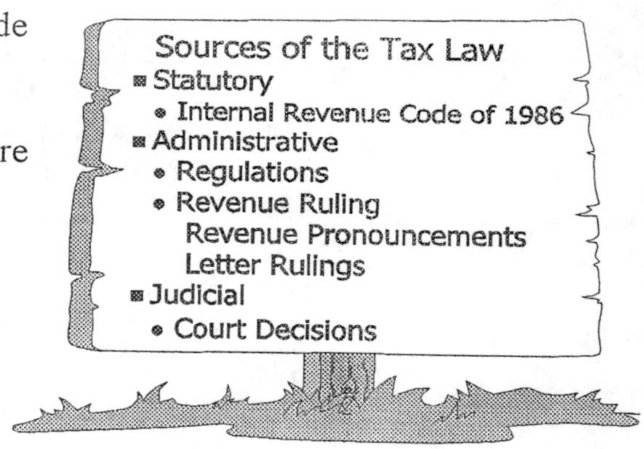


   d. Letter Rulings are issued for a fee at the request of a taxpayer and indicate how the IRS will treat a proposed transaction. Although these were once private, they are now made available for public inspection by private publishing companies.
   e. Other Administrative Pronouncements include:
      (1) *Treasury Decisions* (TDs) issued by the Treasury Department.
      (2) *Determination letters* issued by an IRS Director at the request of taxpayers. The director need not be at the National Office.

(3) The IRS National office issues *Technical Advice Memorandums* (TAMs) weekly. They are like letter rulings but are issued at the request of IRS field personnel during audits.

C. Judicial Sources of the Tax Law

1. If a taxpayer cannot reach a satisfactory remedy to a tax dispute with the IRS, the taxpayer may file with one of four Federal courts. These four trial courts (courts of original jurisdiction) are: *Federal District Court*, *Court of Federal Claims*, *US Tax Court*, and *Small Cases Division of the US Tax Court.*

2. Some of the differences between the four trial courts are listed below.
   a. There is only one Court of Federal Claims (16 judges) and one Tax Court (19 regular judges), but there are many Federal District Courts (one judges for each court).
   b. The Court of Federal Claims meets most often in Washington, D.C., whereas the other courts will hear cases at specified times and places throughout the country.
   c. The Court of Federal Claims has jurisdiction in cases against the United States (tax and nontax). The Tax Court hears only tax cases; whereas, the District Courts hear nontax as well as tax litigation.
   d. District Court is the only court in which a taxpayer can obtain a jury trial.
   e. A taxpayer may go to the Tax Court without first paying the disputed tax deficiency; whereas, with the Court of Federal Claims and the District Courts, the taxpayer must first pay the tax deficiency and then sue for a refund.
   f. Appeals from the Tax Court and the District Court are taken to the Court of Appeals. Appeals from the Court of Federal Claims are taken to the Federal Circuit Court of Appeals. No appeals are available from the Tax Court's Small Cases Division.

3. There are 13 circuits in the Court of Appeals: 11 numbered geographical Circuit Courts, District of Columbia Circuit Court, and Federal Circuit Court. Each geographical circuit has several states within its jurisdiction.

4. The trial courts must abide by the *precedents* set by the Court of Appeals of their jurisdiction. All courts must follow the Supreme Court decisions.

5. The Tax Court follows the *Golsen* rule when making decisions in different parts of the country.

6. The Supreme Court does not hear appeals automatically, rather, it hears only cases it feels are of importance (e.g., to resolve conflicts among the Court of Appeals). If the Supreme Court accepts jurisdiction, it will grant a *Writ of Certiorari*.

7. If the IRS loses in any court other than the Supreme Court, it can publish its acquiescence (agrees) or nonacquiescence (disagrees) with the holdings.

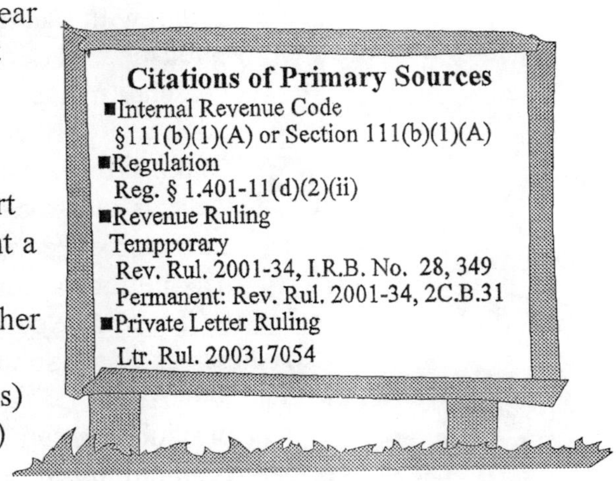

8. The Tax Court (formerly the Board of Tax Appeals) issues two types of decisions: *Regular* and *Memorandum*.
    a. The regular decisions are published by the government in a series designated *Tax Court of the United States Reports* (T.C.).
    b. The memorandum decisions are published by Commerce Clearing House in *CCH Tax Court Memorandum Decisions* and by Research Institute of America in *RIA T.C. Memorandum Decisions.*
    c. Starting in 1999, both regular and memorandum decisions can be found on the U.S. Tax Court website. Also, as of 2001, U.S. Tax Court Summary Opinions (Small Claims Division decisions) are available on the same website. A warning is provided to remind the readers that these to do not provide precedent.
9. Tax cases heard before the other courts are also printed by CCH in the *US Tax Cases* (*USTC*s) and by RIA in the *American Federal Tax Reports* (*AFTR* series).
10. West Publishing Company publishes all District Court decisions (tax and nontax) in their *Federal Supplement Series.* They publish decisions from the Court of Federal Claims and the Court of Appeals in their reporters--designated *Federal Second Series* and *Federal Third Series.* West's *Supreme Court Reporter* contains all of the Supreme Court decisions.
11. US Government Printing Office also publishes the Supreme Court decisions in the *United States Supreme Court Reports* (U.S.).

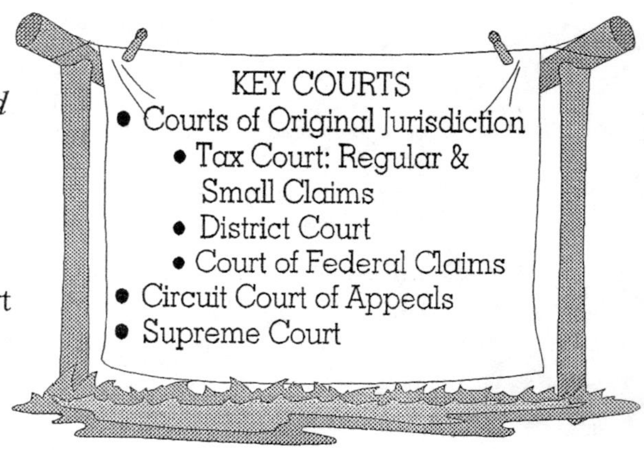


II. Working With the Tax Law -- Tax Research
  A. Tax research involves the following procedures.
    1. Identifying the Problem – Starts with collecting relevant facts for the problem.
    2. Refining the Problem – As information regarding the tax issues is gathered, the problem can be refined until it is clearly defined
    3. Locating the Appropriate Tax Law Sources
        a. Begin with searching the tax services using either an index with a published service or keyword search for electronic services. Simple searches may begin directly with the Code or Regulations.
        b. Ability to perform tax research comes with experience.
        c. Make sure the most current information is collected
        d. Always read the original primary sources of the tax law. Do not rely on tax service's commentaries.
        e. Tax periodicals are another good source of tax information.
    4. Assessing Tax Law Sources – Once the sources have been located, the validity and relevance of the sources must be assessed.
        a While the Code is of greatest authority, its language often makes it difficult to interpret.
        b. Regulations are official interpretations of the Code and are entitled to great deference. Courts generally do not question Regulations and the

IRS must follow them. However, occasionally, a court will invalidate a Regulation or portion thereof if it is contrary to the intent of Congress.

c. Revenue Rulings hold less authority than Regulations. However, the IRS will generally follow them as long as they are currently valid.

d. Reliance on court cases is dependent on several factors including the level of the court, legal residence of the taxpayer, type of decision, weight of the decision, subsequent events, and specific facts of the case.

e. When reading court cases it is important to know the following terms.

(1) Plaintiff, petitioner and appellant are generally the taxpayer

(2) Defendant, respondent, and appellee are usually the government.

(3) Holding is the decision of the court and dicta are not.

5. Arriving at the Solution or Alternative Solutions – When arriving at solutions to the tax problem, apply the tax law to the client's factual situation. Take care to consider nontax factors as well as tax factors when identifying solutions.

6. Communicating Tax Research – Effectively communicating the solution(s) to the taxpayer or the taxpayer's representative should include the following.

a. A clear statement of the issue and a short review of the facts.

b. Any assumptions made.

c. A review of the applicable tax law and other references consulted.

d. The recommend solution and the logic supporting the recommendation.

7. Following-Up Procedures – Changes in the facts of the transaction or changes in the tax law can affect the relevance of the solutions proposed.. Follow-up on the solution(s) where appropriate in light of new developments.

B. Computer-Assisted Tax Research

1. Computer based research is becoming standard practice in the field of taxation because accessing tax documents electronically offers important advantages.

a. Materials are generally available earlier through electron systems.

b. Some documents are only available through electronic means.

c. Electronic services, through bundling, offer products at little or no cost that the practitioner would otherwise not acquire.

d. Costs may be comparable with paper tax sources.

e. Convenience, and reliability of electronic research tools make them the dominate means of analyzing tax law.

2. The tax practitioners generally uses one of the following strategies when performing computer-based tax research.

a. *Search* databases using keywords.

b. *Link* to tax documents by entering the documents tax citation.

c. *Browse* the tax databases by examining the various tables of contents and indexes in a traditional manner.

3. Most major commercial tax publishers and some primary sources are available on CD-ROMs, online services, or through the Internet.

a. CD-ROM Services -- At its best, CD-ROM tax library provides the archival data that would be part of a practitioner's core tax library.

b. Online Services -- Online services allow the tax professional immediate access to tax law sources provided by the system. These services may have a price-per-search cost or a flat yearly fee.

c. Internet -- The clear advantage of the Internet is that many of the primary tax law sources are available with no direct cost. However, freely accessed information should not be relied upon without referring to other, more reliable sources.

(1) World Wide Web provides access to sites maintained by accounting and consulting firms as well as access to publishers, tax academics, libraries and governmental bodies. Exhibit 2-4 in the Text provides a list of some outstanding sites.

(2) Newsgroups allow interested parties to exchange tax law information.

> Tax research is increasingly being conducted, not with stacks of books, but solely with electronic materials as the publishers of primary and secondary source materials convert their output to electronic form. Many accounting firms use only electronic tax materials in their practice. To be competitive, the future accounting graduates are going to need highly developed computer research skills and be familiar with searching on the Web.

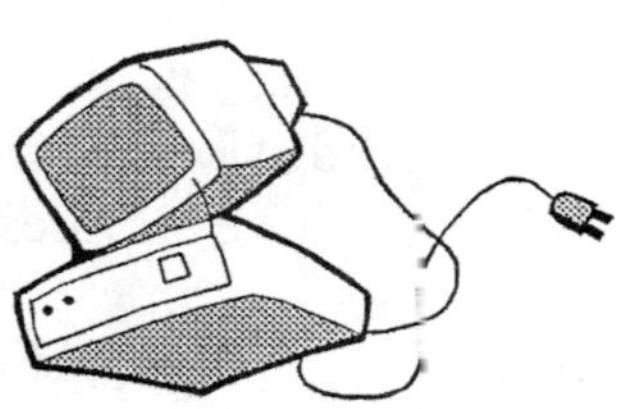

## TEST FOR SELF-EVALUATION -- CHAPTER 2

**True or False**

Indicate which of the following statements are true or false by circling the correct answer.

T F 1. The codification of tax law that is used today is known as the *Internal Revenue Code of 1986*.

T F 2. The Joint Conference Committee is called on to resolve differences between the House Ways and Means Committee version and the full House version of tax legislation.

T F 3. There are 11 Circuit Courts of Appeals throughout the United States.

T F 4. A Temporary Regulation is in effect for 3 years but a Proposed Regulation has no time limitation.

T F 5. Appeals may be made directly from the Court of Federal Claims to the Supreme Court.

T F 6. The courts of original jurisdiction include: the US District Court, the US Circuit Court, and the Court of Federal Claims.

T F 7. The level of the court and the residence of the taxpayers are important factors to consider when assessing the significance of court cases.

T F 8. A jury trial is available in both a District Court and in the Tax Court.

T F 9. When in conflict, tax treaties take precedence over the Internal Revenue Code.

T F 10. Tax research is a process that begins with identifying and refining the problem.

T F 11. Since the tax law changes infrequently, tax research performed in the last 6 months will not need updating before it is communicated to a client.

T F 12. Letter Rulings are issued to taxpayers and therefore are not published by the government.

T F 13. Revenue Rulings provide a more general interpretation of the Code than do Regulations.

T F 14. Electronic tax research via the Internet provides access to the most recent tax changes faster than a printed service..

T F 15. Tax Court Memorandum decisions are issued by the regular division of the Tax Court.

T F 16. In tax cases the plaintiff or petitioner is generally the taxpayer.

**Fill-in-the-Blanks**

Complete the following statements with the appropriate word(s) or amount(s).

1. Federal tax legislation generally originates in the ________ where it is first considered by the ________ Committee.

2. The ________ is the committee in the Senate that considers tax legislation.

3. ________, which may be legislative, interpretive, or procedural by nature, are issued by the ________ under authority granted by Congress.

4. ________ are issued by the ________ of the IRS and are interpretive in nature, but do not carry the same legal force as Regulations.

5. The Internal Revenue Bulletins are gathered and published semi-annually in bound volumes called ________.

6. Appeals from the US Tax Court or the US District Courts are taken to the ________.

7. The ________ hears only tax cases, while the ________ and the ________ trial courts hear nontax litigation as well as tax litigation.

8. For the ________ or ________ to have jurisdiction, the taxpayer must first pay any tax deficiency assessed by the IRS and then sue for a refund.

9. The ________ must abide by the precedents set by the Court of Appeals for their jurisdiction.

10. While the US Tax Court has ________ regular judges, most cases are heard by ________ judge(s).

11. A tax dispute may be heard before the Small Cases Division of the US Tax Court if the amount involved does not exceed ________.

12. When the Senate version of a tax bill differs from that passed by the House, the ________ is called on to resolve these differences.

13. Proposed, final, and temporary Regulations are published in the ________.

14. An ________ by the IRS indicates that it agrees with a decision reached by a court.

15. The role of appellate courts is limited to a review of the record of trial compiled by the ________.

16. The most common search strategies when performing computer-based tax research are ________, ________ and ________ .

17. Paragraph 1 of subsection c of Code Section 362 would be cited as ________ .

## Multiple Choice

Choose the best answer for each of the following questions.

____ 1. Which of the following is not available as an online tax service?
- a. CCH.
- b. RIA.
- c. Kleinrock.
- d. Westlaw
- e. All of these services are available online.

____ 2. The Internal Revenue Code was organized and reorganized in which years? (More than one answer is correct.)
- a. 1913.
- b. 1939.
- c. 1954.
- d. 1986
- e. 1993.

____ 3. Which of the following is not an administrative source of the Federal tax law?
- a. Treasury Department Regulations.
- b. Board of Tax Appeals rulings.
- c. Revenue Rulings.
- d. Treasury Decisions.

____ 4. Which of the following are printed in the Internal Revenue Bulletin? (More than one answer is correct.)
- a. Treasury Decisions.
- b. Private Letter Rulings
- c. Revenue Procedures.
- d. Treasury Regulations
- e. Code Sections.

____ 5. From which of the following courts can a decision *not* be appealed? (More than one answer may be correct.)
- a. Circuit Court of Appeals.
- b. Small Cases Division of the US Tax Court.
- c. US District Court.
- d. Court of Federal Claims.
- e. Supreme Court.

____ 6. Which of the following courts normally meets only in Washington, D.C.? (More than one answer may be correct.)
- a. Court of Federal Claims.
- b. US Tax Court.
- c. US District Court.
- d. US Court of Appeals.
- e. US Tax Court, Smalls Claims Division

____ 7. Which of the following is not an important element in good research communication?
a. A clear statement of the issue.
b. A short review of the fact pattern when the transaction is more complex.
c. A review of the pertinent tax law sources.
d. Any assumptions made in arriving at the solution.
e. All of these are elements in good research communications.

____ 8. Which of the following is true with regards to the Supreme Court.
a. The Supreme Court hears only cases where a *Writ of Certiorari* has been granted.
b. There are 19 judges on the Supreme Court.
c. All cases where there is a conflict between US Courts of Appeal will be heard by the Supreme Court.
d. Only cases appealed by the Commissioner of the IRS will be heard by the Supreme Court.

____ 9. Regular court decisions of the Tax Court are printed in a separate bound series by which of the following publishers:
a. Commerce Clearing House.
b. Research Institute of America.
c. West Publishing Company.
d. The US Government.
e. All of the above.

____ 10. The court cases heard in the US District Court, the Court of Federal Claims, and the US Court of Appeals are reported by which of the following publishers:
a. Commerce Clearing House.
b. Research Institute of America.
c. West Publishing Company.
d. The US Government.
e. All of the above.

____ 11. In the Regulation §1.351-3, what does the "-3" designation indicate?
a. The Regulation is an income tax Regulation.
b. The Regulation discusses the third paragraph of § 351
c. This Regulation was the third one issued on § 351.
d. This Regulation has three major paragraphs.

____ 12. Which of the following statements is *not* true regarding Regulations.
a. An Interpretative Regulation rephrases and elaborates what Congress stated in its Committee Reports.
b. A Legislative Regulation is difficult to overturn because Congress has effectively delegated its legislative powers to the Treasury Department.
c. A Procedural Regulation establishes and explains the procedures provided in the Code.
d. The IRS must give the Code and Regulations equal weight when making determinations.
e. In a challenge of a Regulation, the burden of proof is on the taxpayer.

____ 13. The person initiating a court action can be labeled as which of the following?
a. Plaintiff.
b. Petitioner.
c. Appellant.
d. Any of the above could be a possibility.
e. None of the above.

____ 14. Which of the following statement is *not* true regarding Private Letter Rulings (PLR)
a. PLR are issued only for transactions that have been completed.
b. PLR are issued to taxpayers for a fee.
c. The IRS limits the issuance of PLR to restricted, pre-announced areas of taxation.
d. An example of citation for a PLR issued in 15th week of 2003 would be 200315061.
e. All of the above are true.

____ 15. The IRS considers all of the following as primary sources except:
a. The Constitution.
b. General Counsel Memoranda.
c. Committee Reports.
d. Regulations.
e. Judicial decisions.

____ 16. Which of the following is not a major published tax service?
a. CCH *Standard Federal Tax Reporter*.
b. RIA *Federal Tax Coordinator 2d.*
c. BNA *Tax Management Portfolios*
d. Mertens *West Law's Federal Taxation*
e. All of these services are available in published form.

____ 17. The easiest way to find journal articles on a particular tax topic is through
a. RIA *Accounting and Tax Index*
b. CCH *Federal Tax Articles.*
c. West *Law Review and Tax Journal Index*
d. BNA *Index to Federal Tax Periodicals.*

____ 18. Which of the following is not a factor to consider when assessing the importance of court cases
a. Level of the court and legal residence of the taxpayer.
b. Type of decision and its weight.
c. Subsequent events like changes in the tax law or other case decisions.
d. Whether the IRS or the taxpayer was the initial petitioner.
e. All of the above should be considered.

## SOLUTIONS TO CHAPTER 2 QUESTIONS

### True or False

1. T
2. F The committee is used to resolve differences between the House version and Senate version of a tax bill.
3. F There are 13 Circuit Courts; 11 geographical, 1 for District of Columbia, and 1 for the Federal Circuit.
4. T
5. F Appeals from the Court of Federal Claims are made to the Court of Appeals for the Federal Circuit.
6. F Courts of original jurisdiction (trial courts) do not include the Circuit Court. The trial courts are: District Court, Court of Claims, Tax Court and its Small Cases Division.
7. T
8. F A jury trial is available only in the District Court.
9. F The most recently issued will take precedence.
10. T
11. F The tax law changes daily. Thus, the research would need to be updated.
12. T They are not published by the government but they are published by CCH and RIA.
13. F Revenue Rulings have more specific interpretations than Regulations.
14. T
15. T
16. T

### Fill-in-the-Blanks

1. House of Representatives, Ways and Means
2. Senate Finance Committee
3. Treasury Regulations, US Treasury Department
4. Revenue Rulings, National Office
5. Cumulative Bulletins
6. US Court of Appeals (for the taxpayer's geographical location)
7. US Tax Court, US District Courts, Court of Federal Claims
8. Court of Federal Claims, US District Courts
9. courts of original jurisdiction (or trial courts)
10. 19, 1
11. $50,000
12. Joint Conference Committee
13. Federal Register
14. acquiescence
15. trial courts
16. keyword search, document links, and browse
17. § 362(c)(1)

**Multiple Choice**

1. e
2. b, c, d The tax act of 1939 codified the Internal Revenue Code and the tax acts of 1954 and 1986 reorganized the Code.
3. b The Board of Tax Appeals rulings are judicial sources. The Tax Court was formerly called the *Board of Tax Appeals*.
4. a, c
5. b, e
6. a
7. e
8. a
9. d Since the US Government publishes Tax Court decisions in a series called *Tax Court of the United States Reports*, there is no need for the commercial services to also publish these cases.
10. e
11. c The "-3" indicates it was the third regulation issued on Code Section 351. The "1." of the Regulation indicates its an income Regulation.
12. c Procedural do *not* establish nor attempt to explain the tax law.
13. d All of these are labels for the person initiating the court action. The labels for the party against whom the case is brought are: defendant, respondent and appellee.
14. a PLR are issued for proposed transactions not completed transaction.
15. b General Counsel Memoranda and Letter Rulings while prepared by the government are not considered by the IRS as primary sources.
16. e
17. b
18. d

# Chapter 3
# Gross Income

## CHAPTER HIGHLIGHTS

Gross income is a key component in calculating a taxpayer's income tax liability. The Internal Revenue Code provides an all-inclusive definition of income. However, exclusions from income have evolved over time because of legislative, judicial, or administrative actions. The method of accounting adopted by a taxpayer is important because it generally determines the period in which income is recognized. However, special rules apply in certain situations to various types of income. In any case, all realized income must be recognized for income tax purposes unless a provision in the law specifically exempts the item from taxation. **Changes for the Jobs and Growth Tax Relief Reconciliation Act of 2003 (Tax Act of 2003) have been included in this outline.**

I. The Tax Formula: <u>Components of the Tax Formula</u>
   A. Income broadly conceived -- Tax law provides an *all-inclusive* definition of income. It is essentially equivalent to gross receipts.
   B. Exclusions -- Types of income that for various reasons Congress has chosen not to include in taxable income.
   C. Gross income -- Section 61 provides a definition of gross income: "Except as otherwise provided in this subtitle, gross income means all income from whatever source derived." Gross income is income broadly conceived less exclusions.
   D. Deductions -- Expenditures that are allowable as reductions from gross income are deductions. Deductions include all ordinary and necessary trade or business expenses. Individuals also may deduct some expenses that are personal in nature. Deduction for individuals may be categorized as *for* AGI or *from* AGI. Other taxpaying entities do not have this distinction.
   E. Determining the tax -- The resulting amount from reducing gross income by allowable deductions is taxable income. Tax rates are applied to taxable income. From the tax computed, prepayments and credits are deducted to determine the amount of the taxpayer's refund or tax due to the Federal government.

II. Gross Income – What Is It?
   A. <u>Economic and Accounting Concepts of Income</u>
      1. Economic income reflects the change in the fair market value (FMV) of a taxpayer's net assets during the period. The focus is on the change in net worth. For individuals, the consumption of goods and services during the period is considered part of economic income.

2. Tax laws rely to some extent on the net worth concept. However, the broad application of economic income is seen as impractical for tax purposes.

B. <u>Comparison of the Accounting and Tax Concepts of Income</u> – Differences exist between income tax rules and financial accounting measurement concepts because the goals of accounting and tax differ.

C. <u>Form of Receipt</u> – Income may include any increase in wealth that is received in the form of money, property, or services. It is not limited to the receipt of cash.

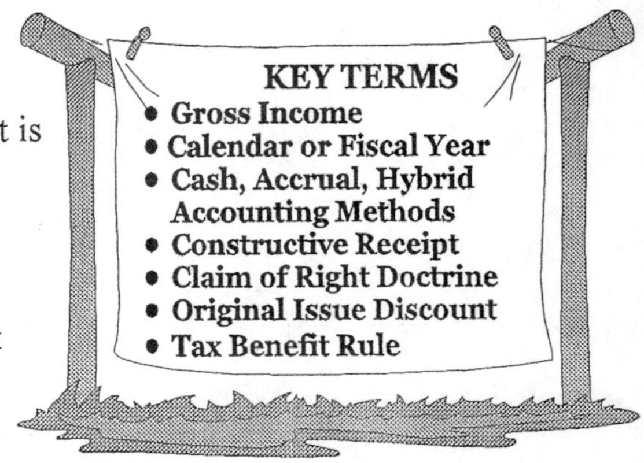


III. Year of Inclusion

A. <u>Taxable Year</u>

1. An annual accounting period or tax year is a basic measurement of time for tax returns.
   a. Generally, taxpayers use a *calendar year* to report income.
   b. Taxpayers who keep adequate books and records may elect to use a *fiscal year* (12 month period ending on the last day of any month) to report income. The fiscal year option is generally not available to partnerships, S corporations, and personal service corporations.
2. Determining the year in which income or deductions are recognized is important because of the impact recognition has on the tax liability.

B. <u>Accounting Methods</u>

1. The year an item of income is reported often depends on the method of accounting a taxpayer uses.
2. Taxpayers generally will use either the *cash receipts and disbursements method*, the *accrual method*, or a *hybrid method* in reporting income.
3. In addition to the overall methods, taxpayer may also use the installment, completed contract, or percentage of completion methods.
4. The IRS may prescribe a method of accounting if a taxpayer has not adopted a method or if the taxpayer's method does not clearly reflect income.
5. Cash Receipts Method
   a. Property or services are included in gross income in the year of actual or constructive receipt. The income need not be reduced to cash; rather, all that is necessary for income recognition is that the property or services received must have a fair market value or a cash equivalent.
   b. The primary advantage of using the cash receipts method is the ability to control the timing of recognition of income and expense.
   c. Most individuals use the cash methods. Personal service corporations and farming businesses may also use the cash method.
   d. The cash method cannot be used for inventory sales or by regular C corporations with three-year average gross receipts greater than $5 million, partnerships with corporate partners, and tax shelters.
6. Accrual Method
   a. Gross income is recognized in the year in which it is earned, regardless of when the income is collected. The income is earned when all events have occurred which fix the right to receive such income (the *all events test*) and its amount can be determined with reasonable accuracy.

b. The measure of the amount of accrual basis income is generally the amount the taxpayer has the right to receive, and not necessarily the fair market value of the receivable.

c. Accrual method *must* be used in determining the gross profit from the purchases and sales of inventory.

d. Most corporations use the accrual method.

7. Hybrid Method

a. The hybrid method is a combination of the accrual method (for computing sales and costs of goods sold) and the cash method (for all other income and expenses).

b. This is primarily used by small businesses.

C. <u>Special Rules For Cash Basis Taxpayers</u>

1. Constructive receipt doctrine

a. *Constructive receipt doctrine* limits a taxpayer's ability to shift income arbitrarily from one year to another. Constructive receipt occurs when:

(1) Income is made readily available to the taxpayer.

(2) Receipt is not subject to substantial limitations or restrictions.

b. Under the *claim of right doctrine*, constructively received income is included in the current year's income.

2. *Original issue discount*

a. *Original issue discount* (OID) is the amount due at maturity of the loan that is greater than the amount of the original loan.

b. OID must be reported as interest income as it accrues by the lender and as an expense by the borrower, regardless of the taxpayer's method of accounting.

3. Amounts received under an obligation to repay (e.g., loans, deposits), are not considered realized income.

D. <u>Special Rules For Accrual Basis Taxpayers</u>

1. General Rule – Prepaid receipts are included in income in the year of receipt, regardless of whether they have been earned. Thus, prepaid rent and prepaid interest are recognized (taxed) on a cash basis (when received).

2. Exceptions to the General Rule

a. Deferral of Advance Payments for Goods – Sellers can elect to defer recognition of income when receiving advance payment for goods if the taxpayer's method of accounting for the sale is the same for both book and tax purposes.

b. Deferral of Advance Payments for Services – Taxpayers can defer income recognition for advance payments for services when the services will be completed by the end of the year following the year of receipt.

> Because the IRS has a computerized matching program for income reported by taxpayers and their employers, taxpayers should verify that the amount of salary and other income reported to the IRS is correct. If W-2s or Form 1099s are incorrect, a taxpayer should have them corrected as soon as possible so the IRS's records agree with the amounts shown on the individual's tax return.

IV. Income Sources

A. Personal Services – The income generated from personal services must be included in the gross income of the person who performs the services. A mere assignment of income does not shift the liability for the tax. (Remember the fruit and tree metaphor).

B. Income from Property

1. Income from property, such as interest, dividends, or rents, must be included in the income of the *owner* of the property.

2. *Interest* is considered to accrue daily. Therefore, if interest bearing property is transferred, the interest must be allocated between the transferor and the transferee based on the number of days that each owned the property.

3. *Dividends* do not accrue on a daily basis because their declaration is at the discretion of the corporation's board of directors. Dividends are taxed to the holder of the stock on the date of record. However, the Tax Court has held that a donor cannot shift the dividend income to a donee if a gift of property is made after the date of declaration and before the date of record.

C. Income Received by an Agent – Income received by a taxpayer's agent is considered to be received by the taxpayer and taxable to the taxpayer.

V. Specific Items of Gross Income

A. Imputed Interest on Below Market Loans

1. Imputed interest is taxable and maybe deductible (see Table next page) even though no exchange has taken place, ie, no realization has occurred.

2. Imputed interest is figured using Federal rates and is compounded semiannually.

3. The imputed interest rules apply to the following below-market loans:

   a. Gift loans,

   b. Compensation-related loans,

   c. Corporation-shareholder loans,

   d. Tax avoidance loans, and loans that significantly affect the borrower's or lender's Federal tax liability.

4. Exceptions and limitations to the imputed interest rules.

   a. Compensation-related loans and corporation-shareholder loans of $10,000 or less do not have interest imputed unless the purpose of the loan is tax avoidance.

   b. Gift loans of $10,000 or less also do not have interest imputed unless the proceeds are used to purchase income producing property.

   c. The interest imputed on loans of $100,000 or less between individuals cannot exceed the borrower's net investment income for the year.

B. Tax Benefit Rule

1. If a taxpayer obtains tax benefit from a deduction in one year and in a later year recovers a portion of the deducted amount, the recovery triggers income in the year of recovery.

**Effect of Certain Below-Market Loans**

| ***Type of Loan*** | ***Lender*** | ***Borrower*** |
|---|---|---|
| *Gift* | *Interest income*<br>*Gift made* | *Interest Expense*<br>*Gift received* |
| *Compensation-related* | *Interest income*<br>*Compensation expense* | *Interest expense*<br>*Compensation income* |
| *Corporation to shareholder* | *Interest income*<br>*Dividend paid* | *Interest expense*<br>*Dividend income* |

2. No income is recognized on the recovery of an expense amount if a tax benefit (deduction) was not received in a prior year.

C. Interest on Certain State and Local Government Obligations

1. Interest income on state and local government obligations is exempt from Federal taxation.
2. The receipts received from state and local governments that are **not** excluded by this provision are as follows.
   a. Interest received on condemnation awards.
   b. Interest paid on overpayments of a state or local income tax liabilities.
   c. Gains on the sale of tax-exempt securities.
3. Private activity bonds are issued by municipalities which use the proceeds to facilitate private business. The use of these securities is limited by the tax law but the interest tends to be tax-exempt for regular tax purposes.

> While most municipal bond interest is not subject to Federal income tax, capital gain income realized on their sale is taxable. An investor should be aware of this when deciding which bonds to buy, and when to sell them. Further, investors should be aware of whether the bonds purchased will be classified as private activity bonds due to the limitations placed on these bonds by Congress.

D. Improvements on Leased Property

1. Leasehold improvements made by a lessee (the renter) to a landlord's (lessor's) property revert to the lessor upon expiration of the lease.
2. The value of these improvements is not income to the landlord when the lease expires. They are taxable only when sold. If improvements are made in lieu of rent, they are taxable as rent.

E. Life Insurance Proceeds

1. General Rule – Life insurance proceeds paid to a beneficiary by reason of the insured's death are exempt from income taxation.
2. Exception to General Rule
   a. If the owner cancels the policy and receives the cash surrender value, the taxpayer recognizes gain equal to the excess of the amount received over premiums paid on the policy.

b. Transfer for valuable consideration – When a life insurance policy is transferred to someone for valuable consideration, the portion of insurance proceeds received in excess of the consideration given (plus any subsequent premiums paid) are included in the gross income of the recipient.

3. Exceptions to Transfer Rule – Exclusion treatment is also allowed for the following transfers.
   a. A partner of the insured.
   b. A partnership in which the insured is a partner.
   c. A corporation in which the insured is an officer or shareholder.
   d. A transferee whose basis in a policy is determined by reference to the transferor's basis (e.g., property received by gift or divorce).

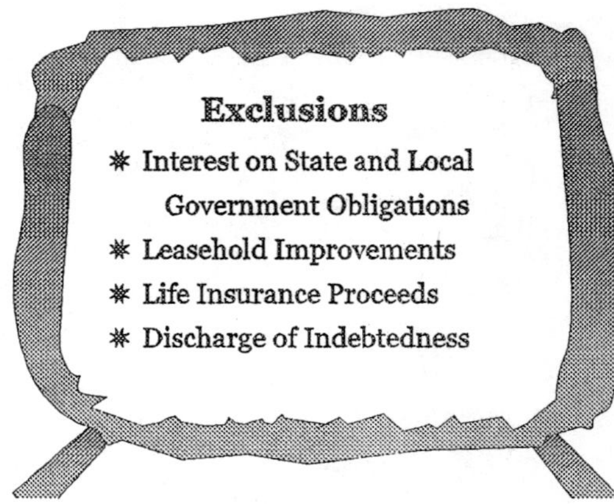


4. Investment earnings from the reinvestment of life insurance proceeds are generally subject to tax.

F. <u>Income from Discharge of Indebtedness</u>

1. The following situations create income for the debtor (the borrower).
   a. The use of appreciated property to pay a debt. This is treated as a sale of the property followed by a payment of the debt.
   b. Foreclosure by a creditor. This is also treated as a sale or exchange.
   c. Cancellation of debt by a creditor.

2. However, the discharge of indebtedness is excluded from income in the following situations.
   a. Creditor Gift – Forgiveness of part or all of the debt due to love, affection, or generosity is treated as a gift to the debtor. Such forgiveness generally arise only on loans between friends or family.
   b. Bankrupt or insolvent – No income is recognized for discharges under Federal bankruptcy law. When the debtor is insolvent the exclusion is limited to the amount of insolvency. However, certain tax benefits must be decreased by the amount of income excluded.
   c. A solvent taxpayer whose farm debt is discharged.
   d. Discharge of *qualified real property indebtedness* – Noncorporate taxpayers may exclude the limited lesser of:
      (1) the excess of the debt over the FMV of the property, or
      (2) the adjusted basis of all real property held.

      The basis of the depreciable real property held by the taxpayer must be reduced by amount excluded.
   e. Seller's cancellation – Indebtedness is treated as a reduction in the selling price of the property. Consequently, the buyer's basis in the property is reduced by the amount of the cancellation.
   f. Shareholder cancellation – Debt of a corporation to its shareholder may be canceled without triggering income to the corporation. The

forgiveness is treated as a contribution to the corporations' capital by the shareholder. The shareholder's basis in the stock is increased by the amount of the forgiven debt.

g. Student loans – Forgiveness of student loans by states under conditions that the student practice a profession within the state are excluded from gross income.

VI. <u>Gains and Losses from Property Transactions</u>

A. The disposition of property produces realized gains or losses. The concept of realized gain or loss (gain/loss) can be expressed as follows:

| Amount realized from the sale | – | Adjusted basis of the property | = | Realized gain or loss |
|---|---|---|---|---|

1. Amount realized: selling price less any selling costs.
2. Adjusted basis: original basis (cost) + capital improvements - capital recoveries (depreciation or cost recovery).

B. All realized gains are recognized (taxed) unless specifically excluded. Realized losses may or may not be recognized (deductible) for tax purposes, depending on the circumstances.

C. When gain/ loss recognition occurs, the character of the gain/loss must be determined.

1. Ordinary gains are fully taxable and ordinary losses are fully deductible.
2. Capital assets, defined in § 1221, are asset *other than* inventory, accounts & notes receivables, and depreciable property or real estate used in a business.
   a. The assets defined by § 1221 as not being capital usually generate ordinary income or losses upon their disposition.
   b. All other assets generally produce capital gains or losses.

D. Tax treatment of capital gains/losses for individuals

1. Individuals net capital gains are subject to the following maximum rates.
   a. Short-term gains (assets held one year or less): 38.6% before the Tax Act of 2003 and 35% after the Act.
   b. Long-term gains (assets held greater than one year): 20% before the Tax Act of 2003 and 15% after the Act.
2. Individual capital losses in excess of capital gains can offset up to $3,000 of ordinary income each year. Remaining losses can be carried forward until used. No time limit on the carryforward of losses.

E. Corporate net capital gains/losses are subject to the following treatment.

1. No special tax rates are provided for net capital gains.
2. Capital losses can only offset capital gains. Net capital losses do not offset ordinary income, rather, they are carried back 3 years and then forward 5 years to offset capital gains occurring in the carryover years.

## TEST FOR SELF-EVALUATION -- CHAPTER 3

**True or False**

Indicate which of the following statements are true or false by circling the correct answer.

T F 1. All realized gains are recognized for income tax purposes.

T F 2. Individuals may carry forward unused capital losses for an indefinite period until they are finally utilized.

T F 3. Corporate taxpayers that incur capital losses may never deduct those losses against ordinary income.

T F 4. Individual taxpayers who incur capital losses may never deduct those losses against ordinary income.

T F 5. The hybrid method of accounting is required when inventory is a substantial income producing factor.

T F 6. Provided a taxpayer maintains adequate books and records, a fiscal year may be selected to report taxable income.

T F 7. An accrual basis taxpayer can defer advanced payments for goods or services to be delivered or performed by the end of the tax year following the year of receipt.

T F 8. If a father "clips" interest coupons from bonds just before interest payments are due and gives the coupons to his son, the father will still have to pay taxes on the interest income.

T F 9. A security deposit received by a landlord (which will be returned if no damages are caused by the renter) must be included in the landlord's income in the year of receipt.

T F 10. A salary check received on the evening of December 31, 20X1 after banking hours is taxable in 20X1.

T F 11. When a $20,000 loan was extended to an employee (who is not a shareholder) by an employer at below-market rates, the employer will recognize imputed interest income and claim a compensation expense, and the employee reports compensation income and may claim an interest deduction.

T F 12. Based on the doctrine of constructive receipt, an item is not brought into income until the taxpayer has actually received cash.

T F 13. Tax accounting rules are not necessarily consistent with generally accepted accounting principles.

T F 14. Life insurance proceeds are always excluded from income.

T F 15. Original issue discount interest is reported when it is earned regardless of the taxpayer's accounting method.

T F 16. Dividends are considered to accrue as income daily in the same manner as interest.

T F 17. The tax benefit rule requires taxpayers to take a deduction when they receive a tax benefit from an expense.

T F 18. Interest received on certain state and local government obligations is excluded from Federal income taxation.

T F 19. Gain realized on the sale of a bond issued by a municipality is not recognized.

T F 20. Generally, a debtor whose debt is forgiven has enjoyed the receipt of income that must be recognized for tax purposes.

**Fill-in-the-Blanks**

Complete the following statements with the appropriate word(s) or amount(s).

1. In determining the realized gain or loss from a sale, the property's ________ must be subtracted from the amount realized from the sale.

2. Once it has been determined that the disposition of property results in recognizable gain or loss, the next step is to classify such gain or loss as ________ or ________.

3. The term income is defined ________ in the Code whereas deductions are defined ________.

4. ________ income is determined by the change in the fair market value of net assets for the year. Thus, the focus is on ________ as a measure of income does not require realization.

5. The ________ doctrine places certain limits on the ability of cash basis taxpayers to arbitrarily shift income from one year to another.

6. Gross income includes income realized in any form, whether in the form of ________, ________, or ________.

7. The imputed interest rules generally apply to various types of ________.

8. Three acceptable methods of accounting are ________, ________, and ________.

9. The IRS may prescribe a taxpayer's method of accounting if a taxpayer's method does not ________.

10. According to financial accounting, revenue is ________ when it is ________.

11. The ________ provides that if a taxpayer obtains a benefit from a deduction in one year and later recovers a portion of that deduction, the recovery produces taxable income in the year received.

12. The income received by a taxpayer's ________ is considered to be constructively received by the taxpayer.

13. The interest earned from certain ________ and ________ obligations is excluded from Federal income tax.

14. When leasehold improvements revert to the landlord upon expiration of the lease, the improvements are included in gross income of the landlord when ________.

15. Generally, debtors ________ income when a debt is canceled. However, if the forgiveness of the debt occurs when the debtor is ________ or if the cancellation results from a ________ proceeding, the debtor may not ________ income.

## Multiple Choice

Choose the best answer for each of the following questions.

____ 1. Sung has the following transactions during the current year: sale of his personal residence at a loss of $4,200; sale of his antique automobile at a gain of $300; and a sale of Skyview Corporation stock at a gain of $2,800. What is the amount of gain or loss to be recognized for the year by Sung?
   - a. $2,800 gain.
   - b. $3,100 gain.
   - c. $1,400 loss.
   - d. $1,100 loss.

____ 2. Margaret had taxable income of $15,000 for the current year not including capital transactions. She had a net short-term capital loss of $1,000 and a net long-term capital loss of $4,000. Calculate Margaret's taxable income after consideration of her capital transactions.
   - a. $15,000.
   - b. $14,000.
   - c. $12,000.
   - d. $10,000.

____ 3. Val and Olga West, who are both over 65, file a joint income tax return which reflects the following.

| | |
|---|---|
| Salary | $10,000 |
| Life insurance proceeds due to death of Olga's father | 25,000 |
| Forgiveness of student loan by Commercial Bank | 2,000 |
| Dividends on stock purchased after the dividend declaration date but before the record date | 19,000 |
| Interest on City of Pullman Bonds | 8,000 |

From the above information, how much gross income do the West's have?
   - a. $10,000.
   - b. $12,000.
   - c. $31,000.
   - d. $39,000.

____ 4. Select the correct statements. (More than one statement may be correct)

a. Tax and accounting rules for income measurement differ because the goals of each are different.

b. Accounting income is based on the recognition principle.

c. The fiscal tax year option is available to all types of corporations.

d. Original issue discount must be reported as income by the lender only for accrual basis taxpayers.

e. Prepaid rents and interest are taxable when received by cash or accrual taxpayers.

____ 5. Raji Inc., an accrual taxpayer, had the following items of revenue during 20X1.

| | |
|---|---|
| Life insurance proceeds from the death of the Treasurer | $100,000 |
| Payments for goods to be shipped in 20X2 | 1,500 |
| Payments for services to be furnished in 20X2 and 20X3 | 6,000 |
| Refund of overpayment of property taxes for 20X0 | 6,000 |

Raji Inc. uses shipment date for reporting income for financial purpose. What is the gross income of Raji Inc. for taxes in 20X1.

a. $000.

b. $12,000.

c. $13,500.

d. $113,500.

e. None of the above.

____ 6. Which of the following statements is true regarding financial accounting and income tax accounting:

a. Unearned income received by accrual basis company is often taxed in year of receipt whereas for financial accounting it is revenue in the year earned.

b. Fiscal year accounting period is allowed for most corporations for tax purposes and any business for financial accounting.

c. Estimates for items such as bad debt are permissible in financial accounting but not for tax purposes.

d. Financial accounting is conservative in recording revenue whereas tax has a broad inclusive view of income.

e. All of the above are true.

____ 7. Which of the following is *not* a reason why determining an annual accounting period for tax purposes is important.

a. Congress may change the tax rate schedule.

b. The entity must file financial statements on a yearly basis.

c. The entity's income may rise or fall between years so that recognizing income in a particular year may mean that the income is taxed at different marginal rates.

d. The entity may undergo a change in status and a different tax rate schedule may apply (e.g., change from a sole proprietorship to a corporation).

e. All of the above are important.

____ 8. On May 1, Jonathan deposited $5,000 in a certificate of deposit (CD) paying 6% interest annually on April 30. On December 27 Jonathan gave the CD to his son. If Jonathan is a calendar year taxpayer, how much interest will Jonathan include in his income for the current year (not a leap year)?

a. $0.
b. $197.
c. $200.
d. $225.
e. None of the above.

____ 9. Nel's savings account at the bank was credited with $120 of interest on December 31, last year. The balance prior to the inclusion of the interest income was $2,400. On February 4, of this year, she withdraws $2,520 from her account. Nel is on the cash basis. What amount must be recognized as income this year?
a. $0.
b. $120.
c. $2,400.
d. $2,520.
e. None of the above.

____ 10. Select the incorrect statement.
a. Appreciation in the market value of an asset would be economic income but not accounting income.
b. For a cash basis taxpayer, the year of payment generally determines the period in which an expense is deductible.
c. An accrual basis taxpayer does not always recognize the same amount of net income for book and tax purposes.
d. As long as a taxpayer follows generally accepted accounting principles, the Commissioner of the IRS cannot prescribe a change in accounting methods.
e. None of the above.

____ 11. The Drayer Corporation, an accrual basis calendar-year taxpayer, sells its services under 12, 18, and 24 month contracts. The corporation services each customer when requested. On May 1 of the current year, Drayer sold the following customer contracts, receiving payment as indicated.

| *Length of Contract* | *Proceeds* |
|---|---|
| 12 months | $9,000 |
| 18 months | 7,500 |
| 24 months | 4,800 |

The Drayer Corporation should recognize taxable income of what amount this year?
a. $4,800.
b. $13,800.
c. $14,133.
d. $21,300.

____ 12. On April 1, Sandra gives her dependent son $20,000 of stock that pays dividends equal to 5% of the value to owners of record on July 1 and January 1 (i.e., 5% twice a year). Sandra and her son are cash basis taxpayers. How much of the $2,000 in dividends paid during the current year will the son recognize as income?
a. $0.
b. $1,000
c. $1,342.
d. $1,500.

____ 13. Dr. Dogood practices psychology in Virginia. Her patients usually pay their office visit charges on the date of the visit or within one month. Additionally, she makes house calls for some of her patients. The outside visits are billed weekly, and are usually paid within two months after the patients collect from their insurance companies. Dr. Dogood is a cash basis taxpayer. Information relating to this year is as follows.

| | |
|---|---|
| Cash received on the date of office visits | $ 40,000 |
| Collections on accounts receivable | 100,000 |
| Accounts receivable, beginning of year | 25,000 |
| Accounts receivable, end of year | 21,000 |

Calculate Dr. Dogood's gross income from her medical practice for this year.

a. $161,000.
b. $144,000.
c. $140,000.
d. $136,000.
e. None of the above.

ITEMS 14 THROUGH 16 ARE BASED ON THE FOLLOWING DATA.

Carmen had the following cash receipts during the current year (20X1).

| | |
|---|---|
| Interest on life insurance proceeds from her deceased aunt's policy left on deposit with the insurance company | $ 42 |
| Interest on state of Utah bond | 1,000 |
| Net rent from condominiums (condos) | 18,000 |
| Advance rent from condos for last months of the 4-year lease | 3,000 |
| Cleaning deposits paid in 20X1 by the renters of the condos | 1,000 |
| Leasehold improvement made by renter on 10/15/X1 | 1,200 |
| Dividends declared on 11/20/X1 and mailed on 12/31/X1 to holders of record on 12/20/X1. Received in mail on 1/10/20X2 | 720 |

____ 14. How much should Carmen include in her current taxable income for interest?

a. $42.
b. $1,000.
c. $1,042.
d. $0.

____ 15. How much should Carmen include in her current taxable income for rent?

a. $18,000.
b. $19,000.
c. $20,200.
d. $21,000.
e. $23,200.

____ 16. How much should Carmen report as dividend income and in what year?

a. $720 in current year (20X1).
b. $720 in next year (20X2).
c. $480 in 20X1 and $240 in 20X2.
d. Not enough information is given to compute the 20X1 and 20X2 income split.

____ 17. On January 1 of the current year, AstroCorp makes a loan of $300,000 to its President, Andre. The interest rate charged by AstroCorp is 3% when the Federal applicable rate for the year is 8%. How is this transactions treated by Astrocorp and Andre?

a. Astrocorp has $9,000 of interest and Andre has $24,000 of compensation.
b. Astrocorp has $15,000 of interest and Andre has $9,000 of compensation.
c. Astrocorp has $24,000 of interest and Andre has $15,000 of compensation.
d. Astrocorp has $24,000 of interest and Andre has $24,000 of compensation.
e. None of the above.

____ 18. Julia owed Franco $50,000 on an unsecured noted. Julia transfers common stock she bought five years ago for $40,000 to Franco in complete payment of the debt when the stock has a fair market value of $50,000. What is the proper treatment of Julia's loan payment.

a. Franco has been repaid the full amount of the debt and Julia has no income.
b. Franco has a bad debt deduction of $10,000.
c. Julia recognizes $10,000 gain from the discharge of indebtedness.
d. Julia recognizes a capital gain of $10,000.
e. b and c are both correct.

____ 19. The imputed interest rules on below-market loans apply to which of the following types of loans?

a. Gift loans.
b. Compensation-related loans.
c. Corporation-shareholder loans.
d. Tax avoidance loans.
e. All of the above are subject to the imputed interest rules.

____ 20. In 20X1, Jose had taxable income of $400 before considering the effect of a business bad debt of $700. As a result, he properly claimed a deduction of $700 for the uncollectible amount, expecting that the customer would never pay the amount due. However, to his surprise, the amount was fully collected in 20X2. How does Jose treat this recovery?

a. No income in 20X2. File a amended return for 20X1.
b. Adjust allowance for bad debts by $700 in 20X2.
c. Recognize $700 of income in 20X2.
d. Recognize $400 of income in 20X2.

____ 21. If a life insurance contract has been transferred for valuable consideration to another individual who assumes ownership rights, then a portion of the proceeds by reason of death are included in income. An exception to this rule includes a transfer to which of the following?

a. A partner of the insured.
b. A corporation in which the insured is an officer.
c. A fellow shareholder of a corporation.
d. a. and b.
e. a, b, and c.

____ 22. Shontelle received the following interest payments during the year.

| | |
|---|---|
| Interest on refund of Federal income tax for the prior year | $520 |
| Interest on a condemnation award | 460 |
| Interest on municipal bonds | 900 |
| Interest on investment of life insurance proceeds | 650 |

How much should she report as gross income?

a. $0.
b. $980.
c. $1,630.
d. $2,530.
e. None of the above.

____ 23. Which of the following is *not* excluded from a taxpayer's gross income for Federal income tax purposes?

a. Amounts received under an obligation to repay.
b. Gifts received from one's parents.
c. Imputed interest on compensated related loans of less than $10,000.
d. Refund of overpayment of life insurance premiums.
e. All of the above are excluded.

____ 24. Hassan, the owner of a $50,000 life insurance policy, decides to cancel the policy. He has paid premiums of $12,000 during the years the policy has been in force, while the current cash surrender value received on the cancellation is $20,000. Hassan must recognize income of what amount?

a. $0.
b. $8,000.
c. $20,000.
d. $30,000.
e. None of the above.

____ 25. Ivan, the owner of a $50,000 life insurance policy, had planned to cancel the policy. However, he was killed in a tragic automobile accident prior to contacting his insurance agent. He had paid premiums totaling $12,000 during the years since the policy's acquisition. At the time of Ivan's death, the policy had a cash surrender value of $20,000. What amount is taxable on the receipt of the $50,000 proceeds?

a. $0.
b. $30,000.
c. $38,000.
d. $50,000.

## SOLUTIONS TO CHAPTER 3 QUESTIONS

**True or False**

1. F The tax law provides certain exceptions to realized gains being recognized.
2. T
3. T Such losses may only be used to offset capital gains.
4. F Net capital losses may offset up to $3,000 of ordinary income each year.
5. F The accrual method or hybrid method can be used when there is inventory.
6. T However, in many situations partnerships, S corporations, and personal service corporations may not use a fiscal year.
7. F The deferral only applies to services, and not to goods.
8. T The "fruit and tree" doctrine is applicable.
9. F Because the lessor has an obligation to return the money, no income is recognized.
10. T The amount is constructively received, and therefore taxable in 20X1.
11. T
12. F There need not be an actual receipt of cash, only that the amount is available without substantial restrictions.
13. T
14. F Normally this is the case, but exceptions do exist such as when the insured cancels the policy and receives the cash surrender value. The excess received over the premiums paid is taxable. Also when life insurance proceeds are received for consideration.
15. T
16. F Dividends do not accrue daily because their declaration is at Board's discretion.
17. F The tax benefit rule requires that if a taxpayer received a tax benefit from a deduction in one year and then recovers a portion of the amount previously deducted, the taxpayers must recognize income in the year of receipt.
18. T
19. F The exclusion pertains only to the interest income generated by such obligations.
20. T

**Fill-in-the-Blanks**

1. adjusted basis
2. capital, ordinary
3. broadly, narrowly
4. Economic, net worth
5. constructive receipt
6. money, property, services
7. below-market loans
8. cash, accrual, hybrid
9. clearly reflect income
10 recognized, realized
11. tax benefit rule
12. agent
13. state, local or municipal
14. the property is sold.
15. recognize, insolvent, bankruptcy, recognize

**Multiple Choice**

1. b $3,100. 300 + 2,800. Loss from sale of personal residence is not deductible.
2. c $12,000. 15,000 - 3,000 (net capital losses allowed; limited to $3,000 per year).
3. c $31,000. 10,000 + 2,000 + 19,000. Only student loans forgiven by states are not taxable. Dividends are taxable to the owner on the record date.
4. a, e Accounting income is based on the realization principle not the recognition principle. The fiscal tax year option is not available to S corporations and personal service corporations. Original issue discount must be reported as income by all lenders, regardless of accounting method.
5. b $12,000. 6,000 + 6,000. Payment for services occurring beyond the end of the next year and overpayment of property taxes due to the tax benefit rule.
6. e
7. b
8. b $197. 5,000 X 6% X (240/365). Jonathan owns the CD for 240 days.
9. a $0. The interest of $120 would have been recognized last year.
10. d The IRS is not bound to follow generally accepted accounting principles.
11. c $14,133. (8/12 X 9,000) + (8/18 X 7,500) + 4,800.
12. b $1,000. The son was the owner of record only for the July 1 dividend.
13. c $140,000. 40,000 + 100,000.
14. a $42 from life insurance left on deposit is taxable. State bond interest is not taxable.
15. d $21,000. 18,000 + 3,000. The leasehold improvement is not currently taxable.
16. b The dividend is taxable in the year it is received.
17. c $24,000. (300,000 X 3% stated interest) + (300,000 X 5% imputed interest). Imputed compensation is equal to imputed interest.
18. d The use of the stock to pay the loan is a disposition of a capital asset and gain of $10,000 is recognized (50,000 - 40,000).
19. e
20. d Income is recognized in the year of recovery to the extent the deduction reduced taxable income ($400) in the earlier year.
21. d
22. c $1,630. 520 + 460 + 650
23. e
24. b $8,000. 20,000 - 12,000.
25. a

Chapter 4
# Business Deductions

## CHAPTER HIGHLIGHTS

Generally deductions are allowed in determining taxable income for expenses incurred in a trade or business or in the production of income as well as for some items of a personal nature. Deductions may have limitations on the amounts that are deductible and a number of expenditures that may appear to be business costs are not deductible under the Code.

Many assets acquired for use in a trade or business or held for the production of income are not currently deductible because their lives extend substantially beyond the close of the tax year. The tax benefit of these costs are recovered over an asset's useful life or over a specified period of time. Distinctions such as whether an asset is used in business or for personal use, whether it is realty or personalty, or whether it is tangible or intangible, are important when determining their tax treatment. **Changes for the Jobs and Growth Tax Relief Reconciliation Act of 2003 (Tax Act of 2003) have been included in this outline.**

I. Overview of Business Deductions
   A. Ordinary and Necessary Requirement
      1. Section 162(a) allows a deduction for all expenses that are both *ordinary and necessary* and paid or incurred to carry on a trade or business.
         a. An expense is *necessary* if a prudent business person would incur such an expense and if the expense is expected to be appropriate and helpful in the taxpayer's business.
         b. An expense is *ordinary* if it is normal, usual, or customary in the taxpayer's business. The amount cannot be capital in nature and it need *not* be a recurring expenditure.
   B. Reasonableness Requirement
      1. Salaries and other compensation for personal services must be of a *reasonable* amount in order to be deducted.
      2. Further, the courts have held that for other business expenses to be ordinary and necessary, they must also be reasonable in amount. What constitutes reasonable is a *question of fact*.

II. Timing of Expense Recognition
   A. The taxpayer's accounting method controls when an item is deductible in computing taxable income. The method selected must clearly reflect the taxpayer's income and must be applied consistently.

B. Cash Method Requirements

1. Expenses are deductible when the amount is actually or constructively paid with cash, credit card, or other property. However, payment does not assure a current deduction.
2. If an expenditure creates an asset that has a life which extends substantially beyond the close of the tax year (one-year rule), the amount must be capitalized.
3. Not all taxpayers are allowed to use cash method.

C. Accrual Method Requirements

1. Expense are deductible when the *all events test* and the *economic performance test* are met.
2. The all events test denies a deduction for expenses until
   a. all events have occurred to create the taxpayer's liability, and
   b. the amount can be determined with reasonable accuracy.
3. Once the all events test is satisfied, economic performance must occur before a deduction is allowed.
   a. Economic performance test is met when the service, property, or use of property giving rise to the liability is actually performed for, provided to, or used by the entity.
   b. Exceptions to the economic performance test apply in the case of certain recurring items.
   c. Reserves for estimated expenses are generally *not* deductible for tax purposes because the economic performance test cannot be satisfied.

III. Disallowance Possibilities

A. Public Policy Limitation

1. A payment that is in *violation of public policy* is not considered a necessary expense and therefore is not deductible.
2. Nondeductible expenses that fall under this limitation include: illegal bribes and kickbacks, fines and penalties, and two-thirds of the treble damage payments.
3. Legal expenses are deductible only if they are incurred in connection with a trade or business activity, the production of income, or are associated with the determination of a tax liability.
4. The normal expenses of operating an illegal business, other than expenses which are in violation of public policy, are deductible. However, no deductions other than cost of goods sold are permitted for expenditures incurred with regard to illegal trafficking in drugs.

B. Political Contributions and Lobbying Activities

1. The general rule – no deduction is allowed for direct or indirect payments made for political purposes.
2. Exceptions – Deductions are allowed for activities devoted to monitoring legislation and lobbying expenses at the local government level. Further, there is a *de minimis* exception for up to $2,000 of in-house expenditures.

C. Excessive Executive Compensation

1. The *millionaires provision* in the Code applies to compensation paid to officials of publicly held corporations.
2. This provision limits the employer's compensation *deduction* to $1 million annually for the chief executive officer and 4 other highly paid employees.
3. Employee compensation *excludes* the following: commissions, performance-based pay, payments to retirement plans, and nontaxable fringe benefits.

> The millionaires provision was enacted to appease middle-class taxpayers who were angered by the high salaries paid and deducted by large public corporations. Due to the exclusions to the millionaires provision, however, most executives can still receive their high compensation and corporations qualify to deduct them. The "loop hole" is compensation based on performance of the individual or the company are excluded from the limitation.

D. Disallowance of Deductions for Capital Expenditures

1. Amounts paid for buildings or for permanent improvements must be capitalized rather than being currently deducted.
2. When an item is capitalized, the deduction, is generally deferred. Some capitalized costs, however, are not recovered. The deductibility of capitalized costs is covered in the "Cost Recovery Allowances" section of this outline.

E. Investigation of a Business

1. The relevant expenses for investigating a business in the same or similar line of the taxpayer's business are deductible currently.
2. Business investigation expenses that are *not* in the same or similar line of the taxpayer's business are *not* currently deductible. If the new business is acquired, expenses must be amortized over a period of 60 months or more. If the business is not acquired, the expenses are not deductible.

F. Transactions Between Related Parties

1. The tax law has placed restrictions on transactions between *related parties* because of the opportunities to create tax savings from sales or exchanges that have no economic substance.
2. Code § 267 *disallows* loss recognition for property transactions between related parties. The unrecognized loss may be used to reduce any realized gain on the subsequent sale of the property to an unrelated person.
3. Code § 267 defers deductions by accrual basis taxpayers when they are paying a related party who is on the cash basis. The deduction may be taken in the period when the payment is included in the income of the cash basis recipient.

4. Related parties include the following.
   a. Brothers, sisters (including half-blood or adopted), spouse, ancestors, and lineal descendants of the taxpayer.
   b. A corporation owned *more than* 50% by the taxpayer.
   c. Two corporations that are members of a controlled group.
   d. Constructive ownership rules are used in determining whether taxpayers are related. These rules provide that, stock owned by related individuals or entities is *deemed* to be owned by the taxpayer.

G. <u>Lack of Adequate Substantiation</u>
   1. Taxpayers have the burden of proof for substantiating deductible expenditures.
   2. Appropriate documentation and substantiation of events and transactions are therefore advisable, and generally required by law.

H. <u>Expenses and Interest Relating to Tax-Exempt Income</u>
   1. Generally, expenses incurred for purposes of producing tax-exempt income are *not* deductible.
   2. It is often very difficult to show a direct relationship between borrowing and investments in tax-exempt securities. Judicial interpretation generally has tried to show "reasonableness" in the disallowance of expenses under this Code section.

IV. Charitable Contributions

A. Charitable contributions made to qualified domestic organizations may be deducted by individuals and corporations. The IRS publishes a list of organizations qualifying as charities. All these organizations are either
   1. Governmental subdivisions of the US, or
   2. Entities organized within the US as a corporation, trust, community chest, fund or foundation for a variety of acceptable purposes.

B. Time of Deduction
   1. A charitable contribution generally is deductible in the year payment is made.
   2. An accrual basis corporate taxpayer may claim a deduction in the year prior to payment if the actual contribution is made within 2 ½ months of the close of the taxable year *and* the board of directors has authorized such payment prior to the end of the year.

C. <u>Property Contributions</u>
   1. Long-Term Capital Gain Property (held greater than 1 year)
      a. General Rule – The contribution amount is equal to the fair market value (FMV) of the property at date of contribution.
      b. Exceptions – Basis rather than FMV is the contribution amount when:
         (1) Tangible personalty is donated to any charity that does not use the property in its charitable function.
         (2) Property is given to certain private nonoperating foundations.
   2. Ordinary Income Property
      a. Generally the deduction is limited to its basis.
      b. Corporations have two exceptions where they can deduct the basis plus 50% of the appreciation of the property.
         (1) Inventory donated to a charity that uses the contribution in its exempt function of caring for the ill, the needy, or infants.
         (2) Gifts of scientific property donated to colleges and certain scientific research organizations for use in research.

D. Limitations Imposed on Charitable Contribution Deductions
   1. Both corporations and individuals are subject to limitations on their charitable contribution deductions. Individual limitations are covered in Chapter 15.
   2. Corporate taxpayers are limited to 10% of taxable income before deductions for charitable contributions, dividend received deductions, and net operating loss or capital loss carrybacks.
   3. Any amounts contributed in excess of the limitation may be carried forward for up to 5 years. When carried forward, the current year contributions are deducted first then the carryover up to each year's limitations.

V. Research and Experimental Expenditures
   A. Research and experimental expenses are defined in §174 as costs incident to the development of an experimental or pilot model, a plan process, a product, a formula, an invention or similar property and improvements to these existing properties.
   B. Three alternatives for handling *research and experimental expenditures* are permitted.
      1. Expensed in the year paid or incurred.
      2. Deferred and amortized over a period not less than 60 months.
      3. 0Capitalized costs.
   C. Expense Method – Taxpayers can elect to expense all research and experimental expenses as they are incurred. Once this election is made, changing from this method requires permission from the IRS.
   D. Deferral and Amortization Method – Under this method, the costs are amortized ratably over 60 months or more. Amortization begins when the taxpayer first realizes benefits from the costs. This deferral election is also binding.

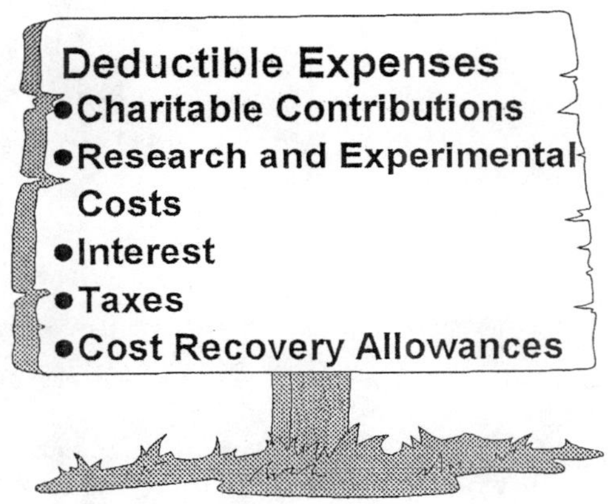


VI. Other Expenses Rules
   A. Interest Expense
      1. Generally, corporations may deduct their interest expense. In contrast, individuals have substantial limitations on their interest deductions. They may deduct interest on loans secured by their home, interest associated with investments to the extent of net investment income and interest on qualified education loans (See Chapter 15).
      2. Since there are limitations on the deductibility of interest associated with certain activities, the IRS provides interest tracing rules for allocating interest expense among activities.
   B. Taxes
      1. Taxes associated with a business or investment activity are generally deductible. Individuals may deduct state income and property taxes.
      2. Federal taxes are not deductible by corporations or individuals.
      3. Real estate property taxes must be apportioned between the buyer and the seller in the year a property is sold.

VII. Cost Recovery Allowances
   A. Overview
      1. Taxpayers may recover the cost of certain assets used in a trade or business or held for the production of income through *cost recovery* (depreciation under

prior law), depletion, or amortization. Generally, no recovery is allowed for assets that do not have a determinable useful life (eg, land).

2. In 1981, depreciation was replaced with the accelerated cost recovery system (ACRS). In 1986, ACRS was replaced with a modified version of ACRS (MACRS). Both of the latter systems provide statutory lives over which the cost of the assets are recovered.
3. The Tax Act of 2002 has modified the MACRS for property acquired after 9/10/2001 and before 9/11/2004. If placed into service before 1/1/2005, an additional first-year cost recovery of 30% is allowed.
4. The Tax Act of 2003 also provides an additional first-year cost recovery. It is 50% for property acquired after May 5, 2003 and before January 1, 2005.
5. If the 50% first-year deduction is claimed on an asset, the 30% cannot also be claimed. Only one of the first-year additional benefits may be used per asset.

B. Modified Accelerated Cost Recovery (MACRS)

1. MACRS provide separate tables for *realty* and *personalty*.
   a. Realty includes land and buildings permanently affixed to land. Cost recovery applies only to buildings because land does not have useful life.
   b. Personalty is defined as any asset that is not realty. Personalty should not be confused with *personal-use* property. Personal-use property are assets *not* used in business or income-producing activity. Cost recovery is not taken on personal-use property.

**Exhibit 4-1**

**DEPRECIATION AND COST RECOVERY: RELEVANT TIME PERIODS**

| System | Date Property is Placed in Service |
|---|---|
| *Section 167 depreciation (pre-ACRS)* | *Before January 1, 1981 and certain property placed in service after December 31, 1980* |
| *Accelerated cost recovery system (ACRS)* | *After December 31, 1980 and before January 1, 1987* |
| *Modified accelerated cost recovery system (MACRS) Section 168* | *After December 31, 1986* |
| *Additional 30% first-year cost recovery* | *After September 10, 2001 and before January 1, 2005* |
| *Additional 50% first year cost recovery* | *After May 5, 2003 and before January 1,2005* |

C. Eligible Property Under MACRS

1. Property for which cost recovery is allowed includes assets used in a trade or business or for the production of income.
2. Assets must be subject to wear and tear, decay, decline, or obsolescence. Assets that do not have a determinable life (land, stock, antiques) are not eligible.

3. The basis of eligible property must be reduced by the cost recovery *allowed* and by not less than the *allowable* amount. Allowed is the cost recovery actually taken, whereas, allowable is the amount that could have been taken under the applicable method, currently MACRS.
4. When personal-use assets are converted to business or income-producing use, the basis for cost recovery is the lower of the adjusted basis or its FMV at the time of conversion.

D. Cost Recovery for Personal Property (Personalty)

1. The classes and methods shown in Exhibit 4-2 are available under the MACRS. In each class, a switch-over is made to the straight-line method when it yields a larger amount of cost recovery.
2. As mentioned previously, additional first-year cost recovery allowances are available for most new personalty property placed into service before 1/1/2005. A taxpayer may elect not to take these additional cost recoveries.
3. Procedurally, the cost recovery is computed by multiplying the asset's basis (reduced by any additional first-year recovery) by the percentages found in the appropriate table at the end of Chapter 4.

**Exhibit 4-2**

**CLASS AND RECOVERY METHOD FOR PERSONAL PROPERTY UNDER MACRS**

| Class | Method |
|---|---|
| *3-year* | *200%DB* |
| *5-year* | *200%DB* |
| *7-year* | *200%DB* |
| *10-year* | *200%DB* |
| *15-year* | *150%DB* |
| *20-year* | *150%DB* |

4. Taxpayers may *elect* the straight-line method to compute cost recovery allowances. The election is available on a class-by-class, year-by-year basis. Further, certain assets do not qualify for accelerated cost recovery methods and must be recovered using the alternative depreciation system (ADS).
5. Half-Year Convention – Under MACRS, all personalty is subject to the half-year convention in the year of acquisition *and* in the year of disposition or retirement.
6. Mid-Quarter Convention
   a. This convention applies instead of the half-year only if more than 40% of the personalty (by value) acquired in the current year is placed in service during the last quarter of the year.
   b. All personalty acquired is treated as if it was placed into service at the mid-point of the quarter in which it was acquired. See Exhibit 4-3 for a list of the months of MACRS allowed for each quarter.

c. The additional cost recovery is available for assets using the mid-quarter convention, even if placed into service on the last day of the year.

**Exhibit 4-3**
**MID-QUARTER CONVENTION**

| Assets Acquired in | Amount of Depreciation |
|---|---|
| *1st Quarter* | *10.5 months* |
| *2nd Quarter* | *7.5 months* |
| *3rd Quarter* | *4.5 months* |
| *4th Quarter* | *1.5 months* |

E. Ccst Recovery for Real Estate (Realty)

1. Cost recovery for realty uses a mid-month convention. Regardless of what day realty acquired, it is allowed ½ month of recovery in its first month of service.
2. Real property placed in service before 1987 is subject to ACRS rules which provide recovery periods still in effect of 18, and 19 years.
3. For residential rental property (at least 80% of the gross rents are from non-transient dwelling units) placed into service after 1986, MACRS recovers costs over 27.5 years on a straight-line basis.
4. Nonresidential real estate placed into service before May 13, 1993 and after 1986, has a MACRS life of 31.5 years, For nonresidential realty placed in service after May 12, 1993, the recovery period is 39 years. MACRS uses a straight-line method for nonresidential property

F. Election to Expense Assets Under §179

1. Prior to the Tax Act of 2003, up to $25,000 of the acquisition cost of *tangible personalty* used in a trade or business may be expenses in the year of acquisition. With the Tax Act of 2003, the amount of the immediate expensing is raised to $100,000 starting January 1, 2003.
   a. This provision is elective and the cost recovery basis of the asset must be reduced by the amount expensed. Any elected §179 deduction is taken *before* the additional first-year cost recovery.
   b. Thus, the adjusted bases to which the standard MACRS cost recovery percentages are applied is the amount of basis after deducting the § 179 expense and additional first-year cost recovery.
   c. The maximum amount that may be expensed varies depending on the taxable year. See Exhibit 4-4 for a list.
2. Annual Limitations -- When the cost of tangible personalty property placed into service for the taxable year exceeds $200,000 ($400,000 after the Tax Act of 2003), the maximum amount of the deduction is reduced dollar-for-dollar by the excess. The amount expensed cannot exceed the taxable income of the taxpayer's trade or business.

**Exhibit 4-4**

**ELECTION TO EXPENSE ASSETS: CEILING AMOUNTS**

| Tax Year Beginning in | Amount |
|---|---|
| *2000* | *$ 20,000* |
| *2001 and 2002* | *$ 24,000* |
| *2003** | *$ 100,000* |

* After passage of Tax Act of 2003

G. <u>Business and Personal Use of Automobiles and Other Listed Property § 280F</u>

1. MACRS deductions are limited for automobiles and other listed property used for both business and personal pleasure.
2. If property is used predominantly for business, the *statutory percentage method* may be taken. Listed property is used predominantly for business if it is used more than 50% of the time in business (not including the time spent for the production of income). However, production of income use is considered when computing the cost recovery.
3. Method for computing business use for automobiles is based on mileage.
4. Listed property includes transportation property (automobiles, planes, etc), property used for entertainment, recreation, or amusement, computers, cellular telephones, and any other property specified by the Regulations.
5. Special limitations on the maximum cost recovery allowed apply to passenger automobiles used for business. If the property qualifies for the additional first-year cost recovery the maximum rates are increased.
6. When the business-use of listed property falls below 50 percent, the property is subject to recapture. The amount recaptured is treated as ordinary income on the taxpayer's return.
7. A taxpayer who leases a passenger automobile must report an *inclusion amount* (computed from an IRS table) in gross income. This provision is intended to prevent taxpayers from circumventing the cost recovery limitations by leasing.
8. Listed property is subject to the substantiation requirements of § 274. However, the substantiation requirements do not apply to vehicles that are not likely to be used more than a *de minimis* amount for personal purposes.

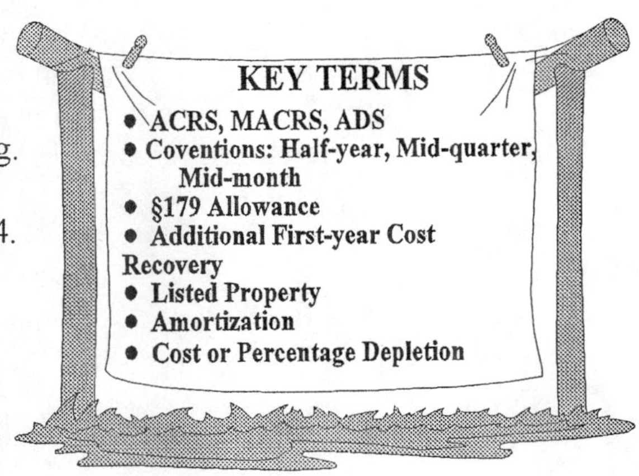


H. <u>Alternative Depreciation System (ADS)</u>

1. *ADS* rules must be used to calculate cost recovery in the following situations.
   a. For the portion of depreciation treated as an adjustment for purposes of the alternative minimum tax.

b. For the depreciation expense for assets used predominantly outside of the U.S., leased by tax-exempt entities, financed with tax-exempt bonds, or imported from certain foreign countries.

c. For depreciation expense when computing corporate Earnings & Profits.

VIII. Amortization

A. Intangible property used in a trade or business or in the production of income may be *amortized* using the straight-line method if the property has a limited life.

B. Taxpayers who acquire goodwill, going-concern value, franchises, trade names, etc, are permitted under § 197 to amortize the costs of these assets over a 15-year period.

IX. Depletion

A. The owner of an interest in a wasting natural resource is entitled to deduct depletion.

1. Depletion is the cost recovery method for natural resources.

2. An owner has a economic interest in the resource.

B. Intangible Drilling and Development Costs (IDC)

1. Costs associated with drilling an oil or gas well.

2. They may either be charged off as an expense in the year they are incurred or capitalized and written off through depletion. Generally it is more advantageous to expense the IDC costs than deplete them.

C. Depletion Methods

1. Depletion may be calculated using either cost depletion and percentage depletion. The choice between the two methods is made by an annual election and generally the method producing the *higher* expense would be taken.

a. Cost Depletion – It is calculated by dividing the adjusted basis of the property by the expected units of resource extraction. The depletion amount per unit multiplied by the number of units sold equals the cost depletion deduction for a given year.

b. Percentage Depletion – This is calculated by multiplying a specified percentage provided in the Code by the gross income received from the natural resource during a given year.

(1) In no event should the depletion deduction computed by this method exceed 50% of taxable income from the property.

(2) Since this depletion is not linked to the adjusted basis of the property, percentage depletion can be taken after the basis of the property has been reduced to zero.

## TEST FOR SELF-EVALUATION -- CHAPTER 4

**True or False**

Indicate which of the following statements are true or false by circling the correct answer.

T F 1. Legal fees pursuant to a criminal defense are deductible if the taxpayer is declared not guilty.

T F 2. Code § 267 operates to disallow or defer losses and deductions between related parties.

T F 3. Interest expenses incurred are always deductible by corporate taxpayers.

T F 4. An accrual basis taxpayer may claim a deduction for an amount owed to a related cash basis taxpayer if the amount is paid within two and a half months of the accrual taxpayer's year-end.

T F 5. As a general rule, cash basis taxpayers cannot expense capital expenditures.

T F 6. Charitable contributions made in any one year which are in excess of the appropriate limitation may be carried over until used.

T F 7. The amount of a charitable contribution depends on the type of property contributed.

T F 8. For an accrual basis taxpayer, economic performance must occur before an expense is deductible for tax purposes.

T F 9. Research and experimental expenditures must be expensed in the year in which they are incurred.

T F 10. With the Tax Act of 2003, the amount that may be expensed under the § 179 election has been increased to $100,000 for 2003.

T F 11. Goodwill is amortizable for tax purposes over a period that is selected by the taxpayer.

T F 12. The *millionaires provision*, applicable to publicly held corporations, limits the amount that can be paid to the chief executive officer to $1 million.

T F 13. For real property placed in service in the current year, a straight-line method of cost recovery *must* be used.

T F 14. A mid-quarter convention applies to cost recovery of personal tangible property placed in service during the year if more than 40% of the property is placed in service during the last 6 months of the year.

T F 15. The use of the alternative depreciation system is in all cases elective.

T F 16. For intangible property placed in service in the current year, a straight-line method of amortization *must* be used.

T F 17. The mid-quarter convention would apply whether or not the taxpayer uses an accelerated method or the straight-line method of cost recovery.

T F 18. Either of additional first-year depreciations apply to tangible personalty placed into service before January 1, 2005.

T F 19. A passenger automobile is classified as listed property even if it is used exclusively for business.

T F 20. Intangible drilling costs must be capitalized and written off through depletion.

**<u>Fill-in-the-Blanks</u>**

Complete the following statements with the appropriate word(s) or amount(s).

1. The period in which an accrual basis taxpayer can deduct an expense is determined by applying the __________ test and the _________ test.

2. The courts consider expenditures which are in violation of __________ as not being necessary costs and thus are not deductible.

3. Trade or business expenses are deductible only if they possess the following three attributes. Such expenses should be ___________, ___________, and ___________.

4. Automobiles and computers are examples of property meeting the definition of ________ property.

5. The deduction for long-term capital gain property (held greater than ___________) donated to a charity is generally measured by its _________ at the time the contribution is made.

6. A corporation's charitable contribution deduction may not exceed __________ of its taxable income before dividends received deduction, NOL carrybacks and capital loss carrybacks.

7. For charitable contribution purposes, ________ property is any property which, if sold, will result in the recognition of ordinary income.

8. The basis of a depreciable asset is reduced by the depreciation actually ________, but never by a lesser amount than that ________.

9. The two methods available to compute depletion are the ________ method and the ________ method.

10. ________ depletion is computed without regard to basis.

11. For the cash method of accounting, expenses are deductible when they are _______.

12. With the passage of the Tax Act of 2003, the maximum amount of the immediate expensing deduction begins to be phased out when aggregate acquisitions (excluding _________) during the year exceed _______.

13. For listed property to be considered as predominantly used in business, the percentage of use for business must exceed _______.

14. In general lobbying costs are not deductible. However, expenditures for influencing _________ and for activities devoted solely to ___________ are allowed a deduction.

15. All cost recovery deductions for _______ are calculated using the mid-month convention.

16. The amount expensed under § 179 cannot exceed the aggregate amount of_______ derived from the conduct of the trade or business of the taxpayer.

17. The basis for computing MACRS is first reduced by _______ and then _______ before the recovery table percentages are applied.

## Multiple Choice

Choose the best answer for each of the following questions.

____ 1. Which of the following are *not* "related parties" under § 267?
   a. Taxpayer and a great, great grandparent.
   b. Taxpayer and an uncle.
   c. Taxpayer and a child.
   d. Taxpayer and a corporation in which she owns 60% of the stock.
   e. All of the above are "related parties."

____ 2. Mr. Amor, a self-employed massage parlor owner, incurred the following expenses.

| | |
|---|---|
| Rent expense | $ 1,000 |
| Bribes to police | 5,000 |
| Expenses incurred to influence the public on a massage parlor state legislation | 1,000 |
| Wages | 20,000 |
| Interest on loan used to purchase City bonds | 1,000 |

Determine the amount of deductions *for* adjusted gross income that Mr. Amor may take currently.
   a. $22,000.
   b. $23,000.
   c. $26,000.
   d. $27,000.
   e. None of the above.

____ 3. Rich is the president of Masters Corporation and has owned 75% of its outstanding stock since its inception. During the year, Rich purchased from the corporation depreciable property with a cost of $80,000 and an adjusted tax basis of $60,000 for $45,000, its FMV. Masters placed this property in service two years ago. What is the available loss that Masters Corporation can claim for the current year?

a. $35,000 ordinary loss.
b. $35,000 capital loss.
c. $15,000 ordinary loss.
d. $15, 000 capital loss.
e. none of the above

____ 4. Which of the following may be considered a trade or business deduction?

a. Travel expenses incurred by a self-employed CPA.
b. Purchase of manufacturing equipment.
c. Illegal bribes and kickbacks.
d. Fines and penalties.
e. All of the above.

____ 5. An exception to the economic performance requirement for accrual basis taxpayers provides that certain recurring items may be deducted if which of the following conditions are met?

a. Such items are treated consistently.
b. Either expenses are not material in amount or such accrual results in better matching of income and expenses.
c. The all-events test is met.
d. Economic performance occurs within a reasonable period but not more than 8½ months after year-end.
e. All of the above are conditions that must be met.

____ 6. Choose the statement that is *not* correct.

a. Traffickers of drugs may deduct the cost of their goods sold.
b. Expenses for the investigation of a new business are deductible in the year paid when the taxpayer is already in the same line of business.
c. The usual expenses of operating an illegal activity are deductible.
d. Personal legal expenses may be deductible if they relate a criminal defense.
e. Each of the above is correct.

____ 7. Lemar owns and operates a very successful automotive service station. Every weekend and during vacations from school, his son Junior (age 13) works full time, earning $35 per hour. Junior has some mechanic skills. However, on other occasions when Junior cannot work and Lemar has a heavy workload, Lemar hires high school students taking mechanics courses at $10 per hour. With respect to Junior's wages, what amount probably is deductible by Lemar's business?

a. $5 per hour.
b. $10 per hour.
c. $20 per hour.
d. $35 per hour.
e. Lemar cannot deduct payments to Junior because he is a related party.

____ 8. Which of the following is not deductible as a charitable contribution?
a. Donations to a veterans organization.
b. Land given to the City of Pullman.
c. Dog food given to an animal shelter.
d. Gifts to homeless individuals.
e. All of the above are deductible contributions.

____ 9. Cold Corporation contributed the land to the University of Virginia (U of V). Its FMV was $16,000 at the time of the contribution and its basis was $11,000. Cold's taxable income before the charitable contribution was $100,000. U of V sold the land for $18,000 after holding it for several months. What is the *amount* of Cold's charitable contribution?
a. $10,000.
b. $11,000.
c. $13,500.
d. $16,000.

____ 10. Assume the same facts as above. What is Cold's charitable contribution *deduction*?
a. $10,000.
b. $11,000.
c. $13,500.
d. $16,000.

____ 11. The tax law does not allow which of the following alternatives for recovering research and experimental expenditures:
a. Expensing in the year paid or incurred.
b. Deferral and amortization over a period not less than 60 months.
c. Capitalization.
d. Credit of 25% of the current year cost.

____ 12. In January of the current year, Champ Corporation incurred expenses in the amount of $60,000 to determine the feasibility of entering a new business. How much of the expenses are currently deductible?
a. $15,000.
b. $15,000 only if Champ is currently in the same line of business.
c. $15,000 only if Champ acquires the new line of business.
d. $15,000 only if Champ is currently in the same line of business and acquires the new business.
e. None of the above.

____ 13. During 20X1, Amber Corporation incurred research and experimental expenses of $10,000. In 20X2, the business incurred another $40,000 of such expenditures and began to enjoy benefits from the project on July 1, 20X2. If the taxpayer elects the deferral and amortization method, what amount may be deducted in 20X2?
a. $4,000.
b. $5,000.
c. $8,000.
d. $10,000.

____ 14. On September 1, 2003, Sergey acquired equipment for $150,000 for use in his business. The equipment has a 5-year recovery period. Sergey desires to use the maximum cost recovery expensing available to him after the Tax Act of 3003. If this was his sole acquisition for the year, determine his total depreciation expense for 2003.

a. $87,500.
b. $90,000.
c. $110,000.
d. $130,000.
e. None of the above

____ 15. Which of the following statements is *not* true?

a. Automobile cost recovery is subject to special limitations that affect the timing of the available deductions.
b. If an automobile is used for business more than 50% of the time, the first-year cost recovery limitation is increased if the automobile is qualified property.
c. For automobile cost recovery, the straight-line method of depreciation is required if business use is not more than 50%.
d. If an automobile is used for business more than 50% of the time, no restrictive rules are applicable.

____ 16. On September 27, 20X2 Mara sold her home and her mortgage was assumed by the seller. Mara had paid $5,000 in interest on her mortgage during 20X2. The property taxes which Mara paid on September 1 for the full year were $2,000. What is Mara's interest and tax deduction for 20X2 assuming 20X2 is not a leap year?

a. $5,000.
b. $5,250.
c. $6,500.
d. $7,000.
e. None of the above.

____ 17. Patriya purchased improved real property as an income-producing activity on October 25 of the current year. Which of the following is true?

a. The property's cost may be recovered over a 31.5-year period.
b. The mid-quarter convention is required.
c. An accelerated write-off based on the 175% declining balance is available.
d. Patriya must decide whether the property is residential or nonresidential real property before she can compute the cost recovery on the investment.
e. None of the above are true.

____ 18. Javier Corporation donated inventory to a local. The inventory cost Javier $50,000 and its FMV at the date of donation was $75,000. Which of the following statements are true regarding this contribution assuming Javier's net income is $700,000.

a. Javier may deduct $50,000 as a charitable contribution.
b. Javier may deduct $62,500 as a charitable contribution if the charity uses the inventory in its exempt function of caring for infants.
c. Javier may deduct $70,000 as a charitable contribution.
d. Javier may deduct $75,000 as a charitable contribution.
e. More than one of the above answers are correct.

____ 19. Which statement concerning the alternative depreciation system is *not* true?
a. ADS must be used in computing depreciation for earnings and profits purposes.
b. In certain situations, a taxpayer may elect to use ADS.
c. ADS must be used in computing depreciation of all listed property.
d. ADS must be used to compute the depreciation adjustment amount for alternative minimum tax purposes.
e. All of the above are true.

____ 20. On February 26 of the current year, Ivy Corporation placed in service a warehouse costing $1 million. Determine the cost recovery deduction for this year.
a. $34,850.
b. $31,820.
c. $27,780.
d. $22,470.

____ 21. On March 15 of *last* year, Crozet Corporation placed in service an apartment building costing $1 million. Calculate the cost recovery deduction for the current year (ie, the *second* year of cost recovery).
a. $18,181.
b. $28,790.
c. $34,850.
d. $36,360.

____ 22. Jasmen, acquired a 7-year property, in May three years ago at a cost $300,000. Jasmen has been using MACRS accelerated cost recovery. What is the amount of cost recovery for the current year (year 4).
a. $37,470.
b. $42,857.
c. $85,714.
d. Some other amount.

____ 23. Mint Corp. acquired a franchise on January 2 of this year for $150,000. This was its sole acquisition for the year. Calculate the amortization deduction for the current year.
a. $30,000.
b. $15,000.
c. $10,000.
d. $ 5,000.

____ 24. On February 26 of this year, Moonsoo purchased the rights to a depletable asset for $1million. At the time of its acquisition, it was estimated that the number of tons that could be mined would be 250,000. During the year, 50,000 tons were mined and 30,000 tons were sold for $750,000. Expenses other than depletion totaled $500,000. Calculate the maximum cost depletion deduction for Moonsoo?
a. $120,000.
b. $125,000.
c. $165,000.
d. $220,000.

____ 25. Assume the same facts as above. Assume that the depletion rate is 22%. What is the maximum percentage depletion deduction for Moonsoo?
a. $120,000.
b. $125,000.
c. $165,000.
d. $220,000.

## Code Section Recognition

Several important sections of the Internal Revenue Code are described below. Indicate, by number, the appropriate Code section.

1. _____ Allows a deduction for "all ordinary and necessary" business expenses.

2. _____ Disallows losses arising from transactions between related parties.

3. _____ Provides for the amortization of intangibles used in a trade or business.

4. _____ The MACRS rules appear in this section.

5. _____ Permits the direct write-off of up to $100,000 in 2003 of acquisition cost for assets placed into service in a trade or business.

## Short Answer

1. Betty acquires commercial real estate and residential real estate for $100,000 each in March of current year. Assuming that each asset is depreciable, compute the annual cost recovery deduction under MACRS and under ADS for the assets' first two years of use.

| | *MACRS* | *ADS* |
|---|---|---|
| *Commercial* | | |
| Year 1 | | |
| Year 2 | | |
| *Residential* | | |
| Year 1 | | |
| Year 2 | | |

# SOLUTIONS TO CHAPTER 4 QUESTIONS

## True or False

1. F They are deductible only if the crime is associated with the taxpayer's trade or business activity.
2. T
3. F Interest expenses incurred for the production of tax-exempt income would not be deductible.
4. F Such amounts cannot be deducted by the accrual basis taxpayer until payments are made.
5. T
6. F A five-year carryover provision is available.
7. T
8. T
9. F Three alternatives are available: expensing, deferral and amortization, and capitalization
10. T
11. F Goodwill is amortizable over a 15-year period.
12. F The provision limits the amount that is *deductible* not the amount that can be *paid.*
13. T
14. F The convention applies if more than 40% is placed in service during the last 3 (not 6) months of the year.
15. F The ADS rules are required in several situations, including the alternative minimum tax and corporate earnings and profits computations.
16. T
17. T
18. T
19. T
20. F Intangible drilling costs can, at the taxpayers option, be expenses currently.

## Fill-in-the-Blanks

1. all events, economic performance
2. public policy
3. ordinary, necessary, reasonable
4. listed
5. one year, fair market value
6. 10 percent
7. ordinary income
8. allowed, allowable
9. cost, percentage
10. Percentage
11. paid
12. realty, $400,000

13. 50%
14. local legislation, monitoring legislation
15. realty
16. taxable income
17. Section 179 expense, additional first-year cost recovery

**Multiple Choice**

1. b An uncle is not a related party for this purpose.
2. e $21,000. 20,000 + 1,000. Only rent expense and wages are deductible.
3. e No loss is deductible because Rich and Masters are related parties.
4. a Purchase of manufacturing equipment is a capital expenditure.
5. e
6. d Criminal defense expenses are deductible only is related to a trade or business.
7. b $10 per hour. Reasonableness requirement would apply to this situation and prohibit deducting payments to Junior at more than the other workers are paid.
8. d Charitable contributions must be made to organized charities not individuals.
9. d The FMV of the land, $16,000 is the amount of the contribution.
10. a Deduction is limited to 10% of the taxable income, 10,000 = 100,000 X 10%.
11. d
12. e $60,000 is deductible if Champ is in the same line of business. If not in the same line but the new business is acquired the costs are amortized over 60 months ($12,000).
13. b $5,000. (10,000 + 40,000) / 60 months X 6 months.
14. d $130,000.

| | | |
|---|---|---|
| Section 179 | $100,000 | |
| 50% additional first-year | 25,000 | (150,000 – 100,000 = 50,000 X 50%) |
| Standard MACRS | 5,000 | (25,000) (20% X 200% X .5) |
| | $130,000 | |

15. d Luxury automobiles are subject to special restrictions even when they are used predominantly (i.e., more than 50%) for business.
16. e $6,479. 5,000 interest + 1,479 taxes (2,000 X [270/365]). Taxes must be allocated between the buyer and the seller on a per day basis.
17. d
18. e Responses a & b are correct. The deduction is $50,000 as a general rule but special rules for corporations donating inventory allows a deduction of adjusted basis + 50% of the appreciation. 50,000 + [50% X (75,000 – 50,000)].
19. c
20. d $22,470. 1,000,000 X 2.247%. See Table 4-3 in the text for percentage.
21. d $36,360. 1,000,000 X 3.636%. See Table 4-3 in the text for percentage.
22. a $37,470. 300,000 X 12.49%. See Table 4-2 in the text for percentage.
23. c $10,000. 150,000 ÷ 15
24. b $120,000. 1,000,000/250,000 tons = $4/ton.
30,000 tons X $4/ton = 120,000 cost depletion.
25. a $125,000. 22% X 750,000 = 165,000 percentage depletion.
Percentage limit (750,000 - 500,000) X 50% = 125,000.

## Code Section Recognition

1. 162
2. 267
3. 197
4. 168
5. 179

## Short Answer

1.

| | MACRS | ADS |
|---|---|---|
| *Commercial* | | |
| Year 1 | $2,033# | $1,979* |
| Year 2 | $2,564# | $2,500* |
| *Residential* | | |
| Year 1 | $2,879# | $1,979 |
| Year 2 | $3,636# | $2,500 |

# See Table 4-3.
* ($100,000 ÷ 40) X 9.5 months = $1,979; ($100,000 ÷ 40) X 12 months = $2,500.

# Chapter 5
# Losses and Loss Limitations

## CHAPTER HIGHLIGHTS

Businesses incur losses in the normal course of operations. Deductible bad debts occur when a taxpayer has previously recognized income but payment is not received. The amount and timing of deductions for casualties or thefts of business property are determined using special rules. For individuals, there are substantial limitations on the amounts of casualty and theft losses they may deduct. Business net operating losses (NOL), provides no benefit in the current tax year but may be carried over to other taxable years to help reduce the inequalities of requiring tax returns to be computed on an annual basis. The tax law includes two sets of complex rules which limit the numerous tax saving opportunities that were available through tax shelter investments. These rules, the at-risk limitations and the passive loss limitations, are discussed in detail in this chapter.

I. Bad Debts
   A. A bad debt deduction is allowed in the year an account receivable (previously included in income), becomes *worthless*. No such deduction is allowed if the taxpayer uses the *cash basis* of accounting (the amount was not previously included in income).
   B. Specific Charge-Off Method
      1. Most taxpayers are required to use this method for bad debts.
      2. Business bad debts are deductible when the debt becomes partially or wholly worthless.
      3. Nonbusiness bad debts are deductible *only* when the debt total worthlessness is known.
   C. Business versus Nonbusiness Bad Debts
      1. A debt is considered nonbusiness when it is *not* related to the taxpayer's trade or business. Generally, only individuals have nonbusiness bad debts.
      2. A business bad debt is always deductible as an ordinary loss in the year incurred.
      3. A nonbusiness bad debt is treated as a short-term capital loss and is subject to capital loss limitations (i.e., maximum net short-term loss deductible annually by individuals is $3,000).
   D. Loans Between Related Parties – May be viewed as gifts when the amounts are not repaid. If a bona fide debt does occur, bad debt treatment is permitted.

II. Worthless Securities

A. <u>Worthless Securities</u> – Losses resulting from securities becoming completely worthless are deemed recognized on the last day of the tax year in which the worthlessness occurs.

B. Small Business Stock (§ 1244)

1. When § 1244 stock, is disposed of at a loss or becomes worthless, the loss qualifies for special treatment.
   a. An ordinary loss is allowed for up to $50,000 ($100,000 on a joint return) per tax year. Any excess amount of loss is a capital loss.
   b. Only the original individual investors who purchaser stock from the issuing corporation can deduct an ordinary loss under § 1244.
2. Not more than $1million of § 1244 stock can be issued by a corporation.
3. § 1244 stock sold at a gain is treated as a capital gain.

> Knowing that almost nine of every ten new corporations fails within two years, the tax advisor should always counsel the new corporate client to issue stock under §1244. This is a "no-lose" technique, generally adding only one short paragraph to the corporate charter.

III. Casualties and Thefts

A. <u>Definition of Casualty</u>

1. Casualty includes losses caused by fire, storm, shipwreck, or other casualties. Such events must be identifiable, damage the taxpayer's property, and are sudden, unexpected, *or* have a unusual cause.
2. Events That Are Not Casualties
   a. Casualty caused by the taxpayer's willful act or willful negligence.
   b. "Acts of God," that are not sudden such as erosion or most insect damage. These are not sudden, unusual, or unexpected.

B. <u>Definition of Theft</u>

1. Theft includes larceny, embezzlement, and robbery. However, the term does *not* include lost or misplaced items.
2. A theft loss is taken in the year of *discovery,* not in the year of theft, if the two are different.

C. <u>When to Deduct Casualty Losses</u>

1. General Rule – Losses are deductible in the year in which they occur.
   a. A casualty loss is not permitted if a reimbursement claim exists with a reasonable prospect of full recovery.
   b. A partial deduction may be available if the expected recovery is less than casualty amount.
   c. If a reimbursement is received for a loss previously deducted, the taxpayer must recognize income to the extent a tax benefit was received from the prior deduction.
2. Disaster Area Loss Exception – Taxpayer may deduct a loss in the year *preceding* the taxable year in which a disaster occurs if the loss results from a casualty sustained in an area designated as a disaster area by the President of the United States.

D. Measuring the Amount of Loss

1. The computation a casualty loss depends on whether the property is held for personal use or for business use and whether the property was partially or completely destroyed.
   a. The amount of the deduction for partial losses of both business property and for the complete or partial destruction of personal-use property is the *lesser* of the following.
      (1) Adjusted basis of the property.
      (2) Difference between fair market value (FMV) of the property before the casualty and FMV immediately after the casualty.
   b. If business property is completely destroyed or lost, the deduction is equal to the property's adjusted basis at the time of the loss.
   c. Cost of repairs may be used to establish the loss in value if certain conditions are met.
2. Any insurance recovery reduces the casualty loss. However, if an individual chooses not to file a claim with insurance company, *no* amount of deduction will be allowed. If insurance proceeds exceed the amount of the loss, a taxable gain may result.

E. Casualty and Theft Losses of Individuals

1. A casualty & theft loss on *personal-use* property are deductible *from AGI*.
   a. The losses must be reduced by a $100 *per event* when computing the deduction.
   b. Additionally, the aggregate of all personal losses incurred during the year after reduction for the $100 per event floor must further be reduced by 10% of the taxpayer's AGI.

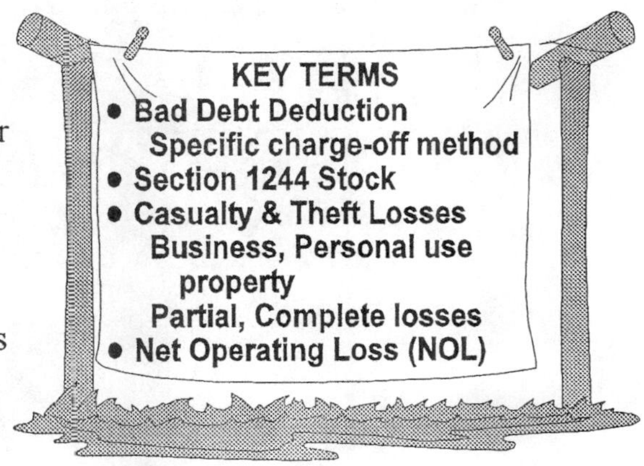


2. Losses in connection with a business or rentals and royalty property are deductible *for* AGI. They are not subject to the $100 per event and 10 %-of-AGI floors.
3. Casualty losses involving investment assets are also not subject to the $100 per event and 10%-of-AGI aggregate floors. They are deductible *from* AGI as miscellaneous itemized deductions and subject to the 2%-of-AGI limitation.

F. Personal Casualty Gains and Losses

1. If personal casualty gains exceed personal casualty losses, the gains and losses are treated as dispositions of capital assets.
2. If the losses exceed the gains, all of the gains and losses (to the extent of the gains) are treated as ordinary items. The excess losses are deductible as personal casualties.

IV. Net Operating Losses (NOL)

A. The net operating loss deduction is designed to provide partial relief from potential inequitable tax treatment which may arise because of the annual tax return filing requirement.

B. Only regular C corporations and individuals are allowed NOL deductions.

C. Computation the NOL

1. For C corporations, the NOL is equal to any negative taxable income with an adjustment for the dividend received deduction.
2. For Individuals, NOL includes only casualties, thefts and business losses. Therefore, an individual NOL is computed by adding back to negative taxable income any personal and nonbusiness deductions in excess of nonbusiness income, personal and dependent exemptions, and net capital losses used in calculating taxable income. Thus, NOLs for individuals include business deductions such as moving expenses, rental losses and ½ of self-employment taxes.

D. Carryback and Carryover Periods

1. A NOL is first applied against income of the 2 preceding taxable years. If the loss is not fully absorbed in the carryback period, it may be carried forward for up to 20 years.
2. A taxpayer may elect to forgo the carryback and only carry forward a net operating loss.

V. The Tax Shelter Problem

A. Under prior law, *tax shelter* investments were successfully used for tax avoidance purposes (i.e., to either avoid or reduce the income tax liability).

B. The *at-risk limitations* and the *passive activity rules* are now intended to curb such abuse. As a result, the term *tax shelter* is now almost obsolete.

VI. At-Risk Limitations

A. Rules apply to individuals and closely held corporations. The rules limit the amount of losses deductible to the amount that the taxpayer has at-risk (i.e., the amount the taxpayer could actually lose) in the activity. These rules apply to losses from business and income-producing activities.

B. Amount At-Risk

1. The initial amount considered at-risk includes the following.
   a. Cash and the adjusted basis of property contributed to the activity.
   b. Amounts borrowed for use in the activity for which the taxpayer has personal liability (*recourse debt*).
   c. Basis of property pledged as security property not used in the activity.
   d. An important exception provides that for real estate activities, taxpayer is considered at-risk for *nonrecourse financing* that is secured by the real property and which the taxpayer is *not* personally liable.
2. The amount at-risk varies as the entity recognizes income and losses, obtains and pays down qualifying debt, and distributes assets (e.g., cash withdrawals) to the owners.

C. Any losses disallowed for given year by the at-risk rules may be deducted in the first succeeding year in which the rule does not prevent the deduction. Such losses are still subject to the passive loss limitations if they are associated with a passive activity.

D. Recapture of previously allowed losses is required to the extent that the at-risk amount is reduced below zero by distributions or when debt changes from recourse to nonrecourse.

VII. Passive Loss Limits

A. <u>Classification and Impact of Passive Income and Loss</u>

1. Classification – The passive loss rules require the classification of income and losses into one of three categories: active, passive, and portfolio.

a. *Active income* includes the following.

(1) Amounts for services rendered (e.g., salary, commissions).

(2) Profit from a trade or business in which the taxpayer is a material participant.

(3) Gain on the disposition of an asset used in a trade or business.

(4) Income from intangible property if the taxpayer's personal efforts significantly contributed to the creation of the property.

b. *Portfolio income* includes the following.

(1) Interest, dividends, annuities, and royalties not derived in the ordinary course of a trade or business.

(2) Gain or loss from the disposition of property that produces portfolio income or that is held for investment purposes.

c. *Passive income or loss* includes the following.

(1) Amounts from any trade or business or production of income activity in which the taxpayer does not materially participate.

(2) Any rental activity regardless of whether the taxpayer materially participates, with limited exceptions.

2. Impact

a. Losses and expenses generated by passive activities are deductible only to the extent the taxpayer has income from other passive activity sources.

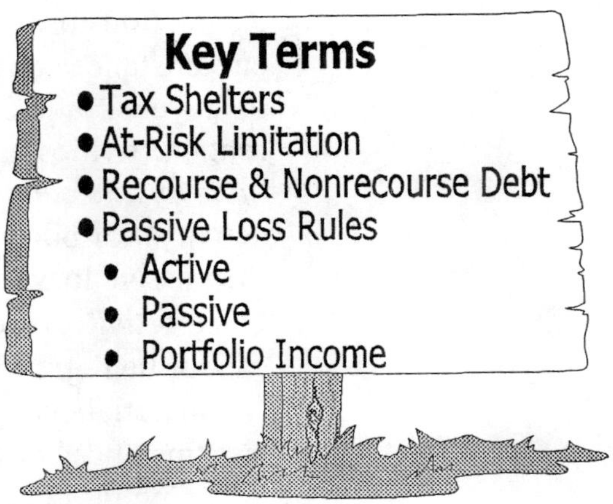


b. Unused passive losses are suspended and carried forward to offset passive income in future years.

c. Upon the taxable disposition of an entire interest in a passive activity, any realized suspended losses may be recognized and used to offset passive and nonpassive income.

3. Carryovers of Suspended Losses – When the taxpayer has more than one passive activity, the amount of loss that must be suspended is allocated to each passive activity using the following formula.

$$\frac{\text{Loss from particular activity}}{\text{Sum of losses from all passive activities}}$$

4. Passive Credits – Passive credits are limited much like passive losses. They can only be utilized against the regular tax caused by passive income.

5. Carryovers of Passive Credits – While unused passive credits can generally be carried forward indefinitely, they can be lost forever when the activity is disposed of in a taxable transaction.

6. Passive Activity Changes to Active – If a activity changes from passive to active for a taxpayer, any suspended losses from this activity may offset active income produced from the activity in the current or future years.

B. Taxpayers Subject to the Passive Loss Rules

1. The passive loss rules apply to individuals, estates, trusts, personal service corporations, and closely held C corporations.
2. For investments in partnerships or S corporations that are passive activities, the passive activity rules are applied at the owner level.
3. Personal Service Corporations (PSCs) – Application of the passive loss limitation to PSCs is intended to prevent taxpayers from avoiding the passive activity rules by creating PSCs and acquiring passive activities at the corporate level then offsetting the ordinary service income produced by the corporation.
4. Closely Held C Corporations – Application of the passive loss rules to closely held (non-personal service) corporations also is intended to prevent individuals from incorporating to avoid the passive loss limitations. These corporations can use passive losses to offset *active* income but not *portfolio* income.

C. Activities Defined

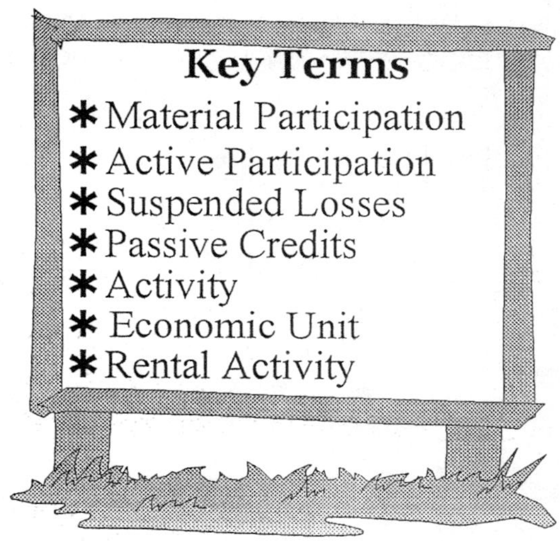


1. Identifying what constitutes an *activity* is of critical importance in applying the passive loss limitations.
2. Regulations provide a facts and circumstances test for grouping a taxpayer's trade or business and rental activities into an *appropriate economic unit* (single activity) for purposes of applying the passive loss limitations.
3. Once activities are grouped, they cannot be regrouped unless there is a material change in the fact and circumstances or the original grouping was inappropriate. The IRS may also regroup activities when appropriate.

D. Material Participation

1. To be a material participant, the taxpayer must participate on a *regular*, *continuous*, and *substantial* basis. If a taxpayer materially participates in a nonrental trade or business activity, losses will be treated as an active loss rather than a passive loss. The seven tests for determining whether a taxpayer is a material participant can be divided into the following categories. (See Exhibit 5-1 on the next page for a list of the test)
   a. *Tests Based on Current Participation* – Four quantitative tests of a taxpayer's participation require measurement in terms of hours of activity during the year.
   b. *Tests Based on Prior Participation* – Two tests allow a taxpayer in certain situations to be classified as a material participant, even though a high level of activity is no longer maintained, if the taxpayer was formerly a material participant.

c. *Facts and Circumstances Test* – In the last test, the criteria of regular, continuous, and substantial participation is used. However, the definition of these terms has not yet been fully developed.

**Exhibit 5-1**
**TESTS FOR MATERIAL PARTICIPATION**

1. Participation in the activity is more than 500 hours for the year.
2. The individual's participation constitutes substantially all of the participation in the activity for all individuals.
3. The individual participates in the activity for more than 100 hours for the year, and this participation is not less than the participation of anyone else.
4. This is a significant participation activity (participation exceeds 100 hours) and the individual's aggregate participation in all significant activities exceed 500 hours.
5. Materially participated in the activity for any 5 taxable years out of the last 10 years.
6. If the activity is a personal service activity, the individual materially participated for any of the 3 preceding years.
7. Based on facts and circumstances, participation was on a regular, continuous, and substantial basis.

2. Participation Defined
   a. Participation is any work performed by an individual in an activity that she or he owns. However, work performed in the capacity of an investor is not counted in applying the material participation tests.
   b. Limited partners generally are not considered to materially participate.
   c. Corporations are considered to materially participate if its owners materially participate.

E. Rental Activities
   1. Rental activities (defined as any activity where payments are received principally for the use of tangible property) are generally treated as passive activities.
   2. Temporary Regulations provide exceptions for rentals of real and personal property that are *not automatically* treated as rental activities. However, the activities are subject to the material participation tests.

F. Interaction of At-Risk and Passive Activity Limits
   1. The at-risk limitations are applied before the passive loss provisions.
   2. Losses suspended because of the at-risk provisions cannot be deducted even if the taxpayer has passive income in the current year.

G. Special Rules for Real Estate
   1. Two exceptions allow all or part of real estate losses to offset active or portfolio income even though the activity may otherwise be a passive activity.
   2. Real Estate Professionals – To qualify for nonpassive treatment, a real estate professional must satisfy both of the following requirements.

a. More than half of the personal services performed by the taxpayer are in real estate trades or businesses in which the taxpayer materially participates.

b. The taxpayer performs more than 750 hours of services in these real estate trades or businesses as a material participant.

3. Rental Real Estate Deduction – The second exception allows individuals to deduct a portion of real estate activities losses against nonpassive income.

a. An annual deduction up to $25,000 is allowed. This amount is phased out over taxpayer's modified adjusted gross income between $100,000 and $150,000

b. Married filing separately have an annual deduction of $12,500 and the phaseout starts at $50,000.

c. In order for the relief provision to apply, a taxpayer must meet the following criteria.

(1) Actively participate in the rental real estate activity. Active participation does not require regular, or substantial involvement. The taxpayer need only participate in making management decisions in a significant sense. Thus, it is a less rigorous standard than material participation.

(2) Own at least 10% of the value of all interests in the activity during the entire tax year or the period during which the taxpayer held an interest.

b. The $25,000 allowance is an aggregate of both deductions and credits in deduction equivalents.

H. <u>Dispositions of Passive Interests</u>

1. Special rules apply to dispositions of passive activities in transactions that are not fully taxable.

2. A transfer of an interest in a passive activity by reason of death results in suspended losses being allowed as a deduction by the decedent to the extent they exceed the amount of the step-up in basis.

3. A disposition of a passive activity interest by gift requires that suspended losses be added to the donee's basis of the property.

# TEST FOR SELF-EVALUATION -- CHAPTER 5

**True or False**

Indicate which of the following statements are true or false by circling the correct answer.

T F 1. The reserve method for bad debts is available for all taxpayers who sell goods or services on credit and use the accrual method of accounting.

T F 2. The net operating loss provisions for individuals apply only to business-related or casualty and theft losses.

T F 3. An individual taxpayer who sells investment stock for less than its cost would always recognize a capital loss.

T F 4. A deduction may be claimed by an individual when stock held for investment becomes partially worthless.

T F 5. The measure of a personal casualty loss deduction is always the decline in the property's fair market value as a result of the casualty event.

T F 6. Business and personal casualty losses are measured in the same manner when there is a partial destruction of a property.

T F 7. A taxpayer may elect to not carry back a net operating loss, but instead to carry it forward only to future years.

T F 8. A deduction is allowed on the partial worthlessness of a business bad debt.

T F 9. Because the deduction for a theft loss must be claimed in the year in which the loss occurs, filing an amended income tax return may sometimes be necessary.

T F 10. The special treatment available for § 1244 stock applies equally to gains and losses.

T F 11. The passive activity rules apply to net losses and tax credits.

T F 12. Net passive income is recognized to the extent of passive losses incurred.

T F 13. The at-risk rules limit the tax deductions from an activity for any taxable year to the amount the taxpayer has at-risk at the end of the year.

T F 14. Rental activities include both real estate rentals and rentals of tangible personal property.

T F 15. When business property is completely destroyed, the loss is equal to the replacement cost of the property at the time of the loss.

T F 16. The passive activity limitations apply only to individuals, estates, trusts, closely held C corporations, and personal service corporations.

T F 17. The amount that a taxpayer has at-risk is limited to the amount the taxpayer has invested in the business or income producing venture.

T F 18. The at-risk rules are an important limitation because if a taxpayer is denied losses for a year by the at-risk rules, they can never be deducted in future.

T F 19 Closely held corporations (other than personal service corporations) may offset passive losses against active income, but not against portfolio income.

T F 20. Cost of repairing a damaged property can be an acceptable method of establishing the loss in value a casualty property.

**Fill-in-the-Blanks**

Complete the following statements with the appropriate word(s) or amount(s).

1. A business bad debt is deductible as a(n) ________ loss in the year incurred, whereas a nonbusiness bad debt is always treated as a(n) ________ loss.

2. Casualties or losses sustained in area designated by the President as a ________ may be claimed in the taxable year ________ the year of the actual loss.

3. A taxpayer may deduct an ordinary loss of up to ________ (________ if filing a joint return) in the year of disposition of § 1244 stock.

4. The NOL deduction is generally be carried back ________ years and then any unused amounts may be carried forward ________ years.

5. The amount of a casualty loss for personal use property must be reduced by a ________ per event floor as well as the ________ percent-of-AGI aggregate floor.

6. If personal casualty gains and losses net to a gain, all of the assets involved in the casualty events will be considered to be ________ assets.

7. Casualty losses connected to rental or royalty property are deductible ________ AGI.

8. Transfers of funds between related parties raise the issue of whether the transfers were bona fide loans or ________.

9. A business bad debt deduction may not be claimed by taxpayers using the ________ method of accounting.

10. Before Congress limited their effectiveness, ________ were popular investments for tax avoidance purposes.

11. In certain situations involving rental real estate activities, an individual taxpayer may deduct up to __________ of losses against nonpassive income. However, for taxpayers filing jointly, the allowance is completely phased out once the taxpayers' AGI exceeds __________.

12. __________ are recognized on a taxable disposition of an entire interest in a passive activity.

13. In terms of the interaction of at-risk and passive activity limits, determination of whether a loss is suspended under the _________ rules is made before the application of the __________ rules.

14. The passive activity rules require classification of income into one of three categories: __________ income, __________ income, and __________ income.

15. To be a material participant, the taxpayer must participate on a __________, __________, and __________ basis.

16. The passive activity rules apply to any trade or business if the taxpayer does not __________.

17. In terms of levels of participation in an activity by a taxpayer, __________ participation requires more involvement than does __________ participation.

18. As a general rule, taxpayers who are subject to the passive loss limitations cannot offset passive losses against __________ income or __________ income.

19. The ________ method is required for tax purposes when accounting for bad debts for most taxpayers. However, some financial institutions may use the ________ method.

20. The __________ rules are designed to prevent a taxpayer from deducting losses in excess of the actual economic investment in an activity.

## Multiple Choice

Choose the best answer for each of the following questions.

____ 1. Jamie uses the cash receipts and disbursements method in her business and has the following income, expenses, and deductions during the year.

| | |
|---|---|
| Gross receipts | $ 30,000 |
| Business expenses | $ 32,000 |
| Uncollectible customer accounts | $ 4,000 |

For financial accounting, Jamie's allowance for bad debt is 5% of gross receipts. Compute Jamie's bad debt deduction.

a. $0.
b. $2,000.
c. $4,000.
d. $6,000.
e. None of the above.

____ 2. Refer to the preceding problem. If Jamie uses the accrual method of accounting, what would be her net operating loss for the year?

a. $0.
b. $2,000.
c. $6,000.
d. $8,000.
e. None of the above.

____ 3. During the year, Wayne had the following personal casualty losses which were fully covered by an insurance policy and which all resulted from the same casualty. His AGI for the year was $20,000.

| | | Fair Market Value | |
|---|---|---|---|
| Asset | Adjusted Basis | Before | After |
| Auto | $5,000 | $3,000 | $ 0 |
| Boat | 1,600 | 2,400 | 1,900 |
| Television | 600 | 800 | 0 |

What is Wayne's casualty loss deduction for the year, assuming he does not request a reimbursement from his insurance company?

a. $2,000.
b. $2,200.
c. $4,200.
d $6,100.
e None of the above.

____ 4. Assume the same facts as in the problem #3 above, except Wayne did not have insurance coverage for the assets. What is Wayne's casualty loss deduction?

a. $2,000.
b. $2,200.
c. $4,200.
d. $6,100
e. None of the above.

____ 5. Assume the same facts as in problem #4 except that Wayne is a corporation. What is the casualty deduction for Wayne, Inc.?

a. $2,000.
b. $2,200.
c. $4,200.
d. $6,100
e. None of the above.

____ 6 Braun dies when he has suspended passive activity losses of $20,000. The activity to which the suspended losses are from has an adjusted basis to Braun of $40,000 and a FMV for estate purposes of $55,000. Braun's son, Rick receives the property. What is the proper treatment of the suspended losses?

a. $20,000 loss deduction on Braun's final return.
b. $5,000 loss deduction on Braun's final return.
c. $20,000 loss deduction on Rick's return.
d. The benefit of the suspended loss is lost when Braun dies.

____ 7. On February 1, last year, Hohokam Corporation and Ed (a single taxpayer) each purchased $75,000 worth of stock in the newly formed Johnson Corporation. On January 31 of the current year, the company suddenly declared bankruptcy and the stock became totally worthless. The stock was § 1244 stock. How should the loss be reported, assuming Hohokam and Ed both are calendar year taxpayers?

| | Hohokam Corporation | Ed |
|---|---|---|
| a. | $25,000 LTCL<br>$50,000 Ordinary Loss | $75,000 STCL |
| b. | $75,000 Ordinary Loss | $75,000 Ordinary Loss |
| c. | $75,000 LTCL | $50,000 Ordinary Loss, $25,000 LTCL |
| d. | $50,000 Ordinary Loss<br>$25,000 LTCL | $50,000 Ordinary Loss, $25,000 STCL |

____ 8. Womack and Co., a professional accounting corporation, extended a loan of $10,000 last year to one of its trusted employees, Charles, who promptly and permanently left the country at the beginning of this year. As a consequence, the loan will never be collected. Womack and Co. may deduct what amount?

a. $10,000 ordinary loss this year.
b. $3,000 short-term loss this year and has a $7,000 carryover.
c. $10,000 ordinary loss on last year's tax return.
d. This does not qualify as a bad debt for a business and is not deductible.

____ 9. Margaret operates a pet shop that specializes in the sale of rare breeds of cats. During 20X1, she has sales of $300,000. She estimated that her bad debts would be 2% of sales. However, at the end of the year, she determined that $8,000 of this year's sales will never be collected. Assuming Margaret uses the accrual method of accounting in her business, she may claim the following bad debt deduction.

a. $0.
b. $6,000.
c. $8,000.
d. $14,000.
e. Some other amount.

____ 10. Assume the facts of the preceding problem, but Margaret misjudged the integrity of one of her customers, Sue, whose account had been written-off. Sue paid her full debt of $2,400 in 20X2 year. How does Margaret report this on her tax return.

a. She does not need to report this on her tax return.
b. $2,400 of income in 20X2.
c. Amend 20X1 and reduce bad debt deduction by $2,400.
d Margaret reduces her bad debt deduction in 20X2 by $2,400.
e. Some other treatment.

____ 11. A taxpayer in the 25% tax bracket with $5,000 of tax credits from a passive activity would have a deduction equivalent of what amount?

a. $1,250.
b. $5,000.
c. $20,000.
d. There is no concept of deduction equivalent.

____ 12. Meghan and Travis loaned $4,000 to their next door neighbor, Dan, so that he could buy some new living room furniture. Dan's business, his sole source of income, fell on "hard times" and he informed Meghan and Travis that he could not repay the loan. What are the tax consequences to Meghan and Travis in the year of the loss, assuming the only other items on their income tax return are their salaries?

a. No deduction is available.
b. $3,000 STCL.
c. $4,000 STCL.
d. $4,000 ordinary loss.
e. $4,000 itemized deduction.

____ 13. Ross is in the business of lending money. Two years ago Ross lent $3,000 to Carlos. Last year, Carlos declared bankruptcy, but expected to be able to pay all of his creditors at the rate of 60¢ on the dollar. However, this year, Carlos was only able to pay in final settlement 10¢ on the dollar. How should Ross treat the loss on *this year's* return?

a. No deduction is available.
b. $900 ordinary loss.
c. $2,700 short-term capital loss.
d. $2,700 ordinary loss.
e. None of the above.

____ 14. On May 30 of last year, Kathleen (married filing jointly) acquired Concord Corporation stock (§ 1244 stock) from the corporation for $150,000. On March 31 of this year, she sold the stock for $40,000. How is her loss treated?

a $110,000 ordinary loss.
b. $110,000 short-term capital loss.
c. $60,000 short-term capital loss and $50,000 ordinary loss.
d. $10,000 short-term capital loss and $100,000 ordinary loss.
e. Some other treatment.

____ 15. A passive activity is defined as which of the following.

a. Any trade or business in which the taxpayer does not materially participate.
b. Any rental activity, subject to certain exceptions.
c. Both a and b are passive activities.
d. None of the above.

____ 16. Material participation is achieved by meeting any one of seven tests. Which of the following is not one of those tests?

a. Individual participates in the activity for more than 500 hours during the year
b. Individual's participation in the activity for the taxable year constitutes substantially all of the participation in the activity of all individuals for the year.
c. The individual participates in the activity for more than 100 hours during the year, and the individual's participation in the activity for the year is not less than the participation of any other individual for the year.
d. Based on all of the facts and circumstances, the individual participates in the activity on a regular, continuous, and substantial basis during such year.
e. Each of the above is a qualifying test.

____ 17. Benito has investments, acquired during the current year, in three passive activities with the following income and losses for the year.

| | |
|---|---|
| Activity X | ($40,000) |
| Activity Y | ( 30,000) |
| Activity Z | 20,000 |
| Net passive loss | ($50,000) |

Which of the following statements is true for the current year?

a. Deductible loss is $40,000 from Activity X and $30,000 from Activity Y.
b. Deductible loss is $10,000 from Activity X and $10,000 from Activity Y.
c. Suspended loss is $40,000 from Activity X and $30,000 from Activity Y.
d. Suspended loss is $15,000 from Activity X and $5,000 from Activity Y.
e. None of the above.

____ 18. Mahout, a joint filer, actively participates in a rental activity (a beach cottage) that has reported a $60,000 loss from current operations. Mahout owns a 50% interest in this property. Assuming Mahout and his spouse's AGI before this loss is $75,000 (solely from salary), what is the amount of Mahout's current deduction from this property?

a. $0.
b. $12,500.
c. $25,000.
d. $30,000.
e. None of the above.

____ 19. Assume the same facts as in the preceding problem, except their AGI in the current year (solely from salary), exclusive of the rental loss, is $125,000. What amount of the loss is currently deductible?

a. $0.
b. $12,500.
c. $25,000.
d. $30,000.
e. None of the above.

____ 20. Xio made an investment in three passive activities during the current year. The activities have only nonrecourse debts. The following income and losses resulted from operations during the year.

| | Investment | Income (Loss) |
|---|---|---|
| Activity X | $ 30,000 | ($60,000) |
| Activity Y | 40,000 | (10,000) |
| Activity Z | 100,000 | 50,000 |
| Total | $170,000 | ($20,000) |

What is the amount of loss that is deductible in the current year?

a. $0.
b. $20,000.
c. $40,000.
d. $50,000.
e. None of the above.

____ 21. Manuel, who earned a salary of $60,000, invested $25,000 for a 50% interest in a partnership venture. The entity acquired assets worth $3 million through the use of $2,400,000 in nonrecourse financing. Manuel's share of the partnership's loss for the current year was $80,000. Assuming he was a material participant, how much may Manuel deduct this year?

a. $0.
b. $25,000.
c. $60,000.
d. $80,000.

____ 22. Due to the at-risk limitations, Iris has a $40,000 suspended loss from a real estate partnership in which she is a 50% partner. However, this year, Iris invests an additional $5,000 in cash, the partnership generates a net income of $10,000 and incurs a $20,000 recourse debt. What amount of the loss carryover Iris may take this year, assuming Iris materially participates in the venture?

a. $5,000.
b $15,000.
c $20,000.
d. $35,000.

____ 23. Orange Corporation, a closely held C corporation (not a personal service corporation), has $45,000 of passive losses from a rental activity, $30,000 of active income, and $25,000 of portfolio income. What amount of the passive losses may be deducted this year by Orange?

a. $45,000.
b. $30,000.
c. $25,000.
d. $0.

____ 24. Sia owns the following businesses and participates in each of the indicated activities.

| Activity | Hours of Participation |
|---|---|
| 1 | 70 |
| 2 | 130 |
| 3 | 300 |
| 4 | 250 |

In which activities is Sia considered to be a material participant?

a. None of them.
b. All of them.
c. Only activities 3 and 4.
d. Activities 2, 3, and 4.

____ 25. Vasanta's adjusted basis in a passive activity is $20,000 at the beginning of the year. Her loss from the activity during the year is $15,000. She has no other investments in passive activities. Which of the following is true?

a. $5,000 year-end basis; $0 deductible loss.
b. $20,000 year-end basis; $0 deductible loss.
c. $5,000 year-end basis; $15,000 deductible loss.
d. $20,000 year-end basis; $15,0000 deductible loss.

**Short Answer**

1. Hector, who is single, owns 100 shares of stock in Blue Corporation which he purchased four years ago for $200,000. The stock meets all of the requirements of § 1244. How will the following transactions be treated for tax purposes under the following scenarios?

   a. In the current year, he sold the stock for $75,000.

   b. In the current year, he sold the stock for $225,000.

2. Molly incurs the following personal casualty losses in separate incidents during the year. Calculate the casualty loss for each item before application of the 10 percent-of-AGI limitation.

| Asset | Adjusted Basis | FMV Before Casualty | FMV After Casualty | Insurance Recovery |
|---|---|---|---|---|
| A | $500 | $600 | $400 | $200 |
| B | $500 | $600 | $ 50 | $150 |
| C | $500 | $600 | $400 | $400 |
| D | $500 | $600 | $250 | $300 |

## SOLUTIONS TO CHAPTER 5 QUESTIONS

### True or False

| | | |
|---|---|---|
| 1. | F | The reserve method is not available for most income tax purposes by taxpayers. |
| 2. | T | |
| 3. | F | Dispositions of § 1244 stock at a loss produce ordinary loss within certain limitations. |
| 4. | F | The stock must be fully worthless in this situation. |
| 5. | F | The deduction is equal to the property's adjusted basis if such amount is less than the decline in fair market value. |
| 6. | T | |
| 7. | T | |
| 8. | T | |
| 9. | F | The theft loss deduction is claimed in the year in which the loss is discovered. |
| 10. | F | The special treatment only applies to losses. |
| 11. | T | |
| 12. | F | There is no limitation on the recognition of passive income. |
| 13. | T | |
| 14. | T | |
| 15. | F | Complete loss of business property is measured by the adjusted basis of the property. |
| 16. | T | |
| 17. | F | The at-risk amount also includes debts for which the taxpayer has personal liability. |
| 18. | F | Losses disallowed under the at-risk rules generally can be carried over and used in future years to the extent an at-risk basis becomes available. |
| 19. | T | |
| 20. | T | |

### Fill-in-the-Blanks

1. ordinary, short-term capital
2. disaster area loss, preceding
3. $50,000, $100,000
4. 2, 20
5. $100, 10
6. capital
7. For
8. gifts
9. cash
10. tax shelters
11. $25,000, $150,000
12. Suspended losses
13. at-risk, passive loss
14. active, portfolio, passive
15. regular, continuous, substantial
16. materially participate
17. material, active
18. active, portfolio
19. specific charge-off, reserve
20. at-risk

**Multiple Choice**

| | | | |
|---|---|---|---|
| 1. | a | A bad debt expense deduction is not available to cash basis taxpayers. | |
| 2. | b | $6,000. 30,000 - (32,000 + 4,000) | |
| 3. | e | No deduction for such a loss would be allowed unless a timely insurance claim is filed. | |
| 4. | a | Individuals use the lower of decline in value or adjusted basis for all losses. | |
| | | Auto (3,000 - 0) | $3,000 |
| | | Boat (2,400 - 1,900) | 500 |
| | | Television | 600 |
| | | | 4,100 |
| | | Less: Statutory floor per event | -100 |
| | | Less: 10% of AGI | -2,000 |
| | | Deduction | 2,000 |
| 5. | d | Corporations are not subject to the $100 or 10% of AGI floor. For total losses, corporations use the adjusted basis of the asset. | |
| | | Auto | $5,000 |
| | | Boat (2,400 - 1,900) | 500 |
| | | Television | 600 |
| | | Deduction | 4,100 |
| 6 | b | $5,000 deduction on final return. 20,000 – (55,000 - 40,000). Loss is allowed on final return to extent the basis in the activity did not increase. | |
| 7. | c | Worthless stock is treated as sold on last day of current year making it a long-term asset. Corporations are not extended the benefits of § 1244. Since Ed is single, he is allowed only $50,000 of ordinary loss for the year under § 1244. | |
| 8. | a | Business bad debts produce ordinary loss deductions. | |
| 9. | c | The specific write-off method is required. | |
| 10. | b | Income must be recognized in the year of recovery to the extent the amount produced a tax benefit in a previous year. | |
| 11. | c | $20,000. 5,000 ÷ 25%. | |
| 12. | b | The nonbusiness bad debt is treated as a STCL and limited to $3,000 in the year of the loss. | |
| 13. | b | Total loss (3,000 X 90%) | $2,700 |
| | | Less: Loss claimed last year (3,000 X 60%) | -1,800 |
| | | Current year's loss (3,000 X 30%) | $ 900 |
| | | Business bad debts are ordinary losses | |
| 14. | d | The § 1244 applies to stock that has decreased in value. The ordinary loss for married filing jointly is $100,000. The remaining loss (10,000) is short-term because it was held less than one year. | |
| 15. | c | | |
| 16. | e | | |
| 17. | e | Passive losses can only be taken to the extent of passive income. The passive loss deduction must be allocated proportionately between the activities.<br>Activity X: Deduction (20,000 X [40,000/70,000]) = $11,429 Suspended = $28,571<br>Activity Y: Deduction (20,000 X [30,000/70,000]) = $ 8,571 Suspended = $21,429 | |
| 18. | c | This loss qualifies under the rental real estate activity exception, but only $25,000 of his share of the current loss (i.e., 30,000) is deductible this year. | |
| 19. | b | $12,500. 25,000 - [50% (125,000 - 100,000)]. | |
| 20. | c | $40,000. Activity X loss limited by at-risk to $30,000. Activity Y loss is $10,000 | |

21. b The loss deduction is limited to the amount at-risk, the $25,000 investment.
22. c $20,000. 5,000 + (50% X 10,000) + (50% X $20,000).
Nonrecourse debt adds to at-risk for real estate activities.
23. b $30,000. Passive losses may offset active income, but not portfolio income.
24. d Material participation is achieved based on Test 4 for activities 2, 3, 4. Activity 1 does not have 100 hours of participation.
25. a Passive loss is deductible only to the extent of passive income which is zero.

**Short Answer**

1. a. Of the total $125,000 loss on the sale of § 1244 stock, §1244 treats $50,000 as an ordinary loss while the remaining $75,000 loss is capital.

   b. The stock is sold at a $25,000 gain. Gain is treated as a capital gain because the stock is a capital asset to Hector. Section 1244 has no impact when stock is sold at a gain.

2.

| Asset | Loss | Insurance Recovery | Net Gain/Loss before $100 floor | $100 floor | Net Gain or Loss |
|---|---|---|---|---|---|
| A | ($200) | $200 | $ 0 | $ 0 | $ 0 |
| B | ($500) | $150 | ($350) | $100 | ($250) |
| C | ($200) | $400 | $200 | $ 0 | $200 |
| D | ($350) | $300 | ($ 50) | $100 | $ 0 |

# Chapter 6
# Property Transactions:
# Basis, Gain and Loss, and Nontaxable Exchanges

## CHAPTER HIGHLIGHTS

Tax consequences generally result when a sale or other disposition of property occurs. In such cases, any gain or loss realized will be recognized. However, in some tax situations realized gains or losses are not recognized in the year of disposition. Examples of this nonrecognition include like-kind exchanges, involuntary conversions, and sales of personal residences. Thus, these nonrecognition provisions, which may or may not be mandatory, can provide for temporary deferral of gain or loss recognition. Further, the personal residence provisions allow a permanent exclusion of a substantial amount of the realized gain on the sale of a home.

I. Determination of Gain or Loss

A. Realized Gain or Loss

1. A *realized gain* or *loss* is measured by the difference between the amount realized from the sale or other disposition of property and its adjusted basis on the date of disposition.
2. A realized gain results if the amount realized exceeds the property's adjusted basis. A loss is realized if the adjusted basis exceeds the amount realized.
3. The term *sale or other disposition* includes virtually any disposition of property, such as trade-ins, casualties, exchanges, or condemnations.
4. *Amount realized* from a property disposition is the sum of money, plus the FMV of property received, plus the release of any liability, less selling expenses relating to the sale.
5. The *adjusted basis* of a property is the original basis (usually cost), plus capital additions or improvements, less capital recoveries. The result reflects the unrecovered cost of the property on the date of disposition.
6. Capital additions, which may be distinguished from ordinary repair and maintenance expenditures, include the cost of capital improvements and betterments made to property by a taxpayer.
7. Examples of capital recoveries (i.e., reductions in an asset's basis) include:
   a. Depreciation, amortization, and cost recovery allowances.
   b. Casualties and thefts.
   c. Certain corporate distributions.
   d. Amortizable bond premium.

B. Recognized Gain or Loss

1. *Recognized gain* is the amount of realized gain that is included in a taxpayer's gross income.
2 *Recognized loss* is the amount of realized loss that is tax deductible.
3 As a general rule, all realized gains and losses are recognized.

C. Nonrecognition of Gain or Loss

1. Several situations where realized gains and/or losses are not recognized are discussed later in the outline.
2. Losses realized on personal use assets are not recognized unless they are the result of thefts or casualties.

D. Recovery of Capital Doctrine

1. A taxpayer is entitled to recover the cost or other basis of property and, therefore, is not taxed on that amount.
2. The cost or other basis is recovered through annual cost recovery methods.
3. On a sale or other disposition, the unrecovered cost (adjusted basis) is subtracted from the amount realized to determine gain or loss.

II. Basis Considerations

A. Determination of Cost Basis

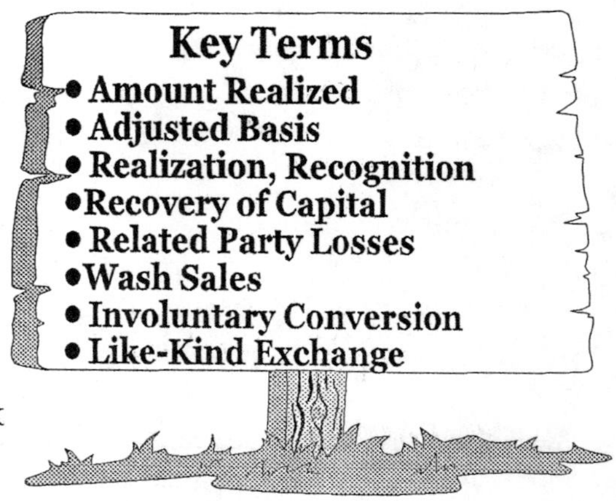


1. The basis for property is generally its cost – amounts paid for the property in cash or other property. However, the basis of property received in a *bargain purchase* is its FMV.
2. Cost identification problems are frequently encountered in securities transactions. Unless a taxpayer can adequately identify the particular stock that is sold, security sales presume the first lots purchased are the first sold (i.e., a FIFO presumption).
3. When multiple assets are acquired in a lump-sum purchase, the purchase price must be allocated among the assets for basis determination. The basis allocation is based on the relative FMV of the individual assets acquired.
4. If a business is purchased and *goodwill* is acquired, the special residual allocation rule must be used. It provides the following order for allocating basis to individual assets.
   a. First, cash and demand deposits.
   b. Next, marketable securities, Certificates of deposit & foreign currency.
   c. Then, all other assets, except § 197 intangible assets.
   d. Lastly, goodwill and other § 197 assets.
5. A special allocation of basis to newly acquired stock is necessary when *nontaxable stock dividends* are received.

When selling shares of stock or interests in a mutual fund, be certain that the asset's basis is properly stated. Income and capital gains distributions that have been reinvested in more stock over the years increase the investment's basis. The effect of the increase in basis is to reduce the gain or increase the of loss to be reported.

B. Gift Basis

1. Since there is no cost to the donee (recipient) on the receipt of a gift, a basis must be assigned to the property. In general, the donee's basis depends on the following.
   a. Date of the gift.
   b. Basis of the property to the donor (giver).
   c. Amount of the gift tax paid.
   d. Fair market value (FMV) of the property.
2. Basis Rules
   a. If the FMV of the asset at the date of gift is greater than the donor's adjusted basis and no gift tax is paid, the donee's basis carries over from the donor, that is the donee's basis is the same as the donor's.
   b. If the FMV of the asset at the date of gift is less than the donors adjusted basis, the donee cannot determine the property's basis until disposition of the asset occurs (See Exhibit 6-1).
      (1) When the disposition of the property results in a loss, the basis to the donee is its FMV on the date of the gift.
      (2) When the disposition of the property results in a gain, the basis to the donee is the donor's adjusted basis.
      (3) If the amount realized on disposition is between the basis for gain and the basis for loss (1 and 2 above), no gain or loss is recognized for tax purposes. Basis equals the amount realized.
3. Basis Rules with Gift Tax Paid
   a. The amount of the gift tax added to donee's basis is equal to the amount of tax attributed to the *net unrealized appreciation* at the date of the gift. Use the following formula to compute this amount.

$$\text{Donee's Basis} = \text{Donor's Adjusted Basis} + \left( \frac{\text{Unrealized Appreciation}}{\text{Taxable Gift}} \times \text{Gift Tax Paid} \right)$$

Where Taxable gift is FMV of gift less per donee annual exclusion

   b. Note that no appreciation can be added to the donee's basis if the asset's FMV at the date of gift is less than the donor's adjusted basis.
   c. For gifts made *prior to* 1977, the full amount of the gift tax paid is added to the donor's basis, up to the FMV of the property.
4. Holding Period
   a. Generally the holding period for the donee includes the holding period of the donor.
   b. However, when the donee's adjusted basis in the gifted property is the FMV at the date of gift, the holding period starts at the date of gift.
5. The basis for cost recovery on depreciable gift property is the donor's adjusted basis (i.e., the donee's basis for gain).

C. Property Acquired from a Decedent

1. The basis in property acquired from a decedent is generally its FMV at the date of the decedent's death.

2. An estate's executor may elect the *alternate valuation amount*, which uses the property's FMV 6 months after the decedent's death (alternate date of death). This valuation date must provide an overall lower estate valuation. If the alternate date is selected and assets are distributed before this date, the basis to the beneficiary is the FMV at the distribution date (See Exhibit 6-1).
3. Giving an appreciated asset to a dying person with an understanding that the donor of the gift (or donor's spouse) will inherit the property is called a deathbed gift. The purpose of this transaction is for the donor to get a stepped-up basis when the donee dies. This type of giving is not recognized.
4. Holding period for inherited property is always deemed to be *long-term*.

**Exhibit 6-1**
**BASIS FOR GIFTED OR INHERITED PROPERTY**

| | |
|---|---|
| ***GIFT*** | |
| *FMV of Gift at Date of Gift* | *Donee's Basis* |
| *Greater than Donor's basis* | *Donor's basis + gift tax paid on appreciation* |
| *Less than Donor's Basis:* | |
| *(1) Sell for Gain* | *Donor's basis* |
| *(2) Sell for Loss* | *FMV at date of gift* |
| *(3) Sell between (1) & (2)* | *Sales price, that is no gain or loss* |
| ***INHERITANCE*** | |
| *Valuation date* | *Heir's Basis* |
| *Date of Death* | *FMV at date of death* |
| *Alternate Date of Death (A-DOD)* | |
| *(1) distribution after A-DOD* | *FMV at alternate date of death* |
| *(2) distribution before A-DOD* | *FMV at distribution date* |

D. Disallowed Losses
1. Losses realized from sales or exchanges of property between certain related parties are *not* recognized under §267. Related parties include:
   a. Member of a family.
   b. A corporation and a shareholder who owns, directly or indirectly, more than 50% in value of corporation's outstanding stock.
   c. A partnership and a partner who owns, directly or indirectly, more than 50% capital or profits interest in the partnership.
2. Wash Sales §1091
   a. A realized loss is *not* recognized when the taxpayer disposes of stock or securities and, within 30 days before or after such disposition, acquires *substantially identical* stock or securities.
   b. The loss not recognized is added to the basis of the substantially identical stock or securities acquired. The holding period of the new stock or securities includes the holding period of the old.

E. Conversion of Property From Personal Use to Business or Income-Producing Use
1. The basis for losses on personal use assets converted to business or income-producing use is the *lower* of adjusted basis or FMV at date of conversion.

2. The gain basis for converted property is its adjusted basis at conversion.
3. The basis for losses serves as the basis for depreciating the converted property.

F. Summary of Basis Adjustments
1. Basis of an asset may be determined by: its cost, the basis of another asset, its FMV, or basis of the asset in the hands of another.
2. Concept Summary 6-2 in the text lists many items that affect the basis of an asset.

III. General Concepts of Nontaxable Exchanges

A. In a *nontaxable exchange*, realized gains or losses are not recognized until the property received in the exchange is subsequently disposed of in a taxable transaction. That is, the recognition of such gains and losses are *postponed* or *deferred*.

B. The reasoning for nonrecognition of a gain or loss in a nontaxable exchange is based on the concept that the taxpayers have merely changed the form, but not the substance, of their relative economic position. That is, the property received is viewed as being a continuation of the old investment in a different form.

IV. Like-Kind Exchanges § 1031

A. The like-kind provisions of § 1031 provide the following.
1. No gain or loss will be recognized if the provision applies to the transaction.
2. The like-kind provisions are *not elective* – they are *mandatory* if the following requirements are satisfied.
   a. The form of the transaction is an exchange.
   b. Both property transferred and property received are held for productive use in either a trade or business or for investment.
   c. The property is considered like-kind.
3. Property held for personal use, inventory, partnership interests, or securities do *not* qualify for the like-kind provisions. Further, US real property and foreign real property are not like-kind property under these provisions.

B. Like-Kind Property
1. The words *like-kind* refer to the nature or character of the property and not to its grade or quality.
2. Under this definition, real estate may be exchanged only for other real estate. It is irrelevant whether the real estate is improved or unimproved.
3. Property qualifying as personalty may be exchanged only for other personalty that is within the same general business asset class or productive class.
4. Livestock of different sexes are not like-kind property.
5. Related parties may not dispose of property received in like-kind exchanges for at least two years.

C. Exchange Requirement
1. To qualify as a like-kind exchange, there must be a direct exchange.
2. The sale of property and purchase of new property, even though the properties are like-kind, is generally not an exchange. However, the IRS may treat two transactions as a like-kind exchange if the transactions are mutually dependent.

> Like-kind exchanges are not limited to direct exchanges between two parties. Instead, if an agreement cannot be reached with the person owning property the taxpayer desires, a multi-party exchange can be arranged. This can result in a solution that will satisfy both parties and at the same time achieve a tax deferral.

D. Boot

1. *Boot* is cash or property other than like-kind property used in the exchange.
2. Realized gain is recognized to the extent of any boot received; however, boot received does not cause the recognition of realized losses.
3. Cash given in a like-kind exchange does not cause the *giver* to recognize gain or loss (though the receiver may recognize gain). However, if appreciated or depreciated property is used as boot, gain or loss will be recognized by the giver. The difference between the FMV and basis is the gain/loss recognized on the boot.

E. Basis and Holding Period of Property Received

1. The *basis* of the property received in a like-kind exchange must be adjusted to reflect any postponed gain or loss.
2. The basis of the property may be computed using either of the two methods illustrated in Exhibit 6-2.

**Exhibit 6-2**

**LIKE-KIND EXCHANGE BASIS CALCULATIONS**

| | | |
|---|---|---|
| *Method 1* | *The basis of the property received in the exchange is its FMV less postponed gain or plus postponed loss* | |
| *Method 2* | *Adjusted basis of property surrendered* | |
| | *Plus:* | *Adjusted basis of boot given* |
| | *Plus:* | *Gain recognized* |
| | *Less:* | *FMV of boot received* |
| | *Less:* | *Loss recognized* |
| | *Equals:* | *Basis of like-kind property received* |

3. The *holding period* of the like-kind property given up carries over and "tacks on" to the holding period of the like-kind property received. For any boot received, the holding period will begin from the date of the exchange.

V. Involuntary Conversions § 1033

A. General Scheme

1. A taxpayer suffering an involuntary conversion of property may elect to postpone recognition of gain realized from the conversion if reinvestment in replacement property occurs. Losses on the conversion can be recognized.
2. The basic rules of the provision follow.
   a. If the amount realized (e.g., insurance proceeds) exceeds the amount reinvested in replacement property, realized gain is recognized to the extent of the excess (boot).
   b. If the amount reinvested in replacement property equals or exceeds the amount received, realized gain is *not* recognized.

B. Involuntary Conversion Defined – An *involuntary conversion* is the result of the complete or partial destruction, theft, seizure, requisition/condemnation, or a sale or exchange under threat/ imminence of requisition/condemnation of the taxpayer's property.

C. Replacement Property
   1. A basic requirement is that the replacement property be similar or related in service or use to the involuntarily converted property.
      a. This rule is more restrictive than the § 1031 like-kind rules.
      b. Replacement property is subject to the *functional use test* if acquired by owner-users. This test requires the taxpayer's use of the replacement property be the same as the taxpayer's use of the involuntarily converted property
      c. Owner-investors are subject to the *taxpayer use test* in selecting qualified replacement property. That is, the replacement property must be used by the taxpayer in a similar endeavor as the involuntarily converted property.
   2. Business or investment *realty* need only be replaced by like-kind property if the involuntary conversion is from condemnation.

D. Time Limitation on Replacement – The taxpayer has a 2 year period (3 years for condemnation of realty used in a trade or business or held for investment) to replace the property after the close of the taxable year in which any gain is realized from the involuntary conversion. Thus, the period always ends of December 31.

VI. Other Nonrecognition Provisions

A. Transfer of Assets to Business Entity under § 351 and § 721 – The transfer of assets to a corporation or a partnership in exchange for an ownership interest is a nontaxable transaction if the requirements of the §351 for corporations or §721 for partnerships are met.

B. Exchange of Stock for Property § 1032 – No gain or loss is recognized by a corporation when it receives money or property in exchange for its own stock.

C. Certain Exchanges of Insurance Policies § 1035 – No gain or loss is recognized as a result of the following exchanges.
   1. The exchange of life insurance contracts.
   2. The exchange of life insurance contracts for endowment or annuity contracts.
   3. The exchange of certain endowment contracts.
   4. The exchange of endowment contracts for annuity contracts.
   5. The exchange of annuity contracts.

D. Exchange of Stock for Stock of the Same Corporation § 1036 – No gain or loss is recognized from the exchange of common stock solely for common stock or from the exchange of preferred stock solely for preferred stock.

E. Rollovers into Specialized Small Business Investment Companies § 1044
   1. If the amount realized on the sale of publicly traded securities is reinvested in the common stock or partnership interest of a specialized small business investment company, the realized gain, subject to limitations, is not recognized.
   2. Any amount not reinvested will trigger the recognition of the realized gain on the sale.

F. Sale of a Residence § 121

1. § 121 permits the exclusion (nonrecognition) of gain from the sale of a taxpayer's *principal residence*. The amount of realized gain excluded is limited to the first $250,000 for single filers or $500,000 for joint filers.
2. For the exclusion to apply, the residence must be owned and used as the taxpayer's primary residence for at least 2 of the 5 years preceding the sale.
3. The exclusion is not available for primary resident sales that occur within 2 years of the last use of § 121.
4. Losses on the sale of a primary residence are never recognized. This treatment is consistent with the treatment for the sale of other personal-use assets.

G. Transfer of Property Between Spouses Or Incident to Divorce § 1041

1. Property transfers made between spouses during marriage, between spouses or between former spouses incident to divorce are nontaxable transactions.
2. For transfers to be as incident to divorce, they must occur within 1 year after the date on which the marriage ceases.
3. The recipient has a carryover basis in the property received.

## TEST FOR SELF-EVALUATION – CHAPTER 6

**True or False**

Indicate which of the following statements are true or false by circling the correct answer.

T F 1. Realized gain or loss is measured by the difference between the amount realized from the sale or other disposition of property and the property's adjusted basis on the date of disposition.

T F 2. Basis for property acquired in a bargain purchase is its fair market value..

T F 3. Realized gains and losses are always recognized for tax purposes.

T F 4. Factors affecting the basis of property received by a gift are the date of the gift, gift tax paid (if any), the basis of the property to the donor, and the FMV of the property on the date of the gift.

T F 5. The basis of property received by gift can be dependent on whether the property is later sold at a gain or a loss.

T F 6. The basis of property acquired from a decedent is always its FMV at the date of the decedent's death.

T F 7. The holding period of property acquired from a decedent is always deemed to be long-term.

T F 8. The like-kind exchange provisions under § 1031 are elective.

T F 9. The nonrecognition provisions for involuntary conversions apply only to gains.

T F 10. A realized loss on the sale of a personal residence is recognized in certain situations.

T F 11. Like-kind treatment under § 1031 is available for exchanges of partnership interests.

T F 12. Partners can transfer assets to a partnership in exchange for a partnership interest without recognizing gain or loss.

T F 13. The wash sale rules disallow the recognition of realized gains and losses for sales or exchanges of stock or securities within 30 days.

T F 14. An exchange of idle farmland for an apartment building could qualify as a nontaxable like-kind exchange.

T F 15. A bakery destroyed in a fire could be replaced by its owner-user with idle farm land in a qualifying nontaxable involuntary conversion.

T F 16. The use of the involuntary conversion provision allowing for the deferral of gain recognition is mandatory.

T F 17. If the amount realized from the sale of publicly traded securities is reinvested in ownership of a specialized small business investment company, the realized gain is not recognized.

T F 18. The opportunity to exclude realized gain on the sale of a personal residence is only available if the taxpayer owned and used the home as a principal residence for at least 5 years.

T F 19. Transfers of property at the time of a divorce is not taxable to either the former husband or wife if they occur within 1 year of when the divorce is final.

T F 20. No gain or loss is recognized as a result of an exchange of a life insurance contract for an annuity contract.

**Fill-in-the-Blanks**

Complete the following statements with the appropriate word(s) or amount(s).

1. If married taxpayers, filing jointly, sell their principal residence, they may elect to exclude up to ________ of the gain from recognition.

2. A corporation does not recognize gain or loss when it receives ________ or other ________ in exchange for its ________.

3. A shareholder can exchange ________ for ________ or ________ for ________ stock in the same company without recognizing a gain or loss.

4. Realized losses from the sale of property between ________ are not recognized.

5. A(n) ________ is the result of the complete or partial destruction, theft, seizure, requisition, condemnation, or the sale or exchange under threat of condemnation of the taxpayer's property.

6. The basis of like-kind property received in an exchange is its FMV ________ postponed gain or ________ postponed loss.

7. With involuntary conversions, a taxpayer normally has ________ years after the close of the taxable year in which the gain is realized to replace the property. However, the time period is ________ years if the conversion is due to ________ of real property used in a business.

8. The ________ rules specify that if a taxpayer sells or exchanges stock or securities and within ________ days before or after the date of such sale or exchange acquires ________ stock or securities, any loss realized from the sale or exchange is not recognized.

9. The holding period of property acquired by gift begins on the date the property was acquired by the donor if the donor's ________ is the basis to the donee. The holding period begins on the date of the gift if the property's ________ serves as the basis to the donee.

10. Section 1031 requires the recognition of gain in some situations, but only if ________ is received by the taxpayer and only if ________ is realized on the transaction.

11. The adjusted basis of a property is its ________ plus ________ less ________.

12. For personal property converted to business or income-producing use, the loss basis is the lower of the property's ________ or ________ on the date of conversion, while the gain basis is the property's ________ on the date of conversion.

13. Transfers between spouses ________ or ________ are nontaxable transactions.

14. Under the involuntary conversion rules, the ________ test applies to owner-users and the ________ test applies to owner-investors.

15. In general, the ________ doctrine provides that a taxpayer is entitled to recover the cost or other basis of property without being taxed on that amount.

## Multiple Choice

Choose the best answer for each of the following questions.

____ 1. Edwardo exchanged an office building for an apartment house. The office's adjusted basis is $80,000 and its FMV is $140,000. The apartments have a FMV of $100,000. As a part of the exchange, Edwardo received $10,000 cash and the buyer assumes a $30,000 mortgage on the office. Calculate Edwardo's recognized gain.

a. $0.
b. $10,000.
c. $60,000, this does not qualify as a like-ind exchange.
d. None of the above.

____ 2. Refer to the preceding question. What is Edwardo's basis in the new property?

a. $80,000.
b. $90,000.
c. $100,000.
d. None of the above.

____ 3. Cataria was given a parcel of land this year. The donor had originally purchased the land in 19X0 for $1,500; however, on the date of the gift the land had a FMV of $20,000. The gift tax paid by the donor on the transaction was $2,000. What is the basis of the property to Cataria?

a. $1,500.
b. $3,350.
c. $3,500.
d. $20,000.

____ 4. Marcel inherited grazing land from his long-lost uncle. The land was purchased by the uncle for $25,000, and over the years, the uncle had added $16,000 of improvements to the land. The FMV of the property at the date of the uncle's death was $35,000 and associated estate taxes were $3,000. The basis of the property for Marcel would be what amount if the no special elections were made by the estate?

a. $41,000.
b. $38,000.
c. $35,000.
d. $Zero.
d. None of the above.

____ 5. Assume the same facts as in the preceding problem. Marcel sells the land 6 months after his uncle's death for $33,000. What is Marcel's gain/loss on the sale of the land?

a. No gain or loss.
b. $33,000 short-term capital gain.
c. $2,000 short-term capital loss.
d. $8,000 long-term capital loss.
e. None of the above.

____ 6. Refer to the preceding problem. If the alternative date of death valuation has been elected by the executor, what would be Marcel's gain/loss on the sale of the land?

a. $8,000 long-term capital loss.
b. $2,000 short-term capital loss.
c. No gain or loss.
d. Cannot be determined from the information given.
e. None of the above.

____ 7. Which of the following statements is *not* one of the rules regarding the relationship between recover of capital doctrine and realization or recognition of gain or losses.

a. A realized gain that is never recognized results in the permanent recovery of more than the taxpayer's basis for tax purposes.
b. A realized gain on which recognition is postponed results in the temporary recovery of more than the taxpayers basis for tax purposes.
c. A realized loss that is never recognized results in the permanent recovery of more than the taxpayer's basis for tax purposes.
d. A realized loss on which recognition is postponed results in the temporary recovery of less than the taxpayers basis for tax purposes.
e. None of the above.

____ 8. Which one of the following statements regarding the exclusion on the sale of a personal residence is *true*.

a. All gain on the sale is excluded.
b. This exclusion applies only to gain and not to losses.
c. The exclusion is available only to taxpayers 55 years of age or older.
d. The exclusion applies to the sale of a taxpayer's principal residence and one other residence.
e. All of the above statements are true.

____ 9. Uchila sold an apartment building this year that had an adjusted basis of $150,000. The buyer agreed to pay $60,000 in cash, assumes the $140,000 mortgage on the building, and pay $50,000 plus interest at the current market rate one year from the date of the sale. What is Uchila's gain or loss realized on the sale?

a. $40,000 loss realized.
b. $50,000 gain realized.
c. $60,000 gain realized.
d. $100,000 gain realized.
e. Cannot be determined from this information.

____ 10. Ramon purchased the following lots of Xenon stock:

| Date Purchased | Number of Shares | Cost Per Share |
|---|---|---|
| 6/15/X1 | 100 | $ 85 |
| 8/20/X1 | 150 | 100 |
| 2/10/X2 | 100 | 125 |

On May 8, 20X2 Ramon sells 150 shares for $150 a share. Ramon can not specifically identify which shares he sold. The amount of his gain is:

a. $5,000.
b. $6,000.
c. $7,500.
d. $9,000.

____ 11. This year, David made gifts to his two daughters, Cory and Emily. To Cory he gave 100 shares of ABC stock which had a basis to him of $5,000 and a FMV of $4,000 at the date of the gift. To Emily he gave XYZ stock which had a basis of $3,000 and a FMV of $4,000 at the date of the gift. Late in the same year, both Cory and Emily sold their stock to unrelated third parties for $3,500 and $4,500, respectively. What gains or losses must Cory and Emily recognize in the year of disposition?

| | Cory | Emily |
|---|---|---|
| a. | $1,500 loss | $1,500 gain. |
| b. | $500 loss | $500 gain. |
| c. | $0 gain or loss | $1,500 gain. |
| d. | $500 loss | $1,500 gain. |

____ 12. Select the *incorrect* statement.

a. Corporations recognize gains but no losses on the sale of treasury stock.
b. The amount realized from the sale of property includes related liabilities assumed by the buyer.
c. When a taxpayer acquires multiple assets in a lump-sum purchase, the taxpayer must allocate the cost among the individual assets because some may be depreciable and others not.
d. Gift taxes paid by the donor which are attributable to the net unrealized appreciation at the date of the gift are added from the basis of the property given to the donee.
e. All of the above statements are correct.

_____ 13. Which of the following statements is *incorrect*?

a. Realty business property which has been condemned may be replaced by "like-kind" property within 3 years and qualify for treatment under involuntary conversion rules.

b. In involuntary conversions and "like-kind" exchanges, the recognized gain may never exceed the realized gain.

c. A taxpayer who sells property because of threat of condemnation may defer gain on a sale under the involuntary conversion rules.

d. A taxpayer who exchanges a tract of land held for investment for an apartment building may elect to either recognize gain on the exchange or defer gain under the like-kind rules.

e. All of the above statements are correct.

_____ 14. The § 121 exclusion available to single taxpayers on the sale of a principal residence is limited to what amount?

a. $150,000.

b. $250,000.

c. $500,000.

d. The amount is not limited.

_____ 15. This year, Nadia gave her son common stock with a FMV of $50,000 and paid $10,000 of gift tax on the transfer. She purchased the stock 4 years earlier for $20,000. The son subsequently sells the stock to an unrelated third party late in the current year for $40,000. What is the son's recognize a gain or loss on the transaction?

a. $10,000 short-term capital gain.

b. $14,000 long-term capital gain.

c. $30,000 long-term capital gain

d. $10,000 short-term capital loss.

_____ 16. Mirla converted her personal residence to rental property. At the time of the conversion, the property had an adjusted basis of $75,000 (land $5,000, building $70,000) and a FMV of $50,000 (land $5,000, building $45,000). What is Mirla's gain basis, loss basis, and basis for depreciation?

a. Gain basis $50,000; loss basis $50,000; depreciation basis $50,000.

b. Gain basis $50,000; loss basis $75,000; depreciation basis $45,000.

c. Gain basis $75,000; loss basis $50,000; depreciation basis $45,000.

d. Gain basis $75,000; loss basis $75,000; depreciation basis $75,000.

_____ 17. Fox Co. and Wolf Co. exchanged machinery used in their separate businesses. The machine Fox transferred had an adjusted basis of $150,000 and was subject $60,000 mortgage that Wolf assumed. In return Fox received a machine with a FMV of $190,000 (adjusted basis $100,000) and cash of $50,000. What is Fox Co.'s recognized gain?

a. $110,000.

b. $90,000.

c. $60,000.

d. None of the above.

____ 18. On 3/17/20X0, Lothar purchased 1000 shares of Ace, Inc. stock for $31,000. He sold all of the stock for $15,000 on 2/22/20X1. Receiving a hot tip from his broker, he repurchased 500 shares for $6,000 on 3/12/20X1 and sold these shares on 6/30/20X1 for $28,000. Marvin. How much gain or loss should Marvin recognize in 20X1 for these transactions?

a. $0 gain or loss.
b. $16,000 long-term loss and $22,000 short-term gain.
c. $22,000 short-term gain and no loss.
d. $8,000 long-term loss and $14,000 short-term gain.

____ 19. A rental office building owned by Britton was condemned by the state on September 12, 20X0. However, the condemnation award was not received until February 26, 20X1. In order to defer any gain realized on the involuntary conversion, what is the latest date on which Britton can purchase qualified replacement property?

a. December 31, 20X4.
b. February 26, 20X3.
c. December 31, 20X3.
d. September 12, 20X4.

____ 20. On August 7, 20X5, Shenna sold land for $60,000. She received the land from her father as a gift on June 9, 20X5, when its FMV was $62,000. Her father paid $6,000 of gift tax on the transfer. He had purchased the lot 20X0 for $65,500. What is Shenna's loss on the sale of the lot?

a. $2,000 long-term capital loss.
b. $2,321 short-term capital loss.
c. $5,500 long-term capital loss
d. $8,000 short-term capital gain.
e. None of the above.

____ 21. Carry contributed assets with a FMV of $102,000 and adjusted basis of $80,000 to Zio Corporation. Carry received 850 shares of the 1,000 shares outstanding. The other 150 shares of Zio belong to Sid who acquired the shares for $5,000 over10 years ago. After Carry's contribution, Zio had a FMV of $120,000 and the par value of the stock was $100. What is the amount of gain(loss) to Carry, Zio and Sid caused by the contribution by Carry.

a. Carry $22,000; Zio $18,000; Sid $13,000.
b. Carry $22,000; Zio $20,000; Sid $13,000.
c. Carry $22,000; Zio $Zero; Sid $13,000.
d. Carry $Zero; Zio $Zero; Sid $Zero.
e. None of the above.

____ 22. The following information applies to the acquisition of a new piece of machinery received by Eyad in a like-kind exchange. Eyad is a self-employed bricklayer, and the machine is used 100 percent in his business.

| | |
|---|---|
| Original cost of machinery traded in | $17,000 |
| Adjusted basis of machinery traded in | 7,000 |
| FMV of new machinery | 21,000 |
| Cash payment made by Eyad | 12,000 |

What amount of gain must Eyad recognize on the exchange?
a. $0.
b. $2,000.
c. $4,000.
d. $9,000.

____ 23. In October 19X0, Dawn bought her principle residence for $150,000. In 20X3, Dawn sold the residence for $500,000. during the time she lived in the house, she made $40,000 of improvements to the house. How much gain should Dawn report on the sale of her home?
a. $0.
b. $60,000.
c. $310,000.
d. $350,000.
e. None of the above.

____ 24. Willie died this year leaving his entire estate to his sister, Serena. The executor of Willie's estate properly made the alternate valuation date election. Willie's estate included 1,000 shares of ABC Co. stock for which Willie's basis was $200,000. The stock was distributed to Serena 4 months after Willie's death. FMV for the stock were as indicated below.

| | |
|---|---|
| On the day Willie purchased the stock | $200,000 |
| On the date of Willie's death | 356,000 |
| 4 months after Willie's death | 272,000 |
| 6 months after Willie's death | 270,000 |

What is Serena's basis in the stock?
a. $200,000.
b. $270,000.
c. $272,000.
d. $356,000.

____ 25. Rashad made a gift to Ella, his wife, of 3,000 shares of stock. His basis in the stock was $2,000 and the FMV at the date of gift was $50,000. Which of the following statements is true regarding this gift.
a. The amount on which to compute the gift tax is the FMV of the stock less the annual exclusion.
b. Ella's basis in the stock will be a $2,000 plus a proportion of the gift tax paid on the appreciation.
c. Ella's basis will be $50,000 because gift tax will be paid on the FMV of the stock at the date of gift.
d. No gift tax will be paid on this gift as it is between a husband and wife.
e. None of the above.

## Code Section Recognition

Several important sections of the Internal Revenue Code are described below. Indicate, by number, the appropriate Code section.

1. _____ Gains and losses are not recognized on a like-kind exchange.

2. _____ Gains are not recognized on involuntary conversions.

3. _____ The transfers of assets to a corporation in exchange for stock is a nontaxable transaction if the control requirements are met.

4. _____ The transfers of assets to a partnership in exchange for ownership interest is a nontaxable transaction.

5. _____ The permanent exclusion of gain on the disposition of a principal residence is provided.

6. _____ Losses are not recognized if a taxpayer sells stock and purchases substantially identical stock within 30 days.

7. _____ Realized losses from transactions between related parties are not recognized.

8. _____ Corporations have no recognition when it receives money or property in exchange for its own stock.

9. _____ Taxation of rollovers of stock gains into specialized small business investment companies are postponed.

10. _____ Transfer of property between spouses incident to divorce are not taxable.

## Short Answer

1. Calculate the gain or loss recognized on the disposition of the properties in the following transactions.

   a. Judy disposes of stock for $5,000 which had been received as a gift 5 years ago when its value was $3,000. The donor purchased the stock for $2,000 and paid no gift tax on the transfer.

b. Judy disposes of stock for $5,000 which had been received as a gift 5 years ago when its value was $3,000. The donor purchased the stock for $4,000 and paid no gift tax on the transfer.

c. Judy disposes of stock for $2,000 which had been received as a gift 5 years ago when its value was $3,000. The donor purchased the stock for $4,000 and paid no gift tax on the transfer.

d. Judy disposes of stock for $42,000 which had been received as a gift 5 years ago when its value was $33,000. The donor purchased the stock for $22,000 and paid $6,000 in gift taxes on the transfer.

2. Franco, sells his warehouse for $150,000 during the current year. He had received the warehouse as a bequest from his mother when it was worth $115,000. His mother had purchased the building 20 years prior to her death for $45,000. One year after the sale of the warehouse, Franco purchases another warehouse for $145,000.

a. Calculate the gain or loss recognized on the sale.

b. Assume that Franco exchanges his inherited warehouse for the new warehouse valued at $145,000 and $5,000 cash. Determine Franco's gain or loss on the exchange and his basis in the new warehouse.

## SOLUTIONS TO CHAPTER 6 QUESTIONS

**True or False**

1. T
2. T
3. F There are certain situations (e.g., like-kind exchanges) when realized gains and losses are not recognized on realization.
4. T
5. T
6. F An election may be made in certain situations to value the estate using the alternate valuation date. In such cases, the basis of property to the recipient normally is its FMV six months following the decedent's death.
7. T
8. F Like-kind exchange provisions *are* mandatory.
9. T
10. F Realized loss on the sale of a personal residence is *never* recognized.
11. F
12. T
13. F The wash sale rules apply only to transactions on which *losses* occur.
14. T It is immaterial whether real estate is improved (apartment building) or unimproved (farmland).
15. F The functional use test would require owner-users to replace the bakery with another facility of similar functional use.
16. F It is elective treatment.
17. T
18. F Taxpayers must own and use the property for 2 out of last 5 years.
19. T
20. T

**Fill-in-the-Blanks**

1. $500,000
2. money, property, stock
3. common, common, preferred, preferred
4. related parties
5. involuntary conversion
6. less, plus
7. two, three, condemnation
8. wash sale, 30, substantially identical
9. adjusted basis, FMV
10. boot, gain
11. original basis, capital improvements, cost recoveries
12. adjusted basis, FMV, adjusted basis
13. during marriage, incident of divorce
14. functional use, taxpayer use
15. recovery of capital

**Multiple Choice**

1. d $40,000. The realized gain of $60,000 (140,000 – 80,000) is recognized to the extent of boot received.(10,000 cash + 30,000 liability assumed)
2. a $80,000. 100,000 (FMV) – 20,000 (gain not recognized (60,000 - 40,000).
3. b $3,350. 1,500 + [(20,000 – 1,500) ÷ 20,000] X 2,000].
4. c $35,000. FMV at the date of the uncle's death.
5. e $2,000 long-term capital loss (33,000 - 35,000). Inherited property is always long-term
6. c At the alternative date of death (6 months after the date of death) the FMV (and Marcel's basis) would be $33,000.
7. c A realized loss that is never recognized results in the permanent recovery of *less* than the taxpayer's basis for tax purposes.
8. b Personal losses are not excluded but they are also not recognized for tax purposes.
9. d $100,000. Amount Realized is 250,000: Cash 60,000 + Mortgage 140,000 + Note 50,000. Less Adjusted Basis 150,000 = 100,000 realized gain.
10. d $9,000. [$150 X 150] – [(100 X $85) + (50 X $100)]
11. d Cory: ($500). 3,500 - 4,000 ( basis = FMV at date of gift);
    Emily: $1,500. 4,500 - 3,000. (basis = donor's basis).
12. a No gains or losses are recognized.
13. d Because this qualifies as a like-kind exchange, the deferral of gain realized is mandatory, not elective.
14. b
15 b $14,000. 40,000 - 26,000. Gift tax added to extent paid on appreciation. [(50,000 - 20,000) ÷ 50,000] X 10,000 + 20,000.
16. c $75,000, $50,000, $45,000. land is not depreciable.
17. a $110,000. Amount Realized: 190,000 + 60,000 + 50,000 = 300,000.
    Gain Realized: 300,000 – 150,000 = 150,000.
    Gain Recognized to extent of boot, (60,000 + 50,000).
18. d The 2/22/20X1 sale is treated as two sales each of 500 shares for $7,500 apiece. One sale has a recognized loss of $8,000 [7,500 – ½ (31,000)] and the other is a wash sale with a unrecognized loss of $8,000. The 6/30/20X1 sale has a gain of $14,000 (28,000 – 6,000 basis – 8,000 unrecognized wash sale loss).
19. a Three years from the end of the year in which gain is realized (20X1).
20. e $2,000 short-term capital loss. 60,000 - 62,000; basis is FMV at date of gift and holding period starts at date of gift.
21. d This transaction meets the requirements of § 351 and § 1032.
22. a $Zero. No boot was received by Eyad, therefore any gain realized is not recognized in the like-kind exchange.
23. b $60,000. 500,000 – (150,000 + 40,000) – 250,000 exclusion.
24. c $272,000. Value is at alternative date of death but distributed earlier.
25. d.

**Code Section Recognition**

1. 1031
2. 1033
3. 351

4. 721
5. 121
6. 1091
7. 267
8. 1032
9. 1044
10. 1041

**Short Answer**

1. a.

| | |
|---|---|
| Sales price | $ 5,000 |
| Less: Basis to Judy | - 2,000 |
| Gain on the disposition | $ 3,000 |

b.

| | |
|---|---|
| Sales price | $ 5,000 |
| Less: Basis to Judy | - 4,000 |
| Gain on the disposition | $ 1,000 |

c.

| | |
|---|---|
| Sales price | $ 2,000 |
| Less: Basis to Judy | - 3,000 |
| Loss on the disposition | $ 1,000 |

d. Judy's basis in the stock is $24,000 figured as follows:

$$\$22{,}000 + \frac{\$33{,}000 - \$22{,}000}{\$22{,}000} \times \$6{,}000 = \$24{,}000$$

| | |
|---|---|
| Sales price | $42,000 |
| Less: Basis to Judy | - 24,000 |
| Gain on the disposition | $18,000 |

2. a.

| | |
|---|---|
| Amount realized | $150,000 |
| Less: Adjusted basis | -115,000 |
| Recognized gain | $ 35,000 |

Purchase of another apartment building has no effect on the recognized gain.

b. Realized gain is $35,000 and recognized gain is equal to the boot received, $5,000.

Basis is equal to adjusted basis + gain recognized - boot received.
115,000 + 5,000 - 5,000 = $115,000.

OR Basis is equal to FMV of new warehouse less gain not recognized.
145,000 - (35,000 - 5,000) = $115,000.

# Chapter 7
# Property Transactions: Capital Gains and Losses, Section 1231, and Recapture Provisions

## CHAPTER HIGHLIGHTS

Capital gain provisions were enacted originally with the intent that they would help promote the formation of capital investment and risk-taking by investors. These provisions allow for beneficial treatment of gains by noncorporate taxpayers on the sale or exchange of capital assets. In addition, on dispositions of certain non-capital assets (e.g., depreciable and real property used in a trade or business) the beneficial treatment associated with a net capital gain also may result. Recapture provisions, however, provide that certain gains, which might have otherwise qualified for the beneficial capital gain treatment, receive ordinary income treatment. Thus, the character of gain or loss as capital or ordinary is significant when computing the tax liability, particularly for noncorporate taxpayers. **Changes for the Jobs and Growth Tax Relief Reconciliation Act of 2003 (Tax Act of 2003) have been included in this outline.**

I. General Considerations
   A. Rationale for Separate Reporting of Capital Gains and Losses
      1. *Net long-term capital gains over net short-term capital losses* of noncorporate taxpayers receive preferential treatment. These net capital gains may effectively be taxed at a lower rates than ordinary gains.
      2. Capital losses initially offset capital gains. If a *net capital loss* results, the deductibility of the loss is limited for corporate and noncorporate taxpayers.
      3. The recapture provisions have eroded some of the benefits of the capital gain provisions for what are called "§ 1231" assets.
      4. Therefore, separating capital asset transactions from other types of transactions is important and required by law.
   B. General Scheme of Taxation
      1. Proper classification of gains and losses depends on the following.
         a. The tax status of the property including the specific type of asset.
         b. The manner of the property's disposition.
         c. The holding period of the property.
      2. There are three possible *tax statuses* of property: Capital assets, Section 1231 assets, and Ordinary assets.
      3. Disposition of property can be by: sale, exchange, casualty, theft, or condemnation.
      4. A capital gain or loss is considered short-term only if the capital asset sold or exchanged has been held for one year or less.

II. Capital Assets

A. <u>Definition of a Capital Asset</u>

1. Investments are the most typical capital assets.
   a. They include stocks, bonds, mutual funds, partnerships interests, government securities, and vacant land.
   b. For individuals, personal use assets such as residences, cars, furniture, and artwork are capital assets. These receive capital treatment if their disposition creates a gain. Losses on these assets are not recognized.
2. The definition of a capital asset is property that is *not* any of the following.
   a. Stock in trade, inventory, or property held primarily for sale in the ordinary course of the trade or business of the taxpayer.
   b. Accounts or notes receivable acquired in the ordinary course of the trade or business of the taxpayer.
   c. Depreciable property or real estate (fixed assets) used in trade or business.
   d. Certain copyrights, literary, musical, artistic compositions, or creative works, letters or memoranda or similar property.
   e. Certain US government publications.
   f. Supplies regularly used or consumed in the ordinary course of business.

B. <u>Statutory Expansions</u>

1. To help reduce uncertainty, Congress has statutorily *expanded* the scope of the general definition of what is a capital asset in several cases.
2. If a *securities dealer* clearly identifies securities as being held for investment purposes by the close of business on the day of acquisition, they are considered capital assets.
3. *Real estate subdivided* by a noncorporate and non-dealer investor who engages in limited development activities may receive capital gain treatment to a limited extent.
   a. The lots sold must be held by the taxpayer for at least 5 years unless the land was inherited.
   b. If the requirements are met, the taxpayer receives capital gain treatment until the year in which the 6th lot is sold. Thereafter 5% of the revenue is treated as ordinary income. This ordinary income can be offset by selling expenses. Generally selling expenses are more than 5%, thus, no ordinary income is recognized.

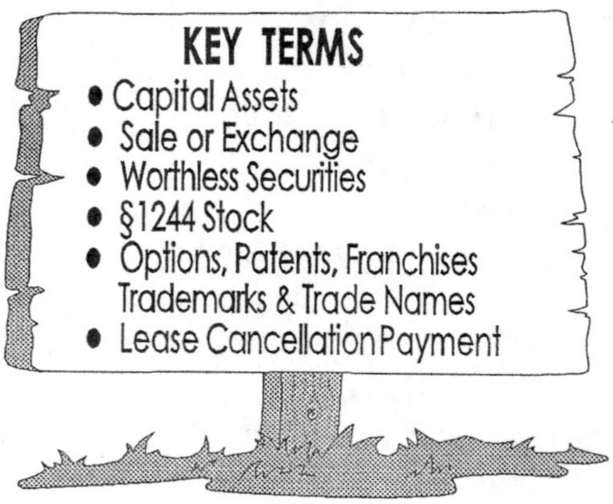


III. Sale or Exchange

A. Recognition of a capital gain or loss usually requires a *sale or exchange* of a capital asset. Although the term sale or exchange is not defined by the Code, a sale generally involves the receipt of money and/or the assumption of liabilities for property, and an exchange involves the transfer of one property for another property.

B. <u>Worthless Securities and § 1244 Stock</u>

1. When a security that is a capital asset becomes worthless, it is treated as if a sale occurred on the *last day* of the taxable year in which it became worthless.

2. Section 1244 allows an *ordinary* loss, instead of a capital loss, on the disposition of small business corporation stock. However, the ordinary loss treatment is limited to $50,000 ($100,000 for joint returns) per year.

C. Retirement of Corporate Obligations

1. Debt obligations (bonds or note payables) may have a tax basis different from their redemption values because of acquiring them at a premium or discount.
2. Generally, collection of a debt obligation will be treated as a sale or exchange and capital gain or loss may be recognized.

D. Options

1. An *option* gives the potential buyer (grantee) the right to purchase property at a set price during a specified time period from the owner (grantor). The grantee pays the grantor for this right.
2. Sale or exchange of an option generally results in capital gain/loss if the property subject to the option would be a capital asset to the grantee.
3. If the option is not *exercised*, the *lapse* is considered a sale on the option expiration date.
   a. Grantee recognizes a capital loss if the property subject to the option would have been a capital asset to the grantee.
   b. The grantor recognizes a short-term capital gain for an option on stock, securities, commodities, or commodity futures. For all other options, the grantor recognizes ordinary income.
4. If an option is *exercised*, the amount paid for the option by the grantee is added to the cost basis of the property subject to the option. With respect to the grantor, the amount received for the option is added to the selling price of the property.

E. Patents

1. If all *substantial rights* relating to a patent are transferred by the qualifying holder, the disposition is automatically considered a sale of a long-term capital asset regardless of whether the patent is a capital asset and regardless of how long the patent was retained by the holder.
2. A qualifying *holder* of a patent must be an *individual* and is usually (but not always) the creator of the invention. The creator's employer and certain parties related to the creator do not qualify as "holders."

F. Franchises, Trademarks, and Trade Names

1. A *franchise* is an agreement that gives the franchisee the right to distribute, sell, or provide goods, services, or facilities within a specified area.
2. The transfer of a franchise, trademark, or trade name is considered a disposition of a capital asset if the transferor does not retain any *significant power, right, or continuing interest*.
3. When the transferor does retain significant powers, rights, or continuing interest, the franchisee's *noncontingent* payments are ordinary income to the transferor. The franchisee capitalizes the payments and amortizes them over 15 years.
4. *Contingent* franchise payments produce ordinary income for the transferor and ordinary deductions for the franchisee in all situations.

G. Lease Cancellation Payments

1. Payments received by a *lessee* (tenant; renter) in consideration of a lease cancellation produce capital gains when the lease is a capital asset.
2. Payments received by a *lessor* (landlord) are always ordinary income because they are considered to be made in lieu of rental payments.

IV. Holding Period

A. Property must be held *more than* 1 year to qualify for long-term capital treatment. If the asset is held for exactly 1 year or less than 1 year, short-term treatment is appropriate.

B. Special Holding Period Rules

1. When the property given is a capital or a § 1231 asset, the holding period of property received in a nontaxable exchange includes the holding period of the formerly owned asset (the asset given).
2. If a transaction is nontaxable and the former owner's basis in the property carries over to the new owner (as in a gift), the holding period of the former owner becomes the present owner's holding period.
3. In situations involving disallowed losses, a new holding period begins when the property is transferred.
4. Property that has been inherited is always treated as held long-term.

C. Short Sales

1. A *short sale* occurs when a taxpayer sells borrowed property and repays the lender with substantially identical property (e.g., other shares of the same stock) either held on the date of the sale or purchased after the sale.
2. The general rule is that the holding period of the property sold short is determined by the how long the property used to close the short sale was held. However, some exceptions to the general rule do exist.

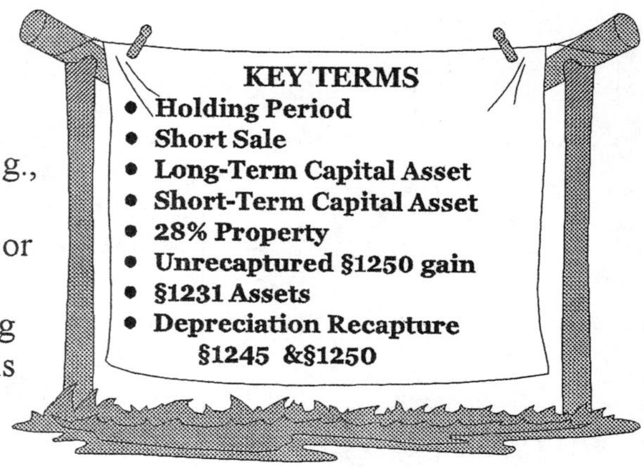


V. Tax Treatment of Capital Gains and Losses of Noncorporate Taxpayers

A. Sales or exchanges of capital assets are taxed at various rates depending on the holding period, general tax bracket of the taxpayer, and type of asset involved.

B. Capital Gains

1. Short-Term (S/T)
   a. Held for one year or less.
   b. Taxed as ordinary income at taxpayers' marginal tax rate. The Tax Act of 2003 changed these tax rates to 10%,15%, 25%, 28%, 33%, 35%.
2. Long-Term (L/T)
   a. Held greater than one year.
   b. Taxed at special *10%* (*5%* after May 5, 2003) for taxpayers in the 10% or 15% brackets and *20%* (*15%* after May 5, 2003) for taxpayers in brackets in excess of 15%.
3. 28% Property
   a. Collectibles held more than 1 year.
   b. Taxable half of the gain on sales of *qualified small business stock.*
   c. Taxed ordinary tax rates for taxpayers in the 28% or below tax bracket and 28% for those in brackets above 28%.
4. Unrecaptured § 1250 gain
   a. Applies to residential and commercial real estate held greater than 1 year.

b. Some of the gain attributable to depreciation deductions is taxable at a maximum rate of 25% rather than the capital rate of 20% (15% after May 5, 2003). Those sellers in the tax brackets of 25% or below receive no capital gains tax benefit.

**Exhibit 7-1**

**SUMMARY OF CAPITAL GAIN RATES**

| Type of Asset | 2003 Applicable Rate | |
|---|---|---|
| Short-Term | Ordinary Tax Rates: 10, 15, 25, 28, 33 & 35% | |
| Long-Term -- | | |
| 28% Property (Collectibles) | Maximum 28% | |
| Urecaptured § 1250 Gain | Maximum 25% | Before May 6, 2003 |
| Other Capital Assets | 5% and 15% | 10% and 20% |

C. Capital Losses

1. Have short-term, long-term, and 28% property losses but cannot have unrecaptured §1250 loss because the latter only applies to gains.
2. Netting Process

   Step 1: Group all gains and losses by category (ie, short-term (S/T), long-term (L/T), 28% property, and unrecaptured § 1250).

   Step 2: Net gains and losses within each category. This will result in a net S/T, net L/T, net 28% property, and/or net unrecaptured §1250 gain.

   Step 3: Within long-term held group (ie, 28% property, unrecaptured § 1250, and L/T capital), offset any net losses against the highest taxed gains first. Thus, a L/T capital loss first offsets 28% property gain and then unrecaptured § 1250 gains. A 28% property net loss first offsets a unrecaptured § 1250 gain then a L/T capital gain.

   Step 4: Offset the results of step 3 against the net S/T gain or loss from Step 2, if appropriate (eg, one is a gain and the other is a loss).
3. To the extent that capital losses exceed capital gains after the netting process, an individual taxpayer can deduct up to $3,000 of capital losses against ordinary income. Any excess is carried forward to future years.
4. When there are more than $3,000 of net capital losses, first use short-term, then 28% property, and lastly, regular long-term capital losses.

D. Small Business Stock

1. A special 50% exclusion is available for capital gains from the exchange or sale of *qualified small business stock*. The taxable portion is subject to a maximum tax rate of 28% (ie, small business stock is 28% property).
2. There are several restrictions on stock receiving this beneficial treatment. Even if the restrictions are met, the amount of gain eligible for the exclusion is limited to the greater of 10 times the stock's basis or $10 million per taxpayer per company.

VI. Tax Treatment of Capital Gains and Losses of Corporate Taxpayers
   A. Capital gains are taxed at the ordinary corporate tax rates. Long-term gains are subject to a maximum rate of 35%.
   B. Capital gains can offset capital losses without limit. However, capital losses in excess of capital gains cannot be used as a deduction against ordinary income.
   C. Net capital losses are allowed a 3 year carryback and 5 year carryforward. The carrybacks and carryforwards are always treated as short-term, regardless of their original nature.

VII. Section 1231 Assets
   A. Relationship to Capital Assets
      1. Section 1231 assets are trade or business property held greater than 1 year.
      2. Sales or exchanges of these assets receive favored treatment; capital treatment for net gains and ordinary treatment for net losses.
   B. Rational for Favorable Tax Treatment
      1. The economic circumstances of World War II set the stage for the enactment of the favorable treatment of assets used in a business.
      2. Years after the end of World War II, Congress curtailed the benefits of §1231 by enacting the depreciation recapture provisions.
   C. Property Included
      1. Depreciable or real property used in business
      2. Property held for the production of income if involuntarily converted.
      3. Timber, coal, or domestic iron ore.
      4. Livestock held for draft, breeding, dairy, or sporting purposes.
      5. Unharvested crops on land used in business.
      6. Certain *purchased* intangible assets (such as patents and goodwill) that are eligible for amortization.
   D. Property Excluded
      1. Property *not* held for more than 1 year (except unharvested crops and certain livestock).
      2. Properties where casualty losses exceed casualty gains.
      3. Inventory and property held primarily for sale to customers.
      4. Other property such as copyrights, literary compositions, and certain U.S. Government publications.
      5. Accounts and notes receivable arising in the ordinary course of business.
   E. Casualty or Theft and Nonpersonal-Use Capital Assets
      1. Nonpersonal-use assets are virtually any capital asset of an entity because entities (corporations, partnerships, etc) cannot use assets personally.
      2. Casualty gains and losses from § 1231 assets and the casualty gains and losses from long-term *nonpersonal-use* capital assets are netted together.
         a. If the result is a *net gain*, the gain is treated as a § 1231 gain.
         b. If the result is a *net loss*, the loss is deducted outside of § 1231.
      3. Condemnations are not treated as a casualty. They receive § 1231 treatment.
      4. Individual taxpayer's treatment of casualties of § 1231 and nonpersonal use assets need additional consideration.
         a. Net gains are added to other § 1231 gains.
         b. Net losses are split into their components and treated as follows.
            (1) Gains as ordinary gains.
            (2) Losses from § 1231 assets are deductible *for* AGI.

(3) Losses from nonpersonal-use asset are deductible *from* AGI subject to the 2%-of-AGI limitation.

c. Personal use property casualty gains/losses are not subject to § 1231.

F. <u>General Procedure for § 1231 Computation</u>

Step 1: Net all recognized long-term gains and losses from casualties of § 1231 assets and nonpersonal use capital assets.

a. For individuals, use the rules in E. 4. above.

b. For entities, net gains are added to other § 1231 gains and losses are ordinary losses.

Step 2: Net § 1231 gains and losses including net casualty gains from Step 1

a. If gains exceed losses, excess is treated as a long-term capital gain.

b. If losses exceed gains, all gains produce ordinary income and all losses are deductible either *for* or *from* adjusted income, as appropriate.

Step 3: Lookback Provisions –

a. The net § 1231 gains must be offset by the *nonrecaptured* net § 1231 losses for the 5 preceding years (i.e., the *§ 1231 lookback*).

b. Capital gain treatment results only after the non-recaptured § 1231 losses from the preceding years have been offset.

VIII. Section 1245 Recapture

A. Section 1245 was enacted to prevent taxpayers from receiving the dual benefits of depreciation deductions which offset ordinary income plus long-term capital gain treatment provided under § 1231.

B. Section 1245 provides that gain recognized from the disposition of § 1245 property will be treated as *ordinary income* to the extent of depreciation previously taken. Any gain in excess of the recaptured depreciation may be treated as § 1231 gain.

C. Recapture rules do not apply to losses. Generally, the loss will be a § 1231 loss unless the form of the disposition is a casualty.

> Very few depreciable personalty assets subject to § 1245 generate § 1231 gain upon their disposal. Section 1231 gain results only when the asset's market value increases while its owned by the taxpayer. In most cases, § 1245 assets do not appreciate in value. Consequently, any gain realized is recognized fully as ordinary income due to the § 1245 recapture.

D. <u>Section 1245 Property</u>

1. All depreciable personalty including depreciable livestock.
2. Amortizable personalty such as goodwill, patents, copyrights, leaseholds, professional football and baseball player contracts.
3. Expensing of costs to remove architectural and transportation barriers that restrict the handicapped and/or elderly.
4. Certain depreciable tangible real property employed as an integral part of the manufacturing and production process.
5. Pollution control facilities, railroad grading and tunnel bores, on-the-job training, and child care facilities on which amortization is taken.
6. Single purpose agricultural and horticultural structures and petroleum storage facilities.

7. Certain real property placed in service after 1980 and before 1987 if the statutory percentage ACRS method is used and is not subject to § 1250.

E. Observations on Section 1245
1. Section 1231 gain will not result unless the § 1245 property is disposed of for *more* than its original cost.
2. Recapture applies to the total amount of depreciation allowed or allowable.
3. Recapture applies regardless of the holding period of the property.
4. Losses normally receive § 1231 treatment.
5. Gains from the disposition of § 1245 assets may also be treated as passive activity gains.

IX. Section 1250 Recapture

A. The § 1250 recapture was enacted for *depreciable real property* for reasons similar to those supporting the enactment of § 1245.
1. Section 1250 property is depreciable real property and intangible real property (leaseholds) that is not subject to § 1245.
2. The § 1250 provides for the recapture of additional depreciation deducted by the taxpayer. Additional depreciation is the excess of accelerated depreciation actually taken over the depreciation that would have been allowed had the straight-line method been used.

3. Since real property placed in service after 1986 can only be depreciated using the straight-line method, there will be no § 1250 depreciation recapture on such property.
4. Section 1250 does not apply to losses or alter § 1231 treatment of realized losses.
5. If the property is held for one year or less, *all* depreciation taken, even under the straight-line method, is additional depreciation.

B. Computing Recapture on Nonresidential Real Property
1. The gain treated as ordinary income is limited to the lesser of the gain recognized or the post-1969 additional depreciation (accelerated in excess of straight-line).
2. Any gain not recaptured as ordinary income is § 1231 gain.

C. Computing Recapture on Residential Rental Housing
1. Recapture is computed the same as for other §1250 property, except only post-1975 additional depreciation needs to be recaptured.
2. Gain in excess of the required recapture is § 1231 gain.

D. Unrecaptured §1250 Gains
1. Noncorporate taxpayers pay a maximum rate of 25% on their unrecaptured §1250 gains.
2. Unrecaptured §1250 gains are equal to the depreciation that is not recaptured by §1250 (ie, the straight-line depreciation).

3. Computation of unrecaptured §1250 gains involves 3 steps.
   Step 1: Determine gain attributable to prior depreciation taken.
   Step 2: Determine §1250 recapture.
   Step 3: Subtract Step 2 from Step 1. This is unrecaptured §1250 gain.

E. Additional Recapture for Corporations
   1. Corporations selling depreciable real estate may have ordinary income in addition to that required by § 1250.
   2. The Code § 291 requires an ordinary income adjustment equal to 20% of the excess of § 1245 potential recapture over § 1250 recapture amount.

X. Exceptions to §§ 1245 and 1250
   A. Gifts – However, the recapture potential carries to the donee.
   B. Death – Recapture potential does *not* carry over from a decedent to an estate or heir. Recapture potential disappears.
   C. Charitable Transfers – The recapture potential reduces the amount of the charitable contribution deduction.
   D. Certain Nontaxable Transactions – In certain nontaxable transactions, such as formation of an entity, reorganizations, and liquidations of subsidiaries, the recapture potential carries over to the transferee.
   E. Like-Kind Exchanges and Involuntary Conversions – To the extent gain is recognized, the nature of such gain may be governed by §§ 1245 or 1250. Any remaining recapture potential carries over and attaches to the property received.

XI. Reporting Procedures
   A. Noncapital gains and losses are reported on Form 4797: Sales of Business Property.
   B. When there has been a casualty, Form 4684: Casualty and Thefts, will need to be completed before Form 4797 can be file.

## TEST FOR SELF-EVALUATION – CHAPTER 7

**True or False**

Indicate which of the following statements are true or false by circling the correct answer.

T F 1. Short-term capital losses are preferable to long-term capital losses on an individual's income tax return.

T F 2. The principal capital assets held by individuals include personal residences, personal-use automobiles, and corporate stock held for investment.

T F 3. If a security which is a capital asset becomes worthless during the taxable year, the resulting loss is treated as a loss from the sale or exchange of a capital asset on the last day of the taxable year.

T F 4. As a general rule, the sale of an option results in capital gain or loss if the property subject to the option is a capital asset in the hands of the grantor of the option.

T F 5. Patents have not been given capital asset treatment because Congress believes that by doing so would inhibit technological progress.

T F 6. A capital asset acquired on the last day of any month must not be disposed of until on or after the first day of the thirteenth succeeding month to be considered held long-term.

T F 7. Special tax rate benefits are provided to most individual taxpayers in the taxation of net capital gains.

T F 8. Collectibles are considered regular long-term capital property if held one year.

T F 9. Gain on § 1245 property, to the extent that it exceeds all recapture potential, will be § 1231 gain.

T F 10. Casualty and theft gains and losses of personal use property are subject to the provisions of § 1231.

T F 11. Real estate capital gains but *not* capital losses can be classified into the unrecaptured §1250 category.

T F 12. The depreciation recapture rules have an impact on the nature of gain recognized rather than on the timing of the recognition of gain.

T F 13. For depreciable real property placed in service by a noncorporate taxpayer after 1986, the depreciation recapture rules of § 1245 apply.

T F 14. As a general rule, securities held by a dealer are considered to be inventory and therefore, are *not* subject to capital gain or loss treatment.

T F 15. Capital gains from the sale of so-called 28% property category is taxable at a flat rate of 28%.

T F 16. The treatment provided to capital gains and losses is identical for both corporate and noncorporate taxpayers.

T F 17. For individual taxpayers, personal-use assets are never capital assets.

T F 18. A franchise is an agreement that gives the franchisee the right to distribute, sell, or provide goods, services, or facilities within a specified area.

T F 19. Short-term capital losses receive the same treatment as ordinary losses.

T F 20. The holding period for inherited property is always long-term.

**Fill-in-the-Blanks**

Complete the following statements with the appropriate word(s) or amount(s).

1. Since straight-line method is used under MACRS for real property purchased after 1986, gain to the extent of this depreciation taken will fall in the ______ gain category.

2. The transactions which do not trigger depreciation recapture under §§ 1245 or 1250 include ________, ________, and ________.

3. To obtain capital gain/loss treatment, two characteristics are required: the transaction must be a ________ and the item disposed of must be a ________.

4. Noncapital gains and losses are reported on Form ________ whereas casualties and thefts are reported on Form ________.

5. Corporate capital losses in excess of capital gains ________ be used as a deduction against ordinary income. Net capital losses are allowed a ________ carryback and ________ carryforward.

6. The assets considered 28% property include ________ held more than one year and the taxable portion of the gain on the sale of ________ .

7. A patent produces a ________ capital gain when all ________ rights are transferred by the holder. The holder must be a(n) ________.

8. In the capital loss netting process, a net capital losses offset against the ________ first.

9. The deduction of net capital losses in excess of net capital gains in any one year for individuals is limited to ________.

10. Section 1244 allows __________ deduction when stock is sold for a loss whereas the __________ provisions determine on which date valueless stock is considered sold.

11. Condemnations are not treated as a __________. They receive __________ treatment.

12. Capital assets do not include ________, ________, depreciable assets, creative works, ________, and supplies.

13. While ________ are created by an individual they are treated as a capital asset when sold.

14. Real estate subdivided by a __________ and __________ investor who engages in limited development activities may receive __________ treatment to a limited extent.

15. The lookback provisions associated with § 1231 require net § 1231 gains be offset by ________ for the ________ preceding taxable years.

**Multiple Choice**

Choose the best answer for each of the following questions.

____ 1. In the current year, Dakota had the following capital transactions.

| | |
|---|---|
| Long-term gain | $ 4,000 |
| 28% property gain | 6,000 |
| Short-term gain | 8,000 |
| Short-term loss | 11,000 |

Calculate Dakota's final net gains/losses and their categories.

a. $4,000 long-term, $6,000 28% property, ($3,000) short-term.
b. $4,000 long-term, $3,000 28% property.
c. $1,000 long-term, $6,000 28% property.
d. None of the above.

____ 2. Select the *correct* statement.

a. Dealers in real estate treat the sale of their first 5 lots as gains or losses from capital assets.
b. Collection of a debt obligation is not a recognition event.
c. A security dealer that identifies certain securities as being sold for investment purposes by the close of the day of disposition will receive capital gain treatment.
d. When the requirements for a qualified small business stock sale are met, the amount eligible for exclusion cannot be greater than 50% of the stock's basis.
e. None of the above.

____ 3. Ira sells a business apartment building for $125,000 which he purchased in 1985 for $100,000. Ira took $46,875 of accelerated depreciation. Straight-line depreciation for the same period would have been $45,000. What is the amount and character of Ira's gain on the sale of the business asset.

a. $45,000 § 1231; $25,000 unrecaptured §1250 gain; $1,875 §1250.
b. $25,000 § 1231; $45,000 unrecaptured §1250 gain; $1,875 §1250.
c. $71,825 §1231.
d. Some other amount.

____ 4. Megna had the following capital gains and losses.

| | | | | | |
|---|---|---|---|---|---|
| LTCG | $15,000 | STCG | $1,000 | Unrecaptured § 1250 | $10,000 |
| LTCL | 5,000 | STCL | 15,000 | | |

Calculate Megna's net capital gains or losses.

a. NLTCG $10,000; NSTCL $4,000.
b. NLTCG $6,000; Unrecaptured § 1250 $10,000.
c. NLTCG $6,000
d. Unrecaptured § 1250 $6,000

____ 5. Ella had the following recognized gains and losses during the year.

- Theft loss of a painting from her home, $700 (net of the $100 floor)
- An $8,000 gain from an insurance recovery on a business machine, owned for two years with $5,000 § 1245 recapture potential.
- Sale of a business machine for $40,000. The machine was purchased two years ago for $45,000. Total depreciation on the machine was $7,000.

Calculate Ella's net § 1231 gain or loss. Assume the § 1231 lookback procedure does not apply.

a. $10,000.
b. $9,300.
c. $4,300.
d. $3,000.

____ 6. Carpenter Corporation sold an automobile on March 27, 20X2 for $5,000 when its adjusted basis was $2,000. The automobile had originally been purchased on the December 31, 20X1 for $4,000. How should Carpenter Corporation report the transaction?

a. $1,000 § 1231 gain and $2,000 §1245 gain.
b. $2,000 § 1231 gain and $1,000 §1245 gain.
c. $3,000 § 1231 gain.
d. None of the above.

____ 7. Refer to the preceding problem. Assume the same facts except the automobile was purchased on January 15, 20X1. How should Carpenter Corporation report the transaction?

a. $1,000 § 1231 gain and $2,000 §1245 gain.
b. $2,000 § 1231 gain and $1,000 §1245 gain.
c. $3,000 § 1231 gain.
d. None of the above.

____ 8. Roberto acquired nonresidential real property in 20X1 to be used in his business. The building cost $70,000. Roberto utilized the MACRS method of cost recovery and claimed $22,000 of cost recovery deductions. If the building is sold during the year for $80,500, before considering the § 1231 lookback rules, how should Robert report the transaction?

a. $22,000 § 1250 recapture; $10,500 unrecaptured §1250 gain.
b. $22,000 unrecaptured §1250 gain; $10,500 § 1231 gain.
c. $32,500 § 1231 gain.
d. $32,500 ordinary income.

____ 9. Uma gives her mother § 1245 property which was used in her business. She bought the property for $50,000 and took $25,000 in accelerated depreciation before gifting it to her mother this year. Which of the following statements is correct?

a. Uma will recapture $25,000 as ordinary income at the time of the gift.
b. The mother recaptures $25,000 as ordinary income upon receipt of the gift.
c. The mother will recapture the excess of accelerated depreciation over straight-line depreciation as ordinary income on the sale of the property.
d. The first $25,000 of the realized gain will be ordinary income to the mother when she sells the property.

____ 10. Which of the following is *false* regarding § 1245 recapture?

a. The amount of a charitable contribution deduction is reduced by § 1245 recapture potential.
b. It can apply to gains recognized in like-kind exchanges.
c. It applies to the full amount of gains on tangible personalty.
d. It can apply to gains recognized in involuntary conversions.
e. All of the above are true.

____ 11. Sanjay had the following transactions during the current year.

| | |
|---|---|
| January 15 | Theft of bicycle he purchased for $250 two years ago. Not insured. |
| February 21 | Sold personal auto for $1,000. Purchased for $6,000 many years ago. |
| March 1 | Sold 100 shares of IBM stock for $3,000; the stock was purchased on September 1 of last year for $1,500. |
| May 15 | Theft of a diamond ring he received as gift on April 15, of last year. Adjusted basis was $60,000. Insurance reimbursement was $70,000. |

What should Sanjay report on his current year return?

a. LTCG $3,500; itemized deduction $250.
b. Section 1231 gain $10,000; STCL $1,500; LTCL $5,000.
c. Section 1231 gain $8,500; itemized deduction $250.
d. LTCG $3,350.
e. None of the above.

____ 12. Which is not § 1245 property?

a. Single-purpose agricultural structures.
b. Professional baseball and football contracts.
c. Buildings and their structural components placed into service in 1990.
d. Costs of removing architectural barriers for the benefit of the handicapped.
e. All are or could be § 1245 property.

____ 13. On May15 of last year, Alfonso, single, purchased on a national stock exchange 3,000 shares of stock in Heights Corp., for $50 per share. On March 29 of the current year the Heights Corp. stock was considered worthless. What type and amount of deduction should Alfred take in the current year assuming no other capital transactions?

a. $3,000 capital loss deduction and $147,000 STCL carryforward.
b. $50,000 ordinary loss deduction and $100,000 LTCL carryforward.
c. $3,000 capital loss deduction and $147,000 LTCL carryforward.
d. $50,000 ordinary loss deduction, $3,000 capital loss and $144,000 LTCL carryforward.

____ 14. On January 6 of this year, Jamal sold some § 1245 business equipment which had an adjusted basis of $5,000. He purchased the equipment for $10,000 five years ago. If he sold it for $8,000, how should Jamal treat the transaction?

a. Section 1231 gain of $3,000.
b. Section 1245 gain of $3,000.
c. Section 1231 loss of $2,000 and Section 1245 gain of $3,000.
d. Capital gain of $3,000.

____ 15. On January 1, Marie sold machinery for $68,000. The machinery was purchased on March 1, four years earlier, for $60,000 and using accelerated depreciation had an adjusted basis of $30,000 at time of sale. Using the straight-line method, the adjusted basis would be $40,000. In the year of sale, how should Marie treat the transaction?

a. Section 1231 gain of $28,000 and § 1250 recapture of $10,000.
b. Section 1231 gain of $38,000.
c. Ordinary income of $38,000.
d. Section 1231 gain of $8,000; ordinary income of $30,000.
e. None of the above.

____ 16. Last year, Alli sustained a § 1231 loss of $4,000 and was able to deduct the loss in full as an ordinary loss. This year, Alli realized a $5,000 gain on the disposition of a § 1231 asset. Assuming there were no other property transactions, how should this year's transaction be treated?

a. $5,000 capital gains.
b. $5,000 ordinary income.
c. $4,000 ordinary income and $1,000 capital gain.
d. $4,000 capital gain and $1,000 ordinary income.

____ 17. The following assets were owned by the Gray Corporation at year end.

| | |
|---|---|
| Delivery Truck | $11,000 |
| Inventory | 15,000 |
| Trade Accounts Receivable | 6,000 |

The capital assets total the following.

a. $0.
b. $11,000.
c. $17,000.
d. $32,000.

____ 18. Which of the following statements are *false*.

a. Proper classification of gains and losses depends on the manner in which the property is disposed.
b. Because of a special loss limitation, it is important to separate capital transactions from other types of transactions.
c. A capital gain or loss is considered short-term only if the capital asset sold or exchanged has been held for one year or less.
d. Disposition of property can be by sale, exchange, gift, casualty, theft, or condemnation.

_____ 19. Black Corporation had the following § 1231 gains and losses for the past 6 years.

| Year | X1 | X2 | X3 | X4 | X5 | X6 |
|---|---|---|---|---|---|---|
| Gain | $3,000 | | | $3,000 | | |
| Loss | | $2,000 | $4,000 | | $3,000 | $1,000 |

In the current year Black Corporation had a § 1231 potential gain of $8,000. How should Black treat the gain on its tax return?

a. $4,000 § 1231 gain and $4,000 ordinary income.
b. $8,000 ordinary income.
c. $1,000 § 1231 gain and $7,000 ordinary income.
d. $8,000 § 1231 gain.

_____ 20. Gary purchases stock options for $300 to purchase 500 shares QCV at $40 per share. Two months later, Gary exercises the options and purchases the shares of QCV. The grantor purchased the stock 5 years ago for $15,000. What is the proper treatment for Gary and the grantor of the options?

a. Gary's basis is $20,000; grantor has a $5,000 LTCG and $300 STCG.
b. Gary's basis is $20,300; grantor has a $5,300 LTCG.
c. Gary's basis is $20,300; grantor has a $5,000 LTCG and $300 ordinary income.
d. None of the above.

_____ 21. On January 1 of the current year, Pierre owned the following assets.

| | |
|---|---|
| Personal residence | $65,000 |
| ABC Corporation stock | 6,000 |
| Antique automobile | 12,000 |

Pierre's capital assets total to the following.

a. $83,000.
b. $77,000.
c. $71,000.
d. $18,000.

_____ 22. Bintong bought land in 20X0 for $180,000 and is going to engage in limited development of the land. Bintong would like to receive capital gain treatment when he sells the land. Which one of the following is *not* a requirement under § 1237 to be eligible for capital gain treatment.

a. The taxpayer is not a real estate dealer.
b. The taxpayer is not a corporation.
c. Substantial improvements have been made to the lots sold.
d. The lots sold were held for at least 5 years, unless the land was inherited.

_____ 23. Isabella purchased an apartment building in 1985. She has been taking depreciation on an accelerated basis. Straight-line depreciation would have produced deductions of $50,000 less than what she has actually claimed. In the current year, when Isabella's basis in the building was $150,000, she exchanged it for an office building worth $275,000. What is Isabella's reportable gain on this transaction?

a. $50,000 § 1250 gain and $75,000 § 1231 gain.
b. $125,000 § 1231 gain.
c. $125,000 long-term capital gain.
d. $0.

____ 24. Brawn purchased a 10 year corporate bond with a face value of $10,000 in 20X0 for $9,700. The bond was redeemed early in 20X6 and a premium was paid due to the early redemption. Brawn received $10,400. How does Brawn treat the redemption?
a. Brawn has a $700 LTCG.
b. Brawn has $700 ordinary income (interest).
c. Brawn has a $300 ordinary income and $400 STCG.
d. The redemption is not a taxable event because it is not a sale or exchange.
e. None of the above.

____ 25. Craft Company purchased options on shares of stock that it planned to hold as an investment. The options cost $2,000 and gave it the right to buy the stock at $200,000 at anytime during the next 3 months. If the option lapses, which of the following treatments results?
a. Craft Company has an ordinary loss of $2,000.
b. Craft Company has a long-term capital loss of $2,000.
c. Craft Company has a § 1231 loss of $2,000.
d. Craft Company has a short-term capital loss of $2,000.
e. None of the above.

## Code Section Recognition

Several important sections of the Internal Revenue Code are described below. Indicate, by number, the appropriate Code section.

1.________ Defines a capital asset.

2.________ Allows capital gain treatment to non-dealers in real estate that have only limited development activities.

3.________ Provides that in certain cases, long-term capital gain treatment applies to sales and exchanges of business assets.

4.________ Provides for depreciation recapture on the disposition of all depreciable personal property.

5.________ Provides for depreciation recapture on the disposition of depreciable realty acquired before 1987.

**Short Answer**

1. Calf Mountain Company sells depreciable property during the year which is subject to § 1245 recapture. The property had been used for three years. The relevant data follow:

| | |
|---|---|
| Original cost | $10,000 |
| Depreciation taken | 4,000 |

Determine the amount and nature of the gain or loss in the following situations.

a. The property is sold for $8,000.

b. The property is sold for $12,000.

c. The property is sold for $4,000.

## SOLUTIONS TO CHAPTER 7 QUESTIONS

### True or False

1. F Both types of net capital losses may be used by individuals to offset up to $3,000 of other income.
2. T
3. T
4. F This is true with respect to the option holder, not the option's grantor.
5. F Gains from the disposition of patents *do* receive capital asset treatment.
6. T
7. T
8. F Collectibles are considered 28% property if held more than one year.
9. T However, one must remember to consider the § 1231 lookback procedure.
10. F Gains and losses of personal use property are netted separately. Casualties on nonpersonal use property is netted with § 1231 gains and losses.
11. T
12. T
13. F The disposition by a noncorporate shareholder of depreciable real property placed in service after 1986 is not subject to depreciation recapture.
14. T
15. F The 28% property can be taxed at the rates below 28% as well.
16. F Corporations do not receive special lower tax rates on capital gains. They also cannot offset ordinary income with capital losses as individuals can.
17. F The opposite is true.
18. T
19. F Short-term capital losses are initially netted against capital gains. Further, if a net loss results, its current deductibility may be limited.
20. T

### Fill-in-the-Blanks

1. unrecaptured §1250
2. Any three of the following: gifts, deaths, charitable transfers, certain tax-free transactions, like-kind exchanges, and involuntary conversions.
3. sale or exchange, capital asset
4. 4797, 4684
5. cannot, 3 year, 5 year
6. collectibles, qualified small business stock
7. long-term, substantial, individual
8. highest taxed gain
9. $3,000
10. ordinary, worthless securities
11. casualty, §1231 gains
12. inventory, accounts & note receivables, U.S. government publications
13. patents
14. noncorporate, non-dealer, capital gain
15. net §1231 losses, five

## Multiple Choice

| | | |
|---|---|---|
| 1. | b | STCL $3,000 (8,000 - 11,000) first nets with the 28% property gain to result in a 28% property gain of $3,000 (6,000 - 3,000) |
| 2. | e | *Non-dealers* in real estate receive capital gain treatment. Collection of a debts is *treated as a sale*. A security dealer identifying investments by the close of the day of *acquisition* receives capital gain treatment. The amount eligible for exclusion on a qualified small business stock sale is 10 times the basis. |
| 3. | b | Total gain: $71,875 [125,000 - (100,000 - 46,875)].<br>§1250 recapture: $1,875 [46,875 - 45,000].<br>Unrecaptured §1250: $45,000 [46,875 - 1,875].<br>§1231: $25,000 [71,875 - 1,875 - 45,000]. |
| 4. | c | Netting each category: NLTCG $10,000; NSTCL $14,000; Unrecap. §1250 $10,000. Net STCL against the highest taxed gain (Unrecap. §1250) then net remaining STCL against NLTCL. Result = $6,000 NLTCG. |
| 5. | d | The theft of personal use property and depreciation recapture are not included. |
| 6. | e | The gain is ordinary income since the automobile was not held for more than 1 year. |
| 7. | a | Since the automobile was held more than 1 year, §§ 1231 and 1245 apply. |
| 8. | b | There is no §1250 recapture potential for real estate placed into service after 1986. |
| 9. | d | Gifts do not trigger depreciation recapture. Recapture attaches to the property. |
| 10. | c | Tangible personalty sole in excess of its original cost will produce § 1231 gains also. |
| 11. | e | STCG $1,500 on the sale of stock; net personal casualty gain $9,850 (gain 10,000 from the ring - loss 150 from the bicycle, net of 100 floor). The loss on the sale of the personal auto is not deductible. |
| 12. | c | Buildings placed into service after 1986 are not subject to §1245 recapture. |
| 13. | c | Stock does not qualify as §1244 stock because taxpayer is not original purchaser. Worthless stock treated as sold on the last day of the year it becomes worthless |
| 14. | b | Recapture of all depreciation to the extent of the gain. |
| 15. | d | The § 1245 recapture produces ordinary income. |
| 16. | c | The lookback provisions apply. |
| 17. | a | The truck is a § 1231 asset and inventory and receivables are ordinary assets. |
| 18. | d | A gift is not considered a disposition of a property. |
| 19. | c | Lookback provisions apply. |
| 20. | b | |
| 21. | a | |
| 22. | c | No substantial improvements can have been made. |
| 23. | d | The transaction qualifies for like-kind treatment under § 1031. Further, any depreciation recapture potential does not trigger the recognition of any realized gain. |
| 24. | a | |
| 25. | d | |

## Code Section Recognition

1. 1221
2. 1237
3. 1231
4. 1245
5. 1250

## Short Answer

1. a. Net long-term capital gain – subject to tax rates of 10% for taxpayers in the 10% and 15% bracket and 20% for all other taxpayers.
   b. Net short-term capital gain – subject to ordinary income rates.
   c. Net 28% property gain – subject to regular tax rates for taxpayers in the 27% or below tax brackets and 28% for all other taxpayers.
   d. Net unrecaptured §1250 gain – subject to regular rates for taxpayers in the 10% and 15% bracket and 25% for all other taxpayers.
   e. Net capital loss – deductible against ordinary income up to a maximum of $3,000 per year.

2. a. The property is sold for $8,000:

| | |
|---|---|
| Amount realized | $8,000 |
| Less: Adjusted basis | -6,000 |
| Amount of gain recognized | $2,000 |

| | |
|---|---|
| Nature of gain recognized | |
| § 1245 | $2,000 |
| § 1231 | $ 0 |

   b. The property is sold for $12,000:

| | |
|---|---|
| Amount realized | $12,000 |
| Less: Adjusted basis | - 6,000 |
| Amount of gain recognized | $ 6,000 |

| | |
|---|---|
| Nature of gain recognized | |
| § 1245 | $4,000 |
| § 1231 | $2,000 |

   c. The property is sold for $4,000:

| | |
|---|---|
| Amount realized | $4,000 |
| Less: Adjusted basis | -6,000 |
| Amount of loss recognized | $2,000 |

| | |
|---|---|
| Nature of loss recognized | |
| § 1245 | $ 0 |
| § 1231 | $2,000 |

# Chapter 8
# Corporations: Organization, Capital Structure and Operating Rules

## CHAPTER HIGHLIGHTS

Unlike a sole proprietorship, partnership, or Subchapter S corporation, a regular Subchapter C corporation is a taxable entity, separate and distinct from its owners. This results in income having the potential of being double taxed; once at the corporate level and again when it is paid out to the owners in the form of dividends. The formation of a corporation, however, is tax-free, when the person(s) transferring the property are in control of the corporation immediately after the transfer under § 351. At the time of initial formation, determining the capital structure of a corporation is important. Shareholders must be aware of the differences between debt and equity for tax purposes. Although the determination of gross income and many of the deductions are similar to those allowed to individuals, there are many important differences in the tax treatment of corporations. **Changes for the Jobs and Growth Tax Relief Reconciliation Act of 2003 (Tax Act of 2003) have been included in this outline.**

I. Introduction to Corporate Tax
   A. Regular (or C) corporations are governed by Subchapter C and S corporations by Subchapter S of the Code. C corporations are tax paying entities whereas S corporations generally do not pay taxes because they are a flow-through entity.
   B. Comparison of Corporations to Other Forms of Doing Business
      1. After the Tax Act of 2003, The highest tax rate is the same for corporations and individuals, 35%. However, corporate income is taxed twice: once at the corporate level and then again when distributed to the owners as dividends. Dividends are taxed to shareholders at a rate of 15% after May 5, 2003.
      2. Income distributed to C corporation shareholders (as dividends) does not retain its character when reported on their income tax returns as it would for the owners of other types of tax entities.
      3. Losses incurred by a corporation do not pass through to the shareholders. Losses of the other tax entities can be passed through the entity to the owner and deducted on their personal returns.
   C. Nontax Considerations
      1. Nontax considerations may override tax considerations when choosing a business entity form.
      2. Some important factors to consider are:
         a. *Liability* of the owners. Corporate shareholders have limited liability.

b. Ability to *raise large amounts of capital*. Sale of large amounts of stock is possible with corporations. Ownership in a corporation (stock) is *freely transferable*.

c. *Continuity of life*. Corporations have continuity of life whereas other entities do not.

d. Responsibility for management of the business. Corporations have *centralized management* which is essential for the smooth operation of widely owned entities.

D. Limited Liability Companies (LLCs)

1. LLCs have the corporate advantage of limited liability combined with the tax advantage of being taxed as a partnership.
2. All 50 states and the District of Columbia recognize LLCs as a business entity.

E. Entity Classification

1. The classification of a business entity has been greatly simplified by the so-called *check-the-box* Regulations. Eligible entities may elect their classification for tax purposes.
2. When no election is made, single owner businesses will be taxed as sole proprietorships and multi-owned entities will treated as partnerships for taxes.
3. This election is not available to entities that are actually incorporated under state law. However, LLCs are not considered incorporated for this purpose.

II. Organization of and Transfers to Controlled Corporations

A. In General – Under § 351(a), no gain or loss is recognized upon the transfer of property to a corporation by one or more owners, solely in exchange for its corporate stock, if, immediately after the exchange, such owners are *in control* of the corporation.

1. Taxpayers who receive *boot* (money or property other than stock) will recognize gain to the extent of the lesser of boot or realized gain.
2. Character of gain recognized is determined by the type of assets transferred.
3. Losses are never recognized even when boot is received.
4. If nonrecognition applies, assets received by the corporation and the stock received by the owner have a carryover/substituted basis (see II. F. below).
5. § 351 treatment is mandatory. The deferral mechanism applies to both realized gains and losses.
6. Subsequent transfers of assets to a corporation can also receive deferral treatment of § 351 *if* all the requirements can be met. Unless other shareholders are inclined to make contributions, however, subsequent contributions will trigger recognized gain or loss because the shareholder may not meet the 80% control requirement.

B. Transfers of Property

1. The definition of property is very comprehensive.
2. The contribution of services is one of the few items not qualifying as property. Stock received for services is taxable at its FMV.

C. Stock

1. Stock includes common and qualified preferred.
2. Stock does not include stock rights or warrants or unqualified preferred.
3. Debt (bonds) does not constitute stock, therefore, is treated as boot.

D. Control of the Corporation

1. Taxpayers *in control* must own at least 80% of the total combined *voting power* of all classes of stock entitled to vote, *and* 80% of the total *number* of shares of all other classes of stock of the corporation.

2. Control can be held by one or several shareholders if all are part of an integrated transfer to the corporation. Transfers should occur close in time but do not have to be simultaneous.
3. A person who receives stock and does not contribute property (ie, contributes services for stock) can not be considered in determining the control requirement.
4. A shareholder who contributes both property and services can be counted in meeting the 80% control test only if the value of the contributed assets is at least 10% of the value of the contributed services.

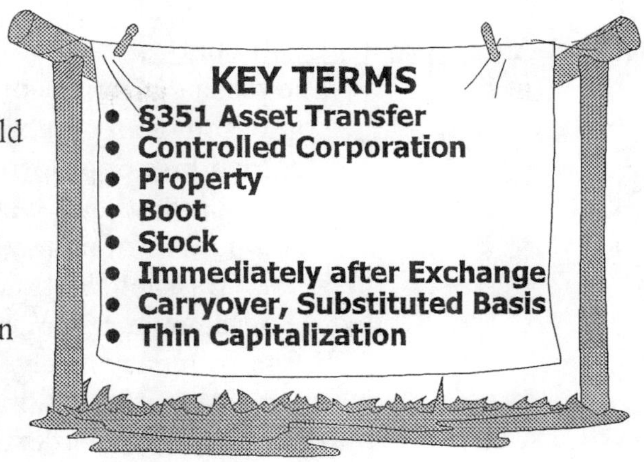


E. <u>Assumption of Liabilities</u> §357

1. Liabilities assumed by the corporation in a § 351(a) transfer usually do not create recognized gain (§ 357), although they decrease the shareholder's basis in the stock received.
2. However, there are two exceptions to this non-recognition rule.
    a. If the primary purpose of the assumption of liabilities is tax avoidance, or if there is no bona fide business purpose behind the exchange, the total liabilities assumed are treated as boot.
    b. If the sum of the liabilities assumed by the corporation exceeds the total of the transferor's adjusted basis in the properties transferred, the excess is taxable to the transferor-shareholder.

F. <u>Basis Determination and Other Issues</u>

1. Shareholder – The basis in the stock received by a shareholder is the same as the basis in the property transferred, increased by any gain recognized, and decreased by boot received and liabilities assumed by the corporation. This is referred to as a *substituted basis*.
2. Corporation – The basis of the property received by the corporation in the transfer is the same as the basis of the property in the hands of the transferor (shareholder), increased by any gain recognized by the shareholder. This is referred to as a *carryover basis*.
3. Services – Corporation recognizes no gain when it issues stock for services. It may be able to deduct the FMV of the stock issued if the services rendered were for a deductible expense.
4. Holding Period – For stock received for a capital asset or §1231 property, the holding period for shareholders includes their holding period for the property they transferred. For transfers of other property (ordinary assets), the stock's holding period starts on the day after the exchange. The corporation's holding period in the property received in a § 351 transfer is always the same as the shareholder's holding period was in the assets transferred.

G. <u>Recapture Considerations</u>

1. When no boot is received, the shareholders are not subject to the recapture of depreciation. Instead, the recapture potential carries over to the corporation.
2. When boot is received, recapture may be triggered.

III. Capital Structure of a Corporation

A. Capital Contributions

1. The receipt of money or property in exchange for stock produces neither gain nor loss to the recipient corporation.
2. Contributions of property by nonshareholders are excluded from gross income of the corporation. The property received has a basis of zero.
3. Contributions of money by a nonshareholder have special rules.
   a. Basis of assets acquired within a 12 month period is reduced by the amount of money received.
   b. If money received is in excess of property described in a. above, the basis of other property held by the corporation is reduced in the following order: depreciable property; amortizable property; depletable property, and lastly other remaining properties.

B. Debt in the Capital Structure

1. Using debt in the capital structure may be advantageous.
   a. Interest is deductible by the corporation.
   b. Shareholders are not taxed on the repayment of debt. An investment in stock cannot be withdrawn tax-free when the corporation has positive earnings and profits.
2. Reclassification of debt as equity by the IRS can occur when the corporation is *thinly capitalized* (ratio of debt to outstanding equity is high) and/or debt has too many of the characteristics of equity. Under § 385, the IRS can reclassify debt as equity or as part equity and part debt.
   a. Reclassification is detrimental because interest and principal payments will be treated as dividends.
   b. The corporation will be denied an interest deduction and the recipient will have taxable dividend income.
3. Since there are no Regulations on the classification of debt, the courts have identified the following factors as important when determining whether an instrument is debt or equity.
   a. Whether the debt is evidenced by a proper instrument, pays a reasonable interest rate, and has a definite maturity date.
   b. Whether debt payments are contingent upon earnings, are made on a timely basis, and whether the debt is subordinated to other liabilities.
   c. Whether the funds were used to finance initial operations or purchase core assets of the corporation.
   d. The relationship between the debt holders and the shareholders. That is, are the debts held by shareholders in the same proportion as their stock ownership.
   e. The relationship of the shareholder debt holdings to equity. If the amount of debt is high relative to the equity, the corporation is thinly capitalized. Both book value and FMV of corporate assets are used to determine debt to equity ratios.

IV. Corporate Operations

A. Deductions Available Only to Corporations

1. Dividends Received Deduction (DRD)

a. A corporation receives a DRD for dividend payments received from other US corporations. The amount of the DRD depends on the percentage the corporation owns in the dividend paying corporation.
   (1) If ownership percentage is less than 20%, DRD is 70%.
   (2) If ownership percentage is at least 20% but less than 80%, DRD is 80%.
   (3) If ownership percentage is at least 80%, DRD is 100%.

b. The DRD percentage is applied to the dividends received to determine the deduction. However, DRD may be limited by the amount of the corporation's taxable income.
   (1) DRD is limited to the DRD percentage times taxable income after charitable contributions, but without regard to any DRD claimed, and carrybacks of net operating losses (NOLs) and/or capital losses.
   (2) The taxable income limit does not apply if: Taxable Income - DRD percentage of dividends received creates or NOL.
   (3) Use the steps listed in Exhibit 8-1 to compute the DRD.

**Exhibit 8-1**

**STEPS IN COMPUTING**
**THE DIVIDENDS RECEIVED DEDUCTION**

| | |
|---|---|
| Step 1: | Multiply dividends by DRD percentage. |
| Step 2: | Multiply taxable income by DRD percentage. |
| Step 3: | Select the lesser of Step 1 or Step 2 unless Step 1 will produce a NOL.<br>If NOL would be produced, use Step 1 amount. |

2. Organization Expenses §248

a. A corporation's organizational expenses are amortizable over 60 months or more, if a timely election is made with the first year's tax return. If the election is not made on a timely basis, organizational expenses cannot be deducted until the corporation ceases to do business or liquidates.

b. Deductible organization expenses which must be incurred by the end of the corporation's first taxable year include: state registration fees, legal and accounting fees, and temporary director fees. Expenses associated with obtaining debt, equity, or assets are not deductible as organization expenses.

c. Start-up costs are different from organizational costs and are covered by § 195. Start-up cost are for investigation of a new business and certain operating expenses incurred before the business begins. They are also amortizable over 60 months or more.

B. Determining the Corporate Income Tax Liability

1. The basic tax rates for regular corporations range from 15% to 35% with phase-outs of the lower tax rate benefits at higher levels of taxable income.
2. Personal Service Corporations (PSC) are taxed at a flat rate of 35%. For this purpose, a PSC is a corporation substantially owned by employees.

C. Tax Liability of Related Corporations

1. Related corporations are subject to limitations in computing their taxes.
2. The following tax attributes are limited for corporations considered to be related parties and in the same controlled group.
   a. Application of the income tax brackets below 35%.
   b. AMT exemption.
   c. The § 179 deduction, the immediate expensing of depreciable assets.

D. Controlled Group

1. The Code includes the *controlled group* provisions, to discourage taxpayers from dividing taxable income amounts among a series of entities, thereby gaining additional tax rate discounts, exemptions, and other limitations.
2. Corporations that are members of the same control group must allocate among the members the tax attributes listed in C. 2. above.

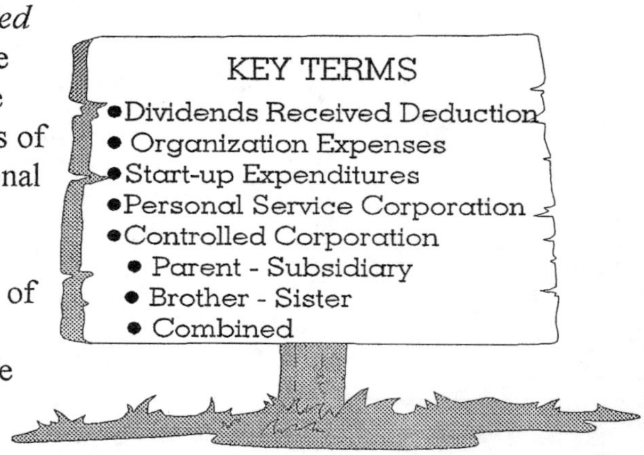


3. Controlled groups include the following.
   a. A *parent-subsidiary* controlled group exists when one corporation owns at least 80% of the voting power or stock value of another corporation.
   b. A *brother-sister* controlled group exists where 5 or fewer individuals, trusts, or estates own at least 80% of the voting power or stock value of two or more corporations. In addition, the aggregate common ownership of the identified shareholders must exceed 50% of the voting power or stock value with respect to all of the corporations.
   c. A combined controlled group includes a combination of parent-subsidiary and brother-sister corporations.
4. IRS can reallocate gross income, deductions, and credits between two or more organizations, trades, or businesses that are owned or controlled by the same interests under § 482.

V. Procedural Matters

A. Filing Requirements for Corporations

1. A corporation must file a tax return regardless of whether it has either taxable income or tax liability.
   a. A regular C corporation files a Form 1120.
   b. A corporation meeting the requirement to be a small corporation files a Form 1120-A.
   c. A corporation electing under Subchapter S files a 1120-S.

2. The tax return for corporations is due 2½ months after the tax year-end which is March 15 for a calendar year-end. By filing an extension, Form 7004, the corporation can get an automatic 6 month extension of time to file.

B. Estimated Tax Payments

1. Quarterly estimated tax payments are required of the corporation unless their tax liability will be less than $500.
2. The total estimated payments must be the lesser of: 100% of the current year's tax liability, or 100% of the preceding year's tax liability.

C. Reconciliation of Taxable Income and Financial Net Income

1. Schedule M-1 – The corporation reconciles financial accounting income with taxable income on Schedule M-1 of Form 1120.
2. Schedule M-2 – The reconciliation of beginning and ending financial Retained Earnings occurs on Schedule M-2 of Form 1120.

# TEST FOR SELF-EVALUATION - CHAPTER 8

## True or False

Indicate which of the following statements are true or false by circling the correct answer.

T F 1. Transferring assets to a corporation by a controlling shareholder usually is a taxable event.

T F 2. Corporations governed by Subchapter C are tax paying entities and are subject to the double tax effect when they make dividend distributions to their shareholders.

T F 3. Start-up costs are included in organizational expenses for amortization.

T F 4. Corporations are considered part of a brother-sister controlled group if 5 or fewer persons own at least 50% of the total ownership and 80% of common ownership.

T F 5. § 351 applies only to contributions that "start up" a new corporation.

T F 6. Unless an election is made, a business with one owner will be treated as sole proprietorships unless it is incorporated under state law.

T F 7. "Boot" refers to any cash, securities, or property other than stock that is received in exchange for property from a controlled corporation.

T F 8. Limited liability companies (LLCs) are partnerships that are taxed like corporations.

T F 9. Liabilities always are considered boot for purposes of determining recognized gain in a § 351 transfer.

T F 10. Depreciation recapture is recognized upon the incorporation of an entity under § 351, when assets are contributed in-kind by the new shareholders.

T F 11. Under the thin capitalization doctrine, the IRS can reclassify proper interest payments as dividends.

T F 12 What constitutes property for § 351 purposes is very broad, however services are specifically excluded from the definition.

T F 13 For § 351 purposes, the term stock does not include some types of preferred stock.

T F 14 A personal service corporations are subject to a flat tax rate of 35%.

T F 15. All C corporations must make estimated payments of their taxes.

**Fill-in-the-Blanks**

Complete the following sentences with the appropriate word(s) or amount(s).

1. A business can be conducted in the form of a ________ ________, ________ corporation, ________ corporation, ________ ________ company, or ________.

2. When § 351 applies, any corporate bonds received by shareholders are treated as ________.

3. The contribution of a liability to a controlled corporation triggers gain recognition if the debt was not incurred for a ________ ________ ________ purpose.

4. When a taxpayer transfers both property and services, the IRS generally requires that the value of the ________ contributed must be at least ________ of the value of the ________ to be included in the control group.

5. The shareholder's holding period for stock received in exchange for ________ or ________ includes the holding period of the assets transferred to the corporation. The holding period for stock received in the exchange of ________ starts on the day ________ the exchange.

6. When a corporation receives non-cash property from a nonshareholder, it assigns a ________ basis to the asset, and it recognizes ________ gross income due to the contribution.

7. When a shareholder receives stock for ________ performed for the corporation, income equal to the ________ of the ________ received is recognized by the shareholder.

8. Gain or loss is not recognized on the transfer of ________ to a corporation solely in exchange for ________ if the person(s) transferring the property are in ________ of the corporation immediately after the transfer.

9. When other property or money is received by a shareholder in an otherwise tax-free § 351 transaction, gain is recognized to the extent of the lesser of ________ or ________.

10. The basis of property received by a corporation in a § 351 transfer is the basis of the property prior to transfer ________ by gain recognized by the ________.

11. In a tax-free transfer of property to a controlled corporation, any depreciation recapture potential ________ to the corporation if not recognized by the shareholder.

12. Some nontax advantages of corporations over general partnerships include the following: ________, ________, and ________.

13. A corporation is allowed a dividends received deduction of ________% for dividends when it owns at least 80%, ________% when it owns less than 20%, and ________% when it owns between 20% and 80% of domestic corporation.

14. The dividends received deduction (DRD) may be limited to applicable DRD percentage times taxable income, unless the DRD will cause a ________ for the year.

15. A corporation can amortize its organization expenses over a period of ________ or more.

16. There are three types of corporate controlled groups: the ________ controlled group, the ________ controlled group, and the ________ controlled group.

17. Usually, the corporation must pay ________% of its tax liability for the year by making ________ estimated payments.

18. On the Form 1120, a corporation reconciles accounting and taxable income amounts on Schedule ________, and beginning and ending retained earnings balances on Schedule ________.

19. A corporation files a tax return by the ________ day of the ________ month following the close of the tax year.

20. Entity classification was simplified when the ________ Regulations were issued.

## Multiple Choice

Choose the best answer(s) for each of the following questions.

USE THE FOLLOWING INFORMATION FOR PROBLEMS 1 - 3.
Rong, a cash basis taxpayer, incorporates her sole proprietorship. She transfers the following items to New Corp. in exchange for 100% of the corporation's stock.

| | Adjusted Basis | Fair Market Value |
|---|---|---|
| Cash | $5,000 | $5,000 |
| Land | 50,000 | 80,000 |
| Mortgage payable (secured by the land) | 70,000 | 70,000 |

____ 1. The gain recognized by Rong is:
a. $0.
b. $10,000.
c. $15,000.
d. $20,000.
e. $30,000.

____ 2. The basis of the land to New Corp. is:
a. $50,000.
b. $65,000.
c. $70,000.
d. $85,000.

____ 3. The basis of the stock to Rong is:
a. $0.
b. $15,000.
c. $55,000.
d. $70,000.
e. $85,000.

____ 4. Which of the following is *not* a true statement about limited liability companies.
a. They are flow-through entities.
b. They are subject to the same possible entity level taxes as S corporations.
c. All 50 states allow LLCs.
d. They provide limited liability to their owners.
e. All of the above are characteristics of limited liability companies.

____ 5. Which of the following statements regarding corporations is *not* true.
a. Under § 482 the IRS can reallocate income and deductions of corporations and its shareholders to prevent avoidance of taxes.
b. Corporations must make estimated tax payments to cover their AMT liability.
c. All corporations must file tax returns regardless of their income.
d. Entities incorporated under state law cannot use the check-the-box Regulations.
e. None of the above statements are true.

____ 6. Lyone plans to start a business. He is expecting to have losses for the first 2 years and then expects the business to become very profitable. In order for the business to grow, the business will need to retain its after tax earnings. Limited liability is also important to Lyone. How should Lyone structure his business?
a. Be a sole proprietorship for 2 years then switch to a limited liability company.
b. Be an S corporation for 2 years then switch to a regular corporation.
c. Be a sole partnership for 2 years then switch to a limited liability company.
d. Be an regular corporation for 2 years then switch to an S corporation.
e. None of the above are acceptable plans.

USE THE FOLLOWING INFORMATION FOR PROBLEMS 7 - 9
Isaac, a cash basis taxpayer, incorporates his sole proprietorship. He transfers the following items to New Corp. in exchange for 100% of the corporation's stock (value $185,000), and $40,000 in cash.

| | Adjusted Basis | Fair Market Value |
|---|---|---|
| Accounts Receivables | $5,000 | $5,000 |
| Land | 90,000 | 190,000 |
| Accounting Services Performed | 000 | 30,000 |

____ 7. Gross income recognized by Isaac is:
a. $0.
b. $30,000.
c. $40,000.
d. $70,000.
e. $130,000.

____ 8. New Corp.'s basis in the total assets is:
a. $95,000.
b. $125,000.
c. $165,000.
d. $195,000.
e. $225,000.

____ 9. The basis of the stock to Isaac is:

a. $0.
b. $95,000.
c. $125,000.
d. $165,000.
e. $225,000

____ 10. Cher, a cash basis taxpayer, incorporates her sole proprietorship. She transfers the following items to New Corp. in exchange for 100% of its stock (value $90,000), and $30,000 in cash.

| | Adjusted Basis | Fair Market Value |
|---|---|---|
| Accounts Receivables | $ 15,000 | $ 15,000 |
| Equipment | 85,000 | 105,000 |

The gain recognized by Cher is:

a. $0.
b. $15,000.
c. $20,000.
d. $30,000.

____ 11. Related corporations are *not* limited in their use of which tax attribute.

a. Accumulated earnings credit.
b. The AMT exemption.
c. The § 179 immediate expensing of depreciable assets
d. The dividend received deduction.
e. The tax rates lower than 35%.

____ 12. Which of the following statements is *not* true with regards to controlled groups.

a. A parent-subsidiary controlled group must have a parent that owns at least 80% of the total voting power of all classes of stock entitled to vote.
b. For a brother-sister controlled group to exist 2 or more corporations must be owned by 5 or fewer individuals or corporations.
c. A combined controlled group includes parent-subsidiary and brother-sister controlled groups.
d. All of the above are true.

____ 13. On January 2, 20X1, Rock Corporation received land and improvements, worth $1 million from Central City, as an incentive to locate a new plant in its local area. How much gross income will Rock recognize due to receiving the improved land?

a. $0.
b. $0 in 20X1, $1 million in 20X2 when the twelve-month period expires.
c. $1 million in 20X1.
d. $500,000 in 20X1, under the Economic Development Act (EDA).

____ 14. Refer to the previous problem. What basis does Rock take in the improved land?

a. $0.
b. $0 in 20X1, $1 million in 20X2.
c. $1 million in 20X1.
d. $500,000, under the terms of the EDA.

____ 15. Goat Corporation has tax liability for the current year of $300,000. Last years tax liability was $350,000. To avoid a penalty, Goat's estimated payments for the current year should have equaled what amount?

a. $350,000.
b. $315,000.
c. $300,000.
d. $270,000.
e. None of the above.

____ 16. Orange Company owns 40% of Banana Company and 15% of Apple Company. The remaining interest in Apple Co is owned by Banana. It also owns 20% of Orange. Lastly, Pumpkin Company owns 65% of Orange Company and 50% of Banana Company. Which of the following statements about these corporations is true?

a. These corporations would be required consolidate into one corporation.
b. These companies form a brother-sister control group.
c. These companies form combined group.
d. These companies form a parent-subsidiary affiliated group.
e. None of the above.

____ 17. Jump Corporation owns 25% of Kick, Inc. Jump had the following income and expenses for the current year.

| | |
|---|---|
| Operating Income | $ 5,000 |
| Kick, Inc. Dividends | 10,000 |
| Operating Expenses | 8,000 |

Jump's dividend received deduction is:

a. $0.
b. $5,600.
c. $7,000.
d. $8,000.
e. None of the above.

____ 18. Refer to the preceding problem. Assume that operating expenses are $6,000 and the Jump corporation owned 15% of Kick, Inc.

a. $0.
b. $6,300.
c. $7,000.
d. $7,200.
e. None of the above.

____ 19. The Schedule M-1 reconciliation of financial accounting income to tax income requires:

a. Federal income tax liability to be added.
b. Tax exempt interest to be added.
c. Excess capital losses to be subtracted.
d. Excess tax depreciation over financial accounting depreciation to be added.
e. All of the above.

____ 20. The treatment taxpayers receive under § 351 is:
a. Beneficial to the corporation being formed but not beneficial to the shareholders.
b. Overridden by the depreciation recapture rules of § 1245 and § 1250.
c. Similar to the treatment under § 1031 for like-kind exchanges.
d. Not available to nonresident aliens.

**Code Section Recognition**

Several important sections of the Internal Revenue Code are described below. Indicate, by number, the appropriate Code section.

1. ____ Gives the IRS the authority to characterize corporate debt as equity or as part debt and part equity.

2. ____ Allows for the tax-free transfer of property to a controlled corporation.

3. ____ Permits the IRS to allocate gross income, deductions, and credits between any 2 or more organizations or businesses that are owned or controlled by the same interests.

4. ____ Determines the consequences of contributing liabilities to a controlled corporation, in a tax-free transfer.

5. ____ Allows the amortization of organizational costs over a period of 60 months or more.

**Short Answer**

1. A Corporation receives $7,000 dividends. Compute its taxable income if:

a. Dividends are from a wholly owned subsidiary. Other taxable income = $60,000.

b. Dividends are from an unrelated domestic corporation in which the recipient corporation owns 50% of the stock. Other taxable income = $60,000.

c. Dividends are from an unrelated domestic corporation in which the recipient corporation owns 15% of the stock. Other taxable income = $60,000.

d. Dividends are from an unrelated domestic corporation in which the recipient corporation owns 50% of the stock. Other taxable income = $(500).

e. Dividends are from an unrelated domestic corporation in which the recipient corporation owns 15% of the stock. Other taxable income = $(500).

f. Dividends are from an unrelated domestic corporation in which the recipient corporation owns 25% of the stock. Other taxable income = $(3,000).

2. Alpha Corporation's taxable income = $200,000. Compute the Federal corporate income tax, if Alpha is NOT a member of any controlled group.

3. Mia Corporation, a calendar year accrual basis entity, was formed on July 1, 20X1. The following items were incurred during 20X1. If Mia makes a timely election to amortize qualifying organizational expenses, what is its 20X1 deduction?

| | |
|---|---|
| Expenses of temporary directors | $2,500 |
| Expenses of printing and selling stock certificates | 1,000 |
| Incorporation fee paid to state | 500 |
| Legal fees for drafting corporate charter and by-laws (paid 2/17/X2) | 3,000 |

4. Keel Corporation is formed, via the following simultaneous activities.

| Taxpayer | RECEIVED | | | CONTRIBUTED | | Corporation Assumed Taxpayer Liabilities |
|---|---|---|---|---|---|---|
| | % and Value of Only Class of Common Stock | Cash | One-Year Note, Fair Market Value | Asset to Corporation (Taxpayer's Basis) | Promoter Services (Fair Market Value) | |
| A | 15% $15,000 | | | $ 8,000 | | |
| B | 15% $15,000 | | | 20,000 | | |
| C | 10% $10,000 | $20,000 | | 5,000 | | |
| D | 10% $10,000 | | $ 5,000 | 3,000 | | |
| E | 10% $10,000 | $ 6,000 | | 15,000 | | |
| F | 10% $10,000 | | | 6,000 | | $4,000 |
| G | 10% $10,000 | | | 7,000 | | 8,000 |
| H | 10% $10,000 | | | -0- | $10,000 | |
| I | 10% $10,000 | | | 5,000 | 500 | |

Complete the schedule below.

| Taxpayer | Gain/Loss Realized | Gain/Loss Recognized | Basis of Assets to Keel Corporation | Basis of Stock to Taxpayer |
|---|---|---|---|---|
| A | | | | |
| B | | | | |
| C | | | | |
| D | | | | |
| E | | | | |
| F | | | | |
| G | | | | |
| H | | | | |
| I | | | | |

# SOLUTIONS TO CHAPTER 8 QUESTIONS

## True or False

1. F
2. T
3. F Start-up costs are separate from organization expenses.
4. F Corporations are part of a brother-sister controlled group if ≤ 5 persons own at least **80%** of the total ownership and **50%** of common ownership.
5. F § 351 can apply to contributions after the creation of the corporation.
6. T
7. T
8. F LLCs are corporations that are taxed as partnerships.
9. F Liabilities usually do not result in gain recognition, although there are some exceptions to this rule.
10. F Depreciation is recaptured only when the shareholder recognizes gain on a § 351 transfer.
11. T
12. T
13. T
14. T
15. F Corporations make estimated payments only f their tax liability for the year will be greater than $500.

## Fill-in-the-Blanks

1. sole proprietorship, C, S, limited liability, partnership
2. boot
3. bona fide business
4. property, 10%, services
5. capital assets, § 1231 property, ordinary property (inventory), after
6. zero, zero
7. services, FMV, stock
8. property, stock, control
9. boot received, realized gain
10. increased, transferor (shareholder)
11. carries over
12. Any three of the following: continuity of life, centralized management, limited liability, free transferability of interests, or ability to raise capital
13. 100, 70, 80
14. net operating loss
15. 60 months
16. brother/sister, parent/subsidiary, combined
17. 100, quarterly
18. M-1, M-2
19. 15th, 3rd
20. check-the-box

**Multiple Choice**

| | | |
|---|---|---|
| 1. | c | $15,000. 70,000 – 55,000. Liabilities – aggregate basis. |
| 2. | b | $65,000. 50,000 + 15,000. Land basis + gain recognized. |
| 3. | a | $0. 55,000 + 15,000 – 70,000. |
| 4. | b | LLCs are not treated like S corporations and are not subject to their taxes. |
| 5. | a | Reallocation under § 482 is between entities that are owned by the same interests. It does not apply to shareholders and their corporations. |
| 6. | b | |
| 7. | d | $70,000. 30,000 + 40,000. Assets transferred meet the 10% of services test, so §351 applies. |
| 8. | c | $165,000. 5,000 + 90,000 + 70,000 gain recognized. |
| 9. | c | $125,000. 5,000 + 90,000 + 30,000 + 40,000 – 40,000. |
| 10. | c | Lesser of boot received (30,000) or realized gain (20,000). |
| 11. | d | |
| 12. | b | Ownership must be by individuals, estates or trusts. No other entities. |
| 13. | a | |
| 14. | a | |
| 15. | c | Lesser of 100% of this year's tax liability or 100% of last year. |
| 16. | d | Banana owns the requisite ≥ 80% of Apple. Each other corporation is owned at least 80% by the other corporations in the group. |
| 17. | d | $8,000. Since a DRD of 8,000 (10,000 x 80%) creates a NOL (7,000 - 8,000), the DRD is not restricted by the taxable income limitation. |
| 18. | b | $6,300. DRD subject to taxable income limitation: 70%(10,000 + 5,000 - 6,000). Full DRD of $7,000 would not create a NOL (9,000 - 7,000). |
| 19. | a | The exempt interest is subtracted; excess capital losses are added; excess tax depreciation is subtracted. |
| 20. | c | |

**Code Section Recognition**

1. 385
2. 351
3. 482
4. 357
5. 248

**Short Answer**

| | | | | |
|---|---|---|---|---|
| 1. | a. | Taxable Income: | $60,000 | Other Income |
| | | | + 7,000 | Dividend Income |
| | | | - 7,000 | 100% Deduction |
| | | | $60,000 | |

b. Taxable Income:

| | |
|---|---|
| $60,000 | Other Income |
| + 7,000 | Dividend Income |
| - 5,600 | 80% Deduction = 80% x $7,000 |
| $61,400 | |

c. Taxable Income:

| | |
|---|---|
| $60,000 | Other Income |
| + 7,000 | Dividend Income |
| - 4,900 | 70% Deduction = 70% x $7,000 |
| $62,100 | |

d. Taxable Income:

| | |
|---|---|
| $ (500) | Other Income |
| + 7,000 | Dividend Income |
| 6,500 | Income before DRD |
| - 5,200 | Limitation on DRD = 80% X 6,500 |
| $ 1,300 | |

e. Taxable Income:

| | |
|---|---|
| $ (500) | Other Income |
| + 7,000 | Dividend Income |
| 6,500 | Income before DRD |
| - 4,550 | Limitation on DRD = 70% X 6,500 |
| $ 1,950 | |

f. The usual 80% deduction creates an NOL. Thus, there is no limitation on the DRD to 80% of Taxable Income.

Taxable Income:

| | |
|---|---|
| $ (3,000.) | Other Income |
| + 7,000. | Dividend Income |
| - 5,600. | 80% Deduction = 80% X 7,000 |
| $ (1,600.) | |

2.

| | | |
|---|---|---|
| 15% x $50,000 | $7,500 | |
| 25% x $25,000 | 6,250 | |
| 34% x $125,000 | 42,500 | |
| 5% x $100,000 | 5,000 | Extra tax on taxable income > $100,000 |
| | $61,250 | |

3. All expenses qualify except those related to printing and selling stock. The $3,000 paid in 20X2 is allowed – the tax year in which the item is incurred dictates the tax treatment.

Organizational Costs:

| | |
|---|---|
| $ 2,500 | Temporary Directors |
| + 500 | Incorporation Fees |
| + 3,000 | Legal Fees |
| $ 6,000 | |

$6,000 ÷ 60 months = $100 deduction per month. For the six months in tax year 20X1, the deduction totals $600.

4.

| Taxpayer | Gain/Loss Realized | Gain/Loss Recognized | Basis of Assets to Keel Corp. | Basis of Stock to Taxpayer |
|---|---|---|---|---|
| A | $ 7,000 | $ 0 | $ 8,000 | $ 8,000 |
| B | (5,000) | 0 | 20,000 | 20,000 |
| C | 25,000 | 20,000 | 25,000 | 5,000 |
| D | 12,000 | 5,000 | 8,000 | 3,000 |
| E | 1,000 | 1,000 ✔ | 16,000 | 10,000 |
| F | 8,000 | 0 | 6,000 | 2,000 |
| G | 11,000 | 1,000 ✚ | 8,000 | 0 |
| H | 10,000 | 10,000 ⌂ | NONE ■ | 10,000 |
| I | 5,000 | 909 ● | 5,000 ○ | 5,909 |

✔ Limited to Gain Realized

✚ Liabilities in Excess of Basis

⌂ Ordinary Service Income

■ Corporation generally is allowed a compensation deduction.

● Ordinary Service Income is equal to Stock that was Issued for Services = $10,000 x $500/$5500 = $909

○ The basis of the contributed property is $5,000, and the corporation generally is allowed a compensation deduction of $909.

Chapter 9
Corporations: Earnings & Profits
and Dividend Distributions

## CHAPTER HIGHLIGHTS

Corporations are taxed on their income. Then the distributions of their earnings are taxed again when corporations pay dividends to their shareholders. Thus, corporate earnings can be subject to double taxation. All distributions by corporations are considered to be dividends, unless the shareholder can prove otherwise. However, a pure stock dividends are not taxable and stock redemptions will not be fully taxable. When a corporation distributes appreciated property as dividend or stock redemption, the corporation must recognize gain to the extent of the unrealized appreciation.

To avoid double taxation, corporations could accumulate earnings rather than pay out dividends. The accumulated earnings tax and personal holding company tax were added to the tax law to keep corporations using this tactic. **Changes for the Jobs and Growth Tax Relief Reconciliation Act of 2003 (Tax Act of 2003) have been included in this outline.**

I. Taxable Dividends – in General
   A. A corporate distribution to shareholders is considered a dividend to the extent of the corporation's current and accumulated earnings and profits (E & P).
      1. The dividend income received by shareholders is equal to the amount of money distributed plus the FMV of any other property distributed, minus any corporate liabilities assumed by the shareholder.
      2. The shareholder's basis in the property is its FMV.
   B. Distributions in excess of current and accumulated E & P are treated first as a return of the shareholders investment to the extent of the stock basis and not taxable. The shareholder's basis in the stock is reduced accordingly but not below zero. Any excess of distribution over the stock basis is treated as a capital gain assuming that the stock is a capital asset to the shareholder.

II. Earnings and Profits (E & P) – § 312
   A. E & P is a concept similar to but not exactly the same as retained earnings.
   B. E & P is the key to dividend treatment of corporate distributions. A distribution is taxed as a dividend only to the extent that the corporation making the distribution has E & P.

C. Computation of Current E & P

1. E&P is not defined explicitly in the Code. Rather, a series of adjustments to taxable income are provided that help identify a corporation's economic income.

2. Corporations must compute at least two E & P accounts.
   a. Accumulated E & P – The total of all previous current E & P since February 28, 1913, reduced by any distributions made from it. The accumulated E & P is computed on the first day of each year.
   b. Current E & P – The portion of E & P attributable to the current year. Its computation starts with Federal taxable income and then is adjusted to more closely estimate the current year's cash flow.
   c. It is important to distinguish between current and accumulated E & P because the taxability of distributions is determined on the balances in these accounts.

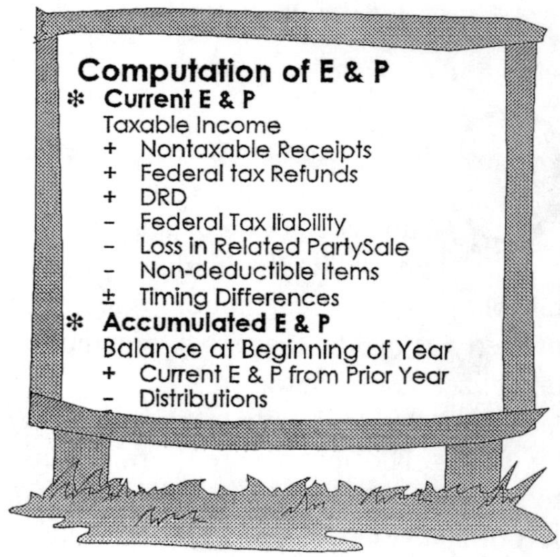


3. Additions to Taxable Income
   a. Non-taxable receipts (e.g., tax-exempt interest income from municipal bonds, proceeds from life insurance policies).
   b. Federal income tax refunds.
   c. Any dividends-received deduction.

4. Subtractions from Taxable Income
   a. Annual Federal tax liability.
   b. Loss on sale between related parties.
   c. Non-deductible items (e.g., premiums on life insurance, excess capital losses, expenses for tax exempt income, fines and penalties).

5. Timing Adjustments
   a. Some adjustments are caused by differences in the timing of inclusion for E & P and for income taxes.
   b. Examples of such items are carryovers (NOL, capital losses, charitable contributions).

6. Accounting Methods Adjustments
   a. Accounting methods used for determining E & P are generally more conservative than those allowed for regular income tax computation.
   b. Installment method is not permitted for E & P.
   c. Alternative depreciation system (ADS) must be used for E & P and none of the additional first-year cost recovery allowed.
   d. The § 179 immediate expensing of assets is taken over 5 years.
   e. A variety of other adjustments are also required for current E & P.

7. A dividend may never reduce E & P below zero. E & P may fall below zero only when the corporation generates a loss.

D. Summary of E & P Adjustments – Concept Summary 9-1 provides a summary of the E & P adjustments.

E. Allocation of E & P to Distributions

1. Distributions are first from current E & P.
   a. These distributions produce dividend income to the shareholder.
   b. If there is more than one distribution during the year, current E & P is allocated pro rata among the distributions.
2. Distributions are from accumulated E & P if current E & P is not sufficient.
   a. This also produces dividend income for the shareholder.
   b. If there is more than one distribution during the year and total distributions are greater than current E & P, accumulated E & P is applied chronologically to the distributions until it is exhausted.
   c. If current E & P is positive but accumulated E & P has a deficit balance at the beginning of the year, distributions are dividends to the full extent of current E & P; the two accounts are ***not*** netted.
   d. If current E & P for the year is less than zero, combine it with accumulated E & P at the date of the distribution to determine whether the distribution is a dividend. The deficit is allocated ratably during the year unless the parties can show otherwise.
3. When the corporate tax year end is different than the shareholders, it may not be possible to determine the amount of current E & P on a timely basis. Consequently, all distributions are presumed to be from current E & P, unless the parties can show otherwise.
4. See Exhibit 9-1 at end of this chapter outline for a summary of the treatment of corporate distributions.

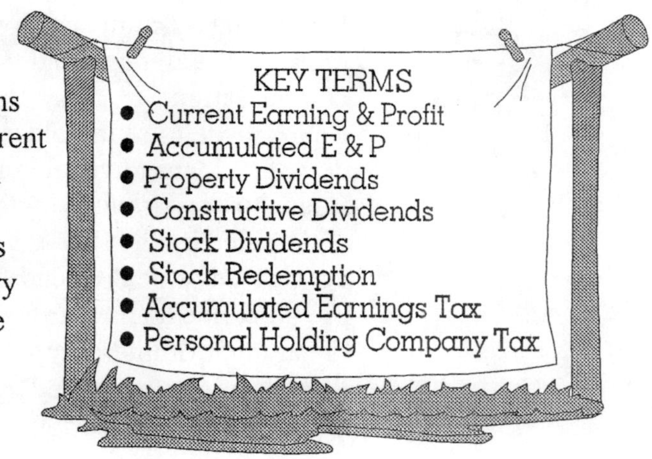


III. Property Dividends

A. Effect on the Shareholder

1. To the extent of corporate E & P, the shareholder has dividend income equal to the FMV of the distributed assets less any liabilities assumed by the shareholder.
2. The shareholder's basis in the distributed property is the fair market value of the assets on the distribution date.

B. Effect on the Corporation

1. A corporation recognizes any realized gain (but not loss) when it distributes property as a dividend to its shareholders. The gain is equal to the difference between the FMV of the asset and its adjusted basis.
2. E & P is increased by any gain recognized on distributed appreciated property.
3. The corporation's E & P is reduced, but not below zero, by the greater of the FMV of the distributed property or its adjusted basis.
4. If the property has a liability that is assumed by the shareholders, the net FMV (FMV less the liability) or net adjusted basis (adjusted basis less the liability) is used to reduce the E & P balance but not below zero.

IV. Constructive Dividends

A. Shareholders can be treated as receiving dividend income even when no dividend has been formally declared and no apparent distribution is made. If shareholders received economic benefit from the corporation, they may have received a *constructive dividend.*

B. <u>Types of Constructive Dividends</u> – Usually arise in closely held corporations.

1. Shareholder's personal use of corporate-owned property. Use of corporate assets at little or no cost to the shareholder. Dividend income is equal to the fair rental value of the property for the period of its personal use.
2. Bargain sale of corporate property to a shareholder. Dividend income is equal to the difference between the FMV of the property and the amount paid by the shareholder.
3. Bargain rental of corporate property. Dividend income is equal to the difference between the fair rental value of the property and the amount paid by the shareholder.
4. Payments for the benefit of a shareholder. This includes forgiveness of debts owed by the shareholder to the corporation. Dividend income is equal to the amounts spent for the benefit of the shareholder or the amount of debt forgiven.
5. Unreasonably compensation to shareholder-employees. Dividend income is equal to the amount paid to the shareholder that is in excess of a reasonable compensation.
6. Loans made to shareholders. When the loans made to shareholders are not bona fide loans, dividend income is equal to the amount of the loan.
7. Loans to corporations by the shareholder. If a loan by a shareholder is reclassified by the IRS as equity then any payments on the loan will be considered to be dividends rather than interest. If the loans by the shareholders are bona fide loans but the interest rate is excessive, dividend income will be the amount of interest paid that is greater than a reasonable rate.

C. <u>Tax Treatment of Constructive Dividends</u>

1. Constructive distributions possess the same tax attributes as actual dividend distributions.
2. Accordingly, constructive distributions result in a taxable dividend only to the extent of the distributing corporation's E & P.

V. Stock Dividends §305

A. Generally, stock dividends are not taxable to the shareholder if they are distributed pro rata on common stock because their proportionate interests in the corporation has not changed.

1. When corporation distributes a nontaxable stock dividend, there is no reduction in the corporation's E & P.
2. With a nontaxable stock dividend, a portion of the basis of the stock on which the dividend is distributed must be allocated to the stock dividend. The allocation is based on the relative FMV of the old and new stock. The holding period of the original stock also attaches to the stock received as a dividend.
3. When the stock dividend is taxable, the corporation treats the distribution the same as other taxable property dividends. The amount of the dividend equals the fair market value of the property received. The holding period starts the date the stock is received.

VI. Stock Redemptions

A. In a stock redemption, the corporation buys back its shares from the shareholders and generally result in dividend income treatment.
   1. The shareholder's basis in the stock redeemed attaches to any remaining shares of the shareholder.
   2. The corporation treats the distribution as a dividend.

B. Stock redemptions can received sale treatment under the conditions provided in § 302. The return of the shareholder's basis in the stock redeemed would be nontaxable and any amounts received in excess of the basis would be taxed as capital gains.
   1. Sale of stock treatment is permitted when:
      a. The shareholder surrenders significant control of the corporation through the redemption.
      b. A shareholder's stock ownership declines by at least 20% because of the redemption and the shareholder owns less than 50% of the stock after the redemption.
      c. All of the shareholder's stock is redeemed.
   2. In the two situations above (a. and b.), ownership of related parties is considered when determining if a reduction in ownership has taken place. In the last situation above (c.) related party are not considered.
   3. The corporation reduces its E & P proportionately for the number of shares redeemed.

C. Stock redemptions may occur for the following reasons.
   1. To liquidate a retiring or deceased shareholder.
   2. As part of a property settlement for divorces.
   3. To increase the per-share price of stock.

VII. Restriction on Corporate Accumulations

A. Two Code provisions were enacted to prevent corporations and shareholders from avoiding double taxation by failing to distribute income in the form of dividends.

B. The *accumulated earning tax* (AET) is imposed on unreasonable accumulations beyond the business needs of the corporation.
   1. The tax is imposed on the current year's earnings retained beyond the reasonable business needs of the corporation.
   2. A minimum accumulated earnings credit of $250,000 is allowed for most corporations which means they do not have to demonstrate reasonable business needs for accumulations of $250,000 or less.
   3. Accumulations beyond the credit amount are allowed for business needs of the corporation, such as: working capital, retirement of debt, loans to or investments in suppliers or customers, and realistic business contingencies.

C. The *personal holding company tax* (PHC tax) discourages the sheltering of certain types of passive, portfolio and personal service income through the use of a corporation. Requirements for personal holding company classification are:
   1. More than 50% of the stock is owned by five or fewer shareholders, and
   2. At least 60% of the corporation's income is passive, portfolio or personal service income.

D. The penalty tax rate for both the AET and the PHC is 15% for tax years beginning after December 31, 2002. Before the Tax Act of 2003, the rate was 38.6%.

**Exhibit 9-1**
**SOURCES OF CORPORATE DISTRIBUTIONS**

**<u>Order of Corporate Distributions</u>**

**Current Earnings and Profits: Taxable***
**Dividend Income**

**Accumulated Earnings and Profits: Taxable****
**Dividend Income**

**Return of Capital: Nontaxable**
**Shareholder reduces the basis in the stock, but not below zero**

**Capital Gain: Taxable**
**To the extent of the distribution in excess of shareholder's basis**

*If there is more than one distribution during the year **and** total distributions exceed current E & P, allocate current E & P pro rata among the distributions, **but** apply accumulated E & P chronologically, until it is depleted.

**If current E & P is less than zero for the entire year, combine it with accumulated E & P **at the date of distribution**.

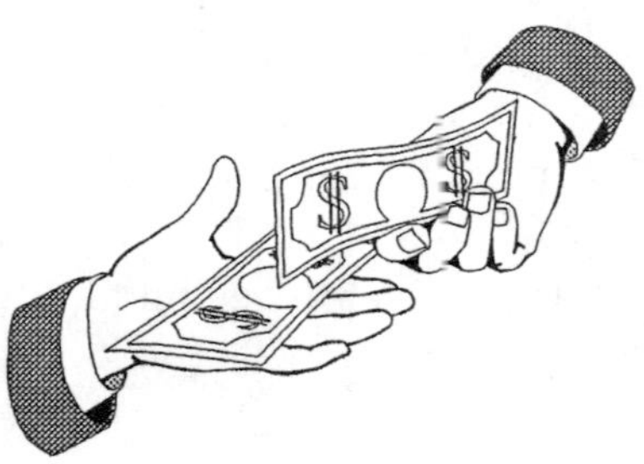

## TEST FOR SELF-EVALUATION - CHAPTER 9

**True or False**

Indicate which of the following statements are true or false by circling the correct answer.

T F 1. When there is a deficit in accumulated E & P and a positive balance in current E & P, the two are netted on the date of a distribution in determining the taxability of the distribution to the shareholder.

T F 2. A dividend distribution of appreciated property results in an increase in E & P that is equal to the difference between the FMV and adjusted basis of the property and a decrease in E & P by the FMV of the property.

T F 3. A distribution of appreciated property to a shareholder always results in the recognition of gain by the distributing corporation.

T F 4. When the IRS determines that a purported loan to a shareholder is actually a constructive dividend, the total amount of the loan will be taxable as dividend income, whether or not there is sufficient E & P to cover the distribution.

T F 5. A dividend may reduce E & P below zero.

T F 6. The accounting methods used for determining E & P are generally more conservative than for regular income tax purposes.

T F 7. A distribution of depreciated property to a shareholder generally results in the recognition of loss by the distributing corporation.

T F 8. A stock dividend that does not change the shareholder's proportionate interest in the corporation is not likely to be taxable.

T F 9. Constructive dividends are treated the same as declared dividends.

T F 10. When computing E & P, corporations add back to taxable income all capital losses taken for regular tax purposes.

T F 11. When distributions are treated as a return of the shareholders' investment, the shareholders must reduce their basis in their stock by the amount received.

T F 12. The accumulated earnings credit allow most corporations to accumulate \$500,000 in earnings without being subject to the accumulated earnings tax.

T F 13. The personal holding company tax was enacted to encourage individuals to incorporate assets that produce passive and portfolio income.

T F 14. A corporation can avoid double taxation by never paying out dividends and have no adverse consequences from this action.

T F 15. In a stock redemption, the corporation buys back its stock from its own shareholders.

**Fill-in-the-Blanks**

Complete the following statements with the appropriate word(s) or amount(s).

1. When computing E & P, the timing adjustments shift the effect of a transaction from the year of its inclusion in ________ to the year in which it has an ________ effect on the corporation.

2. Interest income on municipal bonds ________ E & P and Federal income taxes paid ________ E & P.

3. __________ are not explicitly defined in the Code but the concept is similar to that of __________ .

4. For a shareholder, the amount of a property dividend is the ________ of the asset distributed.

5. The amount of dividend income that a shareholder must recognize is limited to the corporation's ________ and ________ ________.

6. Distributions in excess of ________ are treated as a ________ of the shareholder's ________.

7. A corporation recognizes any realized ________ but not realized __________ when it distributes __________ as a dividend to the shareholder.

8. When current E & P for the entire year is less than the total of all distributions for the year, it is allocated ________ to all distributions occurring during the year.

9. Accumulated E & P will be applied ________ to the distributions during the year, when no current E & P remains.

10. E & P represents the corporation's _______ ability to pay a dividend without impairing its _______.

11. When a shareholder-employee receives unreasonable compensation, the corporation may be forced to treat a portion of the payment as a ________.

12. Related party _______ is not considered when a shareholder has _______ of her or his shares redeemed by the corporation.

13. The __________ method of accounting is not permitted in calculating earning and profits.

14. The ________ tax and the ________ tax are both penalty taxes that are imposed at a rate of 15% for 2003 (after the changes made by the Tax Act of 2003).

15. Corporations reduce E & P by the amount of money distributed or by the greater of the ________ or ________ of property distributed less any ________ on the property assumed by the shareholders.

## Multiple Choice

Choose the best answer for each of the following questions.

____ 1. Cat Corporation distributes a property dividend to its sole shareholder, Ty. He receives property with a basis to Cat of $6,000 and a fair market value of $20,000. Cat's E & P before the distribution is $8,000. How much of the distribution is treated as a dividend for Ty?

a. $6,000.
b. $8,000.
c. $14,000.
d. $20,000

____ 2. Refer to the previous question. What is the balance of E & P after the distribution?

a. $6,000.
b. $2,000.
c. $0.
d. ($12,000).

USE THE FOLLOWING INFORMATION FOR QUESTIONS 3-5.

Worm Corporation made three distributions during the year, of $10,000 each, on April 30, July 31, and September 30 to its sole shareholder. Current E & P for the year is $18,000. Accumulated E & P at the beginning of the year was $3,000.

____ 3. How much of the September 30 distribution was from current E & P?

a. $0.
b. $2,000.
c. $6,000.
d. $10,000.

____ 4. How much of each of the April 30 and July 31 distributions were from accumulated E & P?

| | *April 30* | *July 31* |
|---|---|---|
| a. | $0 | $0. |
| b. | $1,000 | $1,000. |
| c. | $1,500 | $1,500. |
| d. | $3,000 | $0. |

____ 5. How much of the distributions constituted return of capital, if the shareholder's basis in the stock totaled $6,000 before the distributions?

| | *April 30* | *July 31* | *September 30* |
|---|---|---|---|
| a. | $ 0 | $ 3,000 | $ 3,000 |
| b. | $ 2,000 | $ 2,000 | $ 2,000 |
| c. | $ 1,000 | $ 4,000 | $ 1,000 |
| d. | $ 1,000 | $ 4,000 | $ 4,000 |

____ 6. Bird Corporation, a calendar-year taxpayer, had accumulated E & P of $15,000 on January 1. The following transactions took place during the year:

| | |
|---|---|
| Taxable Income (TI) | $16,500 |
| Tax liability | 2,500 |
| Capital losses included in TI | 4,000 |
| Charitable contribution carryover deducted currently | 900 |
| Premium on key-employee life insurance | 1,200 |
| Installment gain from sale in prior year included in TI | 10,700 |
| Tax-exempt interest | 200 |
| Proportionate stock dividend | 3,000 |

What was the balance of Bird's current and accumulated E & P on December 31?

| | Current | Accumulated |
|---|---|---|
| a. | $0 | $19,200. |
| b. | $17,900 | $15,000. |
| c. | $3,200. | $15,000. |
| d. | None of the above | |

USE THE FOLLOWING INFORMATION FOR QUESTIONS 7 - 11

Duck Corporation, which has E & P of $100,000, distributes land to Rahman as a dividend in-kind. Duck's adjusted basis in this land is $3,000. The land has a fair market value of $12,000 and is subject to a mortgage of $5,000, which was assumed by Rahman.

____ 7. How much does Duck recognize as gain on the distribution?

a. $9,000.
b. $7,000.
c. $4,000.
d. $0.

____ 8. How much of the distribution was taxable to Rahman as a dividend?

a. $3,000.
b. $7,000.
c. $9,000.
d. $12,000.

____ 9. Rahman's basis in the land is:

a. $3,000.
b. $7,000
c. $9,000.
d. $12,000.

____ 10. What is the balance of Duck's E & P after the distribution?

a. $88,000.
b. $93,000.
c. $97,000.
d. $102,000.

____ 11. If Duck's E & P prior to the distribution had been a negative $10,000, what is the balance in E & P after the distribution?
a. $4,000.
b. $2,000.
c. $0.
d. ($8,000).

USE THE FOLLOWING INFORMATION FOR QUESTIONS 12-14.

Llama Corporation, which has E & P of $9,000, distributes equipment to Calvin as a dividend in-kind. Llama's basis in the equipment was $10,000 and, the equipment had a fair market value of $2,000.

____ 12. What is the balance of E & P after the distribution?
a. $7,000.
b. $0.
c. $1,000.
d. ($1,000).

____ 13. As a result of the distribution, Llama Corporation recognizes:
a. $0 gain or loss
b. $1,000 loss.
c. $7,000 loss.
d. $8,000 loss.

____ 14. How much of the distribution was taxable to Calvin as a dividend?
a. $0.
b. $2,000.
c. $9,000.
d. $10,000.

____ 15. Cougar Corporation has 2,500 shares of stock outstanding. Of these shares, 1450 are owned by Ching and the remaining 1050 shares are owned by Faisal. Ching receives 580 shares of stock and Faisal receives 420 shares as a dividend distribution when the FMV of each share is $50. Cougar's current E & P is $30,000 and its accumulated E & P is $10,000. What is the amount of Ching's taxable dividend.
a. $0.
b. $8,700.
c. $15,000.
d. Cannot be determined from the information given.

____ 16. Which of the following is not a redemption that will qualify for sale of stock treatment?
a. Sole shareholder has 60% of her stock redeemed.
b. Majority shareholder surrenders significant control of the corporation.
c. All of the shareholder's stock is redeemed.
d. Minority shareholder owns 70% of the shares that she owed before the redemption.

## Short Answer

1. Complete the chart below, indicating the proper tax treatment for each of the following independent fact situations. In each case, the shareholder is an individual taxpayer.

| Question | Distributed Property | E & P Before Distribution | Amount of Dividend | Effect on E & P |
|---|---|---|---|---|
| a | Cash, $10,000 | $25,000 | | |
| b | Cash, $10,000 | $8,000 | | |
| c | Land, Basis $10,000<br>FMV $13,000 | $30,000 | | |
| d | Land, Basis $10,000<br>FMV $3,000 | $30,000 | | |
| e | Land, Basis $3,000<br>FMV $15,000 | $0 | | |

2. Indicate the effects on Yak Corporation's E & P and taxable income for each item below.

| Question | Item | Effect on Yak Corporation's E & P | Gain/Loss Recognized by Yak Corporation |
|---|---|---|---|
| a | Current-year Taxable Income = $65,000<br><br>*NOTE: This amount includes any gain/loss recognized by Yak as a result of property distributions* | | |
| b | Cash dividends paid = $6,000 | | |
| c | Federal income tax liability = $11,250 | | |
| d | Key-Employee Life Insurance:<br>Premiums Paid = $3,000<br>Increase in cash surrender value = $1,400<br>Proceeds received, net of cash surrender value = $75,000 | | |
| e | Accelerated depreciation claimed = $8,000<br>[Straight-line amount = $5,000] | | |

| Question | Item | Effect on Yak Corporation's E & P | Gain/Loss Recognized by Yak Corporation |
|---|---|---|---|
| f | Sale of Depreciable asset for $1,400:<br>Original basis = $15,000<br>Accumulated MACRS deductions = $12,000<br>[Accumulated straight-line depreciation would be $8,500] | | |
| g | Distribution of inventory:<br>Fair market value $3,800<br>LIFO basis $1,000<br>FIFO basis would be $1,800 | | |
| h | Distribution of land:<br>Fair market value $3,800<br>Basis $1,800 | | |
| I | Distribution of land:<br>Fair market value $3,800<br>Basis $1,800<br>Subject to liability $1,300 | | |
| j | Distribution of land:<br>Fair market value $2,000<br>Basis $1,800<br>Subject to liability $2,300 | | |
| k | Distribution of land:<br>Fair market value $1,800<br>Basis $3,800 | | |
| l | Distribution of §1245 asset:<br>Fair market value $6,600<br>Original basis $7,200<br>Accumulated straight-line depreciation $2,800 | | |

# SOLUTIONS TO CHAPTER 9 QUESTIONS

## True or False

| | | |
|---|---|---|
| 1. | F | Only when there is a deficit in current E & P and a positive balance in accumulated E & P are the two netted on the date of distribution. |
| 2. | T | |
| 3. | T | |
| 4. | F | In all situations, a distribution is dividend income only to the extent of the corporation's E & P. |
| 5. | F | A dividend cannot reduce E & P below zero. |
| 6. | T | |
| 7. | F | Loss is never recognized. |
| 8. | T | |
| 9. | T | |
| 10. | F | Capital losses in excess of capital gains are *subtracted* when computing E & P. |
| 11. | T | |
| 12. | F | The accumulated earnings credit is $250,000 |
| 13. | F | The personal holding company tax was enacted to *discourage* incorporation of assets that produce passive and portfolio income. |
| 14. | F | The accumulated earnings tax can be imposed on corporations that accumulated earnings beyond reasonable business needs |
| 15. | T | |

## Fill-in-the-Blanks

1. taxable income, economic
2. increases, decreases
3. Earnings and profits, retained earnings
4. fair market value
5. current, accumulated earnings and profits
6. earnings and profits, return, investment
7. gain, loss property
8. proportionally
9. chronologically
10. economic, capital
11. constructive dividend
12. ownership, all
13. installment
14. accumulated earnings, personal holding company
15. fair market value, adjusted basis, liability

## Multiple Choice

| | | | |
|---|---|---|---|
| 1. | d | $20,000. | corporate E & P: (20,000 − 6,000) + 8,000 = 22,000. |
| 2. | b | $2,000. | 22,000 (see #1 above) − 20,000. |

3. c $6,000. 18,000 X (10,000 ÷ 30,000).
4. d $3,000, $0. Accumulated E & P is applied chronologically.
5. c $1,000, $4,000, $1,000. 6,000 basis – 1,000 – 1 = 1,000 September 30 distribution
6. c $3,200, $15,000. 16,500 – 2,500 + 900 – 1,200 – 10,700 + 200. Capital losses that are not in excess of capital gains do not affect E & P and the stock dividend is not taxable thus, E & P is not reduced for such distributions.
7. a $9,000. 12,000 – 3,000.
8. b $7,000. 12,000 – 5,000.
9. d $12,000. Basis is equal to fair market value.
10. d $102,000. 100,000 + 9,000 – (12,000 – 5,000).
11. c $0. – 10,000 + 9,000 gain – 0 for distribution. Dividends cannot reduce E&P below zero.
12. b Distribution reduce E & P by the greater of FMV or adjusted basis but not below zero.
13. a Loss is not recognized on a property distribution.
14. b The dividend is equal to the FMV of the distributed property. E & P is not affect by the disallowed loss therefore its balance is $9,000 before the distribution.
15. a A stock dividend is not taxable if the shareholder's proportionate ownership does not change.
16. a A sole shareholder cannot qualify for stock redemption treatment.

**Short Answer**

1.

| Question | Distributed Property | E & P Before Distribution | Amount of Dividend | Effect on E & P |
|---|---|---|---|---|
| a | Cash, $10,000 | $25,000 | $10,000 | -$10,000 |
| b | Cash, $10,000 | $8,000 | $8,000 | -$8,000 |
| c | Land, Basis $10,000<br>Fair market value $13,000 | $30,000 | $13,000 | +$3,000 gain recognized<br>-$13,000 FMV distributed property |
| d | Land, Basis $10,000<br>Fair market value $3,000 | $30,000 | $3,000 | -$10,000<br>$0 loss recognized on distribution |
| e | Land, Basis $3,000<br>Fair market value $15,000 | $0 | $12,000 | $12,000 gain recognized on distribution<br>-$12,000 dividend can not reduce E & P below zero |

2.

| Question | Item | Effect on Yak Corporation's E & P | Gain/Loss Recognized by Yak Corporation |
|---|---|---|---|
| a | Current-year Taxable Income = $65,000<br><br>*NOTE: This amount includes any gain/loss recognized by Y as a result of property distributions* | +$65,000 | No effect |
| b | Cash dividends paid = $6,000 | -$6,000 | No effect |
| c | Federal income tax liability = $11,250 | -$11,250 | No effect |
| d | Key-Employee Life Insurance:<br>Premiums Paid = $3,000<br>Increase in cash surrender value = $1,400<br>Proceeds received, net of cash surrender value = $75,000 | <br>-$3,000<br><br>+$1,400<br><br>+$75,000 | No effect |
| e | Accelerated depreciation claimed = $8,000<br>[Straight-line amount = $5,000] | +$3,000 | |
| f | Sale of Depreciable asset for $1,400:<br><br>$15,000<br>- $12,000 MACRS<br>$3,000 Regular Tax Basis<br>- $1,400 Sales Price<br>- $1,600 Regular Tax Loss<br><br>$15,000<br>- $ 8,000 Straight Line Depreciation<br>$7,000 E & P Basis<br>- $1,400 Sales Price<br>$5,600 E & P Loss | Taxable Income0 includes recognized loss $1,600<br>E & P shows recognized loss $5,100<br>Thus, necessary adjustment is:<br>-$3,500<br>$5,100 – $1,600 | |
| g | Distribution of inventory:<br>Fair market value $3,800<br>LIFO basis $1,000<br>FIFO basis would be $1,800 | -$3,800 | $2,800 gain recognized |
| h | Distribution of land:<br>Fair market value $3,800<br>Basis $1,800 | -$3,800 | $2,000 gain recognized |

| Question | Item | Effect on Yak Corporation's E & P | Gain/Loss Recognized by Yak Corporation |
|---|---|---|---|
| I | Distribution of land:<br>Fair market value $3,800<br>Basis $1,800<br>Subject to liability $1,300 | - $3,800<br>+ $1,300<br>$2,500 | $2,000 gain recognized |
| j | Distribution of land:<br>Fair market value $2,000<br>Basis $1,800<br>Subject to liability $2,300<br>The FMV is deemed = liability in this case | - $2,300<br>+ $2,300<br>$0 | $500 gain recognized |
| k | Distribution of land:<br>Fair market value $1,800<br>Basis $3,800 | -$3,800 | $0 loss recognized |
| l | Distribution of §1245 asset:<br>Fair market value $6,600<br>Original basis $7,200<br>Accumulated straight-line depreciation $2,800 | -$6,600 | $2,200 gain recognized |

# Chapter 10
# Partnerships and
# Limited Liability Entities

## CHAPTER HIGHLIGHTS

A partnership is not a taxable entity. Rather, income of the partnership flows through to the partners. Income is allocated to partners according to the partnership agreement. Most tax items retain their character as they flow through to the partners and items that could affect each partner's income differently must be separately allocated to the partners. All items not requiring separate allocation are netted before they flow through to the partners.

A partner's initial basis in the partnership is a substituted basis from the property contributed, plus any gain recognized on the transfer, and includes the partner's share of partnership liabilities. Subject to a few exceptions, generally no gain or loss is recognized when making contributions to a partnership. The partnership takes a carryover basis in the property received. A partner's basis is adjusted later for changes in liabilities, contributions, withdrawals, profits, and losses.

I. Overview of Partnership Taxation
  A. Forms of Doing Business – Federal Tax Consequences
    1. Partnership may be called a *flow-through* or *pass-through* entity because the owners are taxed on the firms taxable income. Due to its flow-through nature, there is only a single level of taxation for partnerships. This is a tax advantage.
    2. Administrative and filing requirements are simple for partnerships. The tax law governing partnerships can be found in Subchapter K of the Code.
  B. What is a Partnership?
    1. Partnerships are an association of 2 or more taxpayers for the purpose of carrying on a trade or business for the owners mutual benefit.
    2. IRS Regulations allow eligible entities to *check-the-box* on partnership returns to indicate they wish to be taxed as partnerships.
    3. Partnerships may operate in the following forms.
      a. General Partnership – Partner have unlimited liability.
      b. Limited Partnership – Some partners have limited liability but at least one partner must have unlimited liability.
      c. Limited Liability Partnership (LLP) – Used chiefly in the service professions. Partners are not liable for certain acts of other partners.
      d. Limited Liability Company (LLC) – Has the capital structure of a corporation but taxed like a partnership.

C. Partnership Taxation and Reporting

1. Since partnerships are not separate taxable entities they pay no Federal income taxes. The owners show their allocated share of income and losses on their own tax returns.

   a. Many of the income and expense items retain their tax identity as they flow through to the owners. These are called *separately stated items.*

   b. Items not separately stated flow through as ordinary income.

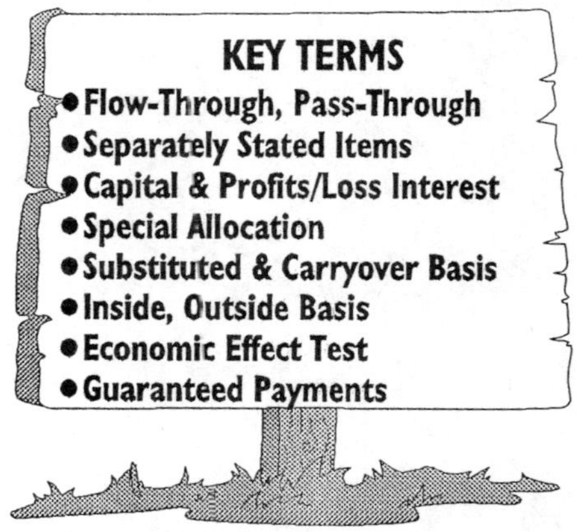


2. A partnership must file an information return (Form 1065) within 3½ months after the end of its taxable year (i.e., April 15th for calendar-year partnership). Each of the partnership's items is reported to the IRS on Schedule K and reported to the partners on Schedule K-1.

D. Partner's Ownership Interest in an Partnership

1. Each partner owns both a *capital interest* and a *profits/loss interest.*

   a. Capital interest measures the partner's *capital sharing ratio.* It usually indicates what percentage of net assets the partner will receive upon liquidation of the partnership.

   b. *Profits/loss interest* indicates the partner's allocation percentage of current operating results.

   c. *Special allocations* of income, expenses, or losses are permitted if they produce nontax economic consequences to the partners.

2. Partners have a basis in their partnership interest as they would in any asset.

   a. The income allocated to the partners increase their basis. Losses allocated to the partners reduce their basis.

   b. Basis is important when determining treatment of distributions from the partnership, establishing deductibility of losses, and calculating gain or loss upon disposition of the partnership interest.

II. Formation of a Partnership: Tax Effects

A. Gain or Loss on Contributions to the Partnership

1. Generally, no gain or loss is recognized by partners or the partnership on contributions made to a partnership in exchange for a partnership interest. The same is true for contributions made subsequent to the creation of the entity.

2. The reasons for the nonrecognition treatment are:

   a. Only the form of ownership and not the substance of the ownership has changed. Taxation of the transfers could make formation of partnerships economically unfeasible.

   b. Owners usually lack the wherewithal to pay taxes on the transfers as the partners receive ownership rather than cash from the formation.

Compare these rules with those of §351. It is much easier for a partner to make a capital contribution subsequent to the formation of a partnership than it is for a shareholder to make later contributions – in the latter case, the 80 percent group of owners must act in concert, not an easy feat in the midst of later business dealings.

B. <u>Exceptions to Nonrecognition</u>

1. The following are exceptions to the nonrecognition rule.
   a. The partnership is used to effect an exchange of assets or a disguised sale of properties. In both situations the realized gain will be taxable to the parties involved.
   b. The partnership interest is received solely for *services* rendered. The fair market value of the interest received is taxable as ordinary income.

C. <u>Tax Issues Related to Contributed Property</u>

1. As with any tax-deferred transaction, the basis is the vehicle used to insure the gain is deferred rather than excluded.
   a. Partners have *substituted basis* in their partnership interest. Their basis in the contributed property is substituted as their basis in their partnership interest.
   b. A partner's *holding period* in the partnership interest is also substituted when § 1231 and capital assets are contributed to the partnership. For other contributed property including cash, the partner's holding period starts on the day the interest is acquired.
   c. The partnership has a *carryover basis* in the contributed assets. The partner's basis in the assets carries over as the partnerships basis. The partner's holding period also carries over to the partnership.
2. When depreciable property is contributed to the partnership, it uses the same cost recovery method and life as was being used before it was contributed.
3. Section 197 intangible assets include goodwill, going concern, information systems, customer or supplier lists, patents, licenses, franchises, trademarks, covenants not to compete, etc. When these assets are contributed by a partner, the partnership "steps into the shoes" of the partner with regard to amortization of the asset.
4. Inventory and receivables contributed to a partnership retain their ordinary asset character. Similar rules apply to capital loss property contributed to the partnership if disposed of within 5 years of contribution.

D. <u>Inside and Outside Bases</u>

1. Each partnership has an *inside basis* and each partner has an *outside basis*.
   a. Inside basis refers to the partnerships basis in each asset, as determined from the partnership's tax accounts. Partners own their proportionate share of the partnership's aggregate inside basis of its assets.
   b. Outside basis represents each partner's investment in the partnership.
2. At formation and in many other situations the total of the partners' outside basis is equal to the partnership's inside basis. The outside and inside basis may be different when a partner buys an interest from an existing partner.

E. <u>Tax Accounting Elections</u>

1. Most of the tax accounting elections are made at the partnership level instead of at the partner level.
2. Each partner is bound by the elections made by the partnership.

3. Partners do make specific elections with regards as to the individual treatment of foreign taxes paid, depletion, and discharge of indebtedness affects on the basis of depreciable property.

F. Initial Cost of a Partnership

1 The initial costs of a partnership are similarly to initial costs of a corporation.

2. Organizational costs & start-up costs– These costs are each amortized separately over a period of 60 or more months.

III. Operations of a Partnership

A. Reporting Operating Results

1. Partnership Form 1065 reports the transactions of the entity. It is due on the 15th day of 4th month after the partnership's year end (usually April 15). Partnerships and partners can be subject to penalties for improper filing.

2. Completion of Form 1065 requires a two-step approach. The separately stated items must be segregated and reported on Schedule K. All other income and expense items appear on the front page of Form 1065 as ordinary income or expenses and are carried over as a single number to Schedule K.

3. The following items must be separately stated and they retain their character as they pass through to the partners.

a. Short- and long-term capital gains/losses, and § 1231 gains/losses.

b. Portfolio income (dividends, interest, royalties) and related expenses.

c. Passive activity items (i.e., income or loss from rental real estate).

d. Expenses that are itemized or non-business deductions to a partner such as charitable contributions, medical, and alimony.

e. Immediately expensed tangible personal property (§ 179 deduction).

f. Items specifically allocated by the partnership agreement.

g. Recovery of previously deducted items (tax benefit rule items).

h. AMT preferences and adjustments.

i. Self-employment income.

j. Intangible drilling and development costs.

k. Foreign country and US possessions taxes.

4. A partnership is not allowed a deduction for net operating losses, dividend received deduction (DRD), or items allowed only to individuals.

5. Withdrawals by partners do not affect the partnership's income and are rarely taxable to the partner.

a. Taxable only when cash received is greater than partner's outside basis.

b. Withdrawals are treated as distributions occurring on the last day of the partnership's tax year.

c. Withdrawals reduce the partner's outside basis.

B. Partnership Allocations

1. Unlike other tax entities, partnerships may make special allocations to partners that are not consistent with the partner's capital interest percentage.

2. Special allocations are permitted as long as they meet the *economic effect test.* The economic effect test requires the following.

a. The allocation must affect the partner's capital account.

b. The capital account must be the basis upon which liquidating distributions are made.

c. Negative capital accounts must be restored upon liquidation.

3. In certain situations, such as with *precontribution gains or losses*, special allocations are required by the tax law.

C. <u>Basis of a Partnership Interest</u>

1. The partner's original interest basis in a newly formed partnership equals the partner's adjusted basis of any property contributed plus gain recognized due to services (at FMV) the partner performed to receive the partnership interest.
2. The items listed in Exhibit 10-1 affect the partner's basis in the partnership.

**Exhibit 10-1**
**COMPUTATION OF PARTNER'S BASIS**

| | |
|---|---|
| ***Initial Basis in Partnership*** | |
| ***Plus:*** | ***Partner's share of partnership liabilities*** |
| ***Plus:*** | ***Partner's share of all types of partnership income*** |
| ***Less:*** | ***Partner's share of all types of deductions and losses*** |
| ***Less:*** | ***Partner's share of reductions in partnership liabilities*** |
| ***Plus:*** | ***Postacquisition contributions of cash or property*** |
| ***Less:*** | ***Postacquisition withdrawals of cash or property*** |
| ***Equals: Ending Basis in Partnership*** | |

3. If the acquisition of a partnership interest is other than at formation, the method of acquisition controls the computation of the partners initial basis.
4. In no case can a partner's basis in the partnership interest be less than zero.
5. Liabilities – There are two types of liabilities or debt:
   a. Recourse debt – The partnership or at least one of the partners is personally liable for the debt.
   b. Nonrecourse debt – The partnership nor any of the partners are liable personally for the debt. Lender can only claim collateral for the debt.
   c. Each type of debt is allocated to the partners in a different manner for the basis computation.
6. Partnership distributions
   a. Cash – A partner's outside basis in the partnership is reduced by the amount of cash distributed but not below zero. If cash is greater than the partner's outside basis, gain is recognized.
   b. Property – A partner's outside basis in the partnership is reduced by the partnership's basis in the asset but not below zero. If the partner's outside basis is not sufficient to cover the partnership's basis in the property, the partner's outside basis will become the basis of the asset received and the partner's outside basis will become zero. No gain is recognized.
   c. Cash & Property – When cash and property are distributed, first reduce the partner's outside basis by the cash received and then by the property.
7. While a partner's basis in the partnership changes from day to day, it usually needs to be computed only at the end of the year or when the interest is disposed of in some manner.

8. Sale of a partnership interest is a taxable event generally resulting in a capital gain or loss. Some capital treatment may be converted to ordinary when a partner is allocated a share of ordinary income items called *hot assets*.

D. Loss Limitations

1. Partnership losses flow through to the partners for deduction on their tax returns. However, there are three different limitations that may restrict the deductibility of the losses. The limitations are applied in the order listed below.
   a. Basis Limitation – A partner can only deduct losses to the extent of its outside basis in the partnership. Basis is determined at the end of the partnership tax year and is adjusted for distributions to partners and partnership gains and income.
   b. At-risk Limitation – Losses are deductible only to the extent of a partner's economic investment, ie, the amount that a partner can actually lose.
      (1) Recourse debt is generally adds to the partner's at-risk.
      (2) *Qualified nonrecourse debt* (indebtedness on real estate) adds to at-risk. Other nonrecourse debt does not add to at-risk.
   c. Passive Loss Limitation – Partnership losses that are classified as passive losses are deductible only to the extent the partner has passive income from this or other passive activities. Partners that materially participate (or actively participate for real estate) avoid this limitation.
2. Losses suspended by any of these limitations are carried forward (never back) until used.

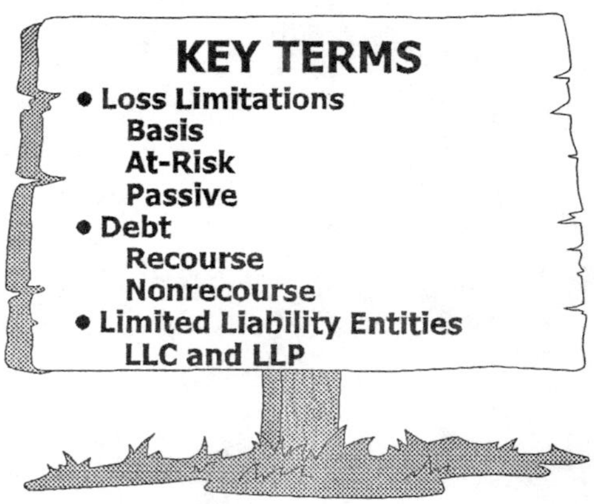


IV. Transactions Between Partner and Partnerships

A. Guaranteed Payments

1. Since a partner is not an employee of the partnership, "salaries" paid to the partners for services performed for the partnership are guaranteed payments. These payments can also be "interest" paid for use of the partner's capital.
2. The payments are usually deductible in computing ordinary income and are separately stated on Schedule K. They may require special allocations.

B. Other Transactions Between a Partner and a Partnership

1. The tax law allows certain transactions between the partnership and a partner to be treated as if the partner was an unrelated party.
2. Examples of transactions treated as arm's length transactions are loans, rent or lease payments, and some sales of property.
   a. No loss is recognized on a sale between a more than 50 % partner and the partnership. The disallowed loss may be used in a future sale.
   b. A gain on a sale between a more than 50% partner and the partnership is ordinary unless the asset is a capital asset to both parties involved.

C. Partners as Employees

1. Partners do not qualify as employees. Thus, partnerships do not pay employment taxes on partners and payments for partner fringe benefits are not deductible.
2. General partners must pay self-employment taxes on their distributive share of partnership ordinary income and guaranteed payments.

V. Limited Liability Entities

A. Limited Liability Company (LLC)

1. Combines partnership taxation with limited personal liability for *all* owners.
2. All states and the District of Columbia permit businesses to function as LLCs.
3. Under the check-the-box Regulations, LLCs are taxed as limited partnerships with no general partners.
4. Comments Regarding LLCs – Since the IRS has not specifically ruled on most aspects of LLC taxation, the following are speculative comments.
   a. Formation of a new LLC, accounting period and method elections, and allocation of its income and losses are treated the same as a partnership.
   b. Same limitations on the deduction of losses would apply.
   c. Contributed built-in gain property can be subject to tax if distributed within five years of contribution.
   d. All liabilities are treated as nonrecourse when allocating to owner's basis because all owners are limited in their liability. The liabilities are not considered to be at-risk unless they are qualified nonrecourse debt.
   e. LLC owner's share of income is not subject to self-employment taxes.
   f. Property distributions are treated the same as a partnership.
5. Advantages of LLC over a Limited Partnership
   a. Limited liability for all partners.
   b. All partners can participate in management even though their liability is limited. With a limited partnership, limited partners cannot participate in the management of the partnership and retain their limited liability.
6. Advantages of LLC over an S corporation
   a. Not limited to 75 owners.
   b. Type of shareholders not limited, ie, corporations, partnerships and nonresident aliens can be owners.
   c. Transfers to the entity do not have to meet a 80% control requirement applied to corporations.
   d. Built-in gains and passive income taxes do not apply to LLCs.
   e. Liabilities can be added to the owners basis for deductibility of losses.
   f. Special allocations are allowed.
7. Disadvantage of LLC
   a. New so administrative and case law is not well established.
   b. Laws governing LLCs vary from state to state.

B. Limited Liability Partnership (LLP)

1. The difference between a general partnership and an LLP is important. In a LLP, partners are jointly and severally liable only for contractual liabilities, whereas in a general partnership the partners are jointly and severally liable for *all* partnership liabilities.
2. An LLP must file formal documents of organization and register with the state. General partnerships need not follow these formalities.

## TEST FOR SELF-EVALUATION - CHAPTER 10

**True or False**

Indicate which of the following statements are true or false by circling the correct answer.

T F 1. Partnerships are subject to individual Federal income tax rates.

T F 2. Each partner can choose a different method of accounting and depreciation computation for purposes of determining its taxable income from the partnership.

T F 3. Any item of income, expense or loss that might affect a partner's personal tax return differently is treated as a separately stated item.

T F 4. Partners are not considered employees of the partnership for purposes of payroll taxes.

T F 5. The period of time that a partner held a capital asset prior to the transfer to the partnership is included in the holding period of the asset for the partnership.

T F 6. A partner may carry over indefinitely any operating losses in excess of its basis in the partnership.

T F 7. Guaranteed payments to partners are treated the same as a withdrawal from the partnership.

T F 8. Capital gains retain their character as they pass through to the partners.

T F 9. Losses on sales between a partner and a partnership always are disallowed.

T F 10. Qualified nonrecourse debt that is considered in computing the at-risk limitation includes indebtedness on real estate and heavy equipment.

T F 11. A limited liability company and a limited liability partnership provide all their partners the same level of limited liability.

T F 12. A partnership must have 2 or more taxpayers as owners.

T F 13. Limited partners in a limited partnership are limited as to their exposure to liabilities and are limited in degree that they can participate in management.

T F 14. Distributions of property that are in excess of a partner's outside basis will cause the partner to recognize a gain to the extent of the excess.

T F 15. The Schedule K provides the totals for each separately stated item appearing on the partners' Schedule K-1s.

## Fill-in-the-Blanks

Complete the following statements with the appropriate word(s) or amount(s).

1. A partnership must file an informational return, Form ________, within ________ months after its year-end.

2. Certain transactions between a partner and a partnership are treated as if the partner was an ________, dealing with the partnership at ________ ________.

3. A properly structured ________ is taxed as a partnership under the ________ Regulations.

4. Losses are disallowed on sales between a partnership and a partner whose interest in the capital or profits of the partnership is more than ________ percent.

5. Generally partners do not ________ when contributing assets to a partnership. However, if the transaction is a disguised ________ or essentially an ________ deferral is not permitted.

6. A partner's ________ basis accounts for the actual investment that the partner has made in the partnership. A partner's ________ refers to the partner's proportionate share of the adjusted basis of each partnership asset.

7. Each partner typically owns a ________ interest and a ________ interest in the partnership.

8. The two types of partnership debt are ________ and ________. The type of debt on which some or all of the partners are personally liable is ________.

9. Partners may allocate specific income, deductions, or credits in any ratio identified in the partnership agreement provided the allocation meet the _____ _____ test.

10. For depreciable and amortizable properties, the partnership merely "________" of the partner and continues the same cost recovery method of the partner contributing the property.

11. A partnership is called a ________ because the owners are taxed on the entity's income.

12. Unlike a corporation, a partnership is not allowed deductions for ________ or ________.

13. An increase in the partnership's liabilities will ________ the partners basis in the partnership, whereas a withdrawal by a partner will ________ the partners basis.

14. The deductibility of partnership losses by partners are restricted by the ________ limitation, the ________ limitation and the ________ rules.

15. When a distribution involves cash and property, the partner reduces its basis in the partnership first by the ________ and then by the ________.

16. Generally the sale of a partnership interest generates a ________ gain or loss. However, hot assets will produce ________ income.

**Multiple Choice**

Choose the best answer for each of the following questions.

USE THE FOLLOWING INFORMATION FOR QUESTIONS 1 - 4.
Tariq and Kareem created the TK Partnership. Tariq contributed cash of $10,000 and property with a basis of $55,000 and a fair market value of $90,000 that is subject to a mortgage of $40,000, for a 60% interest. Kareem contributed $20,000 cash and rendered legal and financial services worth $20,000, for a 40% interest.

____ 1. What is the gain recognized by the TK Partnership as a result of these contributions?
a. $ 0.
b. $ 20,000.
c. $ 35,000.
d. $ 55,000.
e. None of the above.

____ 2. What is the amount of capital gain or ordinary income recognized by Tariq and Kareem?
a. Tariq $0; Kareem $0.
b. Tariq $0; Kareem $20,000.
c. Tariq $35,000; Kareem $20,000.
d. Tariq $75,000; Kareem $20,000.

____ 3. What is the basis of all assets (including services) contributed to the partnership?
a. $45,000.
b. $85,000.
c. $105,000
d. $140,000.

____ 4. What is the basis of Tariq and Kareem's partnership interests?
a. Tariq $25,000, Kareem $20,000.
b. Tariq $25,000, Kareem $40,000.
c. Tariq $49,000, Kareem $56,000.
d. Tariq $65,000, Kareem $40,000.

____ 5. Which of the following items do **not** retain their character as they flow through to partners?
a. Long-term capital gains.
b. Tax-exempt interest.
c. Charitable contributions.
d. Dividend income.
e. All of the above retain their character.

____ 6. Zlata and Vuk own 60% and 40% of the ZV Partnership, respectively. ZV operates a foundry. Zlata sold stock in Boeing with a basis of $4,000 to the partnership for $6,000. The amount and character of gain recognized to Zlata is:
a. $0.
b. $2,000 ordinary income.
c. $2,000 capital gain.
d. $2,000 § 1231 gain.

____ 7. Assume the same facts as previous problem, except that a machine, a capital asset to Zlata, was sold to ZV. The partnership intends to use the machine to manufacture a new product. What is the amount and character of gain recognized to Zlata?

a. $0.
b. $2,000 ordinary income.
c. $2,000 capital gain.
d. $2,000 §1231 gain.

____ 8. Ben and Li-Ming were equal partners in the BL Partnership. Ben's basis in the partnership is $50,000 and Li-Ming's is $30,000. Ben receives a distribution of $20,000 cash and land with a FMV of $20,000. The partnership's basis in the land is $10,000. Li-Ming receives $40,000 cash. What amount of gain or loss recognized by Ben and Li-Ming recognize?

a. Ben $30,000 loss; Li-Ming $Zero gain.
b. Ben $20,000 loss; Li-Ming $10,000 gain.
c. Ben $10,000 loss; Li-Ming $Zero gain.
d. Ben $Zero loss; Li-Ming $10,000 gain.

____ 9. Assume the same facts as in previous problem, what is Ben's basis in the land and what is his basis in the partnership after the distribution?

a. Land $Zero; Partnership $30,000.
b. Land $10,000; Partnership $20,000.
c. Land $20,000; Partnership $10,000.
d. Land $30,000; Partnership $Zero.

____ 10. Jara, Koren, and Leon form the JKL partnership. Jara contributes machinery with a basis of $20,000 and a FMV of $50,000, Koren contributes land with a basis of $15,000 and a FMV of $40,000, and Leon contribute $40,000 of cash. Two months after forming JKL, Jara withdrawals the land and $10,000 cash. She ceases to be a partner. How are these transactions likely to be treated by the IRS.

a. The formation of the partnership is not taxable but the $10,000 cash withdrawn by Jara will be taxable.
b. The formation of the partnership is not taxable and Jara will have a basis in the land of $10,000 and $10,000 cash.
c. On the formation of the partnership, Koren and Leon will be taxed on $5,000 each, the amount by which Jara's contribution is greater than each of theirs.
d. This appears to be a disguised exchange. Jara will be taxed on $30,000 of gain and Koren will be taxed on $25,000 of gain.

____ 11. Mohan and Nella owned 30% and 70% of the MN Partnership, respectively. MN had the following items of income and loss for the year:

| | |
|---|---|
| Sales | $7,000 |
| Cost of sales | 2,000 |
| Dividend income | 3,000 |
| § 1231 loss | 2,000 |
| § 1245 gain | 1,000 |

How much will Nella report as her share of net partnership ordinary income?
a $2,800.
b $3,500.
c. $4,200.
d. $4,900.

____ 12. Which of the following entities will not generally qualify as a partnership for Federal income tax purposes?
a. Limited liability corporation.
b. Limited liability partnership.
c. Subchapter S corporation.
d. All of the above are partnerships for Federal income tax purposes.

____ 13. When capital gain property is contributed to a partnership for a capital and profits interest, the partnership's holding period in the asset:
a. May include the partner's holding period of the contributed property.
b. Always starts the day after the contribution date.
c. Always starts the day the partnership begins.
d. None of the above

____ 14. In which of the following independent situations would the transaction most likely be characterized as a disguised sale?
a. Partner Maria contributes $90,000 of appreciated property to the OM Partnership. Three years later OM distributes $90,000 proportionately to all the partners.
b. Bob contributes property with a basis of $40,000 and a FMV of $100,000 to the CB Partnership in exchange for a 40% interest. CB agrees to distribute $60,000 to Bob in two years, if partnership cash flows from operations exceed $200,000 at that time.
c. Lu contributes appreciated property (adjusted basis $10,000, FMV $50,000) to the BLT Partnership. One week later, he receives a distribution of $40,000 cash. None of the other partners received a distribution at this time.
d. None of the above transactions will be treated as a disguised sale.

____ 15. How are capital withdrawals by a partner during the year treated by the partner and the partnership?
a. Withdrawals are treated as guaranteed payments to the partners and are deductible in computing ordinary income for the partnership.
b. Generally, withdrawals do not affect the partnership's income and are not taxable to the partner unless cash is in excess of the partner's basis in the partnership.
c. Usually, withdrawals are treated as income to the partner in the year in which the withdrawal is received and but does not affect the partnership income.
d. Withdrawals reduce the partner's basis and reduce the partnership's income

____ 16. Which of the following items may be amortized over 60 months or more?
a. Organizational costs.
b. Startup costs.
c. Syndication costs.
d. All of the above.

____ 17. On July 1 Abdul received a 10% interest in the RJ partnership, for past services rendered. RJ's net assets at July 1 had a basis of $140,000 and a FMV of $200,000. What income should Abdul include in his tax return for the partnership interest?
a. $0.
b. $14,000 ordinary income.
c. $20,000 ordinary income.
d. Cannot be determined from the information given.

USE THE FOLLOWING INFORMATION FOR QUESTIONS 18 - 20.

In 20X1, Angelo was admitted to the Best partnership. Angelo's contribution to capital consisted of 50 acres of land, purchased in 19X0 for $20,000, and which had a FMV of $100,000. Angelo's interest in the partnership's capital and profits is 25%. In 20X1, the FMV of the partnership's net assets (after Angelo was admitted) was $400,000.

____ 18. What was Angelo's gain on the exchange of land for a partnership interest?
a. $0.
b. $80,000 ordinary income.
c. $80,000 long-term capital gain.
d. $80,000 § 1231 gain.

____ 19. In 20X3, the partnership sells the land for $110,000. What is Best's recognized gain on the sale?
a. $10,000 capital gain.
b. $10,000 ordinary income.
c. $90,000 capital gain.
d. $90,000 ordinary income.

____ 20. How much of the gain in problem 19 is allocated to Angelo?
a. $2,500
b. $22,500
c. $25,000
d. $82,500

____ 21. The MC partnership sustained an ordinary loss of $84,000 in 20X1. The partnership and its two partners are on a calendar year basis. The partners share profits and losses equally and each materially participates in the partnership's business. On December 31, 20X1, Clark had an adjusted basis of $36,000 for her partnership interest, before considering the loss. She has $24,000 of income from another partnership. On her individual income tax return, Clark should deduct an:
a. Ordinary loss of $24,000.
b. Ordinary loss of $36,000.
c. Ordinary loss of $42,000.
d. No loss is allowed

____ 22. Paloma, a 30% partner in PAA Partnership has a basis in her partnership of $60,000. She receives a distribution of land with a FMV of $100,000 and an adjusted basis to the partnership of $80,000. What is Paloma's gain on the distribution and what is her basis in the land?

a. $0 gain; $60,000 basis in land.
b. $0 gain; $80,000 basis in land.
c. $20,000 gain; $80,000 basis in land.
d. $40,000 gain; $100,000 basis in land.

____ 23. Darth sells his 50% interest in the Empire Partnership to Luke. At the time of the sale, Empire's assets have a FMV of $160,000 and an adjusted basis of $100,000. Darth's outside basis is $60,000. What is Darth's gain/loss on the sale?

a. $100,000.
b. $40,000.
c. $20,000.
d. Cannot be determined from the information given.

____ 24. Assume the same facts as in previous problem, what is Luke's inside and outside basis in the Empire Partnership?

a. Inside $80,000; Outside $60,000.
b. Inside $80,000; Outside $50,000.
c. Inside $50,000; Outside $60,000.
d. Inside $50,000; Outside $80,000.

____ 25. Which of the following is **not** an advantage of a limited liability corporation (LLC) over an S corporation?

a. LLC may have up to 100 owners whereas S corporations can only have 75 owners.
b. S corporations may be subject to built-in gains taxes. LLCs are not subject to this tax.
c. An LLC may make special allocations. S corporations must allocate on a per share pre day basis.
d. Corporations may be partners in an LLC but not in an S corporation.
e. All of the above are advantages of LLCs over S corporations.

## Short Answer

1. ABC Services is owned by individuals A, B, and C. They share profits and losses 40-30-30.

ABC Services data for the tax year is as follows.

| | |
|---|---|
| Sales | $300,000 |
| § 1231 Gain | $30,000 |
| Cost of Sales | 120,000 |
| Municipal Bond Interest | 10,000 |
| Jobs Credit | 3,000 |
| Charitable Contribution | 2,000 |

ABC purchased business equipment, for $80,000. MACRS deductions in excess of the § 179 deduction (only $15,000 taken) are included in Cost of Sales.

a. Allocate ABC's income and other items to the three partners for the tax year. Assume that C received guaranteed payment of $5,000/month for the year.

b. Allocate ABC's income and other items to the three partners for the tax year. Assume that C received guaranteed payments of $7,000/month for the year and B received guaranteed payments of $9,000/month for the year. A received draws from her capital account: $2,500/month.

2. Three individuals form the PST partnership as equal partners. The partner's contributions to the partnership are:

| | |
|---|---|
| P | Cash, $30,000. |
| S | Organizational Services, FMV $30,000. |
| T | Store Building, FMV $90,000; basis to T, $67,500; mortgage of $60,000. |

a. Compute each partner's original basis in the partnership interest.

b. What is the basis of the store to PST?

3. F, an individual, has a 75% interest in the FG Repairs partnership. Both the partners and the partnership use the calendar year for tax purposes. F's basis in the partnership interest on January 1 is $30,000. FG financial data for includes the following.

| | | |
|---|---|---|
| FG ordinary income | | $ 20,000 |
| F's Draws in | | 30,000 |
| 12/31 Cash Distribution to the partners | | 15,000 |
| 12/31 Distribution of Land to F: FMV | 6,000 | |
| Basis to FG | 5,000 | |
| FG Mortgage, January 1 | | 27,000 |
| FG Mortgage, December 31 | | 20,000 |
| FG Municipal Bond Interest Income | | 4,000 |

a. What is F's basis in the FG partnership before the 12/31 distributions? (Assume that the distributions were NOT in liquidation.)

b. What is her basis in the land distributed?

c. What is F's basis in the FG partnership after the distribution?

d. What if the cash distributions were $20,000, instead of $15,000?

e. What if the cash distributions were $5,000, instead of $15,000?

## SOLUTIONS TO CHAPTER 10 QUESTIONS

### True or False

1. F Partnerships are not subject to taxation. The partners, which could be corporations, are taxed on their allocated share of the income.
2. F Accounting and depreciation methods are selected at the partnership, rather than the partner, level.
3. T
4. T
5. T
6. T Assuming that the taxpayer remains a partner in the on-going entity.
7. F Guaranteed payments are treated like paying a salary or interest on the investment.
8. T
9. F Losses are disallowed only with respect to partners whose direct or indirect interest in the capital or profits of the partnership is more than 50%.
10. F Qualified nonrecourse debt does not include indebtedness on heavy equipment.
11. F LLP does not limit the partner's liability for contractual liabilities.
12. T
13 T
14. F Partners only recognized gain when cash in excess of their outside basis is received.
15. T

### Fill-in-the-Blanks

1. 1065, 3½ (the 15th day of the 4th month)
2. outsider, arm's length
3. limited liability company, check-the-box
4. 50
5. recognized gain or loss, sale, exchange
6. outside, inside
7. capital, profits (loss)
8. recourse, nonrecourse, recourse
9. economic substance
10. "steps into the shoes"
11. flow-through or pass-through
12. net operating losses, dividends received deductions
13. increase, decrease
14. basis, at-risk, passive loss
15. cash, partnership's basis in the property
16. capital, ordinary

### Multiple Choice

1. a The partnership does not recognize gain upon the contribution of property.
2. b T has no recognized gain and K recognizes $20,000 for providing legal services.

3. c $105,000. 10,000 + 55,000 + 20,000 + 20,000. Properties basis carries over from partner to the partnership. Services have a $20,000 basis because of the income recognized by K.
4. c T: $49,000; K: $56,000.
   T = 10,000 cash + 55,000 basis - 40,000 liability + 24,000 share of liabilities (60% X 40,000).
   K = $20,000 cash + 20,000 services + 16,000 share of liabilities (40% X 40,000).
5. e
6. c The Boeing stock is a capital asset to the partnership.
7. b The machine is not a capital asset to the partnership.
8. d Ben has no gain because cash is not in excess of his basis. Li-Ming has a $10,000 gain (40,000 −30,000) the cash is in excess of basis.
9. b Ben has a $10,000 basis in the land that is carried over from the partnership. Ben's partnership basis is $20,000 (50,000 −20,000 cash − 10,000 land)
10. d
11. c $4,200. 70% x (7,000 - 2,000 + 1,000)
12. c Subchapter S corporations have their own Federal tax rules and file Form 1120S.
13. a Generally the holding period for the partnership includes the holding period by the partner.
14. d Choice a. is not a disguised sale, because the partner is merely receiving her share of partnership cash flows. Choice b. is not a disguised sale because the distribution is subject to entrepreneurial risk. Choice c. is not a disguised sale because the cash received is less than the FMV of the asset contributed.
15. b
16. a, b Only item c cannot be amortized.
17. c $20,000. 200,000 x 10%. Partnership interest for services is ordinary income.
18. a Generally, no gain is recognized on contributions made to the partnership.
19. c $90,000. 110,000 - 20,000. The partnership's basis is a carryover basis from Angelo. Land is a capital asset to the partnership.
20. d $82,500. 80,000 precontribution gain + 25% X 10,000 post contribution gain.
21. b $36,000. The partner materially participates, therefore, loss deduction limited to partner's basis (36,000) and is not subject to the passive loss limitation.
22. a $0.; $60,000 Paloma substitutes her basis in the partnership for the basis in the land.
23. c $20,000. 50%(160,000 FMV) −60,000 outside basis.
24. d $50,000; $80,000. Inside basis is Luke's proportionate share of the partnership's basis and outside basis is what Luke paid for the partnership interest.
25. a LLCs can have an unlimited number of owners.

**Short Answer**

1. a. Ordinary Income:

| | | |
|---|---|---|
| | Sales | $300,000 |
| | Cost of Sales | -120,000 |
| | Guaranteed Pmts (12 x $5,000) | - 60,000 |
| | Total | $120,000 |

Allocation of tax items for the partners' tax year:

| | A | B | C |
|---|---|---|---|
| Ordinary income | $48,000 | $36,000 | $36,000 |
| Guaranteed Payments | - | - | 60,000 |
| § 1231 Gain | 12,000 | 9,000 | 9,000 |
| Jobs Credit | 1,200 | 900 | 900 |
| Charitable Contribution | 800 | 600 | 600 |
| Muni Bond Interest (for state tax) | 4,000 | 3,000 | 3,000 |
| § 179 Cost Recovery | 6,000 | 4,500 | 4,500 |

There is no special treatment for the regular MACRS deductions. The partnership's elections are effective for all of the partners. All income and deduction items flow through on the last day of the partnership's tax year.

b. Ordinary Income:

| | | |
|---|---|---|
| Ordinary Income: | Sales | $300,000 |
| | Cost of Sales | -120,000 |
| | Guaranteed Pmts (12 x ($7,000 + 9,000) | -192,000 |
| | Total | $(12,000) |

Allocation of tax items for the partners' tax year:

| | A | B | C |
|---|---|---|---|
| Ordinary Income | $(4,800) | $(3,600) | $(3,600) |
| Guaranteed Payments | - | 84,000 | 108,000 |
| § 1231 Gain | 12,000 | 9,000 | 9,000 |
| Jobs Credit | 1,200 | 900 | 900 |
| Charitable Contribution | 800 | 600 | 600 |
| Muni Bond Interest (for state tax) | 4,000 | 3,000 | 3,000 |
| § 179 Cost Recovery | 6,000 | 4,500 | 4,500 |

Ms. A's draws do not affect partnership income. Guaranteed payments can produce a loss for the partnership.

2. a.

| | P | S | T |
|---|---|---|---|
| Cash Contributions | $30,000 | | |
| Basis of Other Property | - | - | $67,500 |
| Gain Recognized on Contribution* | - | $30,000 | |
| Liabilities assumed by the partnership | - | - | -60,000 |
| Partners' share of partnership liabilities | 20,000 | 20,000 | 20,000 |
| Basis | $50,000 | $50,000 | $27,500 |

*Ordinary Income: Compensation for services

b. Basis of Store $67,500

Basis is a carryover from the partner contributing the asset.

3\. a.

| | |
|---|---|
| Basis, 1-1 | $ 30,000 |
| Distributive Share of Ordinary Income (75%) | + 15,000 |
| Share of Tax-exempt Income (75%) | + 3,000 |
| Draws | - 30,000 |
| Share of Decrease in Liabilities (75%) | - 5,250 |
| Basis before 12-31 Distribution | $ 12,750 |

b.

| | |
|---|---|
| Apply Cash Distribution First (75% X 15,000) | - 11,250 |
| Balance: F's Basis in the Land Received | $ 1,500 |

c.

| | |
|---|---|
| F's ending basis in the Partnership | $ 0 |

d.

| | |
|---|---|
| Basis before 12-31 Distribution | $ 12,750 |
| Apply Cash Distribution First (75% X 20,000) | -15,000 |
| Capital Gain Recognized by F | $ 2,250 |
| F's Basis in the Land Received | $ Zero |

F incurs a capital gain of $2,250, because her share of the cash distributions exceeds her predistribution basis in the partnership interest. F's basis in the land and her partnership interest now are zero.

e.

| | |
|---|---|
| Basis before 12-31 Distribution | $ 12,750 |
| Apply Cash Distribution First (75% X 5,000) | - 3,750 |
| Basis after 12-31 Cash Distribution | 9,000 |
| F's Basis in the Land Received | - 5,000 |
| Basis after all Distributions | 4,000 |

F does not incur a capital gain as a result of the distribution, because her share of the cash distributions does not exceed her predistribution basis in the partnership interest. F's basis in the land now is $5,000 (i.e., carryover basis), and her basis in the partnership interest now is $4,000.

# Chapter 11
# S Corporations

## CHAPTER HIGHLIGHTS

Subchapter S is an elective provision of the Code that allows *small business corporations* to become flow-through tax entities. Unlike LLCs however, S corporations are not taxed as partnerships. To received this favorable tax treatment the corporations must meet several restrictive rules regarding the number and type of shareholders and type of stock that can be issued. All of the shareholders must consent to the S election by timely filing with the IRS. The election can be revoked voluntarily or involuntarily by failing to meet the S corporation requirements continually.

Income and losses of the corporation that are passed through are allocated to the shareholders on a per share per day basis. This pass-through of income directly to the shareholders mitigates the effect of double taxation. In addition, shareholders who materially participate in the operations of the business can use the corporate losses to offset any other taxable income on their returns.

While considered a nontaxable entity, the S corporation can be subject to taxes at the corporate level. S corporations may be subject to the built-in gains tax and net passive income tax if they were a regular C corporation prior to the S corporation election.

I. Overview of S Corporations
   A. The S corporation election was enacted to minimize the influence of taxes in the selection of an entity form for the conduct of business.
   B. S corporations are regular corporations in the legal sense but the tax treatment is similar to, but not exactly like, a partnership. They *do not* file a partnership return.
   C. Limited liability companies (LLCs) provide tax results similar to S corporations without the restrictions imposed on S corporations. LLCs are taxed as partnerships.
   D. When to Elect S Corporation Status – Factors that should be considered.
      1. Marginal tax brackets of the owners and likelihood of double taxation of corporate income.
      2. Potential of entity losses and ability of owners to benefit from the losses on their personal return.
      3. Tax costs of changing entity form such as loss of ability to deduct prior NOLs.
      4. Effect on owners of having income and losses flow-through with their tax character retained.
      5. The substantial requirements that limit the applicability of the S corporation election to the owners current and future business.
      6. State and local recognition of the S corporation election.

II. Qualifying for S Corporation Status

A. <u>Definition of a Small Business Corporation</u> – To elect S corporation status, a corporation must qualify as a *small business corporation.* A small business corporation has the following characteristics.

1. A domestic eligible corporation – Foreign corporations, certain banks, or insurance companies do not qualify. The S corporation can have a wholly owed C or S corporate subsidiary.
2 One class of stock – The corporation may have only one class of stock outstanding.
   a. Voting rights differences are permitted but there can be no differences in distribution or liquidation rights.
   b. Straight debt reclassified as stock by the IRS is not considered another class of stock if it meets the safe harbor provisions.
3. Number of shareholders – Limited to 75. Wives and husbands are considered one shareholder for this purpose.
4. Shareholder types limited – Only individuals, estates, and certain trusts. Corporations and partnerships cannot be shareholders because these entities could be used to circumvent the 75 shareholder limitation.
5. No nonresident aliens – Shareholders cannot be nonresident aliens.

B. <u>Making the Election</u>

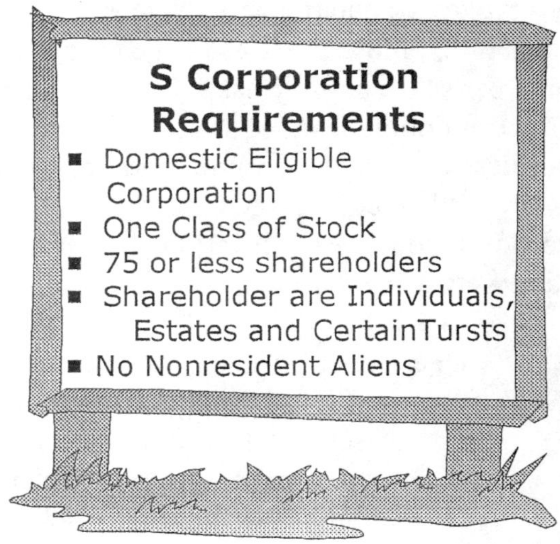


1. To become an S corporation, the shareholders must make a valid election by filing Form 2553 in a timely manner with the IRS.
2. To obtain S status for the current tax year, an election must be made before the 15th day of the 3rd month of the election year, or at any time in the preceding year.
3. The corporation must meet the electing requirements at all times during the taxable year for which the election is made and during all years for which the election is valid.
4. A corporation that does not exist cannot make an S election. Corporations come into existence at the earliest of any of the following events.
   a. When a corporation has shareholders.
   b. When the corporation acquires assets.
   c. When the corporation begins doing business.

C. <u>Shareholder Consent</u>

1. All shareholders must consent in writing to the S election. An extension of time to file is permitted only for filing of consents and *not* for filing the election.
2. A husband and wife who both own stock (even if ownership is because of community property laws) must both consent.

D. <u>Loss of the Election</u> – An S election is terminated when any of the following occur.

1. Voluntary Revocation
   a Shareholders holding a majority of the shares can decide to terminate the election.

b. If filed by the 15th day of the 3rd month of the tax year, the revocation will be retroactive to the first day of the year. Prospective revocation is also permitted.

c. The day on which the revocation occurs is the first day of the C corporation year. Income and losses must be allocated between the S corporation year and the C corporation year either by computing the actual income for each ("closing of the books") or by using a pro rata allocation.

2. Loss of Small Business Corporation Status

a. When a corporation ceases to meet the definition of a small business corporation, the election will be terminated.

b. Termination is effective on the date which the disqualifying event occurs.

3. Passive Investment Income (PII) Limitation

a. Applies only to S corporations that have merged with or were previously C corporations and have earnings and profits (E&P) carried over from C corporation years to the S corporation.

b. The S corporation election is terminated when the corporation's passive income exceeds 25% of gross its receipts for three consecutive years.

(1) Termination is effective beginning of the fourth year.

(2) Passive income for this purpose is interest, dividends, certain rents, royalties and gains/losses from sales of securities.

4. Reelection after Termination

a. After the S election has been revoked, a corporation must usually wait 5 years before reelecting S corporation status.

b. The 5 years waiting period is waived if:

(1) There is a greater than 50% ownership change.

(2) The event causing the revocation was not within the control of the corporation or its majority shareholders.

III. Operational Rules

A. <u>Computation of Taxable Income</u>

1. S corporations file informational Form 1120S which is due by the 15th day of the 3rd month after their taxable year (March 15 for calender year corporation). They may obtain extensions of time to file if needed.

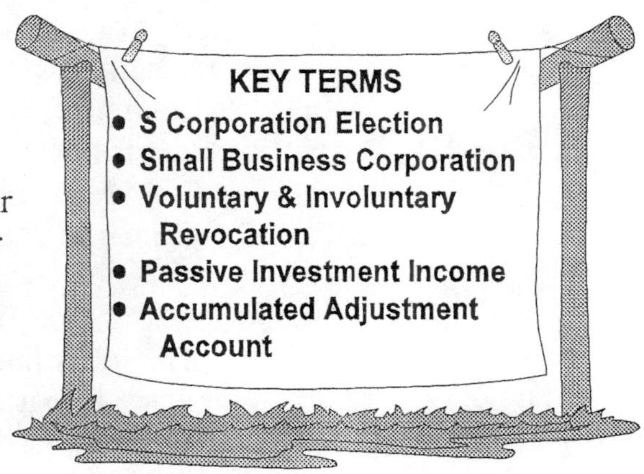


2. The taxable income/loss and separately stated items of an S corporation are determined according to tax rules similar to those applicable to partnerships, except that S corporations must recognize gains (but not losses) on distributions of property to shareholders.

3. The separately stated items for S corporations are identical to those for partnerships (see Study Guide Chapter 10 for a list).

B. <u>Allocation of Income and Loss</u>

1. Income, losses, and separately stated items are passed through to shareholders, on a pro rata per-share daily ownership basis using the following formula.

| S Corporation pass-through item | X | Percentage of shares owned | X | percentage of year owned | = | Amount of item reported |
|---|---|---|---|---|---|---|

2. Short-year election – If a shareholder's interest is terminated during the taxable year, tax items may be allocated under the pro rata approach or all shareholders affected and the corporation may elect to have an interim closing of the books. This will treat the S corporation as having two taxable years.

C. Tax Treatment of Distributions to Shareholders

1. S Corporations do not generate earnings and profits (E&P). Thus, for an S corporation to have accumulated E&P (A E&P) it must have previously been a C corporation and retained the A E&P.
2. No A E&P
   a. First, distributions are tax-free up to the shareholder's stock basis.
   b. Any residual is treated as a gain from the sale or exchange of property.
3. With A E&P
   a. First, distributions are tax-free up to the accumulated adjustments account (AAA) balance, but limited to the shareholder's stock basis at the time of the distribution.
   b. Second, distributions are treated as a taxable dividend to the extent of C corporation A E&P.
   c. Third, any residual amount is a return of capital to the extent of the shareholder's remaining basis in the S corporation's stock.
   d. Fourth, distributions in excess of the shareholder's stock basis are taxable as capital gains.
   e. With the consent of all shareholders, the S corporation may elect to have a distribution treated as made from A E&P first, rather than from the AAA. This is called a *AAA bypass election.*
4. Accumulated Adjustments Account (AAA)
   a. The AAA is a corporate account representing the cumulative total of undistributed net income for S taxable years beginning after 1982.
   b. The AAA is computed at the end of each year by adjusting the beginning balance for this year by:
      (1) Nonseparately stated income and positive separately stated items (except tax-exempt income and related expenses).
      (2) Distributions are deducted, and
      (3) Negative separately stated items are deducted.
   c. The AAA can have a negative balance.
      (1) All losses decrease the AAA balance, even those in excess of the shareholder's stock basis.
      (2) However, distributions may neither increase a negative AAA balance nor take the balance below zero.
5. Schedule M-2, Form 1120S
   a. Provides a reconciliation of the AAA.
   b. The *other adjustments account* column on the schedule is for items that affect shareholder basis but are not included in AAA. Tax-exempt income and its related expenses are such items.

6. Distributions after terminating the S election – Distributions receive special treatment. Rather than being a dividend from the new C corporation, they are tax-free recovery of stock basis to the extent of AAA during the first year after termination. Only cash distributions received this treatment.

D. <u>Tax Treatment of Property Distributions by the Corporation</u>

1. Distributions to a shareholder are measured by the cash and fair market value of other distributed property.
2. The S corporation recognizes gain when it distributes appreciated property to its shareholders. The character of the gain will depend upon the type of asset distributed.
3. Loss is not recognized on the distribution of property.
4. S corporation do, however, recognize both gain or loss on liquidating distributions.

E. <u>Shareholder's Basis</u>

1. Initial basis is computed in the same manner as would be the case for the basis in the stock of a regular corporation.
2. The basis of stock is increased by taxable income, tax-exempt income, and additional shareholder capital contributions
3. The basis of S corporation stock is reduced by cash and property distributions (at FMV), nondeductible expenditures, and deductible expenses and losses.
4. If a loss and a distribution occur in the same tax year, the distribution reduces stock basis first. See Exhibit 11-1 for a summary of shareholder's basis.

**Exhibit 11-1**
**COMPUTATION OF SHAREHOLDER'S BASIS**

| | |
|---|---|
| ***Initial Basis in Corporation*** | |
| ***Plus:*** | ***Postacquisition contributions of cash or property*** |
| ***Plus:*** | ***Shareholder's share of taxable income*** |
| ***Plus:*** | ***Shareholder's share of tax-exempt income*** |
| ***Less:*** | ***Postacquisition distributions of cash or property*** |
| ***Less:*** | ***Shareholder's share of all types of deductions and losses*** |
| ***Equals:*** | ***Ending Basis in of Shareholder but not below Zero*** |
| | ***If Ending Basis is Zero*** |
| ***Plus:*** | ***Shareholder's personal loans to the corporation*** |
| ***Less:*** | ***Remaining deductions and losses*** |
| ***Equals:*** | ***Basis in loans to corporations but not below Zero*** |

5. The shareholder's basis in the stock cannot fall below zero.
   a. Excess basis reductions decrease the shareholder's basis in loans personally made to the corporation (see Exhibit 11-1). Thus, losses can only be deducted to the extent of the shareholder's stock and loan basis. Losses in excess of these are suspended.
   b. When basis is restored (via additional corporate income or shareholder capital contributions), the basis of the loan is restored before the basis of the stock is increased.

5. When a loan repayment amount exceeds the loan's basis, the excess constitutes income. The character of the gain will be capital only if the corporation issued a note as evidence of the debt. Open loan repayments will be ordinary income.

F. <u>Treatment of Losses</u>

1. NOL
   a. NOLs pass through to the S corporation's shareholders and can be deducted for the year in which the corporation's tax year ends.
   b. Deduction of the NOL pass-through is limited to the shareholder's basis as computed in section E. above. NOLs reduce the shareholder's basis but never below zero.
   c. To the extent that the NOL exceeds shareholder basis, the deduction is carried over indefinitely. Any loss so carried is deductible only by the same shareholder when the basis in stock or loans is restored.
2. At-Risk and Passive Loss Limitations
   a. The at-risk rules apply to S corporation shareholders. They are similar to partnership at-risk rules except that the shareholder does not consider any of the corporation's liabilities. Shareholder is at-risk for their basis plus any liabilities associated with the corporation on which the shareholder is personally liable.
   b. S corporation shareholders are also subject to the passive loss/credit rules. Therefore, shareholders who do not materially participate in operating the business apply the S corporation losses and credits only against income from other passive activities.
   c. Both the passive loss and the at-risk rules are outlined in Chapter 10.

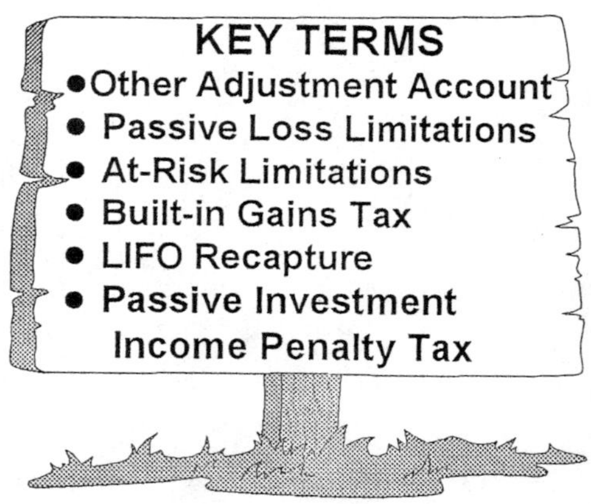


G. Tax on Pre-Election Built-In Gain (BIG)

1. Without the BIG tax, it would be possible for C corporations to avoid double taxation on dispositions of appreciated property by electing S status.
2. The Code imposes the BIG tax on the aggregate net built-in gain (unrealized gain) a corporation has at the time it converts from C status to S status.
   a. Net unrealized built-in gain is the excess of the aggregate FMV of the S corporation's assets over the aggregate adjusted basis for the assets.
   b. The BIG tax is imposed on and paid by the S corporation (not the shareholders) at the highest corporate rate (35%).
3. The yearly BIG tax is limited to the lesser of:
   a. The recognized built-in gains for the tax year; or,
   b. The amount of taxable income the corporation would recognize for the year *if* it were a C corporation (taxable income limitation).
   c. BIG realized but not taxed due to the taxable income limitation is carried forward and recognized in future years.
4. BIG tax applies in the 10 years immediately following the conversion from a C status to S status.

5. BIG tax does not apply to an S corporation that has never been a C corporation.
6. LIFO Recapture Tax
    a. When a C corporation uses the FIFO method for its inventory in the last tax year before making an S election, any built-in gain is recognized and taxed as the inventory is sold.
    b. A C corporation using the LIFO method for its last year before making an S election must include in gross income over a 4 year period the excess of the inventory's value under FIFO over its LIFO basis. No refund is allowed where the LIFO basis exceeds the FIFO value at the time of the election.

H. <u>Passive Investment Income Penalty Tax</u>
1. This penalty tax (at 35%) is imposed on excess passive income of S corporations that have A E&P carried over from C corporation years.
2. The tax is computed on the excess net passive income which is figured as follows.

$$\text{Excess net passive income} = \frac{\text{Passive investment income in excess of 25\% of gross receipts for the year}}{\text{Passive investment income for the year}} \times \text{Net passive investment income for the year}$$

I. <u>Other Operational Rules</u>
1. An S corporation is required to make estimated tax payments for its tax liability that is attributable to the built-in gain tax and passive investment income tax.
2. S corporations may own stock in other corporations but they are not eligible for the dividends received deduction. A C corporation cannot own stock in an S corporation.
3. S corporations are not subject to the 10% of taxable income limitation for charitable contributions. The contributions will pass through to the shareholders.
4. Any family member who renders services or provides capital to the S corporation must be paid reasonable compensation. Unlike partnerships, shareholders of an S corporation can be treated as employees for payments of salaries. Thus, FICA and FUTA taxes are paid by the corporation on the shareholder-employees.
5. The flow-through income from the S corporation is not subject to self-employment tax as it is with a partnership.
6. An S corporation may use the cash method of accounting and must use the cash method for deducting amounts owed to a cash basis related party.
7. S elections are not recognized by the District of Columbia or several states.
8. S corporation may issue § 1244 stock.
9. Flow-through losses are subject to hobby loss rules of § 183.

# TEST FOR SELF-EVALUATION - CHAPTER 11

**True or False**

Indicate which of the following statements are true or false by circling the correct answer.

T F 1. The other adjustment account on Schedule M-2 of Form 1120S keeps track of items that affect basis but not the AAA, such as tax exempt income.

T F 2. A new S corporation shareholder has no power to terminate the election, unless she or he owns 80% or more of the voting stock.

T F 3. A husband and wife are considered to be a single shareholder, for purposes of making an S election on Form 2553.

T F 4. Unlike partnerships, an S corporation is subject to the built-in gains tax.

T F 5. S corporations must make estimated payments with respect to any recognized built-in gain or passive investment income taxes that it will owe for the year.

T F 6. Any gains or losses from the sale of capital assets constitute separately stated income.

T F 7. When an S corporation's election is involuntarily terminated, the entity is taxed as a regular corporation starting on the day after the date on which the disqualifying event occurred.

T F 8. After an S election is voluntarily terminated, there usually is a five-year waiting period before a new election can be made.

T F 9. An S corporation is subject to the same Code sections as a partnership.

T F 10. The passive investment income penalty tax applies to all S corporations.

T F 11. An S corporation cannot own 80% the stock of another corporation.

T F 12. The IRS may permit a corporation to reelect S status prior to the five-year termination waiting period, if there is a more than 50% change in ownership.

T F 13. The AAA is the cumulative total of undistributed separately and non-separately stated items for the S taxable years since 1982.

T F 14. For determining the deductibility of losses, S corporation shareholders may add to their basis their proportionate share of the corporation's liabilities.

T F 15. A "small business" corporation must have assets of less than $1 million and only one class of stock.

**Fill-in-the-Blanks**

Complete the following statements with the appropriate word(s) or amount(s).

1. Shareholders in S corporations may be _________, _________, and _________ .

2. A deductibility of a NOL not greater than the shareholder's stock basis may still be limited by the _________ and _________ limitations.

3. An S corporation election can be made at any time during the preceding taxable year, or by the _________ day of the _________ month of the election year.

4. The one class of stock requirement for an S election permits differences _________ but not in _________ or _________.

5. An S corporation with accumulated earnings and profits from Subchapter C years is subject to a corporate level income tax to the extent that its _________ income exceeds _________ percent of its gross receipts.

6. The order of S corporation distributions is: (1) _________, (2) _________, (3) _________ , and (4) capital gain.

7. An S election can be terminated in any of the following ways: voluntary _________; cessation of small business _________; or the corporation fails the _________ income limitation.

8. No more than _________ individuals can hold shares in the same S corporation.

9. S corporation shareholders receive a ratable share of the corporation's income and losses, based upon their _________ _________ _________.

10. If an S corporation fails the passive investment income for _________ consecutive taxable years, the S election is terminated as of _________ of the _________ year.

11. A shareholder's share of an S corporation's NOL can be _________ to taxable years, to the extent that it exceeds the basis of the shareholder's stock and the loans made to the corporation.

12. The _________ LIFO recapture amount is equal to the excess of the inventory value under _________ over the _________ valuation.

13. A qualified small business corporation must be a _________ corporation and cannot be a _________ corporation, certain _________ or _________ companies.

14. Capital gains and charitable contributions are _________ items when reporting income for an S corporation.

15. After an S shareholder's basis in her stock and loans to the corporation have been depleted by the flow-through of corporate NOLs, corporate income allocated to the shareholder will first restore the basis of her _________.

## Multiple Choice

Choose the best answer for each of the following questions.

____ 1. Which of the following statements *do not* describe a qualifying small business corporation:

a Must have only one class of stock.

b. May not have assets valued in excess of $10 million.

c. May not have another corporation as a shareholder.

d. Must have filed with the IRS for qualifying status.

____ 2. A business that made an S election upon incorporation may be subject to which of the following corporate-level taxes.

a. State corporate income tax.

b. Passive investment income tax.

c. Federal income tax on built-in gains.

d. All of the above.

____ 3. An S election may be terminated when:

a. Gross receipts exceed five million dollars for the year.

b. Any one of the shareholders chooses to revoke the election.

c. A new shareholder forgets to make the election on his own.

d. A new shareholder is a nonresident alien.

____ 4. Which of the following items *do not* retain their tax character as they flow-through to the shareholder from an S corporation.

a. Section 179 immediate expensing of depreciable assets.

b. Portfolio income.

c. §1245 recapture.

d. Tax-exempt income.

e. All of the above are separately stated.

____ 5. On January 1, Don owned 10% of the stock of Electing Corp., which is a calendar-year S corporation. On June 14, Don acquired another 10% of Electing Corp's stock. For calendar year, Electing Corp's nonseparately stated income is $36,500. What is Don's share of Electing Corp's income?

a. $3,650.

b. $5,475.

c. $5,650.

d. Some other amount.

____ 6. Which of the following entities will not qualify as a small business corporation.

a. A corporation that has 100 shareholders, consisting of 30 married couples and 40 individuals.

b. An active corporation that has a wholly-owned subsidiary.

c. A corporation whose straight debt has been reclassified as stock.

d. A corporation that has a partnership as a shareholder.

____ 7. On June 14, Nina acquired a 50% interest in an S corporation due to the death of her father. The corporation earned $100,000 of ordinary income of which $60,000 was earned up to June 14. Which of the following statements is correct regarding a short-year election.

a. Nina will be taxed on $40,000 of S income.
b. Nina will be taxed on $54,167 of S income.
c. Nina will be taxed on $54,795 of S income.
d. A short-year election is not available in this situation because only 50% of the ownership has changed.

____ 8. Advar, a calendar year S corporation, distributes $500 to its sole shareholder, Ayako, on 12-31-20X4. Ayako's basis in the stock is $200 on 12-31-20X4. For 20X4, Advar had $800 of nonseparately stated income, $300 of capital losses and $100 of tax-exempt income. What is Ayako's basis in the stock as of 12-31-20X4?

a. ($200).
b. $0.
c. $200.
d. $300.

____ 9. A shareholder's basis in S corporation stock is:

a. Reduced by the corporation's adjusted basis in property distributed.
b. Decreased by a distribution from accumulated E&P.
c. Originally computed in a manner similar to that used for regular corporations.
d. Unaffected by tax exempt income.
e. All of the above.

____ 10. Deductions for NOLs are limited to:

a. The basis in the stock plus proportionate share of corporate liabilities.
b. Passive income plus $3,000.
c. Basis of stock plus any liabilities owed by the shareholder to the corporation.
d. Basis of stock plus basis of debt owed by the corporation to the shareholder.

____ 11. In which of the following situations may it be desirable to elect S corporation status?

a. The entity is currently a C corporation with NOL carryforwards.
b. The corporation is expected to generate losses in its initial years and the owners are in a high tax bracket.
c. The corporation will not distribute after tax earnings for the next five years.
d. The corporation has a substantial portion of its income from passive sources.
e. All of these situations would benefit from an S election.

____ 12. Which of the following statements is true?

a. Shareholders are treated the same as partners and therefore do not qualify as employees of the S corporation.
b. Since an S corporations is not subject to income tax, they do not make estimated payments.
c. S corporations cannot generate earnings and profits.
d. The LIFO recapture is taxable over a five year period.
e. The S election is currently recognized in all 50 states.

USE THE FOLLOWING INFORMATION FOR QUESTIONS 13 - 15.

Binder, Inc., an S corporation, is owned solely by Sheryl. Her basis in the stock as of January 20X2 is $6,000 and Binder has liabilities outstanding of $10,000. For the calendar year 20X2, Binder has a $20,000 NOL. In January 20X3, Sheryl loans $10,000 to Binder and in December 20X3, Sheryl makes a capital contribution of $28,000. Binder's NOL for 20X3 is $20,000. In 20X4, Binder turns itself around and generates taxable income of $10,000. Binder has made no payments on its liabilities.

____ 13. What is the amount of loss that Sheryl may deduct in 20X2?
a. $Zero.
b. $6,000.
c. $16,000.
d. $20,000.

____ 14. What is the amount of loss that Sheryl may deduct in 20X3?
a. $Zero.
b. $20,000.
c. $34,000.
d. $38,000.

____ 15. What is Sheryl's basis in the S corporation's stock and the loan to the corporation, respectively, at December 31, 20X4?
a. Stock $Zero, Loan $10,000.
b. Stock $4,000, Loan $10,000.
c. Stock $7,000, Loan $7,000.
d. Stock $14,000, Loan $Zero.

____ 16. On January 31, 20X1, Zee Corporation sold all of its stock in its wholly owned subsidiary, Jet Corporation, to individuals Carl and Debra. Jet is a calendar-year corporation and, Carl and Debra filed an S election on March 14, 20X1. The earliest date that Jet's S election will be effective is:
a. January 1, 20X1.
b. February 1, 20X1.
c. March 14, 20X1.
d. January 1, 20X2.

USE THE FOLLOWING INFORMATION FOR PROBLEMS 16 - 18

New Corp., a calendar year taxpayer, was incorporated in 1992 and elected S corporation status for its taxable year beginning January 1, 1995. On that date, it had net unrealized built-in gains of $100,000. In 2004, New Corp. recognized $60,000 from the sale of appreciated assets. If New Corp. was a C corporation, it would have taxable income in 2004 of $50,000.

____ 17. On what amount does New Corp. compute its built-in gains tax for 2004?
a. $50,000.
b. $60,000.
c. $100,000.
d. New Corp. is not subject to the built-in gains tax.

____ 18. What is the built-in gains tax rate applicable to New Corp.?
a. Regular corporate tax rate applied to the total built-in gains.
b. Highest additional corporate tax rate, 39%
c. Highest regular corporate tax rate, 35%.
d. Highest individual tax rate.

____ 19. In 2007 New Corp. recognized $55,000 from the sale of appreciated assets. If New Corp. was a C corporation, it would have taxable income in 2007 of $70,000. On what amount would New Corp. compute its built-in gains tax?
a. $40,000.
b. $50,000.
c. $55,000.
d. New Corp. is not subject to the built-in gains tax.

USE THE FOLLOWING INFORMATION FOR PROBLEMS 20 - 23

Century corporation, had its sole shareholder, Ana, make a timely S election for 20X5. At this time it's a E&P was $10,000 and Ana's stock basis was $40,000. Century has a 85% owned subsidiary from which it receives substantial dividends each year. Century's income & expenses are as follows:

| | Dividends | Gross Sales | COGS | Capital Gain |
|---|---|---|---|---|
| 20X5 | $30,000 | $45,000 | $20,000 | $3,000 |

Century made two distributions of $35,000 each to Ana during 20X5.

____ 20. How are the distributions in 20X5 treated by Ana?
a. None of the distributions are taxable.
b. $60,000 are not taxable and $10,000 are taxable as dividends.
c. $40,000 are not taxable and $30,000 are capital gains.
d. $70,000 is taxable as dividends.
e. None of the above

____ 21. Ana's basis in her stock on January 1 20X6 is:
a. ($10,000)
b. $Zero.
c. $38,000.
d. $40,000.

____ 22. Century's dividend received deduction in 20X5 is:
a. $0.
b. $24,000.
c. $25,500.
d. $30,000.

____ 23. Century's nonseparately stated income in 20X5 is:
a. $25,000.
b. $45,000.
c. $55,000.
d. $78,000.

____ 24. As of July 1, 20X3, Yota corporation converts from a C corporation to an S corporation when it has A E & P of $20,000. Its LIFO inventory is valued at $150,000 and under FIFO its value would be $200,000. For 20X3, Yota has $350,000 of gross receipts including $100,000 of passive income received in November. Expenses associated with the passive income are $20,000. The remaining ordinary income was earned evenly throughout the year. What is the amount of taxes Yota must pay with its final C corporation return due to the converting from a C to an S corporation?

a. $Zero.
b. $4,375.
c. $8,000.
d. $28,000.
e. Cannot be figured from this information.

____ 25. Assume the same facts as Problem 24, what is the amount of the passive investment income tax Yota must pay in 20X3?

a. $Zero.
b. $4,375.
c. $8,000.
d. $28,000.
e. None of the above.

**Short Answer**

1. What are the requirements for a corporation to qualify as a "small" business corporation?

2. Discuss the means by which an S election may be terminated. What are the consequences?

3. Diva Corporation has a valid S election in effect. Diva has no accumulated E&P from C corporation years. On 1-1-X1, Jineng owns all of the 100 outstanding shares in Diva. On 10-1-X1, Jineng sells 20 shares to Ashley for $30,000. All taxpayers use the calendar year.

20X1 Salaries: Jineng $75,000; Ashley $15,000
20X1 Distributions Paid: $10,000 on 5-1-X1 and $10,000 on 11-1-X1

a. Diva's 20X1 Non-Separately-Stated Income = $200,000
LTCG = $30,000, on a sale that was completed 2-1-X1
Charitable Contribution = $55,000, made 12-15-X1
Compute Jineng's and Ashley's 20X1 gross income from Diva Corporation.

b. If Diva Corporation's fiscal year ends on 1-31-X2, what is Jineng's and Ashley's 20X1 gross income from Diva Corporation.?

c. How are the distributions treated by Jineng and Ashley?

4. Rom is sole shareholder in Free Corporation, a valid calendar-year S Corporation. Rom purchased his shares on 1-1-X1, for $100,000. Rom loans Free $17,000 on 2-1-X1. 20X1 activities of Free Corporation include:

| | |
|---|---|
| Non-Separately-Stated Income | $15,000 |
| Net Long-Term Capital Gain | 3,000 |
| Exempt Interest Income | 4,000 |
| Dental Expenses of Rom's mother, paid by Free. | 750 |

a. What is Rom's basis in his Free Corporation shares and loan on 1-1-X2? What is Rom’s taxable income/loss from Free Corporation?

b. Same as a., but 20X1 Non-Separately-Stated Income is ($110,000).

c. Same as a, but 20X1 Non-Separately-Stated Income is ($150,000).

5. Mill Corporation has made a valid S election for 20X3. It has Accumulated Earnings and Profits, from Subchapter C years, of $30,000. During 20X3, Mill recognizes:

| | |
|---|---|
| Sales Receipts | $60,000 |
| Interest Income--AT&T bonds | 40,000 |
| Brokerage Fees | 5,000 |

Compute Mill Corporation's passive income penalty tax.

## SOLUTIONS TO CHAPTER 11 QUESTIONS

**True or False**

1. T
2. F The shareholder must own more than 50% of the S corporation's stock.
3. F Although a husband and wife are considered to be one shareholder for purposes of the number of shareholders requirement, each spouse must consent to the election.
4. T
5. T
6. T Capital gains and losses are separately stated items.
7. F The entity is taxed as a regular corporation starting on the date on which the disqualifying event occurred.
8. T
9. F S corporations are subject Subchapter S of the Code and related regulations. Partnerships are governed by Subchapter K of the Code.
10. F The tax only applies to S corporations that carry over A E&P from a C corporation.
11. F An S corporation may own up to 100% of a C corporation.
12. T
13. T
14. F Only loans made by the shareholder to the S corporation are added to the basis.
15. F There is no asset limitation.

**Fill-in-the-Blanks**

1. individuals, estates, certain trusts
2. passive loss, at-risk
3. fifteenth, third
4. voting rights, distribution, liquidating rights
5. passive, 25
6. accumulated adjustment account, accumulated earnings and profits, return of capital
7. revocation, corporation status, passive investment
8. 75 or 150 if it has 75 married couples as shareholders
9. daily stock ownership
10. three, beginning, fourth
11. carried over
12. taxable, FIFO, LIFO
13. domestic, foreign, banks, insurance
14. separately stated
15. loans

**Multiple Choice**

| | | | |
|---|---|---|---|
| 1. | b | There is no limitation of the value of assets owned by a small business corporation. | |
| 2. | a | A corporation that has always been an S corporation is not subject to the passive investment income tax, or the built-in gains tax. | |
| 3. | d | | |
| 4. | c | | |
| 5. | c | $5,650 = (36,500 x 10%) + 10% (36,500 x 200/365).<br>16 in June +31+31+30+31+30+31 = 200 days. | |
| 6. | d | An S corporation cannot have a partnership as shareholder. | |
| 7. | a | Books are closed as of June 14. | |
| 8. | d | $300 = 200 + 800 − 300 + 100 − 500 (distribution). | |
| 9. | c | | |
| 10. | d | | |
| 11. | b | Losses will pass through to the shareholders and are deductible on their returns. | |
| 12. | c | S corporation can only have A E & P carried over from prior C corporation years. | |
| 13. | b | $6,000. | To extent of adjusted basis. 14,000 loss carryover. |
| 14. | c | $34,000. | 14,000 (20X1 carryover loss) + 20,000 (20X2 loss). Loss not greater than basis. 10,000 + 28,000 = 38,000 basis |
| 15. | b | $4,000; $10,000 | 14,000 = 38,000 basis − 34,000 losses + 10,000 gain. |
| 16. | d | The election is not effective until January 1, 20X2 because the corporation was owned by a regular corporation for part of 20X1, and accordingly, is not eligible to receive S status for 20X1. | |
| 17. | a | $50,000. Lesser of recognized built-in gains or taxable income as if a C corporation. | |
| 18. | c | 35%. | |
| 19. | d | Built-in gains tax only applies for the ten-year period beginning with the first taxable year as an S corporation. | |
| 20. | b | $60,000, $10,000. | AAA = $58,000 (30,000 + [45,000 − 20,000] + 3,000) Distributions are first from AAA ($58,000) and then from A E&P (10,000) and then return of capital (2,000 not taxable). |
| 21. | c | $38,000. | 40,000 + 58,000 −58,000 −2,000. |
| 22. | a | The dividend received deduction is not available to S corporations. | |
| 23. | a | $25,000. | 45,000 − 20,000. Dividends & capital gains are separately stated. |
| 24. | b | $4,375. | [(200,000 − 150,000) X 35%] ÷ 4.<br>The LIFO recapture (FIFO − LIFO) is paid over four years with the first payment due with the last C corporate tax return. |
| 25. | e | $3,500. | [100,000 −(25% X 350,000)] ÷ 100,000 = 12.5%.<br>[12.5% X (100,000 −20,000)] = 10,000 X 35% = 3,500. |

**Short Answer**

1. A qualifying "small" business corporation is a US corporation with 75 or fewer shareholders. For this purpose, a husband and wife are considered to be a single shareholder. The corporation may have only one class of stock outstanding. Only individuals, estates, and certain trusts can be shareholders. Shareholders can not be nonresident aliens. The S corporation may be a member of an affiliated group.

2. The owners of a majority of the shares of the corporation voluntarily may revoke the election. An S election will be terminated at the beginning of the 4th year when the S corporation has Subchapter C accumulated earnings and profits, and passive income exceeds 25% of gross receipts for 3 consecutive years. Lastly, an S election will be terminated when: the corporation ceases to meet the definition of a small business corporation (e.g., because it has too many shareholders or issues a second class of stock). As of the date of this event, the corporation has a "short" taxable year, for which it is subject to the normal Subchapter C provisions. The S election is effective, however, for the days of the taxable year that occur prior to the event.

3. Ownership Weights:
Jineng [100% X 273/365] + [80% X 92/365] = .95
Ashley [20% X 92/365] = .05

| | | *Jineng* | *Ashley* |
|---|---|---|---|
| a. | Salary | $ 75,000 | $ 15,000 |
| | Non-Separately-Stated Income | 190,000 | 10,000 |
| | Long-Term Capital Gain | 28,500 | 1,500 |
| | Charitable Contribution | 52,250 | 2,750 |

b. Salary $ 75,000 $ 15,000
Pass-Through amounts will appear on Jineng's and Ashley's 20X2 returns. Note, the ownership weights would then change.

c. Jineng received a $10,000 distribution on 5-1 and $8,000 on 11-1. None are taxable. Ashley received a $2,000 distribution on 11-1. It is not taxable.

4.

| | | Stock | Loan |
|---|---|---|---|
| a. | Original Basis | $ 100,000 | $ 17,000 |
| | Income | + 18,000 | |
| | Capital gain | + 3,000 | |
| | Exempt Income | + 4,000 | |
| | Non-Deductible Expenditures | - 750 | |
| | Basis of stock, 1-1-X2 | $ 121,250 | $ 17,000 |

Rom's income: $15,000 ordinary income and $3,000 capital gain

| | | | |
|---|---|---|---|
| b. | Original Basis | $ 100,000 | $ 17,000 |
| | Income (−110,000) | - 106,250 | - 3,750 |
| | Capital gain | + 3,000 | |
| | Exempt Income | + 4,000 | |
| | Non-Deductible Expenditures | - 750 | |
| | Subtotal | $ 000 | $ 13,250 |

Rom's income/loss: $110,000 ordinary loss and $3,000 capital gain.

| | | | | Carryover |
|---|---|---|---|---|
| c. | Original Basis | $100,000 | $17,000 | |
| | Income (−150,000) | - 106,250 | 17,000 | $26,750 |
| | Capital gain | + 3,000 | | |
| | Exempt Income | + 4,000 | | |
| | Non-Deductible Expenditures | - 750 | | |
| | Subtotal | $ 000 | $ 000 | |

Deduction for $150,000 NOL is limited to:

| | |
|---|---|
| Basis before NOL (100,000 + 3,000 + 4,000 − 750) | $ 106,250 |
| Basis of Loan to Free Corporation | + 17,000 |
| Deduction Limit | $ 123,250 |

Rom's income/loss: $123,250 ordinary loss and $3,000 capital gain.

5. ENPI X 35% tax rate = Passive income penalty tax

$$\$35{,}000 \text{ X } \frac{40{,}000 \text{ Passive Income} - (25\% \text{ X } 100{,}000 \text{ Gross Income})}{40{,}000 \text{ Passive Income}} = \text{ENPI}$$

Net Passive Income

ENPI = $13,125 13,125 X 35% = $4,593.75 passive income penalty tax

# Chapter 12
# Multijurisdictional Taxation

## CHAPTER HIGHLIGHTS

One of the tax planning tools that has been discussed in the text is shifting income from high-taxing jurisdictions to those taxed at lower rates. Businesses, large and small, make location decisions based in part on the taxes imposed by the jurisdictions. This chapter explores the different sources of tax law for jurisdictions within the United States and throughout the world. Tax issues such as taxing authority and income sourcing for entities with income from a variety of jurisdictions are explored. The importance of transfer pricing and the effects of tax havens are also discussed.

I. The Multijurisdictional Taxpayer
   A. Most businesses must be concerned with the consequences of earning income and paying a variety of taxes in different jurisdictions.
   B. State and local taxes make up over ⅓ of all taxes collected in the U. S.
   C. Global trade represents a major portion of the U.S. economy.

II. U.S. Taxation of Multinational Transactions
   A. From a U.S. perspective, international tax laws should promote the global competitiveness of U.S. enterprises while protecting the U.S. tax revenue base. These two objectives sometimes are in conflict however.
   B. U.S. international tax provisions are primarily concerned with two potential taxpayers.
      1. U.S. persons earning foreign-source income, and
      2. Non-U.S. persons earning U.S. source income.
   C. U.S. taxation of international transactions is organized as follows.
      1. *Outbound taxation* – Taxing foreign-source income earned by U.S. taxpayers.
      2. *Inbound taxation* – Taxing U.S. source income earned by non-U.S. taxpayers.
   D. <u>Sources of Law</u>
      1. U.S. taxpayers operating in other nations are subject to both U.S. law and the laws of the other jurisdictions in which they operate or invest.
      2. For U.S. taxpayers, the Internal Revenue Code addresses the tax consequences of earning income anywhere in the world but local tax law of other nations in which they operate must also be considered.
      3. For non-U.S. persons, U.S. tax law is relevant for income they earn in the U.S.

4. Tax Treaties
   a. Countries enter into *income tax treaties* to provide more tax certainty.
   b. Tax treaties are the result of specific negotiations with each treaty partner, so each treaty is unique but they are generally organized in the same way.
   c. All treaties provide for investment income, business profits from a *permanent establishment* (PE), and exceptions for certain persons.
      (1) Taxpayers have PE when their activities within a country rise beyond a minimal level.
      (2) When a taxpayer has a PE within a country, it is subject to tax in that country.
   d. Treaty provisions generally override the treatment otherwise called for under the Internal Revenue Code or foreign tax statutes.
   e. Where there is no tax treaty, whether a taxpayer is "engaged in a trade or business" within a country replaces the PE determination.

E. Tax Issues

1. Authority to Tax
   a. The United States taxes the worldwide income of U.S. taxpayers.
   b. Others jurisdictions may also tax U.S. persons on income from within their borders, thus, U.S. taxpayers may be subjected to double taxation.
   c. Two methods of mitigating double taxation are:
      (1) Territorial approach – Exempting from taxation income received from sources outside the country's borders.
      (2) Foreign Tax Credit – U.S. provides a *foreign tax credit* for taxes paid to other countries on income also taxed in the U.S.
2. Income Sourcing
   a. Determining income sources is critical in calculating the U.S. tax consequences to both U.S. and foreign taxpayers.
   b. Sourcing rules generally assign income to a geographic location based on where the economic activity producing the income took place.
   c. Deductions are assigned based on their relationship to the income.
3. Foreign Tax Credit (FTC)
   a. The FTC is a dollar-for-dollar reduction of U.S. income tax liability for taxes paid or *deemed paid* to another country.
   b. A deemed-paid credit is available when corporations receive dividends from foreign corporations that pay foreign income taxes. The formula for computing the credit is given below.

$$\frac{\text{Actual or constructive dividend}}{\text{Post-1986 undistributed earnings}} \times \begin{array}{c}\text{Post - 1986}\\\text{Foreign taxes}\end{array} = \begin{array}{c}\text{Deemed Paid}\\\text{Credit}\end{array}$$

   c. Corporations taking a deemed paid credit must *gross up* (add to income) the dividend income by the amount of the deemed paid credit.
   d. FTC is elective. Taxpayers choose to take either a deduction for the foreign taxes or the credit. Generally the credit is more beneficial.
   e. The FTC is the *lesser* of the foreign income taxes actually imposed or the overall limitation amount computed using the following formula.

$$\frac{\text{Foreign-source taxable income}}{\text{Worldwide Taxable Income}} \times \text{US tax before FTC} = \text{Overall limitation}$$

f. Unused foreign tax credits are carried back 2 years and then forward 5 years.
g. To limit the ability to cross-credit foreign taxes, the FTC rules provide for several *separate foreign tax credit limitation categories.* See Figure 12-2 in Text for a summary of the current separate income categories.

4. Controlled Foreign Corporation (CFC)
   a. A CFC is any foreign corporation in which more than 50 percent of the voting stock or the total stock value is owned by U.S. shareholders. Stock owned directly, indirectly, and constructively is counted.
   b. To minimize current U.S. tax liability, taxpayers may try to defer income taxes by shifting income-generating activities to a foreign entity. Income earned is not subject to U.S. tax until it is repatriated.
   c. To thwart potential abuse, the ability to defer foreign income is limited by providing that certain types of *tainted* CFC income is currently included in gross income by U.S. shareholders without regard to actual distributions.
   d. The tainted income generally includes income that can be easily shifted or has little or no economic connection with the CFC's country of incorporation. Examples include:
      (1) Passive income such as interest, dividends, rents, and royalties.
      (2) Sales income where manufacturing activity nor customers are in the CFC's country and supplier or customer are related parties.
      (3) Income from the CFC providing services on behalf of its U.S. owners.

5. Inbound Issues
   a. A *nonresident alien* (NRA) is an individual who is not a citizen or resident of the United States. A person is treated as a resident of the United States for income tax purposes if he or she meets either the green card test or the substantial presence test.
   b. A foreign corporation is one that does not qualify as domestic.
   c. Two important definitions determine the U.S. tax treatment of foreign taxpayers with U.S.-source income: conduct of a U.S. trade or business and effectively connected income.
      (1) For noninvestment income to be taxed in the U.S. the foreigner must be engaged in a U.S. trade or business and have income that is effectively connected with that business.
      (2) Effectively connected net income is taxed at the same rates that apply to U.S. taxpayers.
   d. Some U.S.-source income that is *not* effectively connected with the conduct of a U.S. trade or business is subject to a flat 30 percent tax. This includes certain compensation, passive, and portfolio income.
   e. Several exemptions to taxing foreigners on their U.S. investment income are provided such as for interest and capital gains.

III. Crossing State Lines - State and Local Income Taxation

A. Sources of Law

1. Income taxes can be levied by states, cities, counties, villages, commuter districts, stadium boards, and numerous other bodies that have been granted taxing authority by their states. Each state will have separate tax laws and revenue departments that administer the taxes.

2. The Federal government issued *Public Law 86–272* to protect interstate commerce by exempting from state and local taxation sales of tangible personal property where the only contact within the state is *solicitation* by the taxpayer.

3. Many states are members of the *Multistate Tax Commission* (MTC). This body proposes legislation to the states and localities and issues its own regulations and informational materials.

   a. The Uniform Division of Income for Tax Purposes Act (UDITPA) provide a set of income assignment rules, and it forms the basis for income tax statutes in most of the MTC member states.

   b. If taxing jurisdictions followed MTC rules, taxpayers would be unable to gain any *border advantages*.

B. Tax Issues

1. Authority to Tax

   a. Businesses are taxable in the state in which it resides, or is incorporated.

   b. Businesses also have tax liabilities in jurisdictions where a *nexus* exists.

      (1) A nexus exists when a sufficient presence in the jurisdiction has been established by the business on an ongoing basis.

      (2) The precise activities that create nexus vary from jurisdiction to jurisdiction, although most of the taxing states follow the broad rules of Public Law 86–272 and the regulations of the MTC.

2. Income Sourcing

   a. Multistate businesses must divide up taxable income among the states in which they have a nexus. The template below shows how most states compute their share of the entity's aggregate income.

**Computing State Income Tax Liability**

Federal taxable income
± State modification items
State tax base
± Nonbusiness income/loss (for allocation)
Business income (for apportionment)
X Apportionment percentage for the state
Taxable income apportioned to the state
± Taxable income/loss allocated to the state
State taxable income/loss

State tax, per tax table or rate schedule
− State's tax credits
Net state tax liability

b. States usually base their computations on Federal taxable income but may have some modifications to reflect differences between state and Federal tax laws. Examples of differences include the following.
   (1) Cost recovery schedule differences.
   (2) Tax interest income from its own bonds or from other states.
   (3) Allow a deduction for Federal income taxes paid.
   (4) Disallow deductions for state income taxes.
   (5) Limit net operating loss (NOL) deductions or have different NOL carryover periods.

c. Multijurisdictional businesses need to *allocate* nonbusiness income and loss to the states in which such items are derived.

d. Business income is *apportioned* among the states in which it operates. Most states apply an apportionment procedure involving three factors, each meant to estimate the taxpayer's relative activities in the state.
   (1) The sales factor – In-state sales/total sales.
   (2) The payroll factor – In-state payroll/total payroll.
   (3) The property factor – In-state property/total property.
   (4) The state's apportionment percentage is the average of these three factors.
   (5) Most states add additional weight to the sales factor.

e. Since states do not follow identical rules for weighting factors, the apportionment percentages seldom total to 100 percent.

f. Other aspects of the three-factor approach include the following.
   (1) Assign sales using tax concept of "ultimate destination" (sale is assigned to the state where the purchaser is located).
   (2) Sales in states that are not taxed maybe subject to *throwback rule* causing the sale to be sourced to the seller's state.
   (3) Payroll is usually assigned to the state in which the employee's services primarily are performed.
   (4) Property factor uses an average historical cost basis, net of depreciation. Idle property is ignored, but construction in progress is included.
   (5) Property leased but not owned by the taxpayer is included in the property factor at eight times the annual rentals paid.

g. States use specialized apportionment percentages for industries whose sales and asset profile does not fit the traditional three-factor formula.

h. Some states use a *unitary approach* to computing the apportionment factors. Conglomerates base their computations on the data for all of their affiliated corporations.

IV. Common Challenges

A. Authority to Tax – The notion of *presence* and nexus are becoming less important over time, and the level of resource usage in the host jurisdiction also is declining.

B. Division of Income

1. The multistate apportionment procedures need updating to take into consideration features of the new economy. The sales factor is becoming the preferred income-sourcing device. These sales can be assigned based on a destination test so that the transaction is assigned to the state of the purchaser.

2. Model treaties have been developed by the United States and the Organization for Economic Cooperation and Development (OECD).

C. Transfer Pricing
1. The international trade transfer pricing systems require taxpayers to keep a database of comparable prices and transactions even though this may be difficult.
2. Using advance pricing agreements allows a greater degree of control by the governments in data collection and analysis.

D. Tax Havens
1. When taxpayers perceive effective tax rates as too high, planning usually includes seeking out a tax haven.
2. When governments experience declines in its tax base due movement of assets and income out of the jurisdiction, anti-tax-haven laws are passed.

E. Interjurisdictional Agreements
1. Treaties are documents that address many tax and nontax issues and those involving the United States tend to bilateral.
2. There is little coordination among the states due to the lack uniformity among the states' tax laws and their enforcement efforts.
3. Sharing data, while still respecting the confidentiality needs of the taxpayer and requirements of the governments, represents a technologically sound method of collecting taxes in today's multijurisdictional economy.

## TEST FOR SELF-EVALUATION – CHAPTER 12

**True or False**

Indicate which of the following statements are true or false by circling the correct answer.

T F 1. State and local taxes make up over ⅓ of all taxes collected in the United States.

T F 2. Treaty provisions generally override the treatment otherwise provided in the Internal Revenue Code or foreign tax statutes.

T F 3. The United States retains the right to tax its citizens and residents on their U.S. source income.

T F 4. Determining the source of income is critical in calculating the tax consequences to both U.S. and foreign persons.

T F 5. Although sometimes complex and subject to special exceptions, sourcing rules generally assign income to a geographic source based on where the entity producing the income is located.

T F 6. Since tax treaties are the result of negotiations among several countries, most treaties are very similar.

T F 7. A taxpayer can take a credit and a deduction for the same foreign income taxes.

T F 8. The U.S. limits the amount and type of foreign taxes that can be taken as a foreign tax credit.

T F 9. Worldwide taxable income is the total taxable income reported on the taxpayer's U.S. tax return, not the total worldwide income of a group of related domestic and foreign entities.

T F 10. Foreign corporations, even those controlled by U.S. shareholders, generally are not included in a U.S. consolidated income tax return.

T F 11. U.S. shareholders of a controlled foreign corporation (CFC) lose their ability to defer U.S. taxation of income earned by the CFC.

T F 12. To minimize current U.S. tax liability, taxpayers often attempt to shift the income to foreign entities where the income earned will not be subject to U.S. tax until repatriated.

T F 13. The Code explicitly define a U.S. trade or business.

T F 14. When a foreign taxpayer is engaged in a U.S. trade or business, all U.S.-source income is treated as effectively connected and subject to U.S. taxation.

T F 15. The issues concerning international operations are very different than the issues for businesses with multistate operations.

T F 16. The allocation process for state taxation is very much like the income-sourcing procedures used for international taxation.

T F 17. When computing apportionment percentages, the Federal law requires that all of the percentages add to 100%.

T F 18. Many states use specialized apportionment percentages for industries whose businesses do not fit the traditional three-factor formula.

T F 19. The U.S. Treasury has considered adopting an apportionment approach to the sourcing of international taxable income.

T F 20. Treaties only address tax issues and the computation of income.

**Fill-in-the-Blanks**

Complete the following statements with the appropriate word(s) or amount(s).

1. U.S. international tax address two potential taxpayers:________ earning income from outside the U.S. and________ earning income from inside the U.S.

2. ________ taxation refers to U.S. taxation of foreign-source income earned by U.S. taxpayers. ________ taxation refers to U.S. taxation of U.S.-source income earned by foreign taxpayers.

3. Countries enter into ________ with each other to provide more certainty to taxpayers.

4. ________ is defined in all income tax treaties. Where there is no tax treaty, the more subjective test of whether a person is ________ within a country replaces the PE determination.

5. The U.S. has not adopted a ________ approach in taxing foreign persons.

6. Any foreign tax credit disallowed because of the limitations may be carried back ________ or forward ________.

7. To limit the ability of U.S. taxpayers to ________ foreign taxes, the FTC rules provide for several separate foreign tax credit limitation categories (or________ ).

8. A ________ is any foreign corporation where > 50% of the total voting power or value of the stock is owned by U.S. shareholders on any day during the taxable year.

9. In ________ Congress attempted to bring order to the multistate income tax process. This 1957 pro-________ provision exempts from state taxation sales of tangible personal property where the only contact with the state was the ________ activity of the taxpayer.

10. One of the steps in computing state taxable income is to ________ items of nonbusiness income to the states from which it came. Business income is ________ among the states in which it operates.

11. Many states apply an apportionment procedure involving the following factors:________, ________, and ________.

12. Most states follow the regulations of the ________ and the outline of the________ in defining and applying the apportionment factors.

13. Model treaties developed by the U.S. and the ________ include language relating to the income-sourcing rules and transfer pricing at arm's length, not an apportionment approach.

14 A ________ exists where a business has a sufficient presence in a state on an ongoing basis.

15. Treaties involving the United States tend to be ________.

**Multiple Choice**

Choose the best answer for each of the following questions.

____ 1. Coconut Inc., located in Arkansas, received $20,000 dividend income from Kiwi Corporation, a New Zealand entity, in the current year. Coconut purchased the 30% of Kiwi's stock on the New York stock exchange.
- a. The $20,000 is considered to be U.S.-source income because Coconut purchased the stock in the U.S.
- b. 30% of all taxes paid by Kiwi in New Zealand can be used by Coconut to reduce its U.S. income because it is an owner of Kiwi.
- c. Since Coconut is a U.S. company, the $20,000 it received is U.S.-source income.
- d. The dividends of $20,000 are considered to be foreign-source income.

____ 2. Bobcat Corporation of Arizona had $600,000 of U.S. income generated from $5 million in assets. It also had $400,000 of income generated from its $2.5 million in assets located in Mexico. If Bobcat had $100,000 of interest expense, how much is apportioned to the foreign-source income?
- a. $33,333.
- b. $40,000.
- c. $50,000.
- d. $60,000.

____ 3. Cheeseco, organized in Wisconsin, has operations in the U.S. and in a foreign country. Its worldwide income is $1 million of which $300,000 is from its foreign operations. If U.S. taxes were $340,000 and Cheeseco paid $120,000 in foreign taxes, what is Cheeseco's foreign tax credit?
- a. $100,250.
- b. $102,000.
- c. $105,882.
- d. $120,000.

____ 4. Which statement is *false* regarding international tax laws from a U.S. perspective?
a. Tax laws should promote the global competitiveness of U.S. enterprises.
b. Tax laws should protect the tax revenue base of the United States.
c International tax laws tend to be in direct conflict with the objectives of the Internal Revenue Code.
d The need to meet all of the international tax law objectives contributes to the complexity of the rules governing cross-border transactions.
e. All of the above are true.

____ 5. Companies having permanent establishments in more than one country are subject to double taxation. Which statement is true regarding the mitigation of this double taxation.
a. The U.S. approach is to simply exempt its citizens from tax on any income derived from outside its boarders.
b. The U.S. provides a tax credit against the U.S. taxes for taxes paid or incurred in other countries on the same income.
c. U.S. businesses can use all taxes paid to foreign governments in computing the foreign tax credit which reduces U.S. income taxes.
d. The foreign tax credit is the greater of the taxes paid to the foreign government or the U.S. taxes paid on the same income.
e. All of the above are true.

____ 6. Select the *incorrect* statement.
a. For U.S. taxpayers, tax treaties address the all tax consequences of income earned in other countries.
b. All treaties include provisions for the taxation of investment income, business profits, personal service income, and exceptions for certain persons.
c. Non-U.S. taxpayers must comply with U.S. tax laws relevant to income they earn that is connected to U.S. income-producing activities.
d. The U.S. taxes worldwide income of taxpayers connected to the U.S. through citizenship, residency, or place of organization.
e. Each of the above statements is correct.

____ 7. Daily Corporation purchased 85% of Calendarco for $2 million, thus it qualifies as a controlled foreign corporation. Calendarco earned $300,000 of Subpart F income for the current year and paid $100,000 in taxes on this income. If Daily received no distributions from Calendarco, what is the proper treatment by Daily of these amounts.
a. No income and no foreign tax credit.
b. $15,000 foreign tax credit.
c. $255,000 constructive dividend income and a deemed-paid tax credit for taxes paid on the $255,000.
d. $300,000 deemed income and $100,000 deemed paid foreign tax credit.

____ 8. Which of the following statements is incorrect.
a. The Code defines a foreign corporation as one without U.S. persons as owners.
b. A nonresident alien is someone that is not a citizen or resident of the U.S.
c. Citizenship is determined under U.S. immigration and naturalization laws.
d. Residency is met by either the green card test or the substantial presence test.
e. All of the above are correct.

____ 9. Which of the following is not a component in computing a state taxable income.

a. Nonbusiness income or losses.
b. Taxable income or loss apportioned to the state.
c. Taxable income or loss allocated to the state.
d. State modification items.
e. All of the above are components in computing state income.

____ 10. Which of the following statements does not describe three-factor apportionments.

a. Sales made in a state with no income tax can be subject to throwback rules that cause the sales to be taxed in the seller's state.
b. Property leased by the taxpayer is generally not included in the property factor.
c. Sales are usually assigned to the state of the purchaser.
d. Officer compensation and § 401(k) plan contributions may be excluded from the payroll factor.

____ 11. The unitary approach to computing apportionment factors

a. Considers affiliated corporations to include only those entities whose total stock is held by a parent corporation located within the state.
b. Allows entities such as partnerships and corporations to file combined returns if they are owned by the same group of U.S. taxpayers.
c. Requires less detailed information and therefore are considered to provide a less accurate reflection of the entities' activities within the state.
d. Can require conglomerates to base their taxes on all of their affiliated corporations, not just the legal entities that do business with the state.
e. All of the above.

____ 12. Walnut Corporation had $600,000 in Federal taxable income and Federal taxes of $204,000. Walnut had $10,000 of interest income from State A bonds and $20,000 of net rental income from a building it owns in State B. The bond income is excluded from Federal and State A income, but is taxable in State B. State A allows a deduction for Federal income taxes but not for state taxes and State B allows a deduction only for its own state taxes. Estimate state taxes paid in State A were $30,000 and in State B were $40,000. What are the state modifications that must be made?

| | State A | State B |
|---|---|---|
| a. | $244,000 | $30,000. |
| b. | $70,000 | $10,000. |
| c. | ($224,000) | $40,000. |
| d. | ($244,000) | $60,000. |
| e | None of the above. | |

____ 13. In 2000, the OECD identified these jurisdictions as tax havens that had not cooperated with its campaign to stop harmful global tax practices. As of 2002, which of the following countries is no longer on the list.

a. Andorra.
b. Liberia.
c. Liechtenstein.
d. Monaco.
e. All of these countries remain on the list.

____ 14. Which of the following statements is false.

a The Federal government has not attempted to force states and localities to use a single common tax formula and administrative organization.

b The transfer pricing system used in international trade requires the taxpayer to keep a database of comparable prices and transactions.

c. The activities that create nexus are precisely defined in Public Law 86–272 and elaborated upon in its regulations.

d. When accumulating transfer pricing data for proprietary goods and design, it may be impossible to find comparable goods for determining prices.

e. All of the statements are true.

**Short Answer**

1. Axel Corporation owns and operates two manufacturing facilities, one in State X and one in State Y. Axel's taxable income of $700,000 comes solely from its manufacturing activities in these two states. Further information is listed below.

| | State X | State Y |
|---|---|---|
| Property | $1,200,000 | $300,000 |
| Sales | 720,000 | 480,000 |
| Payroll | 330,000 | 270,000 |

a. Assuming both states use an equally weighted three factor apportionment formula, what is Axel's taxable income in State X and State Y?

b. Assuming State Y double weights the sales factor in its three factor apportionment formula, what would Axel's taxable income be in State Y?

c. Assuming State X uses a single-factor sales only formula and State Y uses an equally weighted three factor formula, what will Axel's total taxable income be?

## SOLUTIONS TO CHAPTER 12 QUESTIONS

### True or False

1. T
2. T
3. F The United States taxes its citizens and residents on their worldwide income.
4. T
5. F Sourcing rules generally assign income based on the location where the economic activity producing the income took place.
6. F Each treaty is unique.
7. F A taxpayer cannot take a credit and deduction for the same foreign income taxes.
8. T
9. T
10. T
11. F A U.S. shareholder of a controlled foreign corporation (CFC) does not necessarily lose the ability to defer U.S. taxation of income earned by the CFC.
12. T
13. F The Code does not explicitly define a U.S. trade or business.
14. F Some U.S.-source interest and capital gains are exempt from U.S. tax.
15. F Many of the issues concerning international operations are similar for businesses with multistate operations.
16. T
17. F Apportionment percentages seldom total precisely to 100%.
18. T
19. T
20. F Treaties address issues other than taxation.

### Fill-in-the-Blanks

1. U.S. persons, non-U.S. persons (foreign taxpayers)
2. Outbound, Inbound
3. income tax treaties
4. Permanent establishment, engaged in a trade or business
5. territorial
6. 2 years, 5 years
7. cross-credit, baskets
8. controlled foreign corporation,
9. Public Law 86–272, interstate commerce, solicitation
10. allocate, apportioned
11. sales factor, payroll factor, property factor
12. Multistate Tax Commission, Uniform Division of Income for Tax Purposes Act
13. Organization for Economic Cooperation and Development
14. nexus
15. bilateral

**Multiple Choice**

| | | |
|---|---|---|
| 1. | d | Kiwi is a non-U.S. taxpayer and it earned its income in New Zealand. |
| 2. | a | $33,333. 2,500,000 ÷ (5,000,000 + 2,500,000) = 33% X 100,000. |
| 3. | b | $102,000. 340,000 X (300,000/1,000,000). |
| 4. | c | The objectives listed in a. and b. are sometimes in conflict with each other. They are not necessarily in conflict with the Internal revenue Code. |
| 5. | b | Only foreign *income* taxes can be used in computing the credit which is the *lesser* of foreign taxes or the U.S. taxes paid on the same income. |
| 6. | a | The Internal Revenue Code addresses the tax consequences for U.S. taxpayers of income from anywhere in the world. |
| 7. | c | $255,000. 85% X $300,000. |
| 8. | a | The Code defines a foreign corporation as one that is not domestic. |
| 9. | e | |
| 10. | b | Property leased is included in the property factor at 8 times annual rentals. |
| 11. | d | |
| 12. | e | ($154,000) State A and $40,000 State B. State A: 70,000 state taxes - 204,000 Federal taxes - 20,000 rent. State B: 10,000 bond interest + 30,000 state taxes. |
| 13. | e | |
| 14. | c | The activities that create a nexus vary from jurisdiction to jurisdiction. Public Law 86–272 provides broad rules not precise rules. |

**Short Answer**

1. Summary information

| | State X | State Y | Total |
|---|---|---|---|
| Property | $1,200,000 | $300,000 | $1,500,000 |
| Sales | 720,000 | 480,000 | 1,200,000 |
| Payroll | 330,000 | 270,000 | 600,000 |

a.

| | State X | % | State Y | % |
|---|---|---|---|---|
| Property | (1,200,000/1,500,000) | .80 | (300,000/1,500,000) | .20 |
| Sales | (720,000/1,200,000) | .60 | (480,000/1,200,000) | .40 |
| Payroll | (330,000/600,000) | .55 | (270,000/600,000) | .45 |
| Total | | 1.95 | | 1.05 |
| Average | | 1.95 ÷ 3 = .65 | | 1.05 ÷ 3 = .35 |
| Income | | 700,000 | | 700,000 |
| | | X .65 | | X .35 |
| Taxable income | | $455,000 | | $245,000 |

b. State Y: .2 +(2 X . 4) + .45 = 1.45 ÷ 4 = .3625 X 700,000 = $253,750

c.

| | |
|---|---|
| State X: | $700,000 X .6 = $420,000 |
| State Y | $245,000 |
| | $665,000 |

# Chapter 13
# Business Tax Credits and Corporate Alternative Minimum Tax

## CHAPTER HIGHLIGHTS

Tax credits are used by Congress to implement social and economic objectives. Tax credits affect the tax liability substantially different than do tax deductions: credits offset a tax liability dollar for dollar, whereas deductions merely reduce the base on which a tax liability is calculated. Some observers contend that credits provide benefits to taxpayers on a more equitable basis than those benefits received as a result of tax deductions.

Also covered in this chapter is the alternative minimum tax (AMT). This tax was designed to insure that every taxpayer with substantial economic income pays at least a minimum amount of tax. The AMT applies to individuals, corporations, trusts, and estates. It represents, in essence, a parallel tax system that is separate and distinct from the regular income tax system. The AMT has become an important tax for corporations and increasingly for individuals as it is increasing becoming a crucial revenue generator for the Federal government. **Changes made by the Jobs and Growth Tax Relief Reconciliation Act of 2003 (Tax Act of 2003) to the AMT have been included in this outline.**

I. Tax Policy and Tax Credits
   - A. A tax credit should not be confused with an income tax deduction. A tax credit is usually worth substantially more to a taxpayer than a deduction of a similar amount since a credit directly offsets the tax liability and a deduction merely reduces taxable income.
   - B. Tax credits, as opposed to deductions, generally provide benefits to taxpayers on a more equitable basis.
   - C. Generally, tax credits are used by Congress to achieve social or economic objectives or to provide equity between different groups of taxpayers.

II. Specific Business-Related Tax Credit Provisions
   - A. <u>General Business Credit (GBC)</u>
     1. The GBC combines a number of credits, each computed separately under its own set of rules, into one amount. This amount is limited in its ability to offset a taxpayer's regular tax liability. See Exhibit 13-1 on next page for list of credits included in GBC.
     2. Any unused credit must first be carried back 1 year, then forward 20 years. A FIFO method is applied to the carrybacks, carryovers, and utilization of credits earned for the year.

3. GBC is limited to the taxpayer's *net income tax* reduced by the greater of:
    a. The *tentative minimum tax*.
    b. 25% of *net regular tax liability* that exceeds $25,000.
4. Definitions
    a. Net income tax is the sum of regular tax and AMT reduced by certain nonrefundable credits.
    b. The tentative minimum tax is reduced by any foreign tax credit allowed.
    c. The net regular tax liability is regular tax reduced by nonrefundable credits.

**Exhibit 13-1**

**GENERAL BUSINESS CREDITS**

***The General Business Credit includes the following credits.***

- *Rehabilitation Expenditure Credit*
- *Business Energy Credits*
- *Work Opportunity Credit*
- *Welfare-to-work Credit*
- *Research Activities Credit*
- *Low-income Housing Credit*
- *Disabled Access Credit*
- *Small Employer Pension Startup Costs Credit*
- *Employer-provided Child Care Credit*

B. Tax Credit for Rehabilitation Expenditures
1. A tax credit is available for rehabilitation expenditures incurred on industrial and commercial buildings and on certified historic structures. However, no credit is allowed for the rehabilitation of personal use property.
2. The credit amounts are:
    a. 10% for nonresidential buildings and residential rental property other than certified historic structures, originally placed in service before 1936.
    b. 20% for nonresidential and residential certified historic structures.
3. Basis of a rehabilitated building is reduced by the amount of the credit taken.
4. To qualify for the credit, a building must be substantially rehabilitated. A building is considered substantially rehabilitated if the rehabilitation expenditures exceed the greater of the following.
    a. The adjusted basis of the property.
    b. $5,000.
5. If rehabilitated buildings are disposed of prematurely (before 5 years) or they cease to be qualifying property, part or all of the credit must be recaptured (See Table 13-1 in the Text).

C. Work Opportunity Tax Credit
1. Enacted to encourage employers to hire individuals from specified targeted and economically disadvantaged groups.

a. Examples of targeted persons include qualified ex-felons, high-risk youth, food stamp recipients, veterans, and persons receiving welfare benefits.

b. The employer must hire the individuals before December 31, 2003.

2. The credit generally is equal to 40% of the first $6,000 of wages (per eligible employee) for the first 12 months of employment.

3. The credit is not available for any wages paid to an employee after the first year of employment However, if the employee's first year overlaps two of the employer's tax years, the employer may take the credit over two tax years.

4. If the credit is elected, employer's tax deduction for wages is reduced by the amount of the credit.

5. For an employer to qualify for the 40% credit, the employees must be certified by a designated local agency and complete at least 400 hours of work for the employer.

6. To qualify for a reduced credit of 25%, the employee must be certified and have worked for 120 hours.

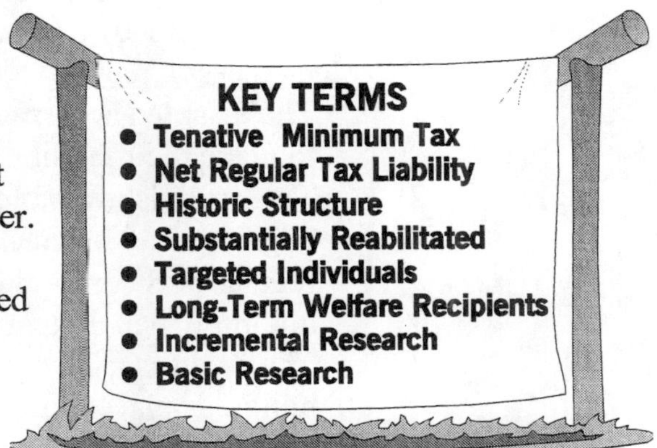


D. <u>Welfare-To-Work Credit</u>

1. This credit is available to employers hiring individuals who have been *long-term recipients* of family assistant welfare benefits.

a. Long-term recipient means receiving aid for an 18-month period ending on the hiring date.

b. The employer must hire the individuals before December 31, 2003.

2. Maximum credit is 35% of the first $10,000 of qualified wages paid in the first year plus 50% of the first $10,000 of wages paid in the second year.

a. If the employee's first two years overlaps two or more of the employer's tax years, the employer may take the credit over applicable tax years.

b. If the credit is elected, employer's tax deduction for wages is reduced by the amount of the credit.

3. Employers cannot take this credit and the work opportunity credit on the wages of the same individuals.

E. <u>Research Activities Credit</u>

1. A business credit is allowed for the purpose of encouraging research and experimentation.

2. The credit is available for qualifying expenditures paid or incurred through June 30, 2004.

3. The credit is the sum of two components: an incremental research activities credit and a basic research credit.

4. Incremental Research Activities Credit

a. Credit is 20% of the excess of qualified research expenses for the current taxable year over the base amount.

b. Not only can the credit be claimed on these costs but the expenditures can also be deducted in the year they are incurred using one of the following methods.

(1) Use the full credit and reduce the deduction for research by 100% of the credit.

(2) Retain the full deduction and reduce the credit by 100% of the credit times the maximum corporate tax rate (35%).

(3) Use the full credit, and capitalize the research expenses and amortize them over 60 months or more.

5. Basic Research Credit

a. A 20% credit is allowed for basic research expenditures incurred in excess of a base amount. Basic research payments are amounts paid to a qualified basic research organization.

b. Basic research is any original investigation for the advancement of scientific knowledge not having a specific commercial objective.

F. Disabled Access Credit

1. The disabled access credit is designed to encourage small business taxpayers to make their facilities more accessible to disabled individuals.

2. The credit is available for eligible access expenditures paid or incurred by an eligible small business (i.e., certain sole proprietorships, partnerships, and regular or S corporations) with gross receipts of not more than $1 million and not more than 30 employees.

3. The credit is calculated at the rate of 50% of the eligible expenditures made on buildings placed into service before November 5, 1990 that exceed $250 but do not exceed $10,250.

4. To the extent the credit is available, no deduction or credit is allowed under any other provision of the tax law (e.g., for depreciation).

G. Credit for Small Employer Pension Plan Startup Costs

1. Small businesses are allowed a nonrefundable credit for up to 50% of the cost of starting and maintaining qualified retirement plans for 3 years.

2. Maximum credit is $500 a year ($1,500 maximum total) and deduction for the startup costs is reduced by the amount of the credit.

3. Qualified small business is one with fewer than 100 employees who earned at least $5,000 of compensation.

H. Credit for Employer-Provided Child Care

1. Employers providing child care facilities for their employees may qualify for an annual credit of up to $150,000.

2. The credit is composed of two components.

a. Qualified child care expenses at a 25% credit rate. These expenditures include costs of acquiring, constructing, refurbishing and operating a child care facility.

b. Child care resource and referral services at a 10% rate. These costs include amounts under contracts to provide child care resource and referral services to employees.

3. The employer's deduction for providing child care is reduced by the amount of the credit taken. The basis of the property acquired, constructed, or refurbished is also reduced by the credit taken.

4. Recapture of a portion of the credit is required if the building ceases to be used as a child care facility within 10 years of when the credit is claimed.

I. Foreign Tax Credit

1. A tax credit (as an alternative to a deduction) may be claimed by individual or corporate taxpayers on income earned and subject to tax in a foreign country or U.S. possession.
2. The credit, which is generally more favorable than a deduction, is designed to mitigate double taxation.
3. The foreign tax credit is the *lesser* of the foreign taxes actually imposed or the overall limitation amount. The overall limitation on the credit is determined by the following formula.

$$\frac{\text{Foreign-source taxable income}}{\text{Worldwide Taxable Income}} \times \text{US tax before FTC} = \text{Overall limitation}$$

4. Unused foreign tax credits is carried back 2 years and then forward 5 years.

III. Corporate Alternative Minimum Tax (AMT)

A. Overview

1. The AMT is to ensure that corporations with substantial economic income pay at least a minimum amount of Federal income taxes.
2. The AMT is an important revenue raiser for the government.
3. Most *small corporations* are not subject to the AMT. A small corporation is:
   a. Initial test – Corporation has average annual gross receipts of no more than $5 million for the preceding 3 years.
   b. Ongoing test – If the initial test is passed, the corporation cannot have average annual gross receipts in excess of $7.5 million for any 3 year period.
   c. A corporation is automatically classified as a small corporation for its first year of existence.

B. AMT Formula

1. The AMT is separate from, but parallel to, the regular income tax system. If it applies, the corporation pays the regular tax and the AMT.
2. Alternative minimum taxable income (AMTI) less the AMT exemption is the base upon which the AMT is calculated.
   a. It starts with regular taxable income and essentially reconciles taxable income to AMTI by accounting for the differences between the regular income tax provisions and AMT provisions. See Exhibit 13-2 for a summary of the AMT formula.
   b. These reconciling items are referred to as AMT *adjustments* and *tax preferences*.

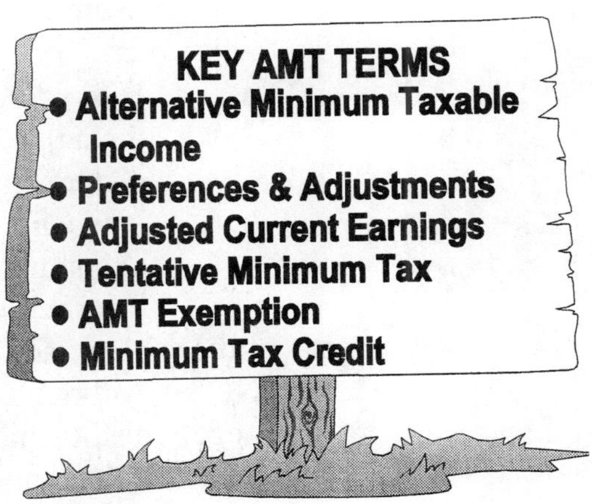

C. Tax Preferences

Always *increase* the AMTI.

Some of the specific preference are:

1. Percentage Depletion. This preference is equal to the excess of regular income tax depletion over the adjusted basis of the property at the end of the taxable year. If the cost of the property is fully recovered, all depletion is a preference item.
2. Private Activity Bond Interest. Tax-exempt interest on private activity bonds net of related expenses is a tax preference item.

**Exhibit 13-2**

**ALTERNATIVE MINIMUM TAX FOR CORPORATE TAXPAYERS**

| | |
|---|---|
| *Regular taxable income before NOL deduction* | |
| *Plus or minus:* | *Adjustments* |
| *Plus:* | *Tax preferences* |
| *Equals:* | *AMTI before AMT NOL and ACE adjustment* |
| *Plus or minus:* | *ACE adjustment* |
| *Equals:* | *AMTI before AMT NOL* |
| *Minus:* | *AMT NOL (possibly limited to 90%)* |
| *Equals:* | *Alternative minimum taxable income (AMTI )* |
| *Minus:* | *Exemption* |
| *Equals:* | *Alternative minimum tax base* |
| *Times:* | *20% rate* |
| *Equals:* | *Tentative AMT before AMT foreign tax credit* |
| *Minus:* | *AMT foreign tax credit (possibly limited to 90%)* |
| *Equals:* | *Tentative minimum tax* |
| *Minus:* | *Regular tax liability* |
| *Equals:* | *Alternative minimum tax (if amount is positive)* |

D. AMT Adjustments

1. With adjustments, it is necessary to determine not only the *amount* of the adjustment, but also whether the adjustment is *positive or negative*.
    a. If the *deduction* for regular tax exceeds the AMT deduction allowed, the adjustment is positive. Generally this occurs in the first years of deduction recognition. Opposite situation causes a negative adjustment.
    b. If *income* reported for regular tax is less than the AMT amount, the adjustment is positive. Generally this occurs in the first years of income recognition. Opposite situation causes a negative adjustment.

Some of the specific adjustments are:

2. NOL – Although the NOL is separately stated in Exhibit 13-2, it is actually a negative adjustment. The NOL cannot exceed 90% of AMTI. Thus it cannot be determined until all other adjustments and preferences are considered.
3. Depreciation of Post-1986 Real Property

a. Applies to real property placed in service after 1986 and before 1999.
b. The AMT depreciation is computed using a 40 year life and regular tax depreciation uses a shorter life (i.e., 27.5, 31.5, or 39 years).
c. The difference between AMT depreciation and regular tax depreciation is treated as a positive adjustment. After assets are fully depreciated for regular tax purposes, they continue to be depreciated for AMT purposes, resulting in a negative adjustment.

4. Depreciation of Post-1986 Personal Property
   a. Applies to personal property placed in service after 1986 and before 1999.
   b. Adjustment is the difference between MACRS deduction and the depreciation deduction using *alternative depreciation system* (ADS), which assumes longer lives and a slower method (150% vs 200%).
   c. The taxpayer may use ADS for regular tax purposes. If this election is made, no adjustments are required, because the depreciation deduction for both would be the same.
5. Pollution Control Facilities
   a. For property placed into service after 1986 and before 1999.
   b. The adjustment is the difference between the regular tax deduction (cost amortized over 60 months) and the AMT deduction (depreciated using ADS over the appropriate class life).
6. Completed Contract
   a. The completed contract method is not allowed for AMT purposes.
   b. Adjustment is the difference between the income that would be reported under the percentage of completion method and the amount reported using the completed contract method.
7. Adjusted Gain or Loss – Given that the basis of property may be different for regular tax and AMT due to the different depreciation systems used, the gain or loss on the disposition of a property will also be different for regular tax and AMT. Consequently, a positive or negative adjustment will be required in the year of a sale or other disposition.
8. Passive Activity Losses – The rules for computing passive losses for AMT proposes differ from those used for regular tax.

E. Adjusted Current Earnings (ACE) Adjustment
   1. ACE rules make up a third, separate but parallel tax system.
   2. The purpose of the ACE adjustment is to insure that large corporations with significant financial accounting income pay a fair amount of income tax.
   3. Corporations are subject to an AMT adjustment equal to 75% of the difference between ACE and AMTI before the ACE adjustment.
   4. The adjustment can be either a positive or negative amount. Any negative adjustment is limited to the aggregate of the positive adjustments under ACE for prior years reduced by the previously claimed negative adjustments.
   5. The starting point for computing ACE is AMTI before the NOL and ACE adjustments. Several adjustments involving excluded income, depreciation, and disallowed items, are made to AMTI in arriving at ACE.
   6. While ACE is similar to current earnings and profits, certain differences do exist.

F. AMT Rate and Exemption
   1. AMT rate is 20% on the AMT base which is equal to AMTI less the exemption.

2. The exemption amount for corporations is $40,000 and is reduced by 25% of the corporation's AMTI that exceeds $150,000. Thus, the exemption is completely phased out when AMTI reaches $310,000.

G. Minimum Tax Credit

1. The *minimum tax credit* treats the AMT like a prepayment of regular taxes for corporations. The regular tax liability may be reduced by AMT paid in previous years through use of the minimum tax credit. The AMT may *not* be offset by the minimum tax credit.

2. The AMT credit cannot be carried back but may be carried forward indefinitely.

H. Other Aspects of AMT

1. Corporations must include their potential AMT liability in the estimated payments of their Federal income taxes.

2. The only credit that can offset tentative minimum tax (TMT) is the foreign tax credit. Further, the credit can only reduce TMT by 90% after considering the AMT NOL.

> If a high-bracket corporation is subject to the AMT in one year and is expected to be subject to the regular tax the next year, income should be accelerated into the AMT year (when the marginal tax rate is relatively lower) and deductions should be deferred into the regular tax year (when the marginal income tax rate is relatively higher). This is the opposite of the classic income tax planning strategy of deferring income and accelerating deductions.

IV. Individual Alternative Minimum Tax

A. The individual AMT is very similar to the corporate AMT with many (but not all) of the adjustments and preferences being the same. While the individual AMT rates and exemptions are different than those for corporations, the objective of the tax is identical.

B. Differences Between Corporate and Individual AMT

1. The AMT rates for individuals are 26 % on the first $175,000 of the tax base and 28% for the tax base in excess of $175,000.

2. The special tax rates in effect for net capital gains (both pre and post Tax Act of 2003) apply when computing the AMT.

3. The Tax Act of 2003 also added special regular tax rates for dividends and these also apply when computing the AMT.

4. The AMT exemption amount for individuals depends on their filing status as indicated below.

| Filing Status | Exemption Amount Before Tax Act 2003 | Exemption Amount After Tax Act of 2003 |
|---|---|---|
| Married, Joint | $49,000 | $58,000 |
| Surviving Spouse | $49,000 | $58,000 |
| Single | $35,750 | $40,250 |
| Head of Household | $35,750 | $40,250 |
| Married, separate | $24,500 | $29,000 |

5. The exemption amount is phased out at a rate of 25% for every dollar that the AMTI exceeds the specified amounts given below.
   a. Married, joint and surviving spouse filers – $150,000.
   b. Single and head of household filers – $112,500.
   c. Married, separate filers – $75,000.
6. There is no ACE adjustment for individuals.
7. Some additional adjustments associated with itemized deductions, are required for individuals.
   a. The standard deduction and personal/dependency exemptions are not allowed for AMT.
   b. Taxes and miscellaneous itemized deductions subject to the 2%-of-AGI floor are not deductible.
   c. Medical expenses threshold is 10% of AGI rather than 7.5% as it is for regular tax.
   d. Interest deductions are also limited.
   e. Accelerating the taxation on incentive stock options.
8. The computation of the minimum tax is more complex because it is only based on the AMT generated as a result of timing differences.

## TEST FOR SELF-EVALUATION – CHAPTER 13

**True or False**

Indicate which of the following statements are true or false by circling the correct answer.

T F 1 A tax credit is always worth more than a tax deduction of an equal dollar amount.

T F 2. One rationale for the use of tax credits as a means of implementing tax policy is that tax credits provide benefits on a more equitable basis than do tax deductions.

T F 3. For a building to qualify as being substantially rehabilitated for purposes of the rehabilitation tax credit, the rehabilitation expenditures must exceed the greater of the adjusted basis of the property or $10,000.

T F 4. The credit for employer-provided child care covers both the costs of child care facilities and cost under contract to provide child care resource and referral services to employees.

T F 5. Unused foreign tax credit may be carried forward indefinitely.

T F 6. Unused general business tax credits must first be carried back for 2 years and then carried forward for 20 years.

T F 7. The welfare-to-work credit is available for the first 12 months of qualified wages of target employees whereas the work opportunity credit apples to the first 2 years of qualifying wages of the target employees.

T F 8. To encourage research activities, a research credit is allowed for expenditures incurred to develop new or improved business components of the taxpayer.

T F 9. The tax preference amount for percentage depletion is the excess of the regular tax deduction over the adjusted basis of the property.

T F 10. A food stamp recipient is one of the types of individuals targeted by the work opportunity tax credit.

T F 11. To prevent employers from receiving double benefits, the pension plan costs credit and the employer provided child care credit require the employer to reduce any expenses deducted by the amounts of the credits.

T F 12. Because the corporate and individual AMT have the same objective, the rules for computing the AMT for each are the same.

T F 13. "Adjustments" to taxable income in arriving at the alternative minimum taxable income may be either positive or negative.

T F 14. The adjustments that apply to corporations also apply to individuals.

T F 15. "Preference" items can either increase or decrease taxable income in arriving at AMTI.

T F 16. The corporate AMT is calculated using the same tax rate as that which applies to the individual AMT calculation.

T F 17. Taxpayers will pay whichever is higher, regular tax or AMT.

T F 18. The depreciation AMT adjustments for real and personalty apply to properties placed into service after 1986 and before 1999.

T F 19. To provide equity to the individual taxpayer, the regular tax liability may be reduced by the minimum tax credit for prior years' AMT liability attributable to timing differences.

T F 20. The adjusted current earnings adjustment is applicable to all businesses regardless of their form.

**Fill-in-the-Blanks**

Complete the following statements with the appropriate word(s) or amount(s).

1. While a tax deduction merely reduces ________, a tax credit reduces the ________.

2. A tax credit is available for rehabilitation expenditures incurred on certain commercial and industrial buildings as well as ________. A ________% tax credit is allowed on these structures.

3. The ________ method is applied to the carryovers, carrybacks, and the utilization of general business credits earned during a particular year.

4. The credit for ________ is equal to 50% of startup or maintaining costs but the credit cannot exceed $500 a year for ________ years. The credit for ________ is limited to 150,000 annually. If within ________ years, the facility ceases to be used for its qualified purpose, a portion of the credit previously claimed will be recaptured.

5. The disabled access credit is available at the rate of ________ percent of the eligible expenditures that exceed ________ but do not exceed ________.

6. A taxpayer may either claim a ________ or a ________ with respect to taxes paid on income earned from foreign sources.

7. For any year, the general business credit is limited to the taxpayers ________ reduced by the greater of the ________ or ________ percent of regular tax liability that exceeds ________.

8. The ________ credit is available to employers hiring individuals who have been ________ recipients of welfare benefits.

9. The research activities credit is the sum of two components: the __________ credit and the __________ credit.

10. The work opportunity tax credit is equal to ________ percent of the first ________ of wages paid per eligible employee for the first year of employment.

11. If a taxpayer claims the work opportunity tax credit or welfare-to-work credit, the ________ for wages is reduced by the amount of the credit.

12. A two-tier rate schedule applies to a noncorporate taxpayer's alternative minimum tax base: _________ percent of the tax base up the first $175,000 and _________ percent of the tax base in excess of $175,000.

13. _________ is the sum of the regular taxable income, plus or minus adjustments, plus tax preferences.

14 A corporation is __________ classified as a __________ corporation for AMT purposes in the first year of its existence.

15. Income from _________ is not included in regular taxable income but is included in AMTI.

16. For the disabled access credit, an eligible small business is one that during the previous year either had gross receipts of not more than ________ or had no more than ________ employees.

17. The objective of the corporate and individual AMT is to make sure that taxpayers who have more ________ than that reflected in their taxable income pay a ________ of Federal taxes.

18. Corporations are subject to an AMT adjustment equal to _________ percent of the difference between ACE and the AMTI before the ACE adjustment.

19. While the long-term contract method of _________ may be used for regular tax , AMT requires the use of_________.

20. A small employer for the pension plan startup costs credit is one that has fewer than _________ employees who earned at least _________ of compensation.

## Multiple Choice

Choose the best answer for each of the following questions.

____ 1. The Sun corporation has a $5,000 expense that it can either take as a deduction or used for a credit. The credit allowable is 30% of the expense. When should Sun use the expense for the credit rather than the deduction?

a. If Sun's marginal tax rate is 25%.
b. If Sun's marginal tax rate is 34%.
c. If Sun is subject to the AMT.
d. Sun should always select a credit over a deduction.

____ 2. Won placed into service a non-historic building 2 ½ years ago. He incurred qualifying rehabilitation expenditures of $800,000 on the building for which he took a rehabilitation tax credit. If Won sold the building at a loss this year, what amount of rehabilitation tax credit recapture is due?
a. $32,000.
b. $48,000.
c. $80,000.
d. None because the building was disposed of at a loss.

____ 3. Select the *incorrect* statement below pertaining to the research activities credit.
a. The credit is allowed for qualifying costs incurred through June 30, 2004.
b. The incremental research activities credit is 20% of the amount of qualified research expenses that exceeds the base amount.
c. Qualifying expenditures eligible for the full research credit, also can be fully expensed in the year incurred.
d. Corporations, but not S corporations or personal service corporations, are eligible for the basic research credit.
e. Each of the above statements is correct.

____ 4. Burk Corporation had $250,000 in income from Scotland which imposes a 50% income tax on income earned within its borders. Burk also had income of $500,000 from within the United States. The tentative U.S. tax on the $750,000 total income is $255,000. What is Burk's foreign tax credit for the year?
a. $0.
b. $80,750.
c. $85,000.
d. $125,000.

____ 5. Lyon Corporation spent $75,000 to rehabilitate a certified historic structure located in the inner city. Lyon had acquired the building early this year for $50,000. What is the amount of the rehabilitation expenditures credit available to Lyon?
a. $7,500.
b. $12,500.
c. $15,000.
d. $25,000.

____ 6. Horn Corporation's general business credit for the year is $85,000. The business's net income tax is $125,000, while the tentative alternative minimum tax is $50,000. Assuming Horn has no other credits for the year, the general business credit allowed for the year is what amount?
a. $85,000.
b. $75,000.
c. $50,000.
d. $25,000.

____ 7. Blue Corporation, a mineral production company, incurred $42,000 of percentage depletion for regular tax purposes $42,000 this year. Blue Corporation's taxable income from the property was $100,000 and its adjusted basis in the property at the beginning of the year was $20,000. Which of the following is correct?

a. No amount is deductible for AMT purposes.
b. A positive adjustment is required.
c. A negative adjustment is required.
d. A positive adjustment is required in this year and a negative adjustment is required next year.

____ 8. The general business credit does *not* include of which of the following credits?
a. Tax credit for rehabilitation expenditures.
b. Disabled access credit.
c. Low-income housing credit.
d. Foreign tax credit.

____ 9. Skyline Corporation, desiring to make their business more accessible to disabled individuals, incurred $8,000 in eligible access expenditures. What is the amount of disabled access credit arising from these expenditures?
a. $4,000.
b. $3,875.
c. $1,938.
d. $1,600.

____ 10. During the current year, Green Hills Corporation had $150,000 in income from Ireland which imposes a 10% income tax on income earned within its borders. Green Hills also had income of $300,000 from within the United States. The tentative U.S. tax on the $450,000 total income is $153,000. How much is Green Hill's foreign tax credit for the year?
a. $0.
b. $15,000.
c. $15,300.
d. $51,000.

____ 11. Good Hands Company hires four individuals who qualify for the work opportunity tax credit. They each earned wages $8,000 during their first year of employment and $10,000 in the second year. What is the amount of the credit and the wages deduction for Good Hands?
a. $8,400; $23,600.
b. $8,400; $32,000.
c. $11,200; $20,800.
d. $11,200; $32,000.

____ 12. Which of the following is *not* a preference item or an adjustment for purposes of computing the alternative minimum tax?
a. Unrealized appreciation element on charitable contributions to public charities made during the year.
b. Passive activity losses utilized in computing taxable income.
c. Depreciation expense claimed for income tax purposes versus depreciation expense calculated over a longer life using a slower rate for AMT purposes.
d. The difference between the income reported under the percentage of completion method and the amount reported using the completed contract method.

____ 13. A married taxpayer filing a joint return has alternative minimum taxable income of $200,000. For purposes of the alternative minimum tax computation, what is the amount of the exemption after the Tax Act of 2003 adjustment?

a. $58,000.
b. $45,500.
c. $45,000.
d. $32,500.

____ 14. Which of the following is *not* true with respect to the alternative minimum tax?

a. The corporate AMT rate is 26%.
b. Corporations are likely to be subject to the AMT if they rely heavily on the cost recovery deduction.
c. The maximum corporate exemption amount is $40,000.
d. Many of the AMT adjustments are merely timing differences in the recognition between regular tax and AMT.

____ 15. As of 12/31/2003, Timothy, a single individual, had the following transactions.

| | |
|---|---|
| Taxable income | $220,500 |
| State income taxes | 20,000 |
| Qualified residential interest | 50,000 |
| Excess depreciation on fixed assets | 52,000 |
| Excess percentage depletion | 40,000 |

Based on the above, what is Timothy's tentative AMT liability for 2003?

a. $64,260.
b. $84,000.
c. $103,600.
d. None of the above.

____ 16. For the current year, Bear Corporation's regular tax liability is $15,000 before considering the AMT. Bear's AMTI is $140,000. Determine the total amount of tax liability for the year.

a. $43,000.
b. $35,000.
c. $20,000.
d. $15,000.

____ 17. Nest Corporation provides the following information.

| | | |
|---|---|---|
| Taxable income | $300,000 | |
| Excess Depreciation on fixed assets | | 40,000 |
| Excess Pollution control facility amortization | | 10,000 |
| Excess charitable contributions | | 25,000 |
| Adjusted Current Earnings | | 380,000 |

Based on the above, what is Nest's AMTI?

a. $350,000.
b. $372,500.
c. $380,000.
d. $385,000.

____ 18. Which of the following is not allowed as an itemized deduction for the individual AMT calculation?

a. Charitable contributions.
b. Miscellaneous itemized deduction subject to the 2%-of-AGI floor.
c. Medical expenses in excess of 10% of AGI.
d. Qualified interest on the taxpayer's principal place of residence.

____ 19. Marcel Corporation constructed a qualified child care facility for $200,000. The salaries for the child care providers amounted to$60,000 and other administrative costs were $30,000. How much is Marcel's employer-provided child care credit?

a. $72,500.
b. $65,000.
c. $50,000.
d. $5,000.

____ 20. Which of the following statements is *not* true?

a. AMT NOL can reduce AMTI by up to 90% and the foreign tax credit can reduce the remaining tentative AMT by up to 90%.
b. Minimum tax credit is computed differently for corporations and individuals.
c. Real property placed into service in the current year is not subject to an AMT depreciation adjustment.
d. The ACE rules make up a third, separate tax system, that parallels both the AMT and regular tax.
e. All of the above statements are true.

____ 21. The taxpayer has a tentative minimum tax of $80,000 and a regular tax of $60,000. Which of the following statements is *not* true?

a. The taxpayer's AMT is $20,000.
b. If the taxpayer has a general business tax credit, it can reduced the tentative minimum tax by up to $71,000.
c. The taxpayer will pay $80,000 in taxes.
d. If the taxpayer is a corporation, its minimum tax credit is $20,000.
e. All of the above are true.

____ 22. If Green Corporation in its first operating year has a taxable income of $200,000, positive adjustments of $190,000 and preferences of $70,000. What is its AMT?

a. $112,000.
b. $84,000.
c. $52,000.
d. $Zero.

____ 23. Boojee Corporation spent $75,000 to rehabilitate a building that had originally been placed in service in 1921 in the inner city. Boojee had acquired the building early this year for $100,000. What is the amount of the rehabilitation expenditures credit available to Boojee?

a. $Zero.
b. $15,000.
c. $17,500.
d. $35,000.

____ 24. AMT adjustments and preferences for which of the following items can be avoided if the taxpayer elects to write off the expenditures for regular tax purposes using the same method as that required for AMT purposes?

a. Depletion.
b. Depreciation of post-1986 personal property.
c. Pollution control facilities costs.
d. Accounting for long-term contracts.
e. All of the above.

____ 25. Rose Corporation began a pension plan for its 40 employees during the current year. The costs of establishing the plan was $1,500. The maintenance cost is $500 each year. What is the maximum pension plan startup costs credit Rose is allowed currently and in the future?

a. Current year $750, future years $250.
b. Current year $750, next two years $250.
c. Current year $500, next two years $250.
d. Current year $500, not available in future years.

**Short Answer**

1. Indicate whether the following AMT items are adjustments or preferences.

a. State and local taxes of individuals who itemized deductions.
b. Tax-exempt interest on private activity bonds.
c. Percentage depletion in excess of the asset's basis.
d. Amortized cost of pollution control facilities placed into service after 1986 and before 1999 that exceeds the depreciation allowed under ADS.
e. Excess MACRS over ADS depreciation on property placed in service after 1986 and before 1999.
f. Miscellaneous itemized deductions that are subject to the 2%-of-AGI limitation.
g. The adjusted current earnings for corporations.
h. Personal and dependency exemptions amounts for individuals.

2. Shawna, who is single, calculates her AMTI to be $230,000 and has a foreign tax credit of $2,000 and a dependent care credit of $400. Her regular tax liability is $47,350. Calculate her AMT for 2003 using exemption amount in effect after the Tax Act of 2003.

## SOLUTIONS TO CHAPTER 13 QUESTIONS

**True or False**

1. T
2. T
3. F The expenditures must exceed the greater of the adjusted basis or $5,000.
4. T
5. F The credit may be carried back 2 years and forward 5 years.
6. F The credit may be carried back 1 year and forward 20 years.
7. F The welfare-to-work applies to the first 2 years of wages and the work opportunity applies only to the first year.
8. T
9. T
10. T
11. T
12. F Corporate AMT has preferences that the individuals do not have such as ACE and there are adjustments that are solely for individuals such as no standard deduction.
13. T
14. F Differences (e.g., ACE adjustment) do exist between the two.
15. F Tax preferences always are added to taxable income in arriving at AMTI while adjustments may be either positive or negative.
16. F The individual rates are 26% on the first $175,000 of the tax base and 28% on the tax base in excess of $175,000, while the corporate rate is 20%.
17. F If the AMT applies, taxpayers pay both the regular tax and the AMT.
18. T
19. T
20. F The adjusted current earnings adjustment applies only to C corporations.

**Fill-in-the-Blanks**

1. taxable income, tax liability
2. certified historic structures, 20
3. FIFO
4. small employer pension plan startup costs, 3, employer-provided child care, 10
5. 50, $250, $10,250
6. deduction, credit
7. net income tax, tentative minimum tax, 25, $25,000
8. welfare-to-work, long-term
9. incremental research activities, basic research
10. 35, $6,000
11. tax deduction
12. 26, 28
13. Alternative minimum taxable income
14. automatically, small
15. private activity bonds
16. $1 million, 30 full-time
17. economic income, fair share

18. 75
19. completed contract, percentage of completion
20. 100, $5,000

## Multiple Choice

1. a — If the marginal rate is 25%, the deduction's reduction in the tax liability is $1,250 = 5,000 X 25%, where as the credit's reduction is $1,500 = 5,000 X 30%. If the marginal rate is higher than 30%, the deduction provides more tax benefit.

2. b

| | |
|---|---:|
| Original credit ($800,000 X .10) | $ 80,000 |
| Recapture percentage | X 60% |
| Recapture tax | $ 48,000 |

3. c — The expense must be reduced by 100% of the credit.
4. c — $85,000. (250,000 ÷ 750,000) X 255,000 = 85,000 and 85,000 < 125,000
5. c — $15,000. 75,000 X 20%
6. b

| | |
|---|---:|
| Net income tax | $125,000 |
| Less: The greater of | |
| ▸ 50,000 (tentative minimum tax) | |
| ▸ 25,000 [25% X (125,000 - 25,000)] | -50,000 |
| Allowable business credit | $ 75,000 |

7. b — Percentage depletion is a preference item and preference items only require positive adjustments.
8. d
9. b — $3,875. (8,000 - 250) X 50%
10. b — $15,000. (150,000 ÷ 450,000) X 153,000 = 51,000. But, the maximum credit is limited to the amount of foreign tax actually paid (i.e., 15,000).
11. a — $8,400, $23,600. 4 X 6,000 X 35% = 8,400. 32,000 - 8,400 = 23,600.
12. a
13. b — $45,500. 58,000 - [(200,000 - 150,000) X .25]
14. a
15. d

| | |
|---|---:|
| AMT Base = 220,500 + 20,000 + 52,000 + 40,000 | $332,500 |
| Exemption amount | 0 |
| Tentative minimum tax liability: 175,000 X 26% | 45,500 |
| (332,500 - 175,000) X 28% | + 44,100 |
| Tentative minimum tax | $ 89,600 |

16. c — $20,000.

| | |
|---|---:|
| AMTI | $140,000 |
| Less: Exemption | - 40,000 |
| AMT Base | 100,000 |
| Rate | X 20 % |
| Tentative AMT | $ 20,000 |

Because the tentative AMT is higher than the regular tax liability, the tentative AMT amount is payable.
15,000 regular tax + 5,000 AMT (20,000 - 15,000).

17. b — $372,500. AMTI before ACE: 300,000 + 40,000 + 10,000 = 350,000.
ACE adjustment: 380,000 - 350,000 = 30,000 X 75% = 22,500.
350,000 + 22,500 = 372,500.

18. b

19. a $72,500. 25% X (200,000 + 60,000 + 30,000).

20. a The NOL plus the foreign tax credit cannot reduce the tentative AMT by more than 90%. Therefore, the foreign tax credit may be limited to less than 90% of tentative AMT.

21. b Foreign tax credit can reduce TMT by up to 90% not the general business tax credit.

22. d Corporations are not subject to the AMT in their first year of existence.

23. a The rehabilitation expenditures credit is not available because the building has not been substantially rehabilitated (i.e., the amount of the expenditures incurred did not exceed the greater of $5,000 or the adjusted basis of the building prior to the rehabilitation).

24. e

25. c $500, $250 for 2 years. Maximum is $500 per year. Maximum credit is 50% of costs for 3 years. 50% X 500 = 250.

**Short Answer**

1.
   a. Adjustment.
   b. Preference.
   c. Preference.
   d. Adjustment.
   e. Adjustment.
   f. Adjustment.
   g. Adjustment.
   h. Adjustment.

2.

| | |
|---|---|
| AMTI | $230,000 |
| Less: Exemption $40,250 - [($230,000 - $112,500) X 25%] | - 10,875 |
| Alternative minimum tax base | 219,125 |
| Times: 26% X $175,000 | 45,500 |
| 28% X ($219,125 - $175,000) | 12,355 |
| Tentative minimum tax before FTC | 57,855 |
| Less foreign tax credit | 2,000 |
| Tentative minimum tax | 55,855 |
| Less regular tax | 47,350 |
| AMT | $ 8,505 |

# Chapter 14
# Comparative Forms of Doing Business

## CHAPTER HIGHLIGHTS

A variety of entity forms are available for conducting business. The decision as to which entity form would be best for the business needs to be based on nontax as well as tax factors. Further, the decision should consider the expected life of the entity. The business form that may be the most effective when the business is young may not be appropriate when the entity has matured. This chapter compares the tax and nontax factors that should be considered when selecting a business form. The entities examined are sole proprietorships, the various partnership forms, limited liability companies, regular C corporations, and S corporations.

I. Forms of Doing Business
   A. <u>Principal Forms</u>
      1. The principal legal forms within which to conduct business are:
         a. sole proprietorship,
         b. partnership,
         c. limited liability entity, and
         d. corporation.
      2. For Federal tax purposes, the same forms are available, however, the corporation can be structured as either of the following forms:
         a. C (regular) corporation, or
         b. S corporation.
      3. Taxpayers are generally bound for tax purposes by the legal form they choose.
         a. An exception is the ability of S corporations and limited liability companies to be taxed similar to partnerships.
         b. Taxpayers may control which set of tax rules apply to their business. Using the so called check-the-box procedures, certain businesses can assure partnership treatment.
      4. Each possible tax entity reports the results of its business operations for the year using the following forms.
         a. Sole proprietorship: Schedule C of Form 1040.
         b. Partnership and limited liability companies: Form 1065.
         c. Corporation: Form 1120.
         d. S corporation: Form 1120S.

B. Limited Liability Companies (LLC)

1. The LLC is a hybrid form of business. It has the corporate characteristic of limited liability for the owners and the tax characteristics of a partnership.
2. All of the states now permit this legal form for conducting business.
3. The most frequently cited benefit of an LLC is the limited liability protection provided to its owners. Some additional benefits of LLCs when compared with other forms of ownership are the following.
   a. Advantages over S corporations
      (1) Greater flexibility in terms of the number of owners, types of owners, special allocation opportunities, and capital structure.
      (2) Inclusion of entity debt in the partner's ownership basis.
      (3) More liberal requirements on recognition of gain on contributions of appreciated property by an owner (determined under § 721 rather than § 351).
      (4) For securities law purposes, an ownership in a LLC is not generally a security but S corporation ownership is a security.
   b. Advantages over C corporations
      (1) Ability to pass tax attributes through to the owners.
      (2) Absence of double taxation.
   c. Advantages over limited partnerships
      (1) Right of all owners to participate in managing the business.
      (2) Ability of all owners to have limited liability (no need for a general partner).
      (3) For securities law purposes, an ownership interest in a limited partnership *is* classified as a security.
   d. Advantages over general partnership
      (1) Ability of owners to have limited liability.
      (2) Greater continuity of life.
      (3) Able to limit an owner's ability to withdraw from the business.
4. Among the disadvantages associated with LLCs are the following.
   a. Absence of a developed body of case law on LLCs.
   b. Most states require that there be at least two owners.
   c. Inability to qualify for § 1244 ordinary loss treatment.

II. Nontax Factors

A. Taxes are one of many factors that should be considered when making an business decision. Above all, a business decision should make economic sense. The following nontax factors are important to the decision of selecting an entity form.

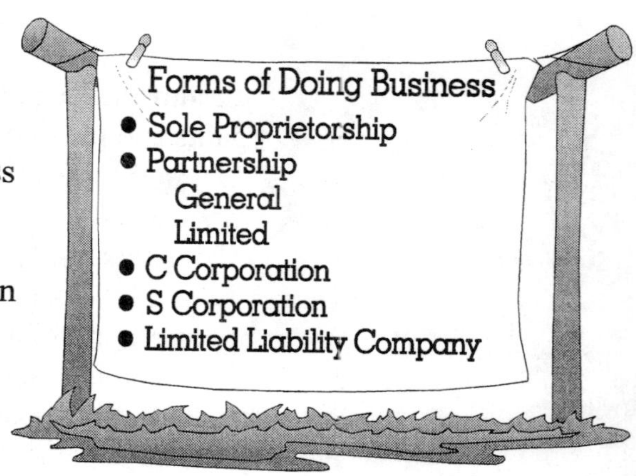


B. Capital Formation

1. The ability of an entity to raise capital varies depending on the entity form selected.
2. Corporate form offers the greatest ease and potential for raising capital. The sole proprietorship offers the least potential.

C. Limited Liability

1. The ability to limit the owner's ultimate financial liability is generally a relevant factor when selecting an entity form.
2. Both the regular corporation and the S corporation forms provide limited liability to their owners but not with regard to the performance of professional services.
3. A limited partnership can achieve this objective for the limited partners. The general partner may also enjoy limited liability when the general partner is a corporation.
4. Sole proprietorships and general partnerships do not possesses this attribute.

D. Other Factors – Nontax factors that may be important in selecting an entity form include:

1. Estimated life of the business.
2. Number of owners and their roles in the management of the business.
3. Freedom of choice in transferring ownership interests.
4. Organizational formality including the related cost and extent of governmental regulation.

III. Single Versus Double Taxation

A. Overall Impact on Entity and Owners

1. Partnerships, limited liability entities, and sole proprietorships are subject to a single layer of taxation.
   a. Owners of these entities, and not the business, are taxed on the earnings.
   b. The entities are not considered as being separate from their owners, therefore, they are tax reporting entities rather than tax paying entities.
2. Corporations, in contrast, are taxable entities. Corporate owners are further subject to tax on any distributions paid out of corporate earning. This is *double taxation.*
   a. Double taxation is the major disadvantage cited of the corporate form.
   b. The S corporation provides a method of avoiding the double taxation on corporations. The S corporation, like a partnership, is a tax reporting rather than a tax paying entity. Thus, the owners are taxed on the entity earnings.
   c. S corporations can be subject to entity level taxes in certain circumstances (see Chapter 11 outline headings for tax on built-in gains and passive investment income penalty tax).

B. Alternative Minimum Tax (AMT)

1. Each form of business is affected by the AMT either directly, as with corporations and sole proprietorships, or indirectly, as with partnerships, limited liability entities, and S corporations.
2. When considering AMT tax rates, corporations have an advantage. The corporate rate is 20% as compared to noncorporate rates of 26% and 28%.
3. However, corporations are subject to a special adjustment for adjusted current earnings (ACE adjustment) which may more than offset any rate advantage corporations enjoy.
4. AMT does not apply to small corporations (about 95% of all corporations) who meet both of the following tests.

a. Average annual gross receipts are less than $5 million for three tax years. New corporations are considered to automatically meet this requirement for their first year.

b. Average annual gross receipts are less than $7.5 million for every subsequent three year period.

C. State Taxation – Besides Federal taxation, state and local taxation consequences should be considered when selecting a business form. For example, not all states recognize an S corporation and will treat it as a C corporation for tax purposes.

IV. Minimizing Double Taxation

A. Only C corporations are subject to double taxation. The following techniques help avoid the double taxation of corporate income.

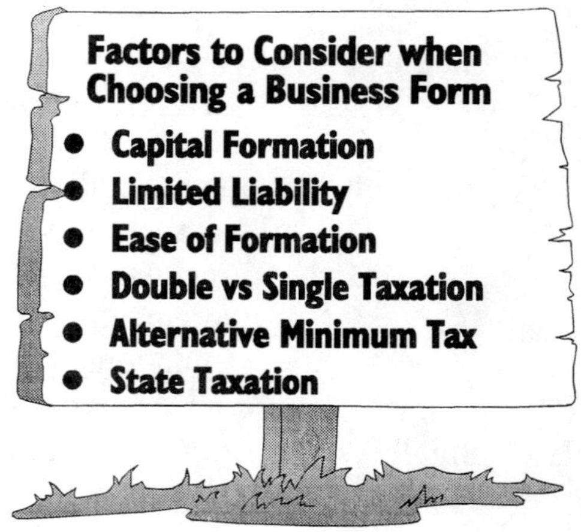


B. Making Deductible Distributions

1. This technique attempts to transfer assets of the entity to the owners in such a manner as to make the transfers deductible at the corporate level. Ideally, this technique is used to reduce the corporate taxable income to zero and effectively avoid the potential for double taxation.

2. Some methods for achieving this goal are the following.

a. Salaries paid to shareholder-employees.

b. Lease or rents paid to shareholders-lessors.

c. Interest payments to shareholder-creditors.

d. All of the above items are subject to the test of reasonableness.

C. Not Making Distributions

1. Corporations and its owners can avoid double taxation by simply having the corporation not make any distributions to the shareholders.

2. The problem with this technique is that the accumulated earnings tax can be applied by the IRS when the accumulations are beyond the reasonable business needs of the corporation.

3. If this method is effective, the second layer of tax can be avoided completely and when the shareholder dies the basis of the stock is stepped-up to its FMV.

D. Return of Capital Distributions

1. The effect of double taxation can be reduced if the distributions to the owners can qualify for return of capital treatment.

2. If distributions are made when E&P is low or negative or the distributions are classified as stock redemptions, return of capital treatment is possible.

3. Recovery of capital or stock basis is tax-free and any excess is a capital gain.

E. Electing S Corporation Status

1. S corporations are pass-through entities and thus avoid the double taxation.

2. There are substantial limitations on a corporation's ability to switch from a C status to S status.

3. The ability of the corporation to continue to meet the S status requirements should be considered before an S election is made.

4. Switching from a C corporation to an S corporation may subject the S corporation to entity level taxes such as the built-in-gains tax and passive investment income tax.

V. Conduit versus Entity Treatment

A. Under the conduit approach, the entity is viewed as merely an extension of the owners, whereas, under the entity approach, the business is regarded as being separate and distinct from its owners.

1. Both of these approaches may be applied to the partnership and the various corporate tax entities.
2. Since the owner and the entity are essentially the same in a sole proprietorship, only the conduit approach is applicable to sole proprietorships.

B. Effect on Recognition at Time of Contributions to the Entity

1. Partnerships
   a. The conduit approach, applied under § 721, allows contributions to a partnership in exchange for a partnership interest, to be tax-free for both the partnership and the partners.
   b. The partnership has a substituted basis in the assets contributed and the partner's have a carryover basis in their partnership interest.
2. Corporations – C and S
   a. Since the entity approach generally applies to corporations, contributions by a shareholder to the corporation would result in recognized gain or loss.
   b. However, if the requirements of § 351 are met, the conduit concept applies and the owners receive similar treatment as partners contributing to a partnership.
3. Special allocations of precontribution gains are mandatory for partnerships and not allowed for C or S corporations.

C. Effect on Basis of Ownership Interest

1. Partnerships and Limited Liability Entities
   a. The profit or loss of the business adds to or reduces the owner's basis in the entity.
   b. The owners also include in their basis their proportionate share of the entity's liabilities. An increase or decrease in the entity's liabilities affects the ownership basis accordingly.
2. Corporations – C and S
   a. The basis in a shareholder's stock is not adjusted for profits, losses, or liabilities of a C corporation.
   b. The S corporation treatment is similar to both partnerships and C corporations. Like a partnership, business profits or losses impact the shareholder's stock basis. Since the shareholders enjoy limited liability protection, like in a C corporation, they generally do not add any of the corporation's liabilities to their basis.

D. Effect on Results of Operations

1. Flow-Through Entities
   a. Flow-through entity (including S corporations) are merely tax reporters and the owners are taxed on the results from operations. Thus, there is only one level of tax on the results from operations.

b. Any item that is subject to special treatment on an owners's tax return must be reported separately by the entity to the owners rather than being reported as part of ordinary income.

2. C Corporations

a. The C corporation income is taxed at the entity level and then at the shareholder when the corporation makes a distribution and of its earnings and profits in the form of a dividend.

b. Distributions that qualify as stock redemptions or as liquidating distributions for C corporations receive sale or exchange treatment and consequently the return of the owner's stock basis is tax-free.

3. S corporations may be subject to tax at the entity level for the built-in-gains tax and passive investment income tax in certain circumstances (see Chapter 11 outline for tax on built-in gains and passive investment income).

E. <u>Effect on Recognition at Time of Distribution</u>

1. Partnerships and Limited Liability Entities

a. As a result of the conduit approach, distributions from the entity to the owners are generally not taxable.

b. The tax-free treatment is limited to the owners basis.

2. Corporations – C and S

a. Distributions from a C corporation are taxable to the extent they are payments out of the corporation's E&P. Distributions of appreciated property trigger gain recognition at the corporate level as well.

b. An S corporation applies both the entity and conduit approach. At the entity level, an S corporation must recognize gain on the distribution of appreciated property. At the shareholder level, the owners are not taxable on the distribution to the extent of their basis in their stock.

F. <u>Effect on Passive Activity Losses (PAL)</u>

1. The PAL rules apply to both flow-through entities at the owner level and to personal service corporations and closely held C corporations at the entity level.

a. A corporation is closely held when more than 50% of the value of the stock at any time during the last half of the year is owned by not more than 5 taxpayers.

b. A personal service corporation is a corporation in which personal services are provided by shareholder-employees who own more than 10% of the corporation.

2. The PAL limitations do not apply to other regular C corporations.

G. <u>Effect on At-Risk Rules</u>

1. The at-risk rules apply to both flow-through entities at the owner level and to closely held C corporations. They do not apply to other regular corporations.

2. The At-risk rules impact partnerships and limited liability entities more than S corporations because owners of partnerships and limited liability entities are allowed to add their proportionate share of the entity's liabilities to their basis. The owners may not be at-risk for this amount.

H. <u>Effect on Special Allocations</u>

1. The advantageous opportunity to make special allocations is available to limited liability entities and partnerships.

2. Special allocations are not permitted for C or S corporations. An S corporation must make allocations on a per-share, per-day basis.

a. The ability to allocate profits, losses, and capital differently.
b. The required allocation for the difference between the adjusted basis and the fair market value of contributed property.
c. The special allocation of any item as long as the allocation has substantial economic effect.
d. Note that most special allocations are elective rather than mandatory.

VI. Disposition of a Business or an Ownership Interest

A. Sole Proprietorships

1. Regardless of the form of the transaction, the sale of a sole proprietorship is treated as the sale of individual assets.
2. Gains and losses must be calculated for each asset separately. The character of the asset (ordinary, § 1231, capital) will determine the treatment of the gain or loss.
3. Goodwill versus Covenant Not to Compete
   a. Excess of the amount realized over the FMV of the assets is goodwill (capital asset) or a covenant not to compete (ordinary income).
   b. Goodwill and covenants not to compete are amortized over 15 years.

B. Partnerships and Limited Liability Entities

1. The form which the sale of an ownership interest takes is important to the seller of the interest.
   a. If structured as the sale of assets, the treatment is the same as that described above for the sale of a sole proprietorship.
   b. If structured as the sale of an ownership interest, the transaction is treated as the sale of a capital asset subject to ordinary income potential for unrealized receivables and substantially appreciated inventory.
2. Form of the purchase transaction takes does not affect the results for the buyer.

C. C Corporations

1. The buyers and the sellers are concerned with the form of the transaction.
2. Sellers will prefer a stock sale because they receive capital treatment for their realized gains, it's a less complex transaction, and a corporate level tax on the sale can be avoided. The buyer's basis in the stock will be equal to the sales price. The basis of the corporation's assets is unaffected by the transaction.
3. Buyers would prefer the transaction to be characterized as the sale of corporate assets so as to receive a stepped up basis in the corporate assets equal to the purchase price. A sale of the assets will cause gain recognition at the entity level as well as the owner (seller) level.

D. S Corporations

1. Since the S corporation is a corporation, the provisions discussed above for a C corporation apply.
2. Any gain realized at the entity level is passed through to the owner and is taxed on their returns.

E. The text Concept Summary 14-1 reviews the tax treatment when disposing of a business.

VII. Overall Comparison of Forms of Doing Business

Concept Summary 14-2 in the text provides a detailed comparison of the tax consequences of the various forms of doing business.

## TEST FOR SELF-EVALUATION - CHAPTER 14

**True or False**

Indicate which of the following statements are true or false by circling the correct answer.

T F 1. When selecting the initial entity form for a business, the entity's expected life cycle should be taken into consideration.

T F 2. The principal legal forms for conducting a business are the same as the forms recognized for Federal tax purposes.

T F 3. To avoid double taxation, without any possible negative tax consequences, a corporation can merely fail to make distributions to its shareholders.

T F 4. A business organized as a sole proprietorship will generally have higher tax rates than a business organized as a S corporation.

T F 5 A LLC offers greater flexibility in terms of types of owners and special allocation opportunities when compared with an S corporation.

T F 6. The ability for raising capital is one of the advantages C corporations have over partnerships and S corporations.

T F 7. Limited liability is possible for all the owners of a partnership when operating as a limited liability entity or when structured as a limited partnership with a corporation as the general partner.

T F 8. Of the flow-through entities, only the S corporation is ever subject to an entity level Federal income tax.

T F 9. Business entities set up as S corporations or limited liability companies use the same tax form for filing their informational returns.

T F 10. Each state now recognizes the S corporation election for state tax purposes.

T F 11. A C corporation is the only entity with the possibility of having its income subject to double taxation.

T F 12. The IRS can challenge the compensation to a shareholder-employee if it does not appear to be reasonable.

T F 13. Both S corporations and partnerships are subject to the built-in gains tax.

T F 14. Corporate distributions to the shareholders can be taxed as ordinary income or as capital gains.

T F 15. When selling a corporate business whose assets have depreciated, the buyer and seller would prefer to structure the transaction as a sale of the assets.

**Fill-in-the-Blanks**

Complete the following statements with the appropriate word(s) or amount(s).

1. An individual conducting a ________ files Schedule C of Form 1040, a ________ files Form 1065, a ________ files Form 1120, and an ________ files Form 1120S.

2. A ________ is a hybrid business form which combines the corporate characteristic of limited liability for the owners with the tax characteristics of the partnership.

3. If an owner of a ________ receives a distribution of appreciated property, gain is recognized at the entity level to the extent of the appreciation.

4. If salary payments to an employee-shareholder are classified as unreasonable, the corporation's taxable income ________ and the shareholder's taxable income ________.

5. The decision as to which entity form is best for a business should be based on ________ and ________ factors.

6. The AMT rate for a corporation is ________ and for noncorporate taxpayers the rates are ________ and ________.

7. Assuming no liabilities are involved in the transaction, after a § 721 contribution by a partner to a new partnership, the partner's basis in the partnership is a ________ basis and the partnership's basis in the contributed assets is a ________ basis.

8. In a ________ and a ________, the owners increase their ownership basis by their share of profits and liabilities, whereas the owners of a ________ increase their ownership basis only by their share of profits and loans made by the owner to the entity.

9. The profits of a ________ do not affect the ownership basis of the owners.

10. The sale of a ________ business is always treated as the sale of the individual asset by the buyer and the seller.

11. While the S corporation generally is tax reporter rather than a taxpayer, it may be subject to tax on ________ and on ________.

12. In 2003, the maximum tax rate for C corporation is ________ than the maximum tax rate for pass-through entities.

13. Ownership redemptions and complete liquidations receive the same treatment for ________ and ________ entities.

14. A closely held corporation exists when more than ________ of the value of the stock during the ________ of the year is owned by not more than ________ individuals.

15. When selling a C corporation, a ________ sale has both the advantage of being less complex and provides a way to avoid ________ taxation on the sale.

**Multiple Choice**

Choose the best answer for each of the following questions.

____ 1. Legal forms available for conducting a business entity include all of the following except:
- a. Limited liability company.
- b. Partnership
- c. Corporation.
- d. S corporation.
- e. All of the above are legal forms.

____ 2. A limited liability company for Federal income tax purposes is:
- a. Taxed as an S corporation.
- b. Taxed as a C corporation.
- c. Taxed as a partnership.
- d. Taxed similar to a partnership but some C corporation rules apply.

____ 3. Which of the following has the least potential for limiting the liabilities of the owner(s)?
- a. Sole proprietorship.
- b. Limited Partnership.
- c. Corporation.
- d. S Corporation

____ 4. Which of the following statements about a limited liability company (LLC) is true?
- a. A LLC provides the corporate characteristic of ability to raise capital.
- b. A LLC may have S corporations, partnerships, and individuals as owners.
- c. The LLC may be subject to double taxation if it was a C corporation prior to becoming an LLC.
- d. A LLC will lose its flow-through character if it has gross receipts greater than $7.5 million for 3 consecutive years.

____ 5. Which of the following is not a technique that a C corporation can use to minimize the possibility of double taxation.
- a. Making distributions to shareholders that are deductible to the corporation.
- b. Making distributions that qualify for return of capital treatment.
- c. Making a check-the-box election.
- d. Not making distributions to the shareholders.

____ 6. Explore Company's income before considering salary payments to its owner/employee (Ali) is $100,000. Which of the following statement is true?
- a. As an S corporation, paying Ali a $100,000 salary will not cause an employment tax liability for Explore because Ali is taxed personally on the income.
- b. As a C corporation, Explore should Ali pay a $100,000 salary. Employment taxes will be paid by Explore but its income tax liability will be zero.
- c. As a C corporation, Explore should pay Ali a deductible dividend of $100,000 to avoid employment taxes and reduce its income tax liability to zero.
- d. As a sole proprietorship, paying Ali a $100,000 salary will cause an employment tax liability for Explore but it will decrease Ali's self-employment tax.

____ 7. Which of the following is a reason why a corporation would want to elect S corporation status?
a. To avoid income being taxed to shareholders at ordinary rates.
b. To avoid the built-in gains tax at the entity level.
c. To make special allocations of income and expenses to shareholders.
d. To pass losses through to the shareholders.

____ 8. Factors that should be considered in making the S corporation election include all of the following except:
a. Are all of the shareholders willing to consent to the election?
b. Can the qualification requirements be satisfied for at least the year of election?
c. For what period will the conditions making an election beneficial prevail?
d. Will the corporate distribution policy create wherewithal-to-pay income tax problems at the shareholder level?

____ 9. Alexandra and Glenn want to create a business entity to develop children's toys. Due to the potential of product liability in this line of business, limited liability for the owners is very important They expect the business to be an immediate success with a net income in the range of $400,000 for the first year. Unfortunately they will have to retain most of the profit for many years into the future for development of new toys. Which form of business entity should they select?
a. Limited liability company.
b. Limited partnership.
c. C corporation.
d. S corporation.

USE THE FOLLOWING INFORMATION FOR QUESTIONS 10 - 13.

Tori contributes property with an adjusted basis of $75,000 and a fair market value of $200,000 to a business entity in exchange for a 25% ownership interest.

____ 10. The transaction occurs as part of an integrated plan with the other owners in the formation of a C corporation. What is the corporation's basis for the asset and what is Tori's basis in the stock?

| | Asset Basis | Stock Basis |
|---|---|---|
| a. | $75,000 | $200,000 |
| b. | $200,000 | $75,000 |
| c. | $75,000 | $75,000 |
| d. | $200,000 | $200,000 |

____ 11. The transaction occurs two years after C corporation's formation. What is the corporation's basis for the asset and what is Tori's basis in the stock assuming Tori is the only shareholder involved in the transaction?

| | Asset Basis | Stock Basis |
|---|---|---|
| a. | $75,000 | $200,000 |
| b. | $200,000 | $75,000 |
| c. | $75,000 | $75,000 |
| d. | $200,000 | $200,000 |

____ 12. The transaction occurs as part of the formation of a partnership. What is the partnership's basis for the asset and what is Tori's basis in the partnership interest?

| | Asset Basis | Partnership Basis |
|---|---|---|
| a. | $75,000 | $200,000 |
| b. | $200,000 | $75,000 |
| c. | $75,000 | $75,000 |
| d. | $200,000 | $200,000 |

____ 13. The transaction occurs two years after the partnership's formation. What is the partnership's basis for the asset and what is Tori's basis in the stock assuming Tori is the only partner involved in the transaction?

| | Asset Basis | Stock Basis |
|---|---|---|
| a. | $75,000 | $200,000 |
| b. | $200,000 | $75,000 |
| c. | $75,000 | $75,000 |
| d. | $200,000 | $200,000 |

USE THE FOLLOWING INFORMATION FOR QUESTIONS 14 - 16.

Khalsa and Rosa decide to form the Sea Front Company. Khalsa contributes beach front property with a fair market value of $150,000 and an adjusted basis of $50,00 for a 50% interest. Rosa contributes $150,000 cash for the other 50% interest. Two years after the formation of the Sea Front Company, the land is sold for $250,000.

____ 14. If Sea is a corporation, how much gain is recognized by Khalsa and Rosa on the sale of the land?
a. $200,000 to Khalsa, $0 to Rosa.
b. $150,000 to Khalsa, $50,000 to Rosa.
c. $100,000 to Khalsa, $100,000 to Rosa
d. $50,000 to Khalsa, $50,000 to Rosa.
e. None of the above.

____ 15. If Sea is a partnership, how much gain is recognized by Khalsa and Rosa on the sale of the land?
a. $200,000 to Khalsa, $0 to Rosa.
b. $150,000 to Khalsa, $50,000 to Rosa.
c. $100,000 to Khalsa, $100,000 to Rosa
d. $50,000 to Khalsa, $50,000 to Rosa.
e. None of the above.

____ 16. If Sea is an S corporation, how much gain is recognized by Khalsa and Rosa on the sale of the land?
a $200,000 to Khalsa, $0 to Rosa.
b. $150,000 to Khalsa, $50,000 to Rosa.
c. $100,000 to Khalsa, $100,000 to Rosa
d $50,000 to Khalsa, $50,000 to Rosa.
e. None of the above.

USE THE FOLLOWING INFORMATION FOR QUESTIONS 17 - 19.

Hung Jun is the owner of a business with the following assets.

| | Adjusted Basis | Fair Market Value |
|---|---|---|
| Accounts receivable | $ 0 | $ 50,000 |
| Inventory | 60,000 | 80,000 |
| Machinery and equipment* | 50,000 | 60,000 |
| Buildings** | 80,000 | 95,000 |
| Land | 40,000 | 90,000 |
| | $ 230,000 | $ 375,000 |

* Potential § 1245 recapture of $10,000.
**Straight-line depreciation was used.

Hung Jun sells the business for $375,000 when her basis in the business is $230,000.

____ 17. Assume that the business is a sole proprietorship. Calculate Hung Jun's recognized gain or loss and classify it as capital or ordinary.

a. $145,000 capital gain.
b. $145,000 ordinary income.
c. $95,000 ordinary income and $50,000 capital gain.
d. $80,000 ordinary income and $65,000 unrecaptured §1250 and capital gain.

____ 18. Assume that the business is a C corporation and the sale is considered a sale of stock. Calculate Hung Jun's recognized gain or loss and classify it as capital or ordinary.

a. $145,000 capital gain.
b. $145,000 ordinary income.
c. $95,000 ordinary income and $50,000 capital gain.
d. $80,000 ordinary income and $65,000 unrecaptured §1250 and capital gain.

____ 19. Assume that the business is a S corporation and the sale is considered a sale of assets. Calculate the Hung Jun's recognized gain or loss (classified as capital or ordinary) on this transaction and the liquidation of the entity.

a. $Zero.
b. $145,000 capital gain.
c. $80,000 ordinary income and $65,000 unrecaptured §1250 and capital gain.
d. $145,000 capital gain on the sale and $145,000 capital gain on the liquidation.

____ 20. Which of the following statements is correct?

a. The buyer and the seller of a partnership are indifferent as to whether the transaction is a sale of the assets or a sale of the business entity.
b. The buyer but not the seller of a partnership is indifferent as to whether the transaction is a sale of the assets or a sale of the business entity.
c. The seller but not the buyer of a partnership is indifferent as to whether the transaction is a sale of the assets or a sale of the business entity.
d. Neither the buyer nor the seller are indifferent as to whether the transaction is a sale of the assets or a sale of the business entity.
e. None of the above.

**Short Answer**

1. Van is establishing a business. He is trying to decide between an C corporation, LLC or a sole proprietorship form. He projects that the business will generate losses of approximately $50,000 each year for the first 2 years and then will generate profits of at least $175,000 each year thereafter. About 30% of profits will be retained in a sinking fund in case of product liability litigation. Product liability problems are very common in this line of business. Advise Van on which tax form he should select.

# SOLUTIONS TO CHAPTER 14 QUESTIONS

## True or False

| | | |
|---|---|---|
| 1. | T | |
| 2. | F | The legal forms consist of the sole proprietorship, partnership, limited liability company, and corporation. |
| 3. | F | The accumulated earning tax can be imposed if a corporation accumulated earnings instead of making distributions. |
| 4. | F | The income from a sole proprietorship and an S corporation are both taxed to the owners at the individual tax rates. |
| 5. | T | |
| 6. | T | |
| 7. | T | |
| 8. | T | In certain circumstances, S corporations are subject to the built-in gains tax and the passive investment income tax. |
| 9. | F | A partnership and a LLC both use Form 1065. An S corporation uses Form 1120S |
| 10. | F | Some states do not permit an S corporation election. |
| 11. | T | |
| 12. | T | Compensation to shareholder-employees must be reasonable. |
| 13. | F | Only S corporations are subject to the built-in gains tax. |
| 14. | T | Dividends can produce ordinary income and stock redemptions and liquidating distributions can produce capital gains. |
| 15. | F | The buyer would prefer a sale of stock to retain the higher basis in the corporate assets. |

## Fill-in-the-Blanks

1. sole proprietorship, partnership, regular C corporation, S corporation
2. limited liability company
3. corporation (S and C)
4. increases, stays the same
5. tax, nontax
6. 20%, 26%, 28%
7. carryover, carryover or substituted
8. partnership, limited liability entity, S corporation
9. C corporation
10. sole proprietorship
11. built-in gains, passive investment income
12. Less, (35% versus 38.6% in 2003)
13. C corporations, S corporations
14. 50%, ½ , 5
15. stock, double

**Multiple Choice**

1. d — S corporation is not a legal form of business. It is a tax form.
2. c — A LLC is considered a partnership for tax purposes.
3. a — A sole proprietorship does not provide limited liability to its owner.
4. b — The LLC has no limit on the type of taxpayers that it can have as owners.
5. c — C corporations cannot make a check-the-box election. They may, however, make an S election to minimize double taxation.
6. b — This is one of the techniques to reduce double taxation. The other three are incorrect. An S Corporation payment of salary would cause an employment tax liability. There are no deductible dividends for C corporations. Sole proprietorships do not pay employment taxes. Rather, the owner pays self-employment taxes
7. d
8. b — Since the qualification requirements are maintenance requirements, these requirements must be satisfied throughout the life of the S corporation.
9. c — The C corporation form permits income the use of the lower corporate tax rates. Since it is not expected to pay out dividends for some time, no double taxation will occur.
10. c — $75,000, $75,000. Under § 351 the carryover basis rules apply.
11. d — $200,000, $200,000. Does not qualify under § 351, thus the transaction is taxable.
12. c — $75,000, $75,000. Under § 721 the carryover basis rules apply.
13. c — $75,000, $75,000. Section 721 applies to this situation also.
14. e — The entity is a corporation, therefore, it will be taxed on the $200,000 of gain. Khalsa and Rosa will not be taxed on any of the gain.
15. b — $150,000, $50,000. For partnerships, precontribution appreciation, $100,000 ($150,000-$50,000), must be allocated to Khalsa. The balance of the recognized gain on the sale of $100,000 would be allocated equally between Khalsa and Rosa.
16. c — $100,000, $100,000. Special allocations are not permitted for S corporations. The gain is allocated on a per-share per-day basis. Since Khalsa and Rosa own the stock 50/50 each is taxed on 50% of the gain, $100,000.
17. d — Since the sale of a sole proprietorship is treated as the sale of individual assets, the gain or loss on each asset must be calculated in order to determine the amount of ordinary income and the amount of capital gain.

| | Recognized Gain | Classification |
|---|---|---|
| Accounts receivable | $50,000 | OI |
| Inventory | 20,000 | OI |
| Machinery and equipment | 10,000 | OI |
| Buildings | 15,000 | Unrecaptured §1250 |
| Land | 50,000 | CG* |

*Actually § 1231 gain, which in this case will be treated as LTCG.

18. a — The sale of stock is treated as a sale of a capital asset.

| | | |
|---|---|---|
| Amount realized | $375,000 | |
| Adjusted basis | | (230,000) |
| Recognized gain | $145,000 | |

19. c — Same treatment as in # 17 above. The gains flow through to Hung Jun and she recognizes them on her return. These recognized gains increase her stock basis to $375,000 by the recognition of gains so no gain or loss on the distribution of the proceeds from the liquidation.
20. b

**Short Answer**

1. The corporation and the LLC both limit Van's personal liability which would be important in this line of business. The sole proprietorship will not provide this protection and, therefore, is not a wise choice for Van.

   If the business operates as a regular C corporation, the projected losses will not benefit Van on his individual tax return. Further, when the business earns a profit it will be taxed at the corporate level. Unless Van employs some tax minimization techniques, the 70 percent of profits not retained within the business will be distributed to Van in the form of dividend and be subject to double taxation.

   If a LLC is selected as the business form, the losses for each of the first 2 years can be passed through to Van and deducted on his individual tax return. In year 3 and thereafter all income generated by the business will be taxed only once on his personal return. He will be taxed on the 30 percent that is retained in the business as well as the 70 percent he receives. In some states, however, a LLC requires at least two owners.

# Chapter 15
# Introduction to the Taxation of Individuals

## CHAPTER HIGHLIGHTS

This chapter describes the various components involved in the computation of Federal taxable income. Generally, all realized income is included in gross income, unless it is specifically excluded by the tax law. Likewise, deductions from income are not allowed unless they are provided by the law. Special deductions, such as the standard deduction and personal exemptions are available only to individual taxpayers. These deductions, in essence, exempt a taxpayer's income from taxation up to specified amounts. After taxable income is determined, the tax liability is computed by reference to tax tables or tax rate schedules. Credits are allowed to reduce the computed tax. Tax prepayments are also subtracted from the gross tax liability to determine a taxpayer's net tax payable or refund due. **Changes for the Jobs and Growth Tax Relief Reconciliation Act of 2003 (Tax Act of 2003) have been included in this outline.**

I. Tax Formula
   A. The Federal individual income tax liability is based on the concept of *taxable income*. Taxable income is determined using the formula shown in Exhibit 15-1 below.
   B. Components of the Tax Formula
      1. Income (broadly conceived) includes all income, both taxable and nontaxable. The term is *not* equivalent to gross receipts.
      2. Exclusions from income have been specifically provided in the law. Congress has chosen to exclude various items from the tax base for equity, social, economic, and other reasons. Certain other items have been excluded by administrative action of the IRS.
      3. Gross income is broadly defined in the Internal Revenue Code as "except as otherwise provided . . . all income from whatever source derived." The "except as otherwise provided" refers to exclusions.
      4. The two categories of deductions applicable to individual taxpayers are deductions *for* adjusted gross income (for AGI) and deductions *from* adjusted gross income (from AGI).
      5. Expenses deductible *for* AGI include, but are not limited to the following.
         a. Ordinary and necessary expenses incurred in a trade or business.
         b. One-half of self-employment tax paid.
         c. Alimony paid.
         d. Payments to deductible individual retirement accounts (IRAs) and Medical Savings Accounts (MSAs).
         e. Moving expenses.
         f. Capital loss deductions (limited to $3,000).

**Exhibit 15-1**

**FORMULA FOR DETERMINING TAXABLE INCOME**

| | |
|---|---|
| ***Income*** | ***Broadly Conceived*** |
| ***Less:*** | ***Exclusions*** |
| ***Equals:*** | ***Gross Income*** |
| ***Less:*** | ***Deductions for Adjusted Gross Income*** |
| ***Equals:*** | ***Adjusted Gross Income*** |
| ***Less:*** | ***Greater of – Standard Deduction, or Total Itemized Deductions*** |
| ***Less:*** | ***Personal and Dependency Exemptions*** |
| ***Equals:*** | ***Taxable Income*** |

6. Adjusted gross income (AGI) is an important subtotal which serves as the basis for computing percentage limitations on certain deductions, such as medical expenses and charitable contributions.
7. Itemized deductions, which tend to be personal in nature, are deductions *from* AGI. They are discussed later in the chapter.
8. Standard Deduction – To determine whether to use the standard deduction or itemize, taxpayers compare their total from AGI itemized deductions with the standard deduction (plus additional amounts if applicable). Taxpayers take the greater of the itemized deductions or the standard deduction.
   a. The *basic* standard deductions and additional amounts are listed by filing status in Exhibit 15-2. The amounts before and after the Tax Act of 2003 are given. These amounts are adjusted for inflation each year.
   b. *Additional* standard deduction amounts are allowed for taxpayers who are elderly (age 65 or over) and/or blind. (Up to two additions per taxpayer or up to four additions for married filing jointly.)
   c. Dependents do *not* qualify the taxpayer for additional standard deduction amounts.
   d. Some taxpayers are not allowed to use the standard deduction (nonresident aliens) or the standard deduction amount is reduced (tax return for less than12 months).
9. Personal Exemption – Taxpayers are allowed to deduct a $3,050 exemption for 2003 ($3,000 for 2002) for the taxpayer, taxpayer's spouse, and for each dependent of the taxpayer in arriving at taxable income.

C. Special Limitations for Individuals Who Can Be Claimed as Dependents

1. If a taxpayer can be claimed by another taxpayer as a dependent, the basic standard deduction for 2003 is limited to the greater of the following.
   a. $750.
   b. The dependent's earned income for the year + $250, but not to exceed the basic standard deduction amount (i.e., $4,750 in 2003 assuming a single dependent).
2. Taxpayers (e.g., children) claimed as dependents on another's (e.g., parents') tax return may *not* claim a personal exemption on their own tax return.

**Exhibit 15-2**

**STANDARD DEDUCTION AMOUNTS FOR 2003**

| ***Filing Status*** | ***Before Tax Act of 2003*** ***Standard*** | ***Additional*** | ***After Tax Act of 2003*** ***Standard*** | ***Additional*** |
|---|---|---|---|---|
| *Single* | *$4,750* | *$ 1,150* | *$4,750* | *$1,150* |
| *Married, filing jointly* | *$7,950* | *$ 950* | *$9,500* | *$ 950* |
| *Surviving spouse* | *$7,950* | *$ 950* | *$9,500* | *$ 950* |
| *Head of Household* | *$7,000* | *$1,150* | *$7,000* | *$1,150* |
| *Married, filing separately* | *$3,975* | *$ 950* | *$4,750* | *$ 950* |

II. Personal and Dependency Exemptions

A. Each personal exemption claimed on a 2003 return is $3,050 ($3,000 for 2002).

B. A personal exemption is allowed for *each* taxpayer and the taxpayer's spouse, if filing jointly. The determination of marital status occurs at the end of the year, except when a spouse dies during the year, then determination is made at date of death.

C. Dependency Exemptions – Allowed for *each* eligible dependent. Five tests must be met in order for an individual to qualify as a dependent.

1. Support Test. Taxpayer provides over 50% of the support of the individual.
    a. Support includes expenditures for food, shelter, clothing, medical and dental care, and education.
    b. Exceptions to the support test.
        (1) Multiple support agreement. Allows one member of the group of individuals furnishing over 50% of the support for a person to claim a dependency exemption for that individual. However, the member claiming the exemption must provide *more than 10%* of the support.
        (2) Divorced parents. The parents can decide in writing who will received the dependency exemption for their children. If there is no agreement, the custodial parent claims the children.
2. The Relationship or Member-of-Household Test. The person to be claimed as a dependent must meet *one* of the following criteria.
    a. The individual must be of a specified relation to the taxpayer or to taxpayer's spouse.
    b. The individual must be a member of the taxpayer's household for the entire taxable year of the taxpayer.
    c. Relationships established by marriage continue regardless of divorce.
3. The Gross Income Test. The dependent's gross income must be less than the exemption amount (i.e., $3,050 in 2003). Excluded income is not considered.
    a. The gross income test does not apply to children under the age of 19 or a full-time student under age 24 and are being claimed by parents.
    b. If the parents claim dependency exemptions for children, the children may *not* claim personal exemptions on their own tax returns.

4. Joint Return Test. Dependents being claimed by another, can not file a joint income tax return with their spouse unless they are joint filing solely to receive a refund of tax withheld, no tax liability would exist for either spouse on separate income tax returns, and neither spouse is required to file a return.

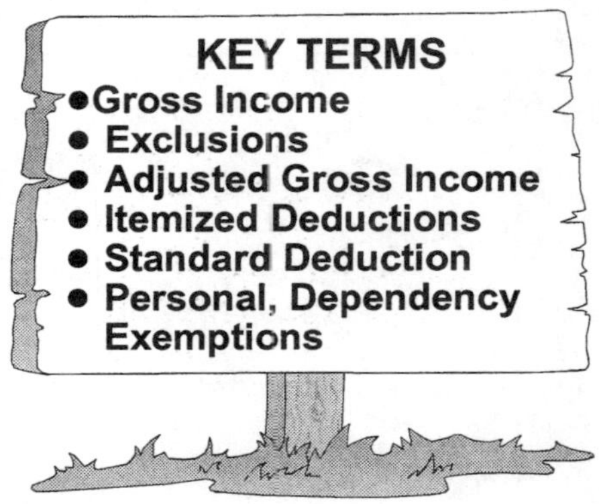


5. Citizenship or Residency Test. Requires that dependents must be either a U.S. citizen or resident, or a resident of Canada or Mexico for part of the tax year.

D. Phaseout of Exemptions

1. Personal and dependency exemptions are phased out as AGI exceeds the specified threshold amounts (indexed for inflation) shown in Exhibit 15-3.
2. Exemptions are phased out at the rate of 2% for each $2,500 or part thereof by which the taxpayer's AGI exceeds the threshold amounts. For married taxpayers filing separately, the phaseout is 2% for each $1,250 or fraction thereof.

**Exhibit 15-3**

**Phaseout OF EXEMPTIONS: THRESHOLD AMOUNTS**

| ***Filing Status*** | ***2003*** | ***2002*** |
|---|---|---|
| *Single* | *$139,500* | *$137,300* |
| *Head of Household* | *$174,400* | *$171,650* |
| *Married, filing jointly* | *$209,250* | *$206,000* |
| *Surviving spouse* | *$209,250* | *$206,000* |
| *Married, filing separately* | *$104,625* | *$103,000* |

III. Tax Determination

Taxes are computed using either the Tax Table method or the Tax Rate Schedule method.

A. Tax Table Method – Taxpayers who are eligible *must* use the Tax Table to compute their tax liability.

B. Tax Rate Schedule Method

1. Prior to the Tax Act of 2003, the six rate brackets for 2003 were 10%, 15%, 27%, 30%, 35%, and 38.6% for each filing status. These higher rates were reduced by the Tax Act of 2003 to 10%, 15%, 25%, 28%, 33%, and 35%.
2. Separate schedules are provided for each filing status (single, married filing jointly, etc). The income ranges to which the rates apply are indexed for inflation and therefore change on a yearly basis.
3. The rates reflect a progressive (graduated) rate structure. A tax system is progressive when higher tax rates are applied as the tax base increases.
4. Special computations limit the effective tax rate on capital gains and dividends after the Tax Act of 2003 (See Chapter 7 for a more complete explanation).

5. Computing a tax using the Tax Rate Schedule may differ slightly from using the Tax Table method because the tax given in the Tax Tables is based on the mid-point income for the particular range of income listed in the Tax Table.

C. Computation of Net Taxes Payable or Refund Due

1. The Federal income tax is a pay-as-you-go system, thus, taxpayers pay their tax liability throughout the year through withholding and/or estimated payments.
2. The total taxes computed is reduced by withholding by employers, estimated tax payments, and various tax credits to derive net taxes payable or refund due.

> Interest-free loan to the government? That's what happens if too much is withheld from an individual's salary and the taxpayer gets a big tax refund once the return is filed. Changing the number of allowances claimed on a Form W-4 will increase the take-home pay and reduce or eliminate the year-end refund.

D. Unearned Income of Children Under Age 14 Taxed at Parent's Rate (Kiddie Tax)

1. A child's unearned income, may be taxable at the parents' highest tax rate.
2. A *child* here is defined as a person who possesses the following attributes.
   a. Has not reached the age 14 by the end of the tax year.
   b. Has at least one living parent.
   c. Has net unearned income of more than $1,500 for the year.
3. *Net unearned income* is computed as follows.

   Unearned income - $750

   Less the *greater* of: $750 standard deduction; **or** allowable deductions directly connected with production of unearned income

   Equals: Net unearned income.
4. Net unearned income is taxed at the parents' marginal tax rate. Parents may report the child's excess unearned income on the parents' tax return (*parental election*) if the following requirements are met.
   a. Gross income is from interest and dividends only.
   b. Gross income is more than $750 but less than $7,500.
   c. No estimated tax has been paid in the name and Social Security number of the child and the backup withholding rules do not apply.
5. If the parental election is made, the child need not file a tax return. Calculations must be made both *with* the parental election and *without* the election to determine whether the election should be made.

> For tax planning purposes, one always should know the marginal tax rate of the taxpayer, as this measures the incremental change in the tax liability due to a planning idea. With the phaseout of the exemptions and itemized deductions, as well as the potential for kiddie tax and alternative minimum tax amounts, the marginal tax rate can be very difficult to determine.

IV. Filing Considerations

A. Filing Requirements

1. Individuals must file income tax returns annually if they have gross income above a minimum level. The filing requirements are based on the sum of the

basic standard deduction, additional standard deduction amount for elderly (but not for blindness), and the allowable personal exemptions.

2. A self-employed individuals with net earnings of at least $400 from self-employment must file an income tax return regardless of their gross income.
3. It is more complex to determine when an individual who can be claimed as a dependent by another taxpayer must file an income tax return.
4. Individual taxpayers file on either Form 1040, Form 1040A, or Form 1040EZ, depending on the complexity of the taxpayer's financial situation.
5. Rather than filing a paper return, taxpayers may file electronically with the IRS either directly (e-filing) or indirectly through a tax professional designated as an electronic return originator (ERO)
6. For a calendar year taxpayer, the appropriate form is due by April 15 of the following year. Extensions for time to file, but not time to pay, may be obtained using Form 4868 (automatic extension) or Form 2688.
7. Tax payments accompanying a return are generally paid by check. However, a debit, credit, or charge card can also be used to pay Federal income taxes.

B. Filing Status

The amount of tax for a given taxable income will vary depending on the filing status of the taxpayer.

1. Single – Unmarried, legally separated, or divorced and does not qualify for any other filing status.
2. Married – Married as of last day of the tax year or spouse dies during the year. Married couples may incur a penalty when both spouses have significant amounts of income. The penalty is equal to the additional income taxes paid by married individuals over the aggregate amount they would pay as single taxpayers. The Tax Act of 2003 alleviates some of the marriage penalty.
3. Surviving Spouse – Joint return rates apply for two years after the year in which a spouse dies if the surviving spouse maintains a household for a dependent child.
4. Head of Household – Unmarried taxpayers who pay over 50% of the cost of maintaining a household that qualifies as a principal home for a dependent.
5. Married Filing Separately – Married on last day of the year but not filing jointly.

V. Overview of Income Provisions Applicable to Individuals

A. Gross income includes almost all receipts of money, property, or services. However, many types of income are excluded from income.

B. Exclusions applying to all taxpayers were discussed in Chapter 3. Most exclusions available only to individuals are for *fringe benefits* and are discussed in Chapter 16.

VI. Specific Inclusions Applicable to Individuals

A. Alimony and Separate Maintenance Payments

1. Alimony payments are taxable to the recipient and tax deductible by the payor.
2. A transfer of property to a former spouse pursuant to a divorce is not a taxable event. Instead, this division of property is considered a property settlement.
3. Child Support. Payment for child support are nondeductible personal expenses. They are not taxable to the person receiving the payments.
4. Amounts paid based contingencies related to the child are considered child support rather than alimony.

B. Prizes and Awards
1. The fair market values of prizes and awards are generally included in income rather than being treated as tax-free "gifts."
2. However, a prize or award is not income if *all* of the following are met.
   a. It is received in recognition of religious, charitable, scientific, educational, artistic, literary, or civic achievement.
   b. The recipient was selected without taking any action.
   c. No substantial future services are required as a condition of the award.
   d. The recipient has the award paid directly to a qualified governmental unit or a nonprofit organization.
3. Another limited exception allows exclusion of certain employee achievement awards of tangible personal property (e.g., a gold watch). Awards must be made in recognition of length of service or safety achievement.

C. Unemployment Compensation – Included in gross income.

D. Social Security Benefits – As much as 50% or 85% of Social Security retirement benefits may be included in a taxpayer's gross income. The amount taxable is determined under rules specified in the Code.

VII. Specific Exclusions Applicable to Individuals

A. Gifts and Inheritances

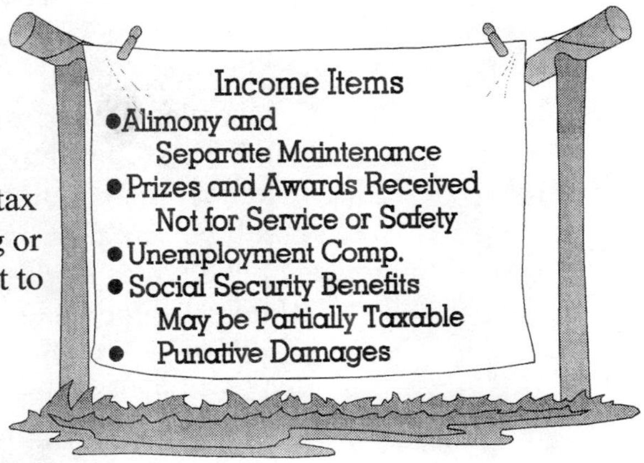


1. The value of a gift or inheritance is excluded from the recipient's gross income. The recipient is subject to tax on any income earned from holding or exchanging the property subsequent to its receipt.
2. A *gift* is "a voluntary transfer of property by one to another without adequate consideration or compensation therefrom." It is made "out of affection, respect, admiration, charity, or like impulses."
3. Business Gifts. Payments are not gifts if they represent compensation for past, present, or future services. Transfers from an employer to an employee *cannot* be excluded as a gift.

B. Scholarships
1. Scholarships are payments or benefits received by a student at an educational institution that are not classified as either gifts or compensation for services.
2. Exclusion is limited to amounts used for tuition, course-required fees, books, supplies, and equipment. Amounts received for room and board are taxable and treated as earned income for calculating the standard deduction.
3. Timing Issues. If the amount eligible for exclusion is not known at the time the scholarship is received, the transaction is held *open* until the educational expenses are paid.
4. Disguised Compensation. The IRS has ruled that scholarships made available by employers solely to children of key employees are taxable income to the parent-employee as disguised compensation.

C. Damages

1. Tax treatment of *compensatory* damages depends on the type of harm the taxpayer has experienced.
2. Reimbursement for the loss of income is taxed in the same manner as the income it replaces.
3. Payment for damaged or destroyed property is treated as income only if the proceeds received exceed the property's basis.
4. For personal damages, the amounts received are intended to make the injured party "whole as before the injury." Tax treatment depends on the type of damage payments received.
    a. Only those *compensatory* damages received due to a physical personal injury or physical sickness can be excluded from gross income.
    b. Under no circumstances may *punitive* damages be excluded from gross income. These are paid not to compensate the injured party but rather to punish the payor causing the harm.

D. Workers' Compensation – Workers' compensation benefits (i.e., fixed amounts for specific job-related injuries) are excluded from gross income.

E. Accident & Health Insurance Benefits – Such benefits received are excludible from gross income if the premiums are paid by the taxpayer. (See Chapter 16 for treatment when premiums are paid by the employer.)

F. Educational Savings Bonds

1. Interest earned on certain Series EE U.S. government savings bonds may be excluded if the following requirements are met.
    a. The savings bonds are issued after December 31,1989 to an individual who was at least 24 years old at the time of issuance.
    b. The bonds are redeemed to pay qualified higher education expenses (tuition and fees) for taxpayer, spouse, or dependent.
2. If the redemption proceeds exceed the qualified expenses (tuition and fees less scholarships and veterans' benefits), only a pro-rata portion of the interest will qualify for the exclusion.
3. The benefit begins being phased out when taxpayers modified AGI exceeds $58,500 for single and $87,750 for joint filers in 2003.

VIII. Itemized Deductions

A. Taxpayers are allowed to deduct limited expenditures as itemized deductions on Schedule A. The expenses fall into three categories.

1. Expenses that are purely *personal* in nature.
2. Expenses incurred by *employees* in connection with their employment.
3. Expenses related to the *production or collection of income* and the *management of property* held for the production of income.

B. Medical Expenses

1. General Requirements – To the extent eligible, nonreimbursed expenses that *exceed* 7.5% of AGI are allowed as an itemized deduction.
2. Medical expenses include:

a. Cost for diagnosis, cure, mitigation, treatment, or prevention of disease, or for the purpose of affecting any structure or body function.
b. Premiums for health care.
c. Prescription drugs and insulin.
d. Lodging while away from home for obtaining medical care.

3. Amounts paid for discretionary *cosmetic surgery* are not deductible medical expenses. Cosmetic surgery deemed to be a medical necessity is deductible.
4. Deductibility of *nursing home* expenses depends on the medical condition of the patient and the nature of the services rendered.
5. Amounts expended for *capital improvements* (e.g., swimming pool, elevator) which are medical in nature are deductible in the year incurred to the extent they do not increase the value of the related property. Costs of operation and maintenance are also deductible.
6. Medical expenses of spouse and dependents are deductible by the taxpayer if paid by the taxpayer for the spouse or dependents. In determining dependency status for this, neither the gross income nor the joint return tests applies.

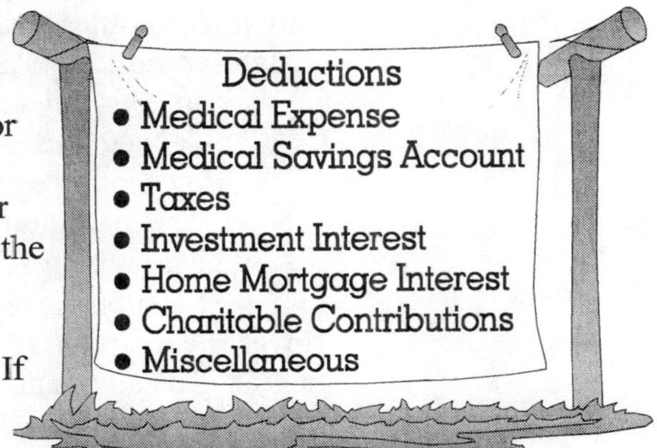


7. Transportation costs to and from medical treatment are deductible. If a personal automobile is used, the deduction is 12¢ per mile or actual out-of-pocket expenses. No deduction for meals in route to treatment.
8. Medical Savings Accounts (MSAs)
   a. MSAs are used with high-deductible medical insurance policies.
   b. MSAs can be created by employers with not more than 50 employees, self-employed taxpayers, or individuals without insurance coverage.
   c. Contributions made by individuals are deductible *for* AGI, while individuals whose employers contribute to MSAs may exclude the contributions from gross income. Further, earnings from MSAs are not included in a taxpayer's income.

C. <u>Taxes</u>

1. Certain state, local, and foreign taxes paid or accrued by a taxpayer are deductible as a relief from multiple taxation.
2. A *fee* and a *tax* are not the same. Fees are not deductible *unless* they are incurred as business expenses or for the production of income.
3. Property Taxes. To be deductible, personal property taxes must be an *ad valorem* tax (i.e., assessed in relation to the value of the property). Real estate taxes are generally deductible.
4. State and Local Income Taxes
   a. State and local taxes imposed on individuals can only be deducted as itemized deductions, even if the taxpayer's sole source of income is from business, rents, or royalties.
   b. Taxes are deductible in the year withheld by the employer or actually paid, even if the taxes relate to a prior or subsequent year.

c. Tax refunds received in a later year must be included in gross income *only* to the extent that deducting the taxes provided a *tax benefit*.

> A taxpayer should be careful not to include too much of a state tax refund in income. State tax refunds are not taxable if the taxpayer did not receive a tax benefit from previously deducting the taxes. For example, if a taxpayer used the standard deduction in the year the taxes were paid, the refunded amount is not taxable.

D. <u>Interest</u>

Interest expense can be divided into five categories.

1. Trade or business interest – fully deductible as an ordinary expense.
2. Personal (consumer) interest – not deductible. Personal interest is generally any interest other business or the three types listed below.
3. Qualified Education Loan Interest
    a. Interest payments on qualified education (student) loans may be deducted for AGI if taxpayer is not married filing separately or claimed by another as a dependent.
    b. The maximum deduction is $2,500.
    c. The benefit is phased out for taxpayers with modified AGI between $50,000 and $65,000 single and $100,000 and $130,000 for joint filers.
4. Investment Interest
    a. The amount of *investment interest* expense (i.e., interest incurred on funds borrowed to acquire investment assets) that is deductible in the current year is limited to net investment income for the current year.
    b. *Net investment income* is the excess of investment income (eg., interest, dividends, annuities, certain royalties and specific net capital gains) over investment expenses.
    c. Investment expenses include those deductible costs directly related to the production of investment income.
5. Qualified Residence Interest
    a. Interest paid or accrued on indebtedness secured by qualified residences (ie, principal residence and one other residence) of the taxpayer or spouse that arises from acquisition indebtedness or home equity loans.
    b. Acquisition Indebtedness
        (1) Debt incurred in acquiring, constructing, or substantially improving a qualified residence.
        (2) Interest paid or accrued on total acquisition indebtedness (both residences combined) of $1 million or less ($500,000 married, filing separate returns) is deductible. Debt amounts in excess of the limit generates nondeductible interest.
    c. Home Equity Loans
        (1) Interest on debt secured by qualified residence of up to $100,000 ($50,000 for married filing separately) is deductible.
        (2) Interest on loans whose outstanding balance exceeds the FMV of the residence less its acquisition indebtedness is not deductible.
        (3) Proceeds from home equity loans can be used for any purpose desired by the taxpayer.

> When buying a new personal car or boat taxpayers may need to take out a loan. If taxpayers use the car or boat as collateral for the loan, the interest will be considered consumer interest and not deductible. However, if taxpayers borrows against the equity in their homes, the interest will be deductible as qualified residential interest. This demonstrates tax avoidance planning.

6. Interest Paid for Services
   a. To qualify as deductible interest, *points* must be compensation to a lender solely for the use or forbearance of money.
   b. The general rule is that points must be capitalized and amortized over the life of the loan. The exception to this rule is when loan proceeds are used to purchase or improvement of a qualified residence. Points on these mortgages are deductible in the year paid.
7. Prepayment Penalties. May be incurred if loans are paid off early. They are considered to be interest in the year paid.
8. Related Parties. When the debtor is on the accrual basis and the creditor is on the cash basis, interest expense must be actually paid by the accrual basis taxpayer in order for a deduction to be taken.
9. Tax Exempt Securities. Interest paid on debts incurred to purchase or carry tax exempt securities is not deductible.
10. Prepaid Interest. The prepayment of interest must be capitalized and allocated to the subsequent periods to which the interest payments relate, even if the taxpayer otherwise uses the cash basis.
11. Classification of Interest Expense. If indebtedness is incurred in connection with a business or for the production of rent or royalty income, the related interest expense is deductible *for* AGI. Otherwise, the related interest expense is deductible *from* AGI.

E. <u>Charitable Contributions</u>

1. Contributions made to qualified organizations are deductible *from* AGI. The government allows contribution deductions to encourage charitable giving by individuals and corporations.
2. Charitable contributions are gifts made to qualified domestic organizations The contributions must have the following elements to qualify: donative intent, no consideration received by the donor, and acceptance by the donee.
3. Benefit Received Rule
   a. To the extent a tangible benefit is derived from a contribution, the value of such benefit cannot be deducted.
   b. Receipt of the right to purchase athletic tickets from a college or university is valued at 20% of the contribution made.
4. Services. A deduction is not allowed for a contribution of one's services to a charitable organization. However, unreimbursed expenses related to the services rendered are deductible. For automobile costs, 14¢ a mile is allowed.
5. The following do *not* qualify as charitable contributions.
   a. Dues or fees paid to fraternal orders, country clubs, or similar groups.
   b. Raffle, bingo, and lottery tickets.
   c. Cost of tuition.
   d. Value of blood given to blood bank.

e. Gifts to individuals or homeowners associations.
f. Rental value of property used by a qualified charity.

6. Time of Deduction. A charitable contribution is generally deductible, by cash or accrual taxpayers, in the year payment is made. A contribution made by check is considered paid on the date of mailing and contributions made by credit card are considered paid on the date charged.

> Since the mailing date is considered the date of payment for a charitable contribution, taxpayers may mail their contributions on the last day of the year, receive a deduction for that year but the checks will not reduce their checking balance until the next year. This timing difference is usually more apparent with contributions charged on credit cards.

7. Record-Keeping and Valuation Requirements
   a. No deduction is allowed for a contribution of $250 or more unless the taxpayer obtains *written substantiation* from the charity. Additional information is required if the value of the donated property is over $500 but not over $5,000.
   b. If a noncash contribution exceeds $5,000 in value ($10,000 for nonpublicly traded stock), an appraisal determining its FMV is required.
   c. Donated property is generally valued at its FMV value at the time of the gift. FMV means: "the price at which the property would change hands between a willing buyer and a willing seller, neither being under any compulsion to buy or sell and both having reasonable knowledge of relevant facts."

8. Limitations on Charitable Deductions
   a. Individuals are subject to deduction ceiling limitations. The limitations are computed as a percentage of the taxpayer's AGI.
      (1) Total contributions of 20% or less of AGI, are fully deductible.
      (2) Total contributions that are more than 20% of AGI, may be limited to either 20%, 30%, or 50% of AGI, depending on the type of property given and the type of organization to which the donation is made.
      (3) In any case, the maximum total charitable deduction may not exceed 50% of AGI for the tax year.
   b. 50% Ceiling. Contributions to public charities may not exceed 50% of AGI. The 50% ceiling also applies to private operating foundations and certain nonoperating foundations.
   c. 30% Ceiling. Contributions of cash and ordinary income property to private nonoperating foundations may not exceed 30% of AGI. This ceiling also applies to contributions of appreciated capital gain property to 50% organizations unless an election is made.
   d. If 30% and 50% property are given in the same year, the 50% is considered first when computing the allowable deduction.
   e. 20% Ceiling. Contributions of appreciated capital gain property made to private nonoperating foundations are limited to 20% of AGI.

f. Contribution Carryover. Any unused excess contributions for a taxable year may be carried forward for up to 5 years. The contributions do not lose their character when carried forward.

F. <u>Miscellaneous Itemized Deductions Subject to 2% Floor</u>

1. A number of miscellaneous expenses are deductible on Schedule A. The expenses are deductible only to the extent that in total the miscellaneous expenses exceed 2% of the taxpayer's AGI.
2. Many of the miscellaneous deductions are for expenditures related to employment. A few examples of the miscellaneous deductions are:
   a. Professional dues and subscriptions to professional journals.
   b. Uniforms.
   c. Tax return preparation fees.
   d. Job-hunting expenses.
   e. Safe deposit box rental.
   f. Investment expenses.
   g. Appraisal fees associated with itemized deductions.
   h. Hobby losses to the extent of hobby income.
   i. Unreimbursed employee business expenses.

G. <u>Other Miscellaneous Deductions</u>

The following Schedule A deductions *not* subject to the 2% of AGI limitation.

1. Gambling losses to the extent of gambling earnings.
2. Impairment-related work expenses of a handicapped person.
3. Federal estate tax on income in respect of a decedent.
4. Deduction for repayments under a claim of right if more than $3,000.

H. <u>Overall Limitation on Certain Itemized Deductions</u>

1. Taxpayers with AGIs exceeding certain levels are subject to a phaseout of their itemized deductions. The phaseout of deductions (the *cutback adjustment*) begins at AGIs in excess of $139,500 ($69,750 for married persons filing a separate return) for 2003.
   a. The limitation applies to these frequently encountered itemized deductions: taxes, home mortgage interest, charitable contributions, and all expenses subject to the 2% of AGI floor including unreimbursed employee expenses.
   b. However, the limitation *does not* apply the following itemized deductions: medical expenses, investment interest, nonbusiness casualty and theft losses, and gambling losses.
   c. The limitation requires itemized deductions to be reduced by 3% of the amount by which AGI exceeds $139,500. However, in no case may the reduction of the itemized deductions be greater than 80%.
   d. This adjustment is applied *after* taking into account other provisions that reduce allowable deductions.

IX. Individual Tax Credits

A. <u>Adoption Expenses Credit</u>

1. The credit assists taxpayers who incur nonrecurring costs associated with the adoption process.

2. Up to $10,160 of costs to adopt a eligible child qualify for the credit. Eligible child is: under 18 years old, or physically or mentally incapable of self care.
3. Amount of the credit is subject to phaseout for taxpayers with AGIs exceeding $152,390, and is phased out completely when AGI reaches $192,390. Credit is computed as follows.

$$\text{Allowable credit X (AGI} - \$152{,}390) \div \$40{,}000$$

B. <u>Child Tax Credit</u>
1. This credit is based solely on the number of the taxpayer's dependent children who are US residents and under the age of 17.
2. Maximum credit was $600 per child. The Tax Act of 2003 increased the amount to $1,000 for the 2003 tax year.
3. This amount begins being phased out when the taxpayer's AGI is $110,000 for joint filers, $55,000 married filing separately, and $75,000 for single taxpayers. The phaseout is at a rate of $50 for each $1,000 (or part thereof) of AGI above the threshold amounts.

C. <u>Credit for Child and Dependent Care Expenses</u>
1. This credit was enacted to benefit taxpayers who incur employment-related expenses for child or dependent care.
2. To be eligible, taxpayer must maintain a household for qualifying individual(s) and have eligible employment-related expenses.
    a. Qualifying individual(s) are: dependents under age 13, or dependents or spouse who is physically or mentally incapacitated.
    b. Eligible expenses include amounts paid for household services and in the home or outside the home care of a qualifying individual(s).
        (1) The amount of expenses qualifying for the credit are limited to an individual's earned income. For married taxpayers, this limitation applies to the spouse with the *lesser* amount of earned income.
        (2) Nonworking spouses who are disabled or are full-time students are deemed to have earned income equal to the maximum costs qualifying for the credit.
3. The credit is equal to a percentage of employment-related expenses up to $3,000 for one qualifying dependent ($250 per month) and $6,000 ($500 per month) for two or more dependents. The percentage (ranging from 35% to 20%) used to compute the credit is dependent on the taxpayer's AGI and the percentage decreases as AGI increases.

D. <u>Education Tax Credit</u>
1. The two education credits, *HOPE scholarship credit* and *lifetime learning credit*, are available to low and middle income taxpayers to help defray tuition costs of higher education. Room, board, and books costs are ineligible for the credits. Both credits are nonrefundable.
2. HOPE Credit
    a. Maximum credit is $1,500 per year; 100% of the first $1,000 and 50% of the next $1,000 of tuition.

b. Available for first two years of higher education.
c. Credit is based on eligible student (taxpayer, spouse, or dependent) who is someone taking at least a half-time course load for one academic term.

3. Lifetime Learning Credit
   a. Maximum credit is 20% of tuition costs for taxpayer, spouse, or dependent up to $10,000 for 2003 (up to $5,000 prior to 2003).
   b. This credit cannot be taken on tuition costs used for the HOPE credit.
   c. This credit is for education beyond the first two years of higher education and since the credit does not require a minimum course load, it is available for seeking new job skills or continuing education.
   d. Credit limit is calculated per taxpayer not per student.
4. Both credits are subject to income limitations and are combined for the limitation calculation. The phaseout begins for AGIs at $41,000 for single taxpayers and $83,000 for joint filers. The phaseout is complete when AGI reaches $51,000 (single) and $103,000 (joint filers).
5. Taxpayers cannot receive a double benefit. If an educational expense is claimed for either credit, it cannot also be deducted or excluded from income as a scholarship or educational assistance benefit. However, amounts distributed from Coverdell Education Savings Accounts can still be excluded from income as long as the amounts distributed were not used for the expenses qualifying for the credit.

E. <u>Earned Income Credit (EIC)</u>
1. The EIC is intended to provide tax equity to the working poor. Therefore, qualifying individuals must have earned income.
2. To be eligible for the credit, the taxpayer must not exceed the income thresholds, and generally have a *qualifying child*. A qualifying child must meet the following three tests.
   a. Relationship test. Child must be a descendent, step-child, adopted, or foster child of taxpayer.
   b. Residency test. Child must live with the taxpayer in the U.S. for more than ½ of the year
   c. Age test. Child must be under age 19, under age 24 and a full-time student, or disabled.
3. EIC also is available for low-income workers who do not have any qualifying children, when the taxpayer is from 25 through 64 years old and cannot be claimed as a dependent on another's return.
4. Computation of EIC
   a. It is determined by multiplying a maximum amount of earned income by the appropriate credit percentage.
   b. The credit begins a phaseout, when the taxpayer's earned income or AGI exceeds a certain amount. The phaseout rates vary depending on the number of the taxpayer's qualifying children.
   c. Since this is a complex calculation, the IRS issues tables that are useful in determining the proper amount of the credit.
   d. If the proper information is provided, the IRS will compute the credit for the taxpayer.
5. Earned income credit is refundable to the extent that it exceeds the taxpayer's tax liability.

6. Eligible individuals may elect to receive advance payments of the earned income credit from their employers. The amount that may be received is limited to 60% of the amount available.

> The earned income credit is unusual in several ways.
> (1) The taxpayer need not compute the credit to receive the benefit,
> (2) The credit can be collected throughout the year by means of a withholding adjustment, and
> (3) The credit is available as a "negative income tax." If the credit exceeds the tax due for the year, the Treasury still pays the difference.

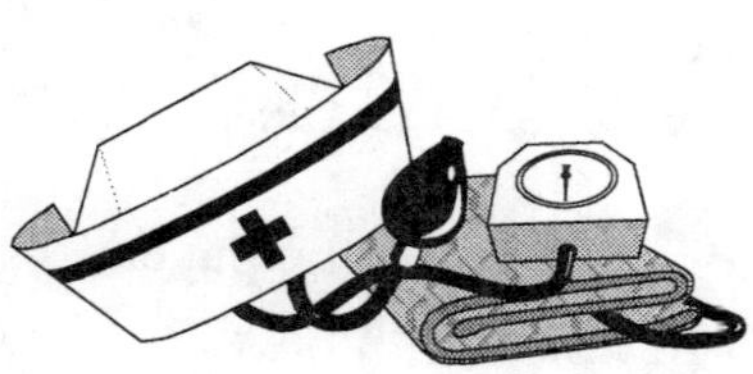

# TEST FOR SELF-EVALUATION – CHAPTER 15

## True or False

Indicate which of the following statements are true or false by circling the correct answer.

T F 1. Income broadly conceived (for tax purposes) includes all income of the taxpayer, both taxable and nontaxable.

T F 2. An additional standard deduction amount is allowed if either the taxpayer or a dependent of the taxpayer is blind or over age 65.

T F 3. The Tax Table and the Tax Rate Schedule are basically the same and taxpayers may choose between the two when calculating their tax.

T F 4. The standard deduction amount in 2003 is limited for a child who may be claimed as a dependent on the parents' tax return to the greater of $750 or the dependent's earned income up to the basic standard deduction amount.

T F 5. Except in situations when a spouse dies during the year, the determination of marital status is made at the end of the taxable year.

T F 6. A taxpayer who can be claimed as a dependent on another taxpayer's income tax return is not allowed a personal exemption when filing a tax return.

T F 7. The dependency exemption for children of divorced parents must always be claimed by the custodial parent.

T F 8. An unmarried taxpayer may claim the head of household status when a child or grandchild lives in the taxpayer's household for more than half of the year and the taxpayer provides over half of the cost of maintaining a household.

T F 9. Gambling losses are allowed as an itemized deduction only to the extent the taxpayer has gambling winnings.

T F 10. The HOPE scholarship credit applies to costs for tuition, books, and supplies associated with the first 2 years of higher education.

T F 11. Greta, 12 years old and a dependent of her parents, received interest income of $2,000. Greta's parents can include her income on their own tax return.

T F 12. Payments properly classified as alimony should always be taken into income by the recipient and deducted by the payor.

T F 13. A professional baseball player receiving a new automobile for being the team's "outstanding fielder" would likely be able to exclude the automobile because it is really an award based on athletic achievement.

T F 14. The standard deduction is not phased-out for individuals with high adjusted gross incomes.

T F 15. With respect to a transfer of appreciated property to a former spouse, no gain or loss is recognized if the transfer is incident to a divorce settlement.

T F 16. For 2003, the child tax credit is based on $3,000 for one child or $6,000 for two or more dependent children of the taxpayer that are under the age of 13.

T F 17. A contestant winning $25,000 on a television game show need not report the amount as income because it is considered a gift for tax purposes.

T F 18. A voluntary transfer of property to another where adequate consideration is not exchanged is included in the recipient's gross income if the transfer is made out of affection, respect, admiration, charity, or like impulses.

T F 19. Interest earned on certain Series EE U.S. government savings bonds may be excluded from income if the proceeds from the bond's redemption are used to pay qualified higher education expenses.

T F 20. Cash bonuses given by employers to their employees generally can not qualify for the gift exclusion.

T F 21. The lifetime learning credit cannot be taken on tuition paid by nontaxable scholarships.

T F 22. Workers' compensation benefits are not taxable.

T F 23. A capital improvement, such as an air cleaning system, which is added to one's personal residence for approved medical reasons, is deducted as a medical expense over 5 years.

T F 24. The term "medicine and drugs" includes only prescribed drugs or insulin.

T F 25. Both state and the Federal income tax are deductible under the Code.

T F 26. The real estate taxes incurred in a year of sale are apportioned between the buyer and the seller of a property.

T F 27. State income taxes paid by individuals are for AGI deductions when the taxpayer's sole source of income is from business, rents and/or royalties.

T F 28. The amount of interest on investment indebtedness that may be deducted is limited to gross investment income.

T F 29. The percentage limits applied to charitable contributions varies depending on the type of property contributed and classification of charity receiving the donation.

T F 30. Qualifying medical expenditures incurred by an individual are normally deductible only to the extent that they exceed 2% of the taxpayer's AGI.

T F 31. Cosmetic surgery cannot qualify as a deductible medical expense.

T F 32. All personalty property taxes must be *ad valorem* in order to be deductible.

T F 33. The investment interest expense deduction includes amounts paid to enable a taxpayer to purchase corporate and municipal bonds.

T F 34. Interest paid on a home equity line may be deducted only if the loan proceeds are used on home improvement projects.

T F 35. For a child to qualify a parent to receive the earned income credit, the child may not be age 24 or older unless the child is permanently disabled.

T F 36. After 2003, the maximum amount of employment-related expenses that qualify for purposes of computing the credit for child and dependent care expenses is indexed for inflation.

T F 37. The earned income tax credit is a form of negative income tax.

T F 38. Eligible employment-related expenses allowable in computing the credit for child and dependent care expenses does not include any amounts paid for household services.

T F 39. The amount of the child tax credit is dependent on the number of the taxpayer's qualifying children.

T F 40. In order to be eligible for the earned income credit the taxpayer must have at least one qualifying child.

**Fill-in-the-Blanks**

Complete the following statements with the appropriate word(s) or amount(s).

1. There are two categories of deductions for individual taxpayers: deductions________ adjusted gross income and deductions ________ adjusted gross income.

2. The filing status of a married taxpayer is generally either ________ or ________.

3. In order for the *kiddie tax* to apply in 2003, the child must have unearned income in excess of ________.

4. To qualify as a dependent, the following tests must be met: ________, relationship or member of the household, ________, joint return, and ________.

5. To meet the support test, over ________ of the support of a dependent must be furnished by the taxpayer.

6. In computing taxable income, taxpayers are allowed to deduct from AGI, the greater of allowable ________ or the ________.

7. In order for a taxpayer to claim a relative as a dependent under a multiple support agreement, the taxpayer must contribute more than ________ of the relative's support.

8. The *kiddie tax* does not apply once a dependent child reaches ________ years of age.

9. The standard deduction amounts in 2003 for single taxpayers and head of household who are neither 65 years old nor blind are ________ and ________, respectively.

10. A taxpayer may not file a 1040EZ if the taxable income is above ________, the taxpayer is more than ________ years of age or the taxpayer claims any ________.

11. Based on a divorce or separation agreement, a taxpayer may receive alimony and child support payments from the former spouse. The receipt of ________ is included in gross income, but a ________ is not.

12. The personal and dependency exemption amount for 2003 is ________ per exemption.

13. The personal exemptions and the itemized deductions are ________ for taxpayers with high levels of AGI.

14. To use the Educational Savings Bonds exclusion the bonds must be issued to a person who is at least ________ years of age at the time of the issuance.

15. A scholarship recipient may exclude from gross income the amount used for ________ and ________ but not the amounts used for ________ and ________.

16. A distinction must be made between a fee and a tax because a ________ is not deductible unless it is incurred as a business expense or incurred in the production of income.

17. Certain miscellaneous expenses are not deductible unless they exceed ________ of AGI.

18. Benefits collected under an accident insurance purchased by the taxpayer are ________.

19. Damages received due to physical injury are excluded from income if they are ________ and taxable if they are ________.

20. Generally, when making a charitable contribution of intangible capital gain property, the amount of the of the deduction is the ________ of the asset.

21. Interest expense on a home equity loan amount that is not greater than ________ may be fully deducted if the proceeds are used for ________.

22. In 2003, transportation for medical purposes is deductible at ________ per mile while transportation for charitable contribution purposes is deductible at ________ per mile.

23. For 2003, expenses of up to ________ incurred to adopt an eligible child may qualify for the adoption expenses credit.

24. The overall limitation on certain itemized deductions requires the taxpayer to reduce the deductions by ________ of the excess of AGI over the threshold amount, in no case may the reduction be for more than ________ of the covered itemized deductions.

25. A qualified individual for the child and dependent care credit is a dependent under the age of ________ or is ________ or ________ incapacitated.

26. A qualified child for the adoption expenses credit must be under __________ years of age or __________ of self care.

27. The two educational credits are the ________ and ________.

28. Eligible individuals may elect to receive ________ of earned income credit from their employers.

29. Taxpayers who claim a(n) ________ credit may not also take a ________ for the expenses on which the credit is based.

30. In 2003, the child credit is ________ per dependent child of the taxpayer that is under the age of ________ .

## Multiple Choice

Choose the best answer for each of the following questions.

____ 1. Which of the following are *not* subject to the overall limitation on itemized deductions (the cutback adjustment)?
   a. Medical expenses.
   b. Investment interest expense.
   c. Nonbusiness casualty losses.
   d. Gambling losses.
   e. All of the above are not subject to the limitation on itemized deductions.

____ 2. Which of the following statements are *false* with regards to the standard deduction.
   a. The basic standard deduction is based on the taxpayer's filing status.
   b. The additional standard deduction is based on characteristics of only the taxpayer and the taxpayer's spouse.
   c. All taxpayer's are allowed to claim some amount of standard deduction.
   d. The amount of the additional standard deduction varies by filing status.
   e. All of the above statements are true.

____ 3. Veljko and Dunja file a joint income tax return for 2003. Veljko is 65 and Dunja is 64. Their eldest son, who generates no income, is legally blind, single, and 29 years of age. He is supported by Veljko and Dunja. What is Veljko's and Dunja's standard deduction?

a. $9,500.
b. $10,450.
c. $10,650.
d. $12,350.

____ 4. Mary McCoy, is single, age 42, and has an 18 year old daughter who lives in the home Mary solely maintains. Mary's AGI is $69,000 and her total itemized deductions are $6,500. What is Mary's taxable income for 2003?

a. $55,900.
b. $56,400.
c. $58,150.
d. $59,500.

69,000
− 4750
64250
6100

____ 5. Mrs. Stooge is supported by her sons, Moe, Larry, and Curly and a dear friend to the following extent

| | | | |
|---|---|---|---|
| Moe | 25% | Larry | 30% |
| Curly | 5% | Friend | 40% |

Assuming a multiple support agreement is filed, who may claim Mrs. Stooge as a dependent?

a. Moe or Larry.
b. Moe, Larry, or Curly.
c. Moe, Larry, Curly or Friend.
d. Moe, Larry, or Friend.

____ 6. Since Ramona's parents provide over 50% of her support while she is full-time college student, the parents claimed Ramona as their dependent. Ramona earned $3,400 from a summer job, $3,100 in dividends from stock she inherited from her grandmother, and $50 in interest on her personal savings account. What is Ramona's taxable income for 2003?

a. $Zero.
b. $1,850.
c. $2,900.
d. $5,800.

____ 7. Veeda's husband died on June 5 of this year. She maintains a household for herself and her unmarried son, Artie. However, Artie does not qualify as a dependent. What is Veeda's filing status for this year and next year?

| | *This Year* | *Next year* |
|---|---|---|
| a. | Married Filing Jointly | Surviving Spouse |
| b. | Surviving Spouse | Head of Household |
| c. | Surviving Spouse | Surviving Spouse |
| d. | Married Filing Jointly | Head of Household |

____ 8. The Harts, joint filers, have two children. Robin,12 years old, received $4,000 interest which is 30% of her support and Butch, 27 years old, is a graduate student and earned $5,000 which is 40% of his support. The Hart's provide the rest of their children's support. In addition, they provide 80% of the support for their cousin, who lives in a nursing home. How many exemptions should the Harts claim on their tax return?

a. 2.
b. 3.
c. 4.
d. 5.

____ 9. Refer to the previous problem. How much of Robin's income will be taxed at her parent's rate?

a. $0.
b. $1,500.
c. $2,500.
d. $3,250

____ 10. Lamar and Ana paid $15,000 to adopt Mohan, 4 years old, in January, 2003. They also paid $3,600 in child care for the full year so Lamar and Ana could work full-time. What is the amount of Lamar's and Ana's credits for 2003 if their AGI is $50,000?

a. $14,760.
b. $11,760.
c. $1,600.
d. $600.

____ 11. Marta received the following amounts during the year.

| | | | |
|---|---|---|---|
| Salary | $40,000 | Unemployment Compensation | $ 1,000 |
| Gifts from parents | 5,000 | Child support payments | 8,000 |
| Prize winnings | 6,000 | Alimony from ex-husband | 10,000 |

What amount must Marta include in the computation of taxable income?

a. $68,000.
b. $63,000.
c. $57,000.
d. $56,000.

____ 12. Which of the following is not a component of the individual tax formula:

a. Income broadly conceived.
b. Exclusions.
c. Personal exemptions.
d. Deduction for dividends received.

____ 13. Which of the following is *not* deductible *from* AGI?

a. Interest on loans to purchase investments.
b. Charitable contributions.
c. Gambling losses to the extent of gambling income.
d. Alimony.
e. All of the above are deductible *from* AGI.

____ 14. Bruno (blind) and Ellie (deaf) have 3 dependent children ages 13, 16, 18, and file a joint return for the year. They have salaries of $100,000, moving expenses of $4,000, home interest of $8,000, property taxes of $2,000 and interest on a car loan $1,000. Calculate their taxable income for the year.

a. $49,750.
b. $50,300.
c. $50,750.
d. $65,000

____ 15. Refer to the preceding problem. What is the amount of child tax credit Ellie and Bruno can take for 2003.

a. $0.
b. $1,000.
c. $2,000.
d. $3,000.

____ 16. Which of the following statements regarding filing status for Federal income tax purposes is *false*.

a. A taxpayer that is unmarried or living apart from her or his spouse at the end of the year is single
b. Joint filing status was originally enacted to establish equity between married taxpayers in common law states and those in community property states.
c. The tax rates for head-of household falls between the rates used for filing jointly and those for filing as single.
d. The tax rates for surviving spouse and married filing jointly are identical.
e. All of the above statements are true.

____ 17. Which statement is not correct regarding Medical Savings Accounts (MSAs)?

a. Contributions made to MSAs by taxpayers are deductible for AGI.
b. Earnings on a MSAs is not taxable when used to pay medical expenses.
c. MSAs are usually created in conjunction with high-deductible medical insurance policies.
d. Distributions are subject to a 10% penalty tax if the amounts are not used to pay medical expenses.

____ 18. During the year, Rosa, an undergraduate majoring in tax accounting, received a $5,000 scholarship from State University. The amount was spent on the following.

| | |
|---|---|
| Tuition | $2,000 |
| Room | 1,000 |
| Board | 1,000 |
| Books | 500 |
| Incidental living expenses | 500 |

How much can Rosa *exclude* from gross income?

a. $5,000.
b. $4,500.
c. $2,500.
d. $2,000.

____ 19. Which of the following statements is true?
a. The amount of tax for a given taxable income can vary depending on the taxpayer's filing status.
b. Child support in excess of $15,000 a year is taxable to the custodial parent.
c. Individuals must file a tax return if their self-employment earnings exceed $250.
d. Amounts received by gift are taxable to the extent of the appreciation.
e. None of the following are true.

____ 20. Joe sustained serious injuries in the course of his employment as a Washington, D.C. hot dog vendor. As a result of his injuries, Joe received the following payments during the current year.

| | |
|---|---|
| Damages for physical personal injuries | $3,250 |
| Worker's compensation | 6,400 |
| Reimbursement from health insurance for expenses paid by Joe but not deducted by him | 2,500 |

Compute his gross income from these items.
a. $Zero.
b. $6,400.
c. $9,650.
d. $12,150.

____ 21. Jin received a $15,000 scholarship from Boatright College to be used for tuition, fees, and related expenses during the 20X3 – 20X4 academic year. She actually incurred qualifying expenditures as follows.

| | |
|---|---|
| August-December, 20X3 | $6,000 |
| January-May, 20X4 | 7,000 |

Compute Jin's gross income.
a. $9,000 in 20X3.
b. $1,500 in 20X3 and $500 in 20X4.
c. $1,000 in 20X3 and $1,000 in 20X4.
d. $2,000 in 20X4.

____ 22. Which of the following is not a deduction for AGI?
a. State income taxes for individuals who are self-employed.
b. Capital losses not in excess of capital gains.
c. Moving expenses.
d. Interest on qualified education loans.

____ 23. Mona is 8 years old and claimed by her parents as a personal exemption. In 2003, Mona receives $2,200 from modeling and $800 in interest from a savings account. How much of Mona's income will be taxed at her parent's tax rate?
a. $1,500.
b. $750.
c. $50.
d. $Zero

____ 24. Which of the items listed below is not deductible from AGI as interest?
a. Mortgage prepayment penalty.
b. Business interest expense.
c. Interest expense incurred to buy or carry corporate securities.
d. Points paid on home acquisition mortgage.

____ 25. Xin paid the following taxes.

| | | | |
|---|---|---|---|
| Car license excise tax | $150 | State income tax | $900 |
| Real estate tax on vacation home | 400 | State gasoline tax | 90 |
| City personal property tax (*ad valorem*) | 60 | | |

Xin's deduction for taxes on her Federal income tax return is:
a. $1,500.
b. $1,450.
c. $1,360.
d. $1,300.

____ 26. During the year, Elmo incurred the following expenses.

| | | | |
|---|---|---|---|
| Over the counter drugs | 200 | Prescription drugs | $ 300 |
| Medical insurance premiums | 600 | Doctors bills | 800 |
| Foreign real property tax | 1,000 | Hospital bills | 1,000 |
| Mortgage interest expense | 4,200 | Credit care interest | 500 |

If Elmo's AGI is $20,000, calculate his itemized deductions for the year.
a. $7,900.
b. $6,900.
c. $6,400.
d. $5,400.

____ 27. Which of the following items may be deducted as a charitable contribution?
a. Ordinary income property donated to a charity to sell in its thrift shop.
b. Cash given directly to the homeless.
c. Value of rent forgone due to letting a charity use the taxpayer's building.
d. Market Value of blood given to the Red Cross.
e. All of the above are deductible.

____ 28. In 2003, Maria made the following contributions to the United Way. She traveled 500 miles in her personal automobile while performing volunteer work. She contributed 10 hours of services as an accountant, valued at $600. She gave stock with a FMV of $14,030 and an basis of $10,400. If Maria's AGI is $80,000, what is the maximum charitable contribution she may take in 2003?
a. $10,070.
b. $10,670.
c. $14,100.
d. $14,700.

____ 29. The Juan Garcias, single, age 40, has an AGI of $50,000. His records indicate the following expenses during the year.

| | | | |
|---|---|---|---|
| Professional Dues | $1,200 | Tax return Preparation Fee | 2,700 |
| State Income Taxes | 5,000 | Safe Deposit Box (for investments) | 80 |
| Job-hunting costs | 500 | Moving Expenses | 3,500 |

What is the amount of Juan's itemized deductions?
a. $7,700.
b. $8,480.
c. $9,480.
d. $11,750.

____ 30. Yenta's AGI is $40,000 and she made contributions to qualified public charities of $7,000 cash, old clothes with a FMV of $600 and cost of $1,400, and land with a FMV of $15,000 and a cost of $3,000. What is the maximum amount Yenta can deduct for charitable contributions this year?
a. $10,600.
b. $11,400.
c. $19,600.
d. $20,000.

____ 31. The Halls, married filing jointly, have the following income and expenses this year.

| | | | |
|---|---|---|---|
| Salaries | $80,000 | Expenses: Uniforms | $2,000 |
| Dividends | 15,000 | Investment interest expense | 20,000 |
| AGI | $95,000 | Investment expenses | 2,500 |
| | | Impairment-related work expenses | 3,000 |

Compute Hal's itemized deductions.
a. $18,100.
b. $20,100.
c. $25,600.
d. $27,500.

____ 32. Which of the following statements is *false*.
a. Tax returns for individuals are due on or before the fifteenth day of the fourth month following the close of the tax year.
b. If a taxpayer is unable to file by the due date, an automatic four-month extension is available.
c. Extension of time to file also extend times to pay taxes.
d. Taxes due can be paid by check, money order, or by debit or credit cards.

____ 33. Ray made a contribution to Central State University's athletic booster club for $1,000. This payment provided Ray the right to purchase tickets in preferred sections of the athletic facilities; and in addition, Ray would be invited to the coaches' luncheons every Monday. Ray felt these benefits were worth $600 to him personally. In addition, Ray forwarded $500 to the school for season football and basketball tickets. What amount may Ray deduct on his return for these expenditures?
a. $0.
b. $400.
c. $800.
d. $1,000.

____ 34. Itemized deductions fall into all of the following categories except
- a. Expenses that are purely personal in nature.
- b. Expenses incurred by employees in connection with their employment.
- c. Expenses related to the production or collection of income.
- d. Management expenses for property held for the production of income.
- e. All of the above.

____ 35. Which of the following is a refundable tax credit?
- a. Adoption expenses credit.
- b. Education tax credits.
- c. Child and dependent care credit.
- d. Earned income credit.
- e. None of the above are refundable tax credits.

____ 36. Sam and Tanya, married filing jointly, have three children under age 6. Their AGI is $24,000 and they spent $3,200 per child for child care. Calculate their child care credit.
- a. $3,360.
- b. $3,200.
- c. $2,700.
- d. $1,800.

____ 37. Susanna, head of household, pays tuition in 2003 for herself and her son Jamal in the amount of $1,500 and $6,000 respectively. Susanna takes one college course each semester to maintain her computer knowledge. She currently hold a degree in History. Jamal is a full-time freshman at State university studying accounting. What is the allowable education tax credit available to Susanna?
- a. $1,800.
- b. $2,000.
- c. $2,700.
- d. $3,500.

____ 38. Assume the same facts as the previous problem, except that Susanna is a full-time graduate student with a tuition of $6,000 and Jamal's tuition is $10,000. Jamal has a scholarship for $9,000 that covers $8,500 of tuition and $500 of book costs. What is the allowable education tax credit available to Susanna?
- a. $3,200.
- b. $3,000.
- c. $2,700.
- d. $2,450.

____ 39. Jane and Bob are both full-time students at State University. They earn $6,000 each and pay $3,000 a year for child-care for their 2 year old. Which of the following credits would Jane and Bob likely *not* qualify for?
- a. Child Tax Credit.
- b. Child Care Credit.
- c. Educational Tax Credit.
- d. Earned Income Credit.
- e. Jane and Bob are likely to qualify for all of the above credits.

____ 40. Which of the following statements concerning the earned income credit is true?
   a. The credit can only be subtracted from any net tax liability after considering withholdings and estimated tax payments.
   b. The credit can only be received by taxpayers with earned income.
   c. The taxpayer must have a dependent child to qualify for the credit.
   d. The taxpayer must file an EIC form to receive the credit.
   e. All of the above are true.

**Short Answer**

1. Chavez and LaToya are married and have 2 dependent children and a pet rabbit. Chavez's and LaToya's earnings from their jobs total $48,000. Their other income consists of the following.

| | |
|---|---|
| Interest income from savings account | $1,000 |
| Unemployment compensation | 500 |
| Municipal bond interest | 600 |
| State lottery winnings | 400 |

They have itemized deductions during the year of $6,000. Calculate their taxable income for 2003.

2. Alma's records reflect the following transactions for the year. How are they to be treated for tax purposes?
   - Receipt of alimony from former husband of $8,000.
   - Workers' compensation of $4,000.
   - Received the door prize at the Chamber of Commerce annual dance valued at $1,000.
   - Gift from parents of $9,000.
   - Award for personal injury paid by employer $30,000.

3. Maret receives a $15,000 scholarship to attend State University during the 20X4-20X5 school year. Maret's records reflect the following expenditures.

| | |
|---|---|
| Tuition | $10,000 |
| Books | 800 |
| Special course fees | 50 |
| Room | 2,000 |
| Board | 2,000 |
| | $14,500 |

Comment on how the scholarship proceeds are taxed.

4. Indicate whether each of the following is subject to the 2% of AGI limitation.
   a. Interest on loan which the proceeds were used to buy stock.
   b. Professional dues.
   c. Tax return preparation fees.
   d. Gambling losses.
   e. Safe deposit box used to store investment-related records.
   f. Hobby losses up to the amount of hobby income.
   g. Deductions for repayment of amounts under the claim of right if more than $3,000.
   h. Federal estate tax on income in respect of a decedent.
   I. Cost of uniforms for employee.

## SOLUTIONS TO CHAPTER 15 QUESTIONS

**True or False**

1. T
2. F The additional standard deduction is allowed only for the taxpayer and the taxpayer's spouse.
3. F Although most taxpayers use the Tax Tables, there are certain situations when the Tax Rate Schedules *must* be used.
4. F The standard deduction is the greater of $750 or earned income + $250 up to the basic standard deduction amount.
5. T
6. T
7. F The noncustodial parent may claim the dependency exemption if the custodial parent agrees in writing to forgo the exemption.
8. T
9. T
10. F The credit does not apply to books and supplies.
11. T
12. T
13. F To be excluded, the award must be for length of service or safety.
14. T
15. T
16. F These rules apply to the child and dependent care credit.
17. F Such amounts are treated as gross income subject to taxation.
18. F Gifts are not included in the recipient's gross income.
19. T
20. T
21. T
22. T
23. F The medical cost of a capital improvement is deductible in the year incurred to the extent that the expenditure exceeds the increase in value of the related property.
24. T
25. F The Federal income tax is not deductible.
26. T
27. F State income taxes imposed on individuals are always deductible as itemized deductions.
28. F The amount deductible generally is limited to *net* investment income.
29. T
30. F A 7.5%-of-AGI threshold applies.
31. F Cosmetic surgery may be deductible if it is considered *necessary*.
32. T
33. F Investment interest does not included the interest on loans where the proceeds are used to acquire tax exempt securities such as municipal bonds.
34. F The use of the proceeds is irrelevant.
35. T
36. F The amounts are **not** indexed for inflation.
37. T

38. F Household service expenses are included.
39. T
40. F A reduced EIC is available if the taxpayer is over age 24 and under age 65.

**Fill-in-the-Blanks**

1. for, from
2. married filing jointly; married filing separately
3. $1,500
4. support, gross income, citizen or residency
5. 50%
6. itemized deductions, standard deduction
7. 10%
8. 14
9. $4,750; $7,000
10. $50,000, 65, dependents.
11. alimony, child support payment
12. $3,050
13. phased out
14. 24
15. tuition, books or related expenses, room, board
16. fee
17. 2%
18. excludible
19. compensatory, punitive
20. fair market value
21. $100,000, any purpose
22. 12¢ , 14¢
23. $10,160
24. 3%, 80%
25. 13, physically, mentally
26. 18, physically or mentally incapable
27. HOPE scholarship credit, lifetime learning credit
28. advance payments
29. educational, deduction
30. $1,000 (Changed by the Tax Act of 2003 from $600), 17

**Multiple Choice**

1. e
2. c Married filing separately cannot take any standard deduction if spouse itemizes.
3. b $10,450. 9,500 (joint filing) + 950 (Veljko is 65).
4. a Mary qualifies as head of household

| | | |
|---|---|---|
| Adjusted gross income | | $69,000 |
| Itemized vs Standard deduction | $6,500 or $7,000 | - 7,000 |
| Personal and dependency exemptions | ($3,050 X 2) | - 6,100 |
| Taxable income | | $55,900 |

5. a Only Moe and Larry provide > 10% of her support <u>and</u> meet the relationship test.

6. c AGI (3,400 + 3,100 + 50) $6,550

Less: Greater of basic standard deduction (750) or earned income + 250 (3,400 + 250) -3,650

Less: Personal exemption - 0

Taxable income $2,900

7. d In the year of the spouse's death, Veeda files married filing jointly. For the next year, Artie does not qualify as a dependent, so Veeda is head of household status.

8. b 3. Son fails gross income test (25 years old) and cousin fails relationship test.

9. c $2,500. 4,000 - 1,500.

10 b $11,760. 10,160 (adoption) +1,000 (child tax credit) + (3,000 X 20%) (child care).

11. c $57,000. 40,000 + 1,000 + 6,000 + 10,000.

12. d Dividends received deduction is for corporations not individuals.

13. d Alimony is deductible for AGI.

14. b Gross income $80,000

Moving expense - 4,000

Less: Greater of Itemized (8,000 + 2,000) or Standard deduction (9,900 + 950) - 10,450

Personal and dependency exemptions (3,050 X 5) -15,250

Taxable income $50,300

15. c $2,000. 1,000 X 2. The 18 year child does not qualify for the credit.

16. a Married taxpayers living apart from their spouse who do not have a decree of divorce or separate maintenance cannot file as single.

17. d Distribution not used for medical costs is subject to a 15% penalty tax if made before age 65, death or disability.

18. c The cost of tuition (2,000) and books (500) may be excluded as a scholarship.

19. a

20. a None of the items are included in gross income.

21. d

22. a State income taxes are always a deduction from AGI.

23. d $Zero. 2,200 + 800 - (2,200 + 250). Up to $750 taxed at child's rate.

24. b Business interest is deductible for AGI.

25. c $1,360. 400 + 900 + 60.

26. c Medical expense deduction [(300 + 600 + 800 +1,000) - (7.5% X 20,000)] $1,200

Foreign real property tax 1,000

Mortgage interest expense 4,200

Total $6,400

27. a

28. c $14,100. (500 miles X 14¢ ) + 14,030. Services rendered are not deductible.

29. b $8,480. 5,000 + [(1,200 + 2,700 + 80 + 500) - (2% X 50,000)].

30. c $19,600. 7,000 + 600 + (30% X 40,000). Land limited to 30% of AGI.

31. a $18,100. [(2,000 +2,500) - (2% X 50,000)] +3,000 (Misc deductions) + (15,000 - 2,500) (net investment income limit) = 2,600 + 3,000 + 12,500.

32. c Time to file does not extend time to pay.

33. c $800. 1,000 X 80%.

34. e

| | | | |
|---|---|---|---|
| 35. | d | | |
| 36. | d | $1,800. | 3,000 X 2 children X 30% |
| 37. | c | $1,800. | 1,500 X 20% (lifetime learning credit) + [100% X 1,000] + [50% X 1,000] (HOPE credit). |
| 38. | d | $2,450. | 6,000 X 20% (lifetime learning credit) + [100% X 1,000] + [50% X $500] (HOPE credit). Amounts paid by scholarship do not qualify for credits. |
| 39. | e | | |
| 40. | b | | |

**Short Answer**

1. Gross income:

| | | |
|---|---|---|
| Salary | | $48,000 |
| Interest income | | 1,000 |
| Unemployment compensation | | 500 |
| State lottery winnings | | 400 |
| Adjusted gross income | | $49,900 |
| Less: The greater of -- | | |
| Itemized deductions | $6,000 | |
| Standard deduction | 9,500 | - 9,500 |
| Less: Personal and dependency exemptions ($3,050 X 4) | | -12,200 |
| Taxable income | | $28,200 |

2. The following amounts are included in Alma's income.

| | |
|---|---|
| Alimony | $8,000 |
| Door prize | 1,000 |
| Total income | $9,000 |

3. Of the $15,000 received, the $10,850 spent on tuition, books, and fees is excluded from taxation. The remaining $4,150 ($15,000 - $10,850) is subject to taxation in 20X5.

4.
a. No – Interest on loan which the proceeds were used to buy stock.
b. Yes – Professional dues.
c. Yes – Tax return preparation fees.
d. No – Gambling losses.
e. Yes – Safe deposit box used to store investment-related records.
f. Yes – Hobby losses up to the amount of hobby income.
g. No – Deductions for repayments under the claim of right if more than $3,000.
h. No – Federal estate tax on income in respect of a decedent.
I. Yes – Cost of uniforms for employee.

# Chapter 16
# Individual as Employees and Proprietors

## CHAPTER HIGHLIGHTS

Discussions concerning the deductibility and treatment of many commonly incurred employee-related and self-employed expenses are included in this chapter. Also presented are items that are specifically excluded from gross income for only employees. These exclusions can provide significant benefits to the employees. Thus, knowing whether an individual is an employee or self-employed is meaningful for tax purposes. Besides ascertaining whether certain benefits are excluded from income, employment status is important in determining the classification of deductions as either *for* or *from* adjusted gross income. The factors to consider when determining whether an individual is an employee or self-employed are therefore presented. Items that specifically relate to being self-employed and using the sole proprietorship business entity are discussed as well as the distinction between having a business and being involved in a hobby.

I. Employee vs Self-Employed
   A. When one person performs services for another, the person performing the service is either an employee or self-employed (i.e., an independent contractor).
   B. Expenses incurred by independent contractors in trade or business are deductible *for* AGI.
   C. Expenses incurred as a result of an employment relationship generally are deducted *from* AGI subject to limitations unless they are part of an accountable plan. With an accountable plan, the employee expenses are deducted *for* AGI.
   D. Factors Considered in Classification – The critical factor in determining the classification of a worker is whether an employer-employee relationship is in existence. The relationship exists when the employer:
      1. Has the right to specify the end result of a task and the ways and means by which the end result is to be achieved.
      2. Can exert will and control over the person regarding what will be done and how it will be accomplished.
      3. Has the right to discharge the person.
      4. Furnishes tools or a place to work.
      5. Bases payment on time spent rather than task performed.

II. Exclusions Available to Employees
   A. Advantages of Qualified Fringe Benefits
      1. These benefits are deductible to the employers and excludible by employees.

2. To qualify for these exclusions the worker must be an employee. They are not available to the self-employed.

B. Employer-Sponsored Accident and Health Plans §105

1. Employees and retired employees may exclude from income premiums paid by their employer for accident or health insurance, disability insurance, and long-term care plans which cover themselves and their dependents.
2. Payments are deductible by the employer.
3. Payments received for medical costs are included in income if the amounts were deducted in a prior year as a medical expense or were for expenses *not* meeting the tax law's definition of medical care.
4. Amounts received as compensation for permanent disfigurement, loss of a body part, or loss of use of a body function body are excluded from gross income.
5. Payments for lost wages due to illness or injury are taxable.

C. Medical Reimbursement Plans

1. Employees reimbursed for medical costs by an employer's self-insurance plan may exclude the reimbursements if the plan is not discriminatory.
2. Small employers can purchase medical insurance with a high deductible for employees and make contributions to the employee's *medical savings account.*

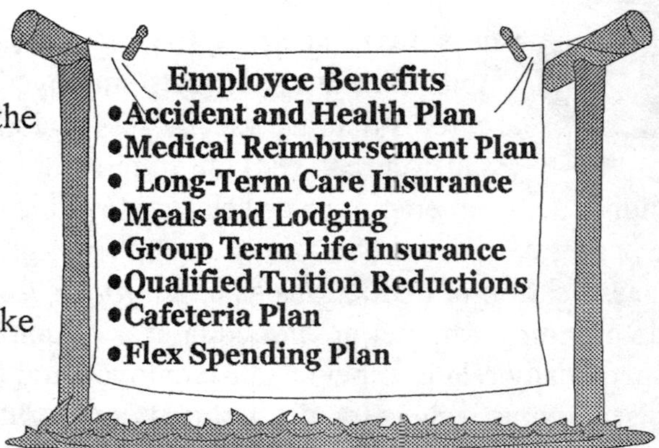


D. Long-Term Care Benefits

1. Long-term care insurance is treated the same as accident and health insurance benefits in that the employee may exclude premiums paid by the employer.
2. However, when policy benefits are received, the exclusion from gross income cannot be *greater* than following amounts.
   a. $220 (for 2003) for each day of long-term care.
   b. The actual cost of the care.
   c. Excludible amounts are reduced by payments received from other parties.

E. Meals and Lodging Furnished for the Convenience of the Employer § 119

1. Value of meals and lodging provided to an employee and dependents are excluded from income if the following requirements are met.
   a. The meals/lodging are *furnished* by the employer, on the employer's *business premises* and for the *convenience of the employer*.
   b. For *lodging*, the employee must also be *required* to accept the lodging as a condition of employment.
2. A partnership is not considered the employer of a partner but some courts disagree.
3. Other housing exclusions are provided for certain employees of educational institutions, ministers of the gospel, and military personnel.

F. Group Term Life Insurance § 79

1. The premiums paid by an employer for the first $50,000 of group term life insurance protection on an employee are excluded from income.
2. For protection received in excess of $50,000, the covered employee must include in income the amount calculated using tables in the Regulations.

G. Qualified Tuition Reduction Plans

1. An employee (including a retired or disabled employee) of a nonprofit educational institution is allowed to exclude a tuition waiver if the waiver is pursuant to a qualified tuition reduction plan.
2. Exclusion applies to the employee, spouse, and dependent children.

H. Other Specific Employee Fringe Benefits

1. The employee can exclude up to $5,000 ($2,500 married filing separate) in value of *child and dependent care services* provided by an employer to enable an employee to work.
2. The value of the use of certain *on-premises athletic facilities* by employees, their spouses,, and dependents are excluded from income.
3. Qualified employer-provided educational assistance at the undergraduate and graduate levels is excludible from gross income up to an annual ceiling of $5,250.
4. The employee can exclude from gross income up to $10,160 of expenses incurred by an employee to adopt a child where the adoption expenses are paid or reimbursed by the employer under a qualified adoption assistance program. The exclusion is phased out as AGI increases from $153,390 to $192,390.

I. Cafeteria Plans

1. The value of certain services or noncash benefits received that are a part of a cafeteria plan may be excluded from the employee's gross income.
2. If cash is selected rather than benefits, the cash is taxable.

J. Flexible Spending Plans

1. Under these plans, the employees agree to reduce their cash compensation in return for the employer agreeing to pay certain costs incurred by the employee (e.g., medical expenses) without the employee recognizing gross income.
2. If the employee's actual expenses are less than the reduction in cash compensation, the employee cannot recover the difference. Thus, these plans are often referred to as *use or lose* plans.

K. General Classes of Excluded Benefits

1. To avoid economic inefficiencies and to create uniform rules for fringe benefits, Congress has specified broad classes of nontaxable employee benefits. These include the following (See Concept Summary 16-1 in text).
   a. No-additional-cost services.
   b. Qualified employee discounts.
   c. Working condition fringes.
   d. *De minimis* fringes.
   e. Qualified transportation fringes.
   f. Qualified moving expense reimbursements.
   g. Qualified retirement planning services.
2. The *nondiscrimination provisions* apply to the no-additional-cost services and qualified employee discounts. These provisions state that if a plan discriminates in favor of highly compensated employees, the exclusion is denied to these key employees.
3. The nondiscrimination rules generally do not apply to *de minimis* and working conditions fringe benefits.

L. Taxable Fringe Benefits

1. Employer provided fringe benefits that do not fall under any of the general classes or specific exclusions are taxable.

2. The amount of taxable income is equal to the benefit's fair market value.

III. Employee Expenses

A. <u>Transportation Expenses</u>

1. Qualified Expenditures
    a. Employees are allowed a deduction *from* AGI for transportation expenses incurred for the purpose of going from one work location to another in the course of a business day.
    b. *Commuting expenses* are nondeductible. However, certain costs incurred when using an automobile to transport heavy tools to work may be deductible. Further, commuting costs between home and a *temporary* work location or between the general work area and a temporary work location outside that area are deductible.
2. Computation of Automobile Expenses – Taxpayers may compute the deduction for automobile expenses in *either* one of two ways.
    a. The taxpayer may deduct the actual operating expenses incurred in the pursuit of business. These expenses include: depreciation (cost recovery), gas, oil, repairs, licenses, and insurance. Records must be kept to document the automobile's personal and business use. Complex depreciation rules apply if the actual expense method is used.
    b. Taxpayers may deduct 36¢ per business mile in 2003. Parking fees and tolls are also allowed when using the automatic mileage method.

B. <u>Travel Expenses</u>

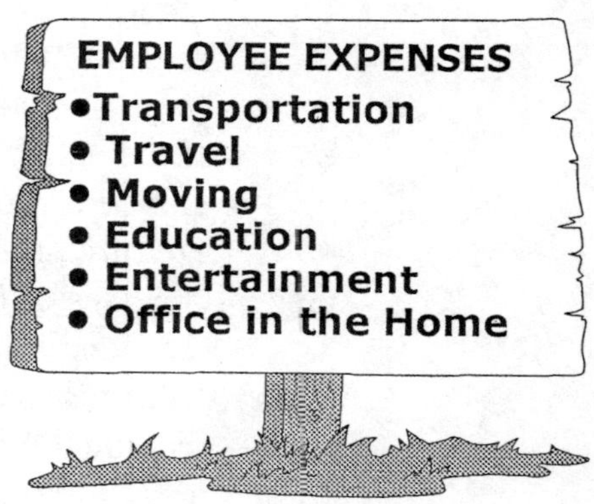


1. Travel expenses are more broadly defined than transportation expenses. In addition to transportation, travel expenses include meals and lodging, reasonable laundry and incidental expenses.
2. Meals and lodging are available only if taxpayers are away from their tax home. Further, meals cannot be lavish.
3. Away-from-Home Requirement
    a. The taxpayer must be *away from home* for substantially longer than an ordinary business day and for a period where rest, sleep, or a relief-from-work period is required.
    b. Time away from home on business must be temporary but not indefinite. A period that exceeds 1 year is not considered temporary.
    c. Tax home is the area in which employees derive their principal source of income. This may be somewhere other than where the employees live.
4. Combined Business and Pleasure Travel – If a trip combines both business and personal objectives, the following points are relevant.
    a. Transportation expenses are deductible (for domestic trips) only if the trip is primarily for business. If the trip is primarily for personal pleasure, transportation is not deductible; however, other expenses incurred which specifically relate to business are deductible.
    b. If the trip is outside the United States (foreign travel), special restrictive rules apply.

C. <u>Moving Expenses</u> §217

1. General Requirements
   a. Moving expenses are deductible when incurred in connection with the commencement of work at a new principal place.
   b. To be deductible, the *distance* and *time tests* must be met.
2. Distance Test
   a. The taxpayer's new job location must be *at least* 50 miles farther from the old residence than the old residence was from the former place of employment.
   b. This test eliminates the deduction for: taxpayers who purchase a new home in the same general area without acquiring new employment; if a new job in the same general area does not necessitate a move; or, if the move is for personal reasons.
3. Time Test
   a. For employees, they must be employed on a full-time basis for 39 weeks in the 12-month period following the move.
   b. If the person is self-employed, he or she must work for 78 weeks during the next two years in the new location.
4. Treatment of Moving Expenses
   a. Qualified moving expenses include *reasonable* expenses incurred for traveling from the former residence to the new residence and moving household goods and personal effects.
      (1) Traveling includes lodging, but not meals, for the taxpayers and members of their household.
      (2) Taxpayers can elect to use actual expenses or an automatic mileage method. In this case, automatic mileage is limited in 2003 to 12¢ per mile for each automobile.
   b. Tax Treatment – Qualified moving expenses are deductible whether the taxpayer starts a new job or was transferred and even if the taxpayer was unemployed prior to obtaining employment in the new area.

D. <u>Education Expenses</u>

1. An employee may deduct education expenses if they are incurred in either of the following situations.
   a. To maintain or improve existing skills required in present job.
   b. To meet the stated requirements of the employer or to meet requirements imposed by law to retain employment status.
2. Education expenses are not deductible in the following situations.
   a. Incurred to meet the minimum educational standards for qualification in the taxpayer's existing job.
   b. If they qualify the taxpayer for a new trade or business.
3. Requirements imposed by law or by employer for job retention, such as the requirements for teachers, qualify under this provision. A deduction for education expenses is allowed if the taxpayers are required by their employer or by law to take additional courses. However, if the required education is the minimum required for the job, no deduction is allowed.
4. Maintaining or Improving Existing Skills – This requirement has been difficult for taxpayers and the courts to interpret. The successful application of the rule is often dependent on subtleties of the particular case under consideration.

5. Educational expenses include expenses for books, tuition, transportation, and travel. Unless the expenses are reimbursed by the taxpayer's employer, the amounts are deductible as miscellaneous itemized deductions, subject to the 2%-of-AGI floor. In addition, the limitation on meals applies.

E. <u>A Limited Deduction Approach</u> §222

1. A deduction for *qualified tuition and related expenses* of up to $3,000 is allowed for higher education expenses for taxpayers with an AGI of less than $65,000 ($130,000, joint filers; $0, married filing separately). Different limitations apply after 2003.
2. The deduction is *for* AGI for those who do not qualify as another's dependent.
3. Deduction must be coordinated with the HOPE and lifetime learning credits to insure you do not receive "double benefits".
4. Qualifying costs are defined the same as for HOPE and lifetime learning credits (See Chapter 15 for discussion of these credits).

F. <u>Entertainment Expenses</u>

1. 50% Cutback
   a. Only 50% of meal and entertainment expenses are allowed as deductions. The limitation applies in both the context of employment or self-employment status.
   b. The reduction is applied *either* to the employer or to the employee, but it will *not* be applied to both.
   c. Transportation expenses are not affected by this provision.
2. Entertainment expenses may be classified into the following categories.
   a. *Directly related to business* – an actual business meeting or discussion takes place during the entertainment.
   b. *Associated with business* – must serve a specific business purpose.
3. There are restrictions on the deductibility of business meals.
   a. The meal must be directly related to or associated with the active conduct of a trade or business.
   b. The expense cannot be lavish or extravagant under the circumstances.
   c. The taxpayer (or employee) is present at the meal.
4. No deduction is allowed for *dues* paid for membership in any type of *club* organized for business, pleasure, or any other purpose. However, this prohibition does not apply to clubs whose primary purpose is public service and community volunteerism (e.g., Kiwanis, Lions, Rotary).
5. Business gifts are deductible to the extent of $25 per donee per year. Records must be maintained to substantiate business gifts.

> The IRS no longer requires substantiation for business expenses under $75. This threshold reduces the documentation businesses and individuals are required to accumulate to support deductions on their returns. Not retaining receipts, however, is not the same as not having to keep records. Adequate records are still required to support all deductions. Receipts are still required for all lodging deductions.

G. <u>Other Employee Expenses</u>

1. Office in the Home
   a. No deduction is allowed unless a portion of the residence is used *exclusively* and on a *regular basis* for one of the following purposes.

(1) As the principal place of business for any trade or business of the taxpayer.
(2) As a place of business which is used by patients, clients, or customers.

b. Employees must meet an additional test: the use must be for the convenience of the employer as opposed to being merely appropriate and helpful.

c. An office in the home will qualify as a *principal place of business* if *both* of the following are met.
(1) The office is used to conduct administrative or management activities of a trade or business.
(2) The trade or business has no fixed location where these activities can otherwise be conducted.

d. Allowable home office expense may not exceed the gross income from the business reduced by all other business expenses attributable to the activity.

2. Certain Expenses for Teachers – The Tax Act of 2002 added a deduction for school supplies, books, equipment and supplementary materials purchased by elementary and secondary teachers for use in the classroom. The *for* AGI deduction ceiling is $250 and is available in 2003.

3. Miscellaneous Employee Expenses – Other employee expenses, which are generally deductible *from* AGI and subject to the 2%-of-AGI limitation, include the following.
a. Union dues.
b. Professional expenses (e.g., dues for organizations, meetings).
c. Expenses for job hunting in the same profession.
d. Special clothing and their upkeep.

H. <u>Classification of Employee Expenses</u>

1. If employee expenses are reimbursed by an employer under an *accountable plan*, they are not reported by the employee.
a. Employees must adequately account for, or substantiate the expenses (with receipts).
b. Employees must return excess reimbursement or allowance to employer.
c. Proper *substantiation* of expenses involves maintaining adequate records which contain the following information.
(1) The amount of the expense.
(2) The time and place of travel or entertainment, or date of gift.
(3) The business purpose of such expense.
(4) The business relationship of the taxpayer to the person entertained or receiving the gift.

2. To reduce paperwork, employers can reimburse employees for travel away from home based on a flat dollar amount per day of business travel (a *per diem*). The amount *deemed substantiated* is equal to the *lesser* of the per diem allowance or the Federal per diem rate.

3. If expenses are reimbursed under a *nonaccountable plan*, they are classified as deductions *from* AGI and only claimed if the employees itemize their deductions.
a. Nonaccountable Plans – A plan in which an adequate accounting and/or return of excess amounts is not required. All reimbursements are fully included in income and deductible like an unreimbursed expenses.

b. Failure of an employee to follow the rules of an accountable plan causes nonaccountable plan treatment

4. Unreimbursed employee expenses – Meals and entertainment expenses are subject to the 50% cutback. Total unreimbursed employee business expenses are reported as miscellaneous itemized deductions subject to the 2%-of-AGI floor.

> The value of a deduction depends on the tax bracket of the taxpayer incurring an expense. For example, if a taxpayer has business expense of $100 is in the 15% tax bracket, the net after-tax cost of a deductible expenditure to the employee is $85. That is the taxpayer is out-of-pocket by $85. This treatment, however, may be dependent on whether the expense is deductible *for* or *from* AGI, and whether the deduction is subject to further limitation (e.g., 2%-of-AGI limitation).

I. <u>Contributions to Individual Retirement Accounts</u>

1. Traditional IRAs
   - a. Employees not covered by another qualified plan may establish their own tax deductible IRAs. Annual deduction is limited to the *lesser* of $3,000 (or $6,000 including spousal IRA) or 100% of compensation.
   - b. If the taxpayer is an active participant in another qualified plan, the IRA deduction limitation is phased out *proportionately* between AGI ranges of $40,000 – $50,000 for unmarried taxpayers and $60,000 – $70,000 for joint filers. Taxpayers are not considered active participants in a plan merely because their spouses are participants.
   - c. Most unemployed spouses may take a full $3,000 deduction unless the couple's AGI is above $150,000.
   - d. Taxpayers at least 50 years old can make catch-up IRA contributions of $500 so the maximum contribution is $3,500 per the taxpayer.
   - e. When a contribution deduction is available, it is a *for* AGI deduction. The deduction cannot be less than $200 (floor limit).
   - f. To the extent individuals are ineligible to make deductible contributions to IRAs, nondeductible contributions may be made to separate accounts.
2. Roth IRAs
   - a. Contributions to a Roth IRA are not deductible when made but the distributions from this IRA are not taxable when received.
   - b. Tax-free withdrawals are available after an initial 5 year holding period if one of the following requirements are satisfied:
     - (1) The taxpayer receiving the distribution is at least age 59½.
     - (2) The distributions is after the death of the participant.
     - (3) The taxpayer becomes disabled.
     - (4) The distribution is used to pay for qualified first-time home buyer's costs.
   - c. Maximum annual contribution rules are similar to traditional IRAs. However, phase-out of the contributions begins at AGIs of $95,000 for single taxpayers and $150,000 for joint filers.
3. Coverdell Educational Savings Accounts (CESAs)
   - a. A distribution from a CESA to pay for qualified higher education expenses receives tax-free treatment. Contributions are not deductible.

b. Qualified higher educational expenses include tuition, fees, books, supplies, related equipment, and room and board if the student's course load is at least ½ time.

c. If the distribution is greater than the qualified costs, part of the excess is treated as a return of capital (not taxable) and part is a distribution of the earnings. The exclusion ratio is calculated as follows.

$$\text{Exclusion} = \frac{\text{Qualified education expenses}}{\text{Total distributions}} \text{ X Earnings}$$

d. The maximum amount that can be contributed to the CESA is $2,000 per designated individual beneficiary. Contributions cannot be made once the beneficiary reaches age 18.

e. Distributions must be completed within 30 days after the beneficiary reaches age 30. Before this, amounts can be rolled over tax-free to another family member's CESA. Person must be under age 30.

f. The maximum contribution phase-out begins at AGIs of $95,000 for single taxpayers and $190,000 for joint filers.

g. A 6% excise tax is imposed on excess contributions and a 10% excise tax is imposed on any distributions that are included in gross income.

h. Coordination of benefit with the HOPE and lifetime learning credits is required to insure you do not receive "double benefits".

IV. Individual as Proprietors

A. Proprietorship as a Business Entity

1. Sole proprietorships are not separate entities from the owner.
2. Net income from operations of a business is reported on the proprietor's Form 1040, Schedule C.
3. Business income and expenses retain their character when reported on the proprietor's Form 1040.

B. Income of a Proprietorship – The general rules regarding the taxability of income and the deductibility of expenses apply to proprietorships as they do to other entities.

C. Deductions Related to a Proprietorship

1. The ordinary and necessary business expense rules under § 162 apply.
2. Health Insurance Premiums – In 2003, self-employed may deduct 100% of medical insurance premiums as a *for* AGI.
3. Self-Employment Tax

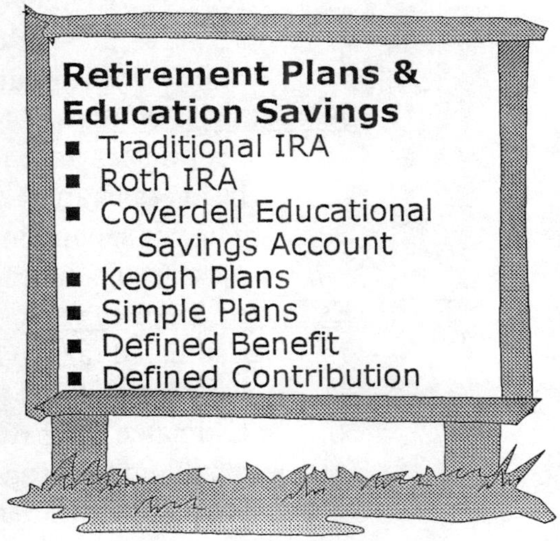


a. The employment taxes (Social Security and Medicare) are imposed on the self-employed individuals with net earnings in excess of $400. For 2003, the employment tax rates are 12.4% of the first $87,000 of net earnings (for Social Security) and 2.9% on the total amount of net earnings (for Medicare).

b. Self-employed are allowed a *for* AGI deduction equal to 50% of the employment taxes paid.

D. Retirement Plans for Self Employed Individuals

1. There are several options for retirement funding available to the self-employed. Individual retirement plans used by employees may also be utilized by self-employed individuals.

2. Keogh Plans

   a. These plans are established by the self-employed to cover themselves. They are required to also cover their employees under the plan.

   b. Investment decisions of the plan may be *self-directed.*

   c. Plans may be set up as either a *defined contribution plans* or a *defined benefit plan.*

   d. The limits on contributions to the plans are as follows:

      (1) Defined contribution plan: the lesser of $40,000 or 100% of earned income.

      (2) Profit sharing or stock bonus: 25% deduction limit applies. For discrimination purposes the limit is computed on the first $200,000 and is limited to $40,000.

      (3) Defined benefit: the lesser of $160,000 or 100% of average net earnings for highest three years.

3. SIMPLE Plans

   a. Employer with no more than100 employers may establish a *savings incentive match plan for employees* also know as a SIMPLE plan. Self-employed individuals may also participate in this type of plan.

   b. Plan is based on a salary reduction arrangement and the employees in 2003 can contribute up to $8,000 per year with employer matching contributions up to 3% of employees' compensation with a $200,000 salary cap. Thus, maximum contribution by employer is $6,000.

   c. There is a catch-up provision for employees age 50 that is like the IRA plan. The amount for 2003 is $500.

   d Employer's deduction for contributions is limited to the greater of 25% of compensation with a $200,000 salary cap.

   e. Distributions from SIMPLE plans are taxed like IRA distributions.

E. Accounting Periods and Methods

1. Proprietors have the same accounting methods available to them as other business entities.

2. The tax accounting period, however, must match that of the proprietor as the income and expenses appear on the proprietors personal return.

F. Estimated Tax Payments

1. Estimated tax payments may be required for self-employed and employees who have income that is not subject to withholding.

2. Estimated tax payments are the amount of income tax (including alternative minimum tax) and self-employment tax an individual expects to owe for the year after considering credits and withholding.

3. If the estimated tax, as defined above, is at least $1,000, quarterly estimated payments must be made.

4. In order to avoid a penalty for failure to timely pay taxes, the taxpayer must have paid in the smaller of the following.
   a. 90% of the current tax liability, or
   b. 100% of last year's tax liability. In 2003, the percentage is increased to 110% when the AGI on last year's return exceeded $150,000.
5. Estimated payments are due on April 15, June 15, and September 15 of the current year and January 15 of the following year.

V. Hobby Losses § 183

A. <u>General Rules</u>

1. If an individual can show that a business or investment activity (that may have personal pleasure attributes) has been conducted with the purpose of earning a profit, then any losses from the activity are deductible in full.
2. The *hobby loss* rules apply if the activity is considered not to be engaged in for profit.

B. <u>Presumptive Rules of § 183</u>

1. A rebuttable presumption in the Code provides that if an activity shows a profit in at least 3 of every 5 consecutive years, then the activity is considered to be profit-seeking and the hobby loss rules do *not* apply.
2. For activities involving horses, its 2 out of every 7 years.

C. <u>Determining the Amount of the Deduction</u>

1. If an activity is deemed to be a hobby, expenses are deductible only to the extent of the income from the hobby.
2. However, some expenses may be deducted in full as allowed by other sections of the Code (e.g., interest and property taxes). These expenses must be considered before other types of expenses in computing the overall hobby loss limitation.
3. Hobby expenditures are deductible *from* AGI as miscellaneous itemized deductions subject to the 2%-of-AGI floor.

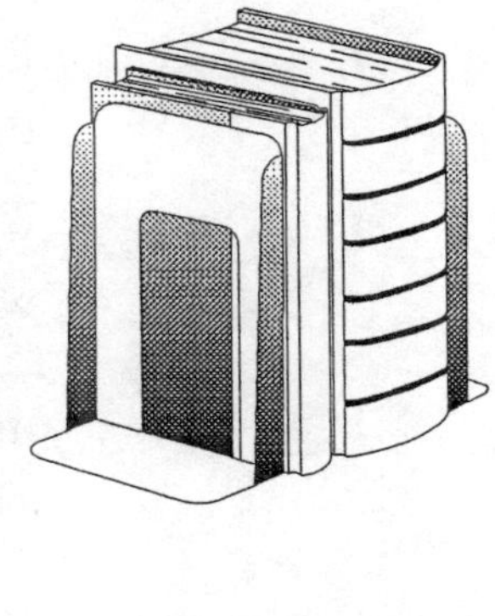

## TEST FOR SELF-EVALUATION – CHAPTER 16

**True or False**

Indicate which of the following statements are true or false by circling the correct answer.

T F 1. Expenses of self-employed individuals incurred in a trade or business are always deductible *for* AGI.

T F 2. The value of a parking space provided by an employer need not be included in the income of an employee.

T F 3. For tax purposes, transportation expenses incurred by an employee are always deductible *for* AGI.

T F 4. For persons who qualify, payments to Individual Retirement Accounts are deductible *for* AGI.

T F 5. Transportation expenses and travel expenses are synonymous terms.

T F 6. Moving expenses are deductible without limit if they are related to an employee's trade or business.

T F 7. Pama's daily cost of traveling from her home in Richmond, VA to her job in Washington, D.C. are deductible because she is traveling out of town.

T F 8. Special clothing, such as that worn by a police officer, may be deductible as a miscellaneous employee expense.

T F 9. All employee expenses reimbursed under a nonaccountable plan by an employer are deductible *for* AGI.

T F 10. A taxpayer may compute car expenses in either of two ways: the taxpayer deducts the actual operating expenses incurred for business, or the taxpayer deducts an automatic allowance for every business mile driven.

T F 11. Like other employee expenses deductible *from* AGI as miscellaneous itemized deductions, unreimbursed moving expenses are subject to the 2%-of-AGI limitation.

T F 12. Premiums paid by an employer for up to $50,000 whole life insurance protection on the employee are excluded from the employee's income.

T F 13. Employees of nonprofit educational institutions can only exclude tuition wavers granted to themselves or their spouses.

T F 14. In order to qualify for exclusion from income, a qualified employee discount for the receipt of services may not exceed 15% of the customer price.

T F 15. Elementary school teachers can deduct up to $250 of classroom supplies as a for AGI deduction.

T F 16. Lavish or extravagant entertainment expenses are limited in deduction to 20% of their cost.

T F 17. For a plan to be accountable, the employee need only render an adequate accounting of expenses.

T F 18. Commuting expenses are never deductible.

T F 19. The for AGI deduction for higher education expenses must be coordinated with the educational credits to insure that the taxpayer does not receive double benefits for the same expense payments.

T F 20. An example of a qualifying educational expense is one that enables an employee to meet the minimum educational standards for qualification in the taxpayer's existing job.

T F 21. With the Roth IRA the contributions are not deductible but the distributions may not be taxable if at least the 5 year holding period requirement is met.

T F 22. One of the requirements that must be met for meals and lodging to be excluded from a recipient's income is that they must be provided for the convenience of the employer.

T F 23. The maximum contribution to a Coverdell Education Savings Account (CESA) is the same as a traditional and Roth IRA.

T F 24. The amount of deductions taken *for* AGI can have an impact on the amount of itemized deductions.

T F 25. Self employed individuals may deduct their health insurance premiums as for AGI deductions just like a business deducts health insurance for its employees.

## Fill-in-the-Blanks

Complete the following statements with the appropriate word(s) or amount(s).

1. Exclusions that are available only to ________ are called ________ benefits.

2. Small employers (________ or fewer employees) can purchase a medical insurance plan with high deductibles and then make contributions to the employee's ________ .

3. To be eligible for the moving expense deduction, a taxpayer must meet two basic tests: ________ and ________.

4. In order to be deductible, entertainment expenses must be categorized as either ________ or ________.

5. Business gifts generally are deductible to the extent of ________ per donee per year.

6. The type of benefits that are so small that accounting for them is impractical are called ________.

7. Generally __________ insurance, which covers expenses such as nursing home costs, is treated the same as accident and __________ insurance benefits.

8. To avoid an underpayment tax penalty, the taxpayer with an AGI under $150,000, must pay in the smaller of ________ of the current year's tax or ________ of last year's tax.

9. No deduction is allowed for a home office unless the office space is used __________ and __________ for trade or business activity.

10. In most situations, _________ and _________ expenses are reduced by 50% of the amount incurred.

11. In order for meals provided by the employer to be excluded from income of the employee, three tests must be met. These tests are (1) _______ (2) _______ (3) _______.

12. For lodging provided by an employer to be excluded from income of the employee, it must meet all three tests listed in # 11 and ________.

13. A _______ plan provision permits a covered employee to choose one or more benefits from among several taxable or nontaxable fringe benefits that may be offered by the employer.

14. Section 183 provides that hobby expenses are deductible only to the extent of ________.

15. The Code provides a rebuttable presumption that an activity (that does not involve horses) is profit-seeking if it shows a profit in at least ________ of any ________ consecutive years ending with the taxable year in question.

16. The exclusion for qualified tuition reduction plans is generally limited to __________ tuition waivers. However, in the case of __________ or __________ assistants, graduate tuition waivers may also qualify for exclusion.

17. __________ operate much like cafeteria plans.

18. For travel expenses to be deductible, the taxpayer must be __________ on a __________ assignment.

19. The distributions from a Coverdell Education Savings Account can be used to pay for tuition, books, supplies and __________ and __________ if the student is taking at least __________ of a full-time course load.

20. A __________ retirement plan is established when a taxpayer decides to make all investment decisions regarding a retirement plan.

21. No quarterly payments of Federal income taxes is required if the taxpayers estimated tax due is less than __________ .

22. In 2003, the self-employment tax is __________ percent on self-employment earning up to __________ for Social Security and __________ percent on __________ earning for Medicare.

23. Estimated payments are due on the following dates (assuming that none of the dates fall on a __________ or __________): __________, __________, __________, and __________ .

24. An employee can exclude from gross income up $5,000 of costs incurred for __________ and $10,160 for __________ that are paid or reimburse by the employer.

25. Alice being able to fly without cost because she works for an airlines is an example of a __________ fringe benefit.

**Multiple Choice**

Choose the best answer for each of the following questions.

____ 1. Katz incurred the following expenses when his employer transferred him from Chicago to New York City.

| | |
|---|---|
| Continental Movers | $1,900 |
| Airline tickets for family to NYC | 700 |
| Installation of carpeting in new home | 800 |
| Real estate commissions on residences | 1,000 |
| Meal costs en route to new residence | 200 |
| Lodging costs en route to new residence | 400 |

Assuming Katz is not reimbursed by his employer, what amount is deductible moving expenses?

a. $4,900.
b. $4,100.
c. $3,100.
d. $2,400.
e. None of the above.

____ 2. Which of the following is *not* a retirement plan.

a. Simple Plan.
b. Roth Plan.
c. Keogh Plan.
d. Coverdell Plan.
e. All of the above are retirement plans.

____ 3. Matt had incurred the following expenses at the Downtown Society Social Club. Matt was not reimbursed by his employer for any of these expenses.

| | |
|---|---|
| Annual dues | $5,000 |
| Meals directly related to business | 1,700 |
| Meals associated with business | 300 |
| Meals on business days | 2,000 |

The deduction attributable to the above before the 2%-of-AGI limitation is:

a. $1,000.
b. $2,000.
c. $3,500.
d. $4,500.

____ 4. Jenette, whose AGI is $40,000 in 2003, teaches French at Central High School. The local school board requires that she take professional development courses to maintain her teaching certification. Jenette had the following expenses related to teaching.

| | |
|---|---|
| Tuition for college course | $ 700 |
| Books for college course | 300 |
| Transportation to college for course (college out of state) | 600 |
| Meals (while out of state at college) | 200 |
| Lodging (while out of state at college) | 400 |
| Trip to France to maintain familiarity with the culture | 1,500 |
| French books bought to use in her high school class | 250 |

Unfortunately, the school board does not reimburse Jenette for any expenditures. What are Jenette's *for* AGI deductions assuming no expenses are used for credits?

a. Zero
b. $700.
c. $950.
d. $1,250.

____ 5. Refer to the proceeding question, what are Jenette's *from* AGI deductions?

a. $600.
b. $800.
c. $1,500.
d. $3,000.

____ 6. Which of the following is not correct about proprietorships.

a. Self-employed can deduct 100% of health insurance premiums as *for* AGI deductions.
b. The requirements that business expenses be ordinary and necessary applies to proprietorships as well as other entities.
c. Self-employed are allowed a deduction from net earnings equal to 50% of their self-employment tax rate.
d. The income on which the self-employed must pay Social Security is twice that of employees.
e. All of the above are deductions related to a proprietorship.

____ 7. In celebration of a hardware store's 100th anniversary, the owners make some business gifts to valued employees based on years of employment. These gifts, which were not considered to be compensation, had the following fair market values: two at $20 each, three at $25 each, three at $50 each, and two at $500 each. What amount pertaining to these gifts is deductible as a business expense?

a. $1,265.
b. $250.
c. $240.
d. These do not qualify as business gifts.

____ 8. Kui is a CPA who works as a public accountant for Shire and Company, CPAs. During the current year she had the following expenses. Her employer's reimbursement procedure is pursuant to the terms of an accountable plan.

| | |
|---|---|
| Airfare for business trips (reimbursed in full) | $800 |
| Use of personal auto for company business (reimbursed $400) | 500 |
| Entertainment (reimbursed $100) | $200 |
| Professional dues (not reimbursed) | 300 |
| Professional clothes (not reimbursed) | 1,500 |

What amount could Kui claim as itemized deduction, before applying any limitations?

a. $400.
b. $450.
c. $1,700.
d. $1,900.

____ 9. Amber, a self-employed CPA has the following expenses

| | |
|---|---|
| Transportation costs for 1,528 miles (use automatic rate) | |
| Entertainment | $ 1,300 |
| Term life insurance ($50,000 face value) | 600 |
| Professional dues | 750 |
| Medical Insurance | 1,000 |
| Supplies | 800 |

What is the amount of Amber's *for* AGI deductions in 2003?

a. $3,000.
b. $3,750.
c. $4,350.
d. $5,000.

____ 10. Which of the following is not a factor in determining employer-employee relationship.

a. The employer has the right to specify the end result of a task and the means by which the end result is to be achieve.
b. The employer can exert control over the person regarding what will be done and how it will be accomplished.
c. The employer determines the amount of compensation the person will receive based on the task performed.
d. The employer had the right to fire the person.
e. All of the above are critical factors.

____ 11. Bing and Yang are married and file jointly. Bing earns $84,000 in 2003 and Yang is not employed. Bing is not an active participant in a qualified retirement plan. What is the maximum amount of traditional IRA deduction for Bing and Yang respectively?

a. $3,000 and $3,000.
b. $3,000 and $0.
c. $0 and $3,000.
d. None of the above.

____ 12. Ramon, single, has a salary of $175,000, no *for* AGI deductions, taxable income of $140,000 and his tax is $36,000. Assuming that last year he had a salary of $160,000, no *for* AGI deductions, taxable income of $110,000 and his tax was $27,000, what is the minimum amount Ramon must have paid through withholding or estimated pavements to avoid an underpayment penalty in 2003?

a. $36,000.
b. $32,400.
c. $29,700.
d. $27,000.

____ 13. The following does *not* qualify as a deductible employee education expense.

a. Expenses incurred to maintain or improve existing skills required in present job.
b. Fees incurred for professional qualification exams.
c. Amounts incurred to meet the express requirements of the employer to retain employment status.
d. Amounts incurred to meet requirements imposed by law to retain certification.
e. All of the above qualify as deductible education expenses.

____ 14. Select the *incorrect* statement below.

a. The tax treatment of employee business expenses generally depends on whether the expenses are reimbursed or unreimbursed.
b. The tax treatment of reimbursed employee business expenses depends on whether the expenses were reimbursed under an accountable plan or a nonaccountable plan.
c. A reimbursement plan is considered an accountable plan if the employee renders an adequate accounting of the expenses and returns any excess reimbursement or allowance.
d. Documentary evidence is required to support all expenditures that are excess of $25.
e. All of the above statements are correct.

____ 15. Records to substantiate expenses incurred need not include which of the following items?

a. The amount of the expense.
b. The time and place at which the expense was incurred.
c. The business purpose of the expense.
d. The business relationship of the taxpayer to the person for whom the expense was incurred.
e. All of the above are necessary.

____ 16. Which of the following is *not* a deductible employee expense?
- a. Expenses for daily travel from home in Connecticut to office in New York City.
- b. Expense of traveling from taxpayer's office to client's office.
- c. Expenses of traveling from one job (a day-time job) straight to another job (an evening job) with different employers.
- d. All of the above are deductible.

____ 17. A self-employed accountant attended a two day tax seminar and had the following costs.

| | | | |
|---|---|---|---|
| Air transportation | $ 500 | Local transportation | $ 40 |
| Meals | 320 | Lodging | 275 |
| Airport parking | 50 | Tickets to Opera | 150 |
| | | Dry cleaning of suit while at seminar | 25 |

The taxpayer may claim a deduction *for* AGI for the following amount.
- a. $1,025.
- b. $1,050.
- c. $1,360.
- d. None of the above.

____ 18. An employed human resource manager attended the same tax seminar discussed in # 17. The taxpayer may claim a *from* AGI deduction before limitations of the following amount.
- a. $1,025.
- b. $1,050.
- c. $1,360.
- d. None of the above.

____ 19. Which of the following employee fringe benefits generally is *not* excluded from taxation?
- a. Parking costing $190 per month paid by the employer.
- b. Personal use of a company car up to $5,000.
- c. A 30% discounts on employer's merchandise.
- d. Payment of $500 of employee's professional dues.
- e. All of the above are excluded from taxation as a matter of policy.

____ 20. Sarah, a cash basis taxpayer, practices law as an employee of a firm where she earns an annual salary of $100,000. She received the following fringe benefits from her employer this year.

| | |
|---|---|
| Personal use of copying machine | $ 45 |
| Free parking (provided only to highly paid employees) | 360 |
| Personal legal service discount (15% discount) | 105 |
| Membership in the U-R-Fit Athletic Club | 500 |
| Personal use of the firm's beach cottage | 150 |

What amount related to the receipt of these fringe benefits must be *included* in Sarah's gross income?
- a. $500.
- b. $605.
- c. $650.
- d. $695.

____ 21. Which of the following statements is *not* correct?

a. A proprietorship must use a calendar year-end.
b. Proprietorships that provide services commonly use the strict cash method.
c. Proprietorships selling inventory are required to use the accrual method for computing the gross profit from sales.
d. Selecting an accounting period for a proprietorship is simpler than for a partnership or S corporation.
e. All of the above are correct.

____ 22. Lane received the following compensation and benefits during the 2003 tax year.

| | |
|---|---|
| Salary | $260,000 |
| Christmas bonus | 12,000 |
| Value of medical insurance coverage | 5,000 |
| Long-term care benefits (200 days) | 50,000 |

What amount is *included* in Lane's 2003 tax computation?

a. $260,000.
b. $272,000.
c. $327,000.
d. None of the above.

____ 23. Elsa is employed as the general manager of a local hotel. Her employer gave her the choice of two compensation arrangements:

(1) Yearly salary of $50,000 plus free food at the hotel (value $7,300), *or*
(2) Yearly salary of $40,000 plus free food at the hotel (value $7,300) and free lodging at the hotel (value $15,000)

If Elsa chose option 2, what amount would be included in her gross income?

a. $40,000.
b. $55,000.
c. $57,300.
d. None of the above.

____ 24. In connection with the hobby loss rules, indicate which of the following is *incorrect*.

a. If a taxpayer can show that an activity has been conducted with the intent to earn a profit, losses from the activity are fully deductible.
b. Hobby expenses are deductible only to the extent of hobby income.
c. The Code provides a rebuttable presumption that an activity is profit-seeking if it shows a profit in two of any five consecutive years.
d. If an activity is deemed to be a hobby, some expenses incurred may be deductible by virtue of other sections in the Code.

____ 25. Which of the following is *not* true about home office expenses.

a. For employees, the office need be appropriate and helpful to the employer.
b. The office can be used for administrative activities if there is no other trade or business location at which these activities can be conducted.
c. Office home expenses cannot exceed the gross income from the business less all other business expenses attributable to the activity.
d. All of the above are true.

____ 26. Which of the following is an educational tax benefit.
a. Employee may deduct education expenses from AGI if they are incurred to qualify the taxpayer for a new trade or business.
b. Employees of a college can exclude tuition waivers for their children if the waiver is pursuant to a qualified tuition reduction plan.
c. A deduction for qualified tuition and related expenses of up to $3,000 is allowed for higher education expenses as long as the HOPE or lifetime learning credits are not taken.
d. Primary, secondary, and college teachers may deduct as a *for* AGI deduction up to $250 in cost for classroom supplies.

____ 27. Ling and Joseph decided to take a second honeymoon to Niagara Falls. Joseph wanted to incorporate some business into the trip in order to be able to deduct a portion of the costs. Luckily, the headquarters office of one of his business clients was located in Niagara Falls. Round-trip airfare from their home to Niagara Falls was $260 per passenger. Hotel costs were $150 per night. Of the ten days out of town, Joseph consulted with his client for two days. How much of the may Joseph treat as business expenses?
a. $560.
b. $352.
c. $300.
d. None of the above.

____ 28. Ari and Shae are married and file jointly. Ari earns $58,000 in 2003 and Shae is not employed. Ari is an active participant in a qualified retirement plan. What is the maximum amount of Roth IRA deduction for Ari and Shae respectively?
a. $1,200 and $3,000.
b. $1,200 and $1,200.
c. $0 and $0.
d. None of the above.

____ 29. Kojo received a distribution from his CESA in the amount of $6,000. His qualified educational costs were $4,000. On the date of the distribution the CESA had a balance of $20,000 of which $14,000 represents contributions. How much of the distribution from the CESA is taxable to Kojo?
a. $2,000.
b. $1,400.
c. $1,200.
d. None of the above.

____ 30. Diega, a self-employed artist, has a defined benefit Keogh plan providing 20% of compensation contribution rate. Diega's net income before the Keogh contribution is $150,000. What is the deductible Keogh contribution for Diega?
a. $25,000.
b. $30,000.
c. $37,500.
d. None of the above.

**Code Section Recognition**

Several important sections of the Internal Revenue Code are described below. Indicate, by number, the appropriate Code section.

1. _______ Provides the $50,000 group term life insurance exclusion.

2. _______ This section covers employer-sponsored accident and health plans.

3. _______ Provides the rules which govern the deductibility of moving expenses.

4. _______ This section excludes the value of meals and lodging from gross income when certain conditions are met.

5. _______ Determines the treatment of expenses incurred in the conduct of an activity not engaged in for profit (i.e., the "hobby loss" rules).

**Short Answer**

1. James, is a self-employed handy-man. He has the following income and expenses for the year 2003:

| | |
|---|---|
| Gross income | $175,000 |
| Deductible transportation costs | 25,000 |
| Employee wages | 40,000 |
| Supplies | 30,000 |
| Business meals (directly related) | 10,000 |

a. Compute the net earnings from the sole proprietorship.

b. Compute the amount of James's self-employment tax.

2. Jane, is an employee of an accounting firm in Gainesville, Florida and has an AGI of $80,000. She is in need of CPE credits to maintain her certification to practice in Florida. Therefore, she attends the AICPA National Tax Education Program held in Washington DC and incurs the following expenses, none of which are reimbursed by her employer.

| | |
|---|---|
| Transportation | $ 600 |
| Tuition and materials | 1,200 |
| Meals | 300 |
| Lodging | 500 |

Compute the amount Jane may treat as an itemized deduction.

3. Identify the seven broad classes of nontaxable employee benefits.

4. Amir has Parkinson's disease and is a patient in a nursing home. The cost of the nursing home in 2003 was $97,250 of which Medicare paid $12,950. Amir received $82,125 from his long-term care insurance policy. How much of the insurance proceeds may Amir exclude from his income?

## SOLUTIONS TO CHAPTER 16 QUESTIONS

### True or False

1. T
2. T Qualifies as a working condition fringe benefit.
3. F Such expenses are deductible *from* AGI.
4. T
5. F Travel expenses are incurred when the taxpayer is away from home and include transportation, lodging, 50% of meals, and business incidentals. Transportation does not include lodging, meals, or incidentals.
6. F Only qualifying unreimbursed moving expenses of a reasonable amount are deductible. Indirect moving expenses (e.g., commissions on the sale of an old residence) and meals are not deductible.
7. F Commuting expenses are not deductible.
8. T
9. F The deductions are classified as deductions *from* AGI and can only be claimed if the employee-taxpayer itemizes.
10. T
11. F Moving expenses are deductible *for* AGI.
12. F Exclusion is for group-term not whole life insurance.
13. F Tuition waivers for employee's dependent children are also excludible.
14. F The discount exclusion may not exceed 20% of the service's price.
15. T
16. F The lavish or extravagant portion of entertainment expenses is not deductible. No percentage is provided.
17. F In addition, the employee must return any excess reimbursement or allowance.
18. F While commuting expenses generally are not deductible, several exceptions exist (e.g., to transport heavy tools, to travel to a second job).
19. T
20. F Educational expenses incurred to meet minimum educational standards of employment are not deductible.
21. T
22. T
23. F Maximum contribution in 2003 is $2,000 per beneficiary to a CESA and $3,000 to a traditional IRA.
24. T For example, as deductions reduce AGI, itemized deductions such as employee business expenses which are reduced by a percentage of AGI, may become deductible to a greater extent.
25. T

### Fill-in-the-Blanks

1. employees, qualified fringe
2. 50, medical savings account.
3. distance, time
4. directly related to business, associated with business

5. $25
6. *de minimis* fringe benefits
7. Long-term care, health
8. 90%, 100%
9. exclusively, on a regular basis
10. meals, entertainment
11. (1) furnished by the employer, (2) furnished on the employer's business premises, and (3) furnished for the convenience of the employer.
12. required as a condition of employment.
13. cafeteria
14. hobby income
15. 3, 5
16. undergraduate, teaching, research
17. Flexible spending plans
18. away from home, temporary
19. room, board, 50%
20. self-directed
21. $1,000
22. 12.4%, $87,000, 2.9%, total
23. Saturday, Sunday, April 15, June 15, September 15, January 15 of next year
24. child and dependent care costs, adoption expenses
25. no-additional-cost

**Multiple Choice**

1. e $3,000. 1,900 + 700 + 400.
2. d Coverdell is an education savings account.
3. a $1,000. (1,700 + 300) X 50%
4. c $950. 700 tuition + 250 secondary teacher supplies.
5. a $600. 300 + 600 + (50% X 200) + 400 = 1,400 – (40,000 X .02) = 600
6. d The amount on which the tax is computed is not double. It is tax rate that is double.
7. c $240. (2 X 20) + (8 X 25)
8. b $450. 100 [unreimbursed auto expense] + 50 [50% X unreimbursed entertainment (100)] + 300 (professional dues).
9. b $3,750. (36¢ X 1,528) + (50% X 1,300) + 750 + 1,000 + 800.
10. c The employer bases payment on time spent rather than task performed is the requirement.
11. a Neither covered by a plan and nonworking spouse is allowed full $3,000.
12. c $29,700 = 27,000 X 110%. Since Ramon's AGI is greater than $150,000 for 2003, he must pay in the lesser of 110% of last year's taxes or 90% of this year's ($32,400).
13. b
14. d Expenditures of more than $75 need documentation.
15. e
16. a
17. b $1,050 = 500 + (320 X .50) + 50 + 40 + 275 + 25.
18. d None of the expenses are deductible. A tax seminar is not related to the human resource employment of the taxpayer.

| | | |
|---|---|---|
| 19. | b | Personal use of company car is taxable. |
| 20. | c | $650. 500 + 150. Parking fringe benefit can be discriminatory. |
| 21. | a | The requirement is that the proprietorship must have the same year-end as the proprietor. This may not be a calendar year-end. |
| 22. | d | $278 000. 260,000 + 12,000 + [50,000 - (220 X 200)]. |
| 23. | b | Since the lodging is not required for employment, it is taxable. Meals are not taxable. |
| 24. | c | Except for horses, a profit must be shown in 3 out of 5 years. |
| 25. | a | |
| 26. | b | Educational expenses cannot qualify the employee for a new trade or business. |
| 27. | d | $300. 150 X 2. None of the airfare is deductible, because the trip was not *primarily* for business. Of the ten days out of town, only two were devoted to business. |
| 28. | c | Roth IRA contributions are not deductible. |
| 29. | d | $600. (20,000 − 14,000) ÷ 20,000 = 30% earning percentage X 6,000 = 1,800 of the distributions is earnings. (4,000 ÷ 6,000) X 1,800 = 1,200. 1,800 - 1,200 = 600. |
| 30. | a | $25,000. 150,000 - .2X = X. 150,000 = 1.2 X 125,000 = X .2 X 125,000 = 25,000. |

**Code Section Recognition**

1. 79
2. 105
3. 217
4. 119
5. 183

**Short Answer**

1. a. The net earnings for James's sole proprietorship is $100,000 computed as follows.

| | |
|---|---|
| Gross income | $175,000 |
| Less: | |
| Deductible transportation costs | 25,000 |
| Employee wages | 40,000 |
| Supplies | 30,000 |
| Business meals (directly related) $10,000 X 50% | 5,000 |
| Net earnings | $ 75,000 |

b. The self-employment tax for James is $10,597 computed as follows.

| | |
|---|---|
| Net earnings | $ 75,000 |
| Multiply by | X 92.35% |
| Result | 69,263 |
| Self-employment tax rate | X 15.3% |
| Self-employment tax | $ 10,597 |

2. Jane itemized deductions are as follows:

| | |
|---|---|
| Transportation | $ 600. |
| Tuition and materials | 1,200. |
| Meals ($300 X 50%) | 150. |
| Lodging | 500. |
| Total | 2,450. |
| Less 2% of AGI | (1,600.) |
| Total Deduction | $ 850. |

3. The seven broad classes of nontaxable employee benefits.
No-additional-cost services.
Qualified employee discounts.
Working condition fringes.
*De minimis* fringes.
Qualified transportation fringe.
Qualified moving expense reimbursement.
Qualified retirement planning services.

4. Amir may exclude $80,300.
Computation:
Exclusion cannot be greater than:

| | | |
|---|---|---|
| Daily statutory amount of $220 X 365 days | | $80,300 |
| OR | | |
| Actual cost of care | 97,250 | |
| Less: Amount received from Medicate | -12,950 | |
| | 84,300 | $84,300 |
| Amount of the Exclusion | | $80,300 |

THE END